Praise for *Rivers of Blood, Rivers of Gold:*

"Thoughtful and thought-provoking, this superbly written book deserves a wide readership."—*Publishers Weekly*

"Cocker's analysis of four European conquests spanning the past five hundred years has important implications for global realities at the dawn of the new century."—*Booklist*

"A passionately written history of four episodes in European imperialism . . . Cocker's fervent and entertaining prose should warn us about how readily we accept progress as an answer to war, conquest, and genocide."—*Kirkus Reviews*

"Eloquent and harrowing . . . A powerful book, communicating its fierce indignation without recourse to polemic . . . Cocker succeeds in finding a tone appropriate to the matter: he has a journalistic sense of impact . . . and a powerful command of historical narrative."—*Sunday Times*

"A beguiling, significant, and in some ways groundbreaking book."
—*Literary Review*

"Here is the other side of Empire. In four concise, well-written and closely argued essays, covering four different European nations' assaults on four different lands, this is the case against colonialism."—*Mail on Sunday*

"This eloquently written and well-researched book serves as a necessary corrective to triumphalist and evasive histories of the rise of the West."
—*The Guardian*

Also by Mark Cocker

RICHARD MEINERTZHAGEN
LONELINESS AND TIME

RIVERS OF BLOOD, RIVERS OF GOLD

Europe's Conquest of Indigenous Peoples

Mark Cocker

GROVE PRESS
New York

First published in Great Britain in 1998 by Jonathan Cape, Random House, London
Published simultaneously in Canada
Printed in the United States of America

Library of Congress Cataloging-in-Publication Data
Cocker, Mark, 1959–
Rivers of blood, rivers of gold : Europe's conquest of indigenous peoples / Mark Cocker.
p. cm.
Originally published: London : J. Cape, 1998.
Includes bibliographical references and index.
ISBN 978-0-8021-3801-9
1. Europe—Colonies—History. 2. Imperialism. 3. Indigenous peoples. 4. Tribes.
I. Title.

JV305 .C63 2000   909—dc21   99-087927

Grove Press
an imprint of Grove/Atlantic, Inc.
154 West 14th Street
New York, NY 10011
Distributed by Publishers Group West
www.groveatlantic.com

13 14 15 16   10 9 8 7 6 5 4 3 2

For Miriam Lucy

Contents

Maps

Illustrations

Acknowledgements

This book started life in 1992 and its completion during the intervening six years has been a long and complicated process. Yet it would undoubtedly have taken much longer had I not received invaluable support and assistance from a great many people.

In the matter of travels, wholly or partly related to the project, I must express my deepest gratitude to the personnel of the Society of Authors and the panel of judges for the K. Blundell Trust Award. Their generous monetary grant enabled me to travel in Southwest USA – an invaluable experience in attempting to unravel the historical, cultural and geographical background to the struggles of the Apache people with the region's first white settlers. I am also especially grateful to Dave Mills of Naturetrek who, during the period of the book's preparation, provided me with opportunities to visit Namibia, Botswana and elsewhere in southern and central Africa, and also Spain and Ecuador.

Needless to say, most of the work was far less exciting than these geographical ventures and involved mainly a mental slog through a large body of literature. This could never have run so smoothly without the kind assistance from the personnel of a number of official organisations, including The Australian Institute of Aboriginal and Torres Strait Islander Studies (Canberra), The Minority Rights Group (London), The Wilderness Society of Tasmania (Hobart, Tasmania) and Survival International (London). The largest and most important contribution of this nature was made by the staff at Norwich Central Library. Tragically, this building burnt down midway through the project and the fire destroyed most of their stock. Yet the staff seemed to cope as calmly with this larger crisis as they did with the weekly barrage of requests that I inflicted upon them over four years. I must have been helped by at least twenty different staff members, yet all showed the same unfailing courtesy and for this they have my deep respect and sincere thanks.

In addition to these conventional channels for information, a range of people have provided individual assistance on particular subjects, either teasing out facts unknown or inaccessible to me, or passing on their expertise or relevant written material, cornering specific details and generally making the writer's life a little less isolated. This list includes my mother and father, Peter and Anne Cocker, Gill Coleridge, Gerald Crowson, Camille Davis, Dan Franklin, Brenda Ferris, Jason Hook, Peter Hulme, David Lovatt Smith, Rod Martins, Jan Morris, Dr Michael Occleshaw, Tony Stones, Alan Wood and Andy Soutter.

Andy also read about a quarter of the book's first draft and made valuable suggestions for improving the text. Gerald Crowson and John Morley both gave freely of their time, reading and making helpful comments on other sections. To all three of them I am deeply grateful. John Morley and Moira Warland also listened patiently as I gave full rein to my views and ideas, which was invaluable in shaping the text, especially the final chapters. My great friends Dr Tony Hare and Amanda Greatorex played that same role of sounding board, then offered many valuable suggestions. They also gave me regular accommodation in London, while Tony provided typically stimulating companionship in Spain. For all of these things I thank them both.

In the later stages of production, the manuscript passed into the hands of the late John Blackwell, who quickly fulfilled his reputation as a brilliant editor and publisher. Sadly John died suddenly while we were finalising the text, but he had already brought to bear upon it his great intellectual rigour and editorial insight. For his expertise, his good humour, tact and thoroughness, I owe him an enormous debt, and it is one of the few regrets of the book that I am not able to thank him personally at its publication. Charlotte Mendelson of Jonathan Cape skilfully excavated all the various layers of amended text and has also been extremely helpful in seeing the book through to completion. I wish to thank her for this contribution, as I do Ann Hobday for the preparation of her excellent maps.

My agent, Gill Coleridge, and my editor, Dan Franklin, have played an enormous part in the project, encouraging my initial interest in the subject, helping to define an approach, reading and making invaluable comments on the text, some parts several times, then waiting patiently as the book crept forward. For their support, intelligent advice and professional tact I am deeply indebted.

Finally I come to the part played by my partner, Mary. She has helped me in too many ways for them all to be listed here. She has been my first critic, reading chapters as they were drafted and then also in a final stage, and always balancing her patient encouragement with perceptive and clear-headed advice. During the course of the book's preparation she has also cared for our two daughters during my long absences, both physical (amounting to more than nine months overseas) and mental. For her infinite patience and support I am eternally grateful.

I need only add that without all these people this book would have been impossible. Its completion is due in large measure to them, yet any failings are mine alone.

Preface

Europe's encounter with and treatment of the world's tribal peoples is an immense theme, sprawling over five centuries and across all the inhabited continents. Yet it is also a phenomenon whose outline retains a fundamental clarity. In essence it is the story of how a handful of small, highly advanced and well-populated nation-states at the western extremity of Eurasia embarked on a mission of territorial conquest. And how in little more than 400 years they had brought within their political orbit most of the diverse peoples across five continents.

It is in equal measure a tale of extraordinary human achievement in adversity, conferring on the victors possession of much of the world's physical resources, and a tragedy of staggering proportions, involving the deaths of many millions of victims and the complete extinction of numerous distinct peoples. In fact, when viewed as a single process the European consumption of tribal society could be said to represent the greatest, most persistent act of human destructiveness ever recorded.

The most obvious challenge that faces any inquirer into this subject is the sheer mass of material. Clearly, no single volume can hope to document every episode. Nor is the book's purpose an exhaustively detailed overview. Yet I believe it is important to attempt to convey the whole picture between two covers, since one can at least suggest both its full time-scale and its international embrace. The method I chose for this purpose is a detailed examination of four widely spaced episodes – the Spanish conquest of Mexico, the British near-extermination of the Tasmanian Aborigines, the white American dispossession of the Apache, and the German subjugation of the Herero and Nama of South West Africa.

These four portraits have several critical and interlocking functions. Most obviously, they imply the global picture, illustrating four different European powers in four separate regions. They span a 400-year period, from the sixteenth to the twentieth centuries, and involve the first and last phases of European military expansion. They also serve as separate close-focus lenses through which I could explore the human story in detail. They convert the abstract theory or idea into concrete reality, they show the generic process as specific incidents and they transmit statistical data as a clear and emotionally engaging, sometimes harrowing story. Yet, the underlying structure of the book enabled me – to continue the cinematographic analogy – to move backwards sometimes from these close-up images to a panoramic vision. It was a balance of two complementary perspectives that I intended to create.

I have also sought to provide in the geographical and temporal spaces between my four portraits a connective tissue of parallels, of recurrent echoes and reverberations, and of linkages both partial and overt. In the confrontation between the civilised and the savage the repetitions are seldom truly exact, but a failure to learn from the past is one indisputable thread running through the many tragedies of this whole saga.

Author's Note

In a comparative work such as this, figures present a particularly obstinate problem, and it seems better to spell out the general approach rather than to enter a caveat in every instance cited.

Estimates of population sizes or losses and of casualty figures, especially from campaigns as distant as the Spanish conquest of Mexico, are always problematic. Often the only reliable principle is that the larger the figure, the less accurate it is likely to be. Even in the war between the Germans and the Herero and Nama of South West Africa, a conflict of less than a century ago and in an age of telegraph and railways, the assessments of dead and wounded differ widely from source to source.

In all four histories I have invariably tried to find and use the most widely accepted numbers. In cases where the variation is itself significant, the matter is more fully aired. In other instances, where a range of estimates exist and each has achieved roughly equal validity I have invariably opted for the more conservative figure. In this tragic story there is no need for exaggeration to indicate its massive scale.

Another problematic area is money, especially when trying to establish modern equivalents for historical sums. Once again, this is especially the case in sixteenth-century Spain, when a number of currencies were in circulation, exchange rates were arbitrary and volatile, and the Spanish economy subject to serious inflation.

Where a useful modern equivalent could be found then I have tried to include it, but have not attempted to impose a table of values overall. The important point is that the value of the treasure trove of the Americas must have been as stupefying to the scribes who first tried to calculate it, as it is irretrievable to the modern imagination.

In the less contentious matter of distances, weights and other measurements I have used the metric system, except in quotations. This makes for some mild incongruities on occasion, but these seemed a worthwhile price for ease of comparison.

Introduction

All Christendom will here have Refreshment and Gain

In the arid hills of Namibia one of the first sounds to register the passing of the African night is the loud, ringing call of the bok-makierie, a bird closely related to the shrikes or butcher-birds of Europe. Against the soft pastel-washed skies and sepia tones of the morning landscape, its notes are so clear and distinct they seem chiselled from the crisp dawn air, and the song acts on the awakening consciousness like an alarm.

On the dawn of 12 April 1893, the bokmakieries were singing as 200 German soldiers, newly arrived from Europe, took up their positions around the small settlement of Hornkranz. The village was the home of an African tribe, the Witbooi, and, although barely 100 kilometres from Windhoek, the fledgling capital of German South West Africa, Hornkranz's occupants had successfully resisted the encroaching imperial power. However on that April morning their village was at peace. Most of its residents were sleeping. Their chief, Hendrik Witbooi, the man who had inspired a bold defiance of the Germans, was quietly seated outside his home, enjoying coffee with his family.

Taking advantage of the tranquillity, the Germans surrounded the settlement and waited for their orders. Only the officers had been told in advance the purpose of the exercise. Now the commanding officer repeated his message to his troops. Their intention that calm, song-awakened morning was 'to destroy the tribe of the Witboois'.[1]

The German soldiers, part of one of the largest and most powerful land armies in the world, started firing from three directions, and within thirty minutes 16,000 rounds had been expended by 200 rifles. By the time this torrent of bullets had ceased it had wrought a dread-

3

ful carnage. Blood-stained bodies and the remains of slaughtered animals were strewn around the settlement. Surveying the aftermath, one eye-witness noted random fragments of the shambles, like the seven Witbooi corpses pressed tightly together in the hollow beneath an overhanging rock, or the shattering reports of ammunition, abandoned in their huts by fleeing Witbooi men, and now exploding as the huts were torched by the Germans.[2] And amidst this deafening noise he recalled the silent, incongruous tableau of two children playing in the dust by the corpse of their mother.

In front of the entire panorama of death the European troops methodically assembled the spoils of their victory, a collection they recorded with all the fastidious attention of a clerk to a column of figures. The list included 212 stirrups, 74 horseshoes, 25 tin cups, 12 coffee-grinders, 12 coffee pots, 9 tin plates, 44 sets of dentures, 3 violins, one harmonium, a pair of opera glasses.[3]

The German captain's official report immediately following the massacre suggested that the Witbooi were neutralised as a fighting force. One cable to Berlin more than a month after the raid suggested that fifty Witbooi soldiers had been killed. Gradually, however, it began to emerge that the attack had not been as effective militarily as had been claimed. In particular, it transpired that able-bodied men constituted only a small portion of the approximately ninety dead. One German participant in the slaughter became particularly incensed by the 'hateful and lying manner' in which some British newspapers 'alleged that our soldiers spared neither wife nor child'. However, as one subsequent English commentator noted, had women and children not been targets why had the Germans attacked a sleeping village without warning, when both were bound to be present?[4]

When it did eventually emerge that many of the victims were, in fact, women and children – seventy-eight according to the Witbooi themselves – and German officialdom was forced to make what it termed 'an undesirable revision', it struck upon a brilliantly inventive reply to the accusations. There had been heavy casualties amongst non-combatants, conceded the Director of the German Colonial Department, but this was owing to the cowardice of the Witbooi men, who took cover behind their womenfolk when fired upon.[5]

The Hornkranz massacre is a unique event in the history of a people. It is also a fragment completely typical of Europe's wider conflict with tribal peoples. One representative ingredient is its smallness, its perceived insignificance in the broader sweep of European history. Another common element is the dispute over the precise nature and number of victims. Casualty statistics in this global war have seldom been a straightforward matter.

One of the major problems is the sheer size of the numbers involved. For out of those small, 'insignificant' massacres like Hornkranz arises an aggregate of monstrous proportions. And this, in turn, has bred its own complications. Those attempting to assess the total numerical cost of Europe's colonial empire have often prefaced any figures with warnings about the dangers of statistical evidence. To concern ourselves, they argue, with converting historical experience into an auditor's column runs the risk of our losing any relationship to the individual tragedies which those numerals so distantly convey. In striving for the Olympian perspective, any real human meaning disappears from view.

And yet however distant from any scale we might recognise in our daily lives, it is the cumulative statistics of Europe's conflict with tribal peoples which most immediately convey its magnitude. It is valuable to repeat that eleven million indigenous Americans lost their lives in the eighty years following the Spanish invasion of Mexico. In the Andean empire of the Incas the figure was more than eight million. In Brazil the Portuguese conquest saw Indian numbers dwindle from a pre-Columbian total of almost 2,500,000 to just 225,000. And to the north of Mexico it has now been widely accepted that Native Americans declined from an original population of more than 8,000,000 to just 800,000 by the end of the nineteenth century. For the whole of the Americas some historians have put the total losses as high as one hundred million.[6]

From the other continents emerge statistics every bit as chilling. In Africa, for example, perhaps the most widely known figure concerns the European traffic in black slaves, of whom eleven million were transported for sale in the Americas. However, less well appreciated are the vast numbers killed en route or abandoned to die before they could be processed as the visible cargo crossing the Atlantic. During the course of its 300-year history, possibly as many as an additional fourteen million Africans fell victim to the slave-trade.[7]

Even less familiar are the figures that relate to colonial policies during the first fifty years of European rule: statistics like the 325,000–375,000 inhabitants who died between 1904 and 1907 in German East Africa (modern-day Tanzania) and German South West

Africa (Namibia), either in wars of resistance or during episodes of famine resulting from these conflicts. Less precise but more damning is the evidence for the hundreds of thousands, and probably millions of Africans who died in the Belgian Congo as a consequence of the Belgian King Leopold's frenzied quest for rubber and ivory.[8]

In Oceania, if the population collapse did not involve the absolute numbers of the other continents, then certainly the pattern of decline was replicated with extraordinary consistency. Typically, Australia's Aborigines slumped from a pre-colonial total of at least a million to just 30,000 by the 1930s, outnumbered even by the 40,000 people of mixed Aboriginal–European descent. Similarly, the Maoris of New Zealand dwindled from more than 250,000 at the time of first European contact to 42,000 by 1890. The Polynesian inhabitants of Tahiti, which had served eighteenth-century Europe as a paradigm of tropical paradise, had gone from an original 40,000 in 1769 to just 6,000 by the 1840s: from Eden to Armageddon in a single lifetime.[9]

Not surprisingly the assessment of these victim numbers, given their scale and implications for European civilisation, has involved an academic feud commensurate with the historical struggles themselves. A single example of the huge discrepancies in the figures accepted by different parties will have to stand for the whole complex debate. It concerns the extinct Arawak populations on the Caribbean island of Hispaniola (comprising the modern-day states of the Dominican Republic and Haiti). Of two important historical works on European conquest of the Americas published in the early 1990s, one author accepted 8,000,000 as the original indigenous population, the other could only suggest that it 'may have been over 100,000'. Both, however, could agree that within a quarter of a century more than ninety per cent of the Arawak were dead, largely as a consequence of Spanish brutality.[10]

Using only the most widely accepted estimates of population loss, one can make projections about the total losses suffered by tribal peoples during their conquest by whites. These dwarf the entire sum of deaths during the First World War and were certainly greater than all European losses during the Second World War. Incidents like Hornkranz, so unmemorable to their European victors, add up to a truly global struggle with a casualty list of more than fifty million human names.

*

And yet, it had not started out like that. When Christopher Columbus first made landfall in the Caribbean on 12 October 1492, his initial reports on American humanity were filled with a sense of wonder and excitement. In a letter to his royal sponsors, King Ferdinand and Queen Isabella of Spain, he wrote of a 'people without number':

[They] all go naked, men and women, just as their mothers bore them . . . They have no iron or steel or weapons, nor are they fitted to use them; not because they are not well built and of handsome stature, but because they are extraordinarily timorous . . . It is true that, after they become reassured and lose this fear, they are so guileless and so generous with all that they possess, that no one would believe it who has not seen it. Of anything they have, if they are asked for it, they never say no, on the contrary they invite the person to share it and display as much love as if they would give their hearts . . .[11]

The meeting on the Caribbean shoreline of two such radically different branches of the human family was for both a psychological moment of overwhelming magnitude. Amidst the exchanges of hand gestures, of mime and awkward laughter, half the world was obliged to embrace its other half in an instant revolution of the imagination. For the Caribbean Arawak it was an encounter as profound as it would be for modern Europeans to receive aliens from outer space. In fact, Columbus wrote, 'wherever I went . . . the others went running from house to house, and to the neighbouring towns, with loud cries of, "Come! Come! See the people from the sky!" So all came, men and women alike, as soon as they were confident about us, not one, small or great, remaining behind . . .'[12]

Elsewhere in the Americas that same deep confusion characterised the indigenes' first notions about Europeans. In the case of the three major pre-Columbian societies – the Mexica, Maya and Inca – each referred to the white invaders initially in terms that suggested supernatural origins. The best-known instance concerned the Mexican emperor, Moctezuma, who entertained notions that his Spanish conqueror, Hernan Cortés, was the returning Mexican culture god, Quetzalcoatl.

Nor were such misidentifications peculiar to the Americas. In nineteenth-century Australia, Aborigines explained the sudden arrival and strange, pale-skinned appearance of whites with the idea that they were the returned ghosts of their deceased kin. The nineteenth-century colonial pioneer George Grey wrote of an occasion when a tearful old Aboriginal woman approached him exclaiming, 'Yes, yes, in truth it is him,' threw her arms around Grey and rested her head upon his breast.

> At last the old woman, emboldened by my submission, deliberately kissed me on each cheek . . . and assured me that I was the ghost of her son, who had sometime before been killed by a spear wound in his breast . . . My new mother expressed almost as much delight at my return to my family, as my real mother would have done, had I been unexpectedly restored to her.[13]

As late as 1926, when increasing numbers of white colonists arrived on the island of Malekula, one of the Vanuatu archipelago in the South Pacific, the indigenous inhabitants consoled themselves with a myth about pale-skinned hero-gods who would restore the island and its people to a new golden age. They continued to cling to this belief even as the Pandora's box of Western ailments drove them rapidly towards extinction.[14]

The idea that they should be received as god-like beings, which initially flattered the pioneers, was later incorporated into a body of imperial myth as further confirmation of Europe's superiority. Yet it is easy to forget that explorers like Columbus were equally capable of mingling extravagant fantasy with their empirical accounts of indigenous peoples. Without a flicker of incredulity he passed on to his royal patrons reports about humans with dogs' faces and only a single eye, of humans with tails and an island inhabited by a martial race of women – the Amazons of legend. More than half a century later, the Spanish conquistador Bernal Diaz recalled how on entering the Mexican capital, Tenochtitlan, the sight of the great stone temples and buildings seemed 'like an enchanted vision from the tale of Amadis. Indeed, some of our soldiers asked whether it was not all a dream.'[15]

However, once the first great gush of excitement and emotion had spent itself, the encounter between natural and civil man was an experience triggering two basic responses in Europeans. On the one hand, as colonists gazed at the naked primitive with his simple weapons and rudimentary technology, they were brought to an appreciation, by contrast, of their own culture's enormous achievement.

From this fundamental reaction it was but a small step to assume that the primitives thereafter must move inexorably out of their backward state, towards the twin blessings of Western science and the Christian faith.

On the other hand, in the elegant sun-bronzed form of the savage, some Europeans beheld a mirror-image of themselves, but an image unencumbered by the many accretions of European civilisation. Looking at the Arawak in the luxury of his Caribbean garden, or the Australian Aborigine amidst an infinity of outback, they were offered a vision of Europe's own past. It was a response that worked along the same axis as the earlier reaction, but it led in completely the opposite direction. While one predicted how the savage must gain on the road to civilisation, the other envisioned what Europe had lost in its own journey out of the wilderness.

The notion that mankind had somehow fallen away from an earlier social ideal was a tradition embedded in European culture. From the Greco-Roman world it had inherited in a variety of forms the myth of a golden age – either an era or a location where humans had existed free from want, strife and from restraint. The Homeric legend of the Lotus-eaters, for instance, depicted a society abundantly supplied by the fruits of the lotus-tree, without cares and indulging a life of forgetful ease. The Roman poet Virgil recreated Arcadia as a rustic paradise of virile shepherds and sylph-like maidens, simple, virtuous and happy. From the Judaeo-Christian tradition Europe had inherited the myth of the garden of Eden, an original terrestrial paradise whose principal constituents, apart from its human pair, were blissful innocence and earthly fecundity.

When Europeans embarked on their global exploration in the fifteenth century, their earliest descriptions of tribal peoples were profoundly influenced by this complex of ideas. One of the most obvious associations was between the tropical luxuriance of the American environment and the exotic foliage entwining Europe's visual representations of Eden. The natural abundance of the Caribbean was amongst the first things Columbus noted. He wrote of islands that were 'fertile to an excessive degree' and 'filled with trees of a thousand kinds and tall, seeming to touch the sky.'[16]

The tribal peoples themselves also deeply impressed some of the early explorers by their physical grace and clear-skinned complexion, free from the signs of disease that so often disfigured European features. The Indians' lifestyle, with its communally based approach to resources, its instinctual reciprocity, the apparent absence of social hierarchy or moral restraint upon the physical aspects of life all made a strong impact on the sexually repressed and class-bound consciousness of the visitors. Just like the sun and water, ran one commentary on Caribbean society, 'the land belonged to all'.

> They live in a golden age, and do not surround their properties with ditches, walls or hedges. They live in open gardens, without laws or books, without judges, and they naturally follow goodness and consider odious anyone who corrupts himself by practising evil.[17]

Equally appealing was the fact that tribal societies had hitherto managed their economies without money. Even the Mexica, a vigorous mercantile nation with highly developed trade networks both internally and at an international level, had no monetary system comparable with that in Europe. This led some to conclude that since tribal society had avoided money, it had also escaped money's corrosive potential. According to one commentator on the Indians of Brazil, they lived 'free from the greed and inordinate desire for riches that are so prevalent among other nations.'[18]

Such conclusions, drawing as they did on the strong currents of association in European culture between natural landscape and natural innocence, presented only a highly selective version of the first Americans. Yet in assessing European views of tribal society it would be wrong to overlook these idealised portraits completely, in favour of the deeply negative, racist attitudes that came to dominate, and equally wrong to underestimate their profound impact on European intellectual life.

Until the moment of first contact, Christian Europe's study of humankind had been simply a question of reflecting upon itself, its classical antecedents and – more rarely – its alien twin, the world of Islam. At the end of the fifteenth century, however, Europeans were forced to confront the existence of human beings fundamentally identical to themselves, yet whose lifestyle, culture, even civilisation were radically other than their own. In the half millennium since Columbus' first encounters in the Caribbean, tribal peoples have served constantly as an imaginative resource for Europeans, as an assemblage of values and ideas, which has evolved in relation to the changing concerns of Europe itself. That fundamental oscillation between their sameness and radical difference, which operated in almost all Western attitudes towards indigenous peoples, presented opportunities for implicit commentary upon European conditions.

A classic example is Thomas More's *Utopia*, the model for any ideal vision of human society and a long-established part of Europe's political lexicon. Written in 1516, it described a fictional community whose experiences of enduring harmony unburdened by want, inequality or excessive work represented conditions radically different from and obliquely critical of those in More's own society. In order to recreate his hypothetical Utopians, the English humanist and statesman drew partly on contemporary accounts of indigenous American society.

One of the key conditions for their social concord was the absence of money, by which 'all nobility, magnificence, worship, honour, and majesty, the true ornaments and honours . . . of a commonwealth, utterly be overthrown and destroyed.'[19] Inverting the norms of Renaissance Europe, where gold was the ultimate insignia of power, Utopians used it to make 'vessels that serve for most vile uses' like chamber pots, or restricted it for the adornment of children, criminals and slaves.[20] This indifference to the precious metal echoed almost perfectly Columbus' historical reports of crew members who exchanged worthless leather straps for substantial quantities of Caribbean gold.[21]

The fact that Utopians held 'virtue to be life ordered according to the prescript of nature' also questioned the conventional Christian dogma on original sin.[22] If allowing what was *natural* in man could result in such an admirable community, then it was perhaps not his inherent sinfulness that produced war and crime, but the operation of society itself.

Another author who expressed the idea even more powerfully and was similarly inspired by his research into pre-industrial society was the French philosopher Jean Jacques Rousseau. Where More had selected facets of pre-Columbian Americans to invent his Utopians, in *A Discourse on Inequality*, Rousseau used the methods of comparative anthropology. Drawing from early accounts of Caribbeans, Native Americans and the Khoikhoi (some of the original inhabitants of southern Africa and ancestors to the Witbooi), he recreated the familiar idealised portrait of pre-civil society. But it assumed new potency and popularity under the guise of Rousseau's 'noble savage'. According to the author, natural man lived in harmony with himself and his surroundings, 'a free being whose heart is at peace and whose body is in health.' With this as a first principle, Rousseau then presented a radical aetiology for the social ills of eighteenth-century Europe. Just as factors within civilised existence itself were the cause of physical disease, so the uneven and distorted arrangements of civil society had poisoned man's primitive inclinations towards goodness and happiness.

Even today such stereotypes of indigenous people continue to resurface in Western society as a means of advancing certain political and cultural views. One modern reincarnation is the feather-crowned, crimson-anointed Yanomami Indian from Brazil, endlessly reproduced by the conservation community both as an eloquent reproach against environmental destruction, especially of the rainforest, and as an icon symbolising sustainable use of such resources.

Although these sympathetic stereotypes have had a generally positive effect on relations with tribal society, they tended to circulate only in an intellectual milieu. Moreover, their influence was greatest within Europe, but it diminished as they drew closer to the place of actual contact between the two communities. At the frontier itself such stereotypes could even have adverse consequences. For when the people they were meant to describe failed to live up to the claims of human perfection, the result could be a kind of post-coital disappointment. Ideas like the 'noble savage' then supplied the sharp edge to a deepening cynicism.

Yet Europe's positive stereotypes concerning indigenous society cannot be blamed for the massacre at Hornkranz, or the diabolic conflagration which consumed the Caribbean in the quarter-century after Columbus, or indeed for any of the destruction which subsequently unfurled across four continents. The attitudes that launched the tragic developments described in this book revolved around a reverse image – an evil twin – of the idea of the noble savage. And the only characteristic it shared with its opposite was that it drew on ancient myths which loomed in the European subconscious with enormous potency.

Ever since the time of the Greeks, Europeans had been accustomed to a binary vision of human societies. On the one hand were the original classical cultures of the Mediterranean and their successors in a wider Europe. These were the ordered realms which civilisation naturally inhabited, but beyond the pale of this rational interior, Europe was besieged by the forces of human darkness or, to use the word of Greek origin, the barbarians – a sound imitative of their unintelligible languages. If the commonwealth of civilised nations was the province of rational government and moral order, then it followed logically that the exterior was a province of irrational savagery and immoral wickedness. And when Columbus reported progress on his search for dog-faced men and other 'human monstrosities', he was articulating Europe's persistent belief in this threatening penumbra at the margins of civilisation.

Coupled with this bipolar view of mankind were Christian Europe's deeply ambivalent attitudes towards the natural world. While the pastoral scenes of Virgil's *Arcadia* might carry associations with innocence, the realm of physical nature was equally the habitat for man's instinctual drives – a panic landscape of procreation and fertility. The earth might yield up her bountiful harvests, but if she were not regulated by some intervening hand, nature would riot and turn the civilised products of mankind back into chaos. Nature was fruitful but she was also wild and threatening, which carried profoundly negative implications for those humans who lived closest to her.

The fact that indigenous Americans or aboriginal Africans and Australians often went naked was confirmation for the West of their deep intimacy with nature and of an un-Christian openness towards the physical body. Even the sultry climate or tropical fertility of their home environment could reinforce the idea of this closeness to the physical earth. These factors led many Europeans to view tribal peoples as having retained the menacing characteristics of wild animals as much as the natural qualities of fellow men. Time and again, Christian Europe defended its transgressions against tribal society on the grounds of the latter's subhuman condition.

It is perhaps as much a measure of the prevalence of such attitudes in the fifty years after Columbus' historic voyage, as it is of papal concern, that Pope Paul III issued a bull in 1537 giving the Catholic Church's official judgement that Indians were indeed 'true men', not beasts. It is equally a measure of how ineffectual such official statements were in challenging attitudes that as late as 1902 a member of the Commonwealth Parliament in Australia felt able to announce that 'There is no scientific evidence that the Aborigine is a human being at all.'[23] Similarly in German South West Africa, when the imperial administration ordered settlers to curb corporal punishment of African workers, the settlers petitioned the colonial department with the plea that 'Any white man who has lived among natives finds it almost impossible to regard them as human beings at all in any European sense.'[24]

Viewing aboriginal society as beyond the pale of humanity had legal and political implications that were deeply sinister for its constituents. It was an axiom of Christian thought, propounded in the opening portion of its most sacred text, the Bible, that all organic life on earth was arranged in a hierarchy, at whose apex stood Christian man. As its appointed masters, Christians could look down upon this entire physical realm as a God-given field for their use and enjoyment. If the savage were not differentiated from the natural environment, then it followed that he too could be incorporated in that utilitarian prospect. Since he was outside the fellowship of Christian civilisation, he would enjoy no greater legal or moral status than any other flora and fauna.

It was in part this ideology which informed Columbus' sweeping announcement in his first letter from the New World, that 'all Christendom will here have refreshment and gain.'[25] And it was on premises like these that he based Europe's earliest moves to dispossess the savage, and claim the Caribbean islands in the name of his Spanish masters. Almost 300 years later, comparable views permitted British colonists to declare the Australian continent an empty land – a *terra nullius* – and dismiss in a single Latinate phrase forty millennia of Aboriginal occupation.

Even when it was acknowledged that indigenous occupants were indeed human, from the sixteenth century onwards Europeans conceived a theory of mankind's social and historical development which helped them to bypass any legal or political rights that tribal society might be presumed to possess. The doctrine held that human beings were accessible to a hierarchical arrangement comparable with that in the Old Testament which ordered all other organic life. Each newly encountered tribe could be assigned to a particular stratum of this pyramid, according to its level of technological and cultural achievement. Naturally, the colonists viewed themselves as having long since progressed through these intermediate stages, while Christian civilisation was the obvious apex and terminal point to which all mankind must inexorably aspire.

A whole battery of specious legal and theological devices were soon advanced that both expressed this determinist schema and reinforced its moral validity. In 1494, for instance, two years after Columbus' first voyage, the Spaniard Rodrigo Borgia, both the father and lover of Lucretia Borgia, had approved the Treaty of Tordesillas in his capacity as Pope Alexander VI. At a stroke he had granted to the Spanish and Portuguese crowns, as the two temporal agents of the Catholic Church, the right to divide the New World between themselves. In the eyes of the *conquistadores*, God had given the Americas to them.

One of the more ingenious justifications for European conquest is worth recalling, if only to demonstrate that the Arawak, with their theory of Columbus' descent from the sky, had no monopoly on the absurd. The Spanish historian Gonzalo Fernandez de Oviedo advanced the thesis that, since the Caribbean islands were really the Hesperides, the fabled Islands of the Blest thought to exist at the western extremity of the earth, and since 3,193 years ago these had belonged to Hesperus, the twelfth King of Spain, Columbus' action had not been a fresh annexation but a reclamation of lost territories.

However, this ecumenical vision of human societies carried hidden complications. If it was in the furtherance of a divinely ordained progress that the *conquistadores* claimed the right to seize and displace in the New World, their fellow theologians at home claimed on behalf of the subjected peoples their right to be absorbed into the bosom of the Christian Church. In 1512 this privilege was encoded in the Laws of Burgos, requiring of the colonists that they convert Caribbean peoples to Christianity. Indigenous Americans were to be offered the eternal blessings of baptism and burial, Christian education (for the sons of chiefs) and compulsory attendance at church. The European faith eventually became for tribal peoples worldwide both an important solace against, and a social bridge into, the alien world of their colonisers. Moreover, the army of genuinely humane missionaries who travelled out to the colonies to evangelise often served as important political champions for their indigenous flock.

Yet the methods of enforced conversion could be a stark violation of the beliefs they were intended to propagate. Typically, in 1513 there was a further addition to the Laws of Burgos, known as the *Requerimiento*. On the occasion of fresh conquests, American communities were to be read a proclamation, providing the audience – albeit in a language and conceptual framework incomprehensible to them – with an outline of Christian history and a request for their formal submission to European authority. Supposedly a means of avoiding bloodshed by allowing Americans to surrender gracefully, it was a statement of Europe's monumental presumption. In practice it usually served as little more than a grotesque subterfuge. Wishing to spare them any possible opportunity for misunderstanding, the *conquistadores* often read the *Requerimiento* from a position where it was inaudible to the hapless people they had always intended to despoil and enslave.

A compelling revelation of the meaning of the Christian message for many tribal peoples is contained in the death-scene of an Arawak chief, Hatuey. Captured in Cuba by the Spaniards in 1511, Hatuey was asked to convert before being executed. His apostasy would have reaped the reward of death by decapitation, rather than being burnt alive. According to an eyewitness:

> The lord Hatuey thought for a short while, and then asked the friar whether Christians went to Heaven. When the reply came that good ones do, he retorted, without need for further reflection, that, if that was the case, then he chose to go to Hell to ensure that he would never again have to clap eyes on those cruel brutes.[26]

Apart from their religion, the other great benefit Europeans sought to bestow upon tribal peoples was the opportunity to participate in an increasingly global economy. The matter of work had always been a key element in Western attitudes towards pre-civil society. Initially, the deep impression made by America's natural abundance led many explorers to conclude that its inhabitants were free from the constant hard labour which ground down such a large proportion of European humanity. The Arawak, surrounded by his lush gardens and the warm, fish-crowded waters of the Caribbean, had merely to reach out to acquire his daily needs. For European audiences, the leisure implicit in this tropical idyll was a source of both envy and admiration. And it is striking that in Thomas More's model society, the Utopians laboured for just six hours a day to acquire their healthy surpluses.

Yet it is remarkable, as the original European sense of wonder gave way to disdain, how any applause for the indigenes' love of leisure quickly turned to scorn for their irresponsible sloth. A seventeenth-century judgement on the southern African Khoikhoi could serve as a universal statement of Europe's contempt for the work capacity of tribal peoples:

> Their native inclination to idleness and a careless life, will scarcely admit of either force or rewards for reclaiming them from that innate lethargick humour. Their common answer to all motives of this kind, is, that the fields and woods afford plenty of necessaries for their support, and nature has amply provided for their subsis-

tence, by loading the trees with plenty . . . So that there is no need of work . . . And thus many of them idly spend the years of a useless restive life.[27]

Disgust at such apathy soon offered a means to challenge tribal society's much-lauded indifference to wealth. This had not arisen out of the innate virtue of the noble savage: 'their contempt for riches,' wrote one French commentator on the Khoikhoi, 'is in reality nothing but their hatred of work.'[28] Another author pointed towards equally sinister conclusions when he noted what a 'great pittie that such creatures as they bee should injoy so sweett a country.'[29]

Statements like these on the lazy, undeserving savage soon cohered in another general principle of Europe's right to dispossess him. John Locke, the seventeenth-century British philosopher, argued in *The Second Treatise of Government* that if two equal portions of land were subjected, one to good English husbandry, and the other to the control of Native Americans, the first would produce crops a thousand times more valuable than the products derived by the occupants of the second. ''Tis labour,' Locke suggested, 'which puts the greatest part of value upon land,' while 'labour, in the beginning, gave a right of property.'[30] From there it was a simple step for colonists in America and Africa to conclude that since hunters and gatherers, like the Indians, or pastoralists, like the Khoikhoi, did not actually work the land in the form of cultivation, they were not therefore in possession of it. The answer was to take it from them. The answer to the indigenous aversion to work itself was to force them to it.

Ever since the classical period, Europe had acquired the historical precedents and cultural beliefs to legitimise this step. Greece and Rome had both been slave economies, and even their most hallowed philosophers had accepted the necessity of slaves. In his *Politics*, Aristotle had reasoned that since the various human races differed 'from one another by as much as the soul differs from the body or a man from a wild beast . . . these [inferior] people are slaves by nature, and it is better for them to be subject to this kind of control.'[31]

By the time the New World had been discovered, slavery was endemic in parts of medieval European society – as indeed it was in Islamic and African society. By 1300, Italians in Cyprus were running sugar plantations with imported forced labour, including some black

Africans. By the early fifteenth century, mainland Italian merchants were doing a flourishing business in Slavs – the origin of the word 'slave' – acquiring their raw human materials from the Black Sea ports of the Tartars. In Venice alone ten thousand slaves were sold between 1414 and 1423.[32] In the same period the Portuguese had started to fill their boats with human cargoes as part of their newly acquired commerce with West Africa. These slaves, in combination with sugar and cash-crop production methods, soon moved out to the Portuguese-controlled islands of Madeira and the Azores, while the Spaniards followed suit in their own Atlantic toehold, the Canaries.

Thus, when Columbus embarked upon the seizure of the Arawak to do the labour of his new-found colony, he was only following a well established tradition. Yet it is deeply ironic that it should have been the great explorer who initiated the enslavement of indigenous Americans, when only a few years earlier he had trumpeted the New World as Europe's opportunity to create a new Christian paradise on earth. How quickly he had exchanged the role of herald for that of serpent in his proclaimed Eden. Within a generation of his actions, the first slave-grown sugar from the Americas was being sold in Europe. However, the Spaniards had soon found 'the effeminate native of Hispaniola' – 'loitering away his hours in idle pastimes under the shadow of his bananas' – poor material for slavery.[33] As Arawak numbers collapsed, so the transatlantic trade in black Africans began.

Slavery was the final step in Europe's ideological debasement of tribal society. Not only were slavery's victims considered subhuman, they had assumed much of the inanimate status of chattels. Slaves were objects that could be traded, exchanged, given away, sexually violated, dismembered or destroyed with impunity. Equally, they could be insured against possible loss like any other physical possession. Some of the most shameful implications of this commodity status are illustrated by the actions of one of the slave-traders plying the Atlantic.

In 1781 Luke Collingwood, captain of the *Zong*, a vessel owned by a Liverpool company, was anxious about the disease carrying off a number of his human cargo. Aware of the laws governing maritime insurance, Collingwood told his officers that 'if the slaves died a natural death, it would be the loss of the owners of the ship; but if they were thrown alive into the sea, it would be the loss of the underwriters.'[34] On the pretext that food and water supplies were insufficient for the full complement of slaves, the captain spurred his crew to sling 131 of them overboard to drown.

Surprisingly, perhaps, the affair did eventually come before the courts. However, while the machinery of the British legal system had been set in motion, it was not to deliver punishment for the cold-blooded murder of 131 Africans. It involved the insurers' refusal to underwrite the losses of the ship's owners, and was to settle a dispute about property and money.

It was not just the inhumanity of the slave system, which was denounced even at the time of the *Zong* incident, but also its massive wastage of human potential that was so destructive. In parts of Britain's North American colony of Virginia, for instance, a quarter of all African slaves died in the first year after transportation. In the West Indies one in three died within three years.[35] However, while this might have been shocking extravagance in terms of human life, on purely economic grounds it was not necessarily inefficient. In the words of Robert Fogel, slavery provided European manufacturers with

> a labour force stripped of every right that could impede their industrial designs. As nearly as the law could bring it about, slaves were to be as compliant a factor of production as the mills that ground the cane or the mules that pulled the carts. Planters had the license to establish whatever institutions and to use whatever force they deemed necessary to achieve that goal.[36]

Once reduced to the condition of economic automata, tribal society made a contribution to the wealth of European nations which is of incalculable magnitude, and even a single example can give some sense of its scale.

When they had imposed control on the former empires of the Mexica and the Inca of South America, the Spaniards discovered underground silver deposits of awesome fertility in both regions. Although the formal enslavement of inhabitants was supposedly outlawed in Spain's American possessions, the imperial authorities instituted systems of obligatory labour barely distinguishable from slavery. The work was so dangerous that an eyewitness to one of the Andean mines noted that if 'twenty healthy Indians enter on Monday, half may emerge crippled on Saturday'.[37] On the approaches to some Mexican silver mines, the dead miners' bones and rotting corpses littered the ground as in the environs of some grotesque human slaughterhouse.[38]

By 1600 the precious metals flowing from these sumps of misery into Spain's coffers had an average annual value of 40,000 ducats – a vast reservoir of wealth that for centuries served as a critical supply for the national economy and as a powerful stimulus to all European trade. For some historians, the silver and gold taken from the Americas, in conjunction with the later, fabulous profits accruing from African-slave-grown sugar and tobacco, were the essential preconditions of the industrial revolution and a foundation of Europe's modern world supremacy.[39]

If Europe's sweeping military conquests across four continents represented the first phase of defeat for tribal society, then the seizure of their possessions, like the German looting at Hornkranz – right down to the sets of dentures and the pair of opera glasses – symbolises a second phase. European dispossession of colonial subjects, the absorption of their most valuable resources and of so much of the product of tribal labour, as well as the orientation of colonial economies towards a Eurocentric goal, are major reasons for the Third World status of much of Africa and South America. Equally, they help explain the massive disparities in wealth and prosperity between the first peoples of Australia or North America and their largely white neighbours.

Yet, rather than confront the realities of their behaviour, the master races of Europe marched forward sheathed in an impenetrable armour of intellectual self-justification. A complex language of projection and inversion has exonerated Europeans for five centuries. These misrepresentations were a vital element not just during the initial military conquest, when they inspired European combatants with a sense of moral crusade and ensured its widest possible sanction by the home audience, but they were equally important in the ensuing centuries of political control and economic exploitation. For in order to maintain tribal peoples and their descendants at the brutal margin of European civilisation it was necessary to reassemble, almost on a daily basis, the fabric of untruths which justified their institutionalised inferiority.

Once again, the events at Hornkranz described in the opening paragraphs exemplify this process of falsification, which amounts to an intellectual conquest and a third phase in Europe's triumph over tribal society. One modern historian, for instance, as if to suggest the Witbooi massacre's prophylactic character, referred to it as a 'preventive raid'.[40]

Preventive? Certainly it prevented the future life and well-being of a significant number of the Witbooi people. But since the tribe, until that moment, had not lifted a hand in anger against the Germans, except to write letters of defiance at their encroachment, and since the principal consequence of the slaughter was to stir them into armed opposition, paralysing the colony and forcing the removal of the commanding officer, it was anything but a preventive raid. Even more preposterous were the claims of the contemporary Berlin authorities, who suggested that it was not the German soldiers who were responsible for the cold-blooded slaughter of so many women and children. It was actually the fault of the Witbooi themselves, hiding beneath the skirts of their womenfolk.

The ubiquity and magnitude of these falsehoods were so great that eventually anything could be laid before a European audience and might be believed. Within the stereotypic image of the savage swirled a miasma of random violence, sexual depravity, clod-like inertia and infantile incompetence. There was little profit in applying the rational faculties of Europe to this vague and inexplicable creature, for it was almost beyond logical analysis.

It is only in the context of this mental climate that one can comprehend the nineteenth-century notion that a mother from the now extinct Yahgan people of Tierra del Fuego would sell her child for a button; or the judgement on the Arawak extinctions in Hispaniola by the nineteenth-century American historian William Prescott. In *The Conquest of Mexico*, still regarded as a classic work on its subject, he wrote:

> The Indians would not labour without compulsion, and . . . unless they laboured, they could not be brought into communication with the whites, nor be converted to Christianity . . . The simple people, accustomed all their days to a life of indolence and ease, sunk under the oppressions of their masters, and the population wasted away with even more frightful rapidity than did the aborigines of our own country, under the operation of other causes.[41]

They faded away, not before a Spanish regime comparable, for its unlicensed rapacity, to that of Nazi Europe, but before the simple demands of an honest day's work. These weak and 'effeminate' beings – Prescott's favoured adjective – were infants in a man's world, sadly but inevitably doomed, a fact clearly confirmed by their defencelessness before the ailments of childhood, like measles and the common cold.

William Prescott, of course, lived in the nineteenth century, the period of the West's greatest geographical expansion and political dominance, and as a writer he was naturally influenced and unsighted by that massive triumph. Some might wish to argue that at the close of the second millennium his work represents no more than an anachronism, a set of Western attitudes that has long ceased to have any meaning.

They might further point to the fact that the last third of this century has seen radical changes in Western treatment of tribal peoples and their modern descendants. In Australasia and throughout North America there has been a wide-ranging restoration of indigenous lands and a redefinition of the legal and moral status of tribal society. In Africa the continent has been returned, from the Mediterranean to the Cape of Good Hope, to the political control of its indigenous inhabitants. Elsewhere, in the last refuges of pre-civil humankind, such as the Zairean jungles of the Efe 'pygmies' or the Brazilian rainforests of the Yanomami, the tribal hunter-gatherer has never enjoyed a higher international profile or greater assistance and protection.

All of these developments, it might be argued, demonstrate how Western society has long since recognised its past injustice and taken a path, if not of penance, then at least of proper adjustment. Yet, while academic histories may have re-evaluated Europe's relationship with tribal peoples in a manner less pleasing to the former, there is still strong evidence to indicate that at many levels, Europeans remain resistant to aspects of their own past and have retained some of their most ancient ideas about the savage.

Even the most popular revisionist histories have not been entirely able to penetrate these recesses. A classic example is Dee Brown's influential and majestic account of the American Indian wars, *Bury My Heart at Wounded Knee*. While presenting the story from the perspective of the defeated Indians and while galvanising Western sympathies like no other book on white–tribal conflicts, Brown's text portrayed indigenous Americans very much in the image of the noble savage – a proud and tragic people inexorably doomed and long since vanished (for consideration of the function of Europe's myth of tribal extinction see Chapter 11). Even had the author intended a more nuanced and rounded portrait, and there is much evidence that he did, many of his readers missed this version in favour of the older pre-existing stereotype.

Yet this inadvertent consequence of Brown's book is of minor significance compared with the levels of distortion encountered elsewhere. One example will have to suffice. English-speaking encyclopaedias, some of the most widely disseminated sources of information and presenting a corporate world view for their audiences, offer a perfect demonstration of these pernicious historical myths. One would search in vain, for instance, in most of these books for a people entitled the Arawak, or for a pre-Columbian population in Hispaniola. They and their extinction at European hands are facts exorcised from the sum of general knowledge. Similarly, on the island of Tasmania the presence of an Aboriginal population is seldom admitted, while their decimation by British settlers is far less likely to be noted than that of the island's strange marsupial predator, the Tasmanian wolf.

If one looks at actual entries, rather than the equally eloquent omissions, then the accounts of the Mexica, or Aztecs as they are more widely known, are highly instructive. In most encyclopaedias, usually within a handful of lines, one encounters phrases like 'great and powerful despotic state', and invariably a sentence such as this: 'They sacrificed human victims, captives of warfare, by ripping out their hearts while they still lived.'[42] The Mexica's frenzied religious blood lust was more than just a cultural feature or historical fact, it is still for many Europeans the sole and critical measure of their entire civilisation. Yet, conversely, in the entry for their Spanish conquerors, there is no similar account of their comparably violent persecution of Central American humanity. Nor, indeed, is there any reflex association of these Iberian people with human sacrifice, which the sixteenth-century Spanish Inquisition practised with equal relish in the guise of exposing heretics.

It goes without saying that an event so small as the murder of ninety Witbooi Africans at Hornkranz would never find its way into any European compendium of facts. But more significant is the almost universal omission of the overall German slaughter in South West Africa, a total a thousand times greater than the Hornkranz figure. Even more compelling still is the fact that in none of these works could one locate the raw data to assemble the statistics of mass death inflicted by European invasion upon its tribal subjects. (Yet when one notes that in almost every work, the Black Hole of Calcutta – for Britons a paradigm of brutality involving the deaths of fewer than fifty of their countrymen and women at Indian hands – is a constant, one begins to realise how much these compendia respond to mythic portraits of national life.)

These books suggest that for large numbers of Europeans and those of European descent, tribal peoples remain a defeated and immaterial branch of humanity entombed in a conspiracy of silence and misrepresentation. Either as rich and vital human societies or even simply as numbers of historical victims, they remain outside of our vision. Even now, in many parts of the world their past experiences at European hands continue to be denied. Tribal peoples have a right to know their own history and we have a duty to make their story a part of our own.

Part I

The Conquest of Mexico

'They thirsted mightily for gold; they stuffed themselves with it;
they starved for it; they lusted for it like pigs.'

MEXICAN EMPIRE

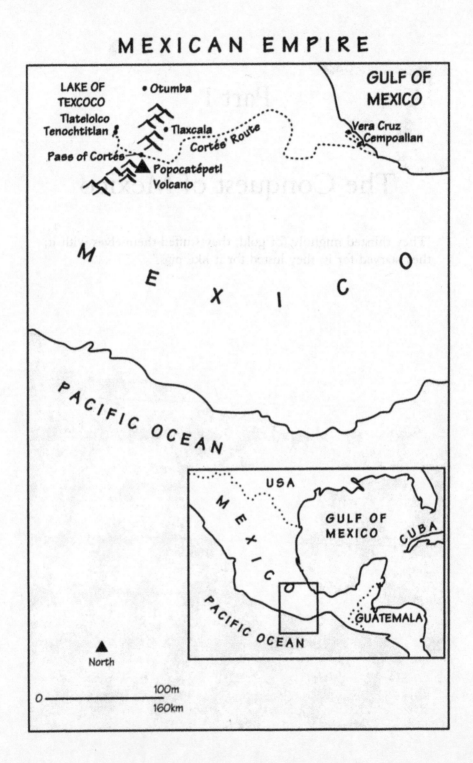

1

The March

Today, from a vantage point on the slopes of the volcano Popocatépetl, all that the modern visitor can normally make out of Mexico City, sixty-five kilometres away on its hinterland of fertile plain, is the muffling cloud of smog. However, on 1 November 1519 the would-be sightseers were foiled by the weather. And it was only on the following morning when the clouds lifted and the sun came out that the Spanish soldiers, gathering on a spot now known as the Paso de Cortés, became the first Europeans ever to have gazed down on this scene.

Below, just sixteen kilometres away, lay the first in a large high-altitude complex of connecting lakes. Beyond, the Spaniards could make out the outline of a city. A city built on water, the largest city in the Americas and the heart of its most powerful military people, the Mexica. Their new capital was immense. Its 108 districts housed a population of some 225,000, bigger than those of Paris and London combined. The largest city of which the newly arrived visitors could boast was Seville with 70,000 inhabitants, at most just a third the size of the Mexican capital. Across the whole of Europe only Naples compared. In fact, Tenochtitlan, the name of this American metropolis, stood amongst the greatest artefacts on earth; and when Hernan Cortés, the Spanish commander gazing down on that morning in November 1519, committed his small army to its conquest, he carried his nation across a historical threshold of momentous importance.

In the half-century before that day Iberian sailors, circling the world's oceans, had enmeshed the globe with their routes like the tentacles of some fantastically enlarged monster from the deep. Even as

Cortés and his forces entered the outskirts of Tenochtitlan, Ferdinand Magellan, sailing under the Spanish flag, was negotiating the straits at the tip of South America that were to bear his name. And only days after the Spanish arrival in the Mexican capital, the great sailor entered the waters of a vast new ocean, which he named the Pacific, before embarking on the first circumnavigation of the planet.

Yet, in the great Renaissance surge for geographical knowledge, it was not the Spaniards who had best profited from all this activity. It was the small sea-faring nation on their western border, the Portuguese, who had gained most. It was they who had pioneered navigational routes down the west coast of Africa, and one of their countrymen who had rounded its southernmost tip at the Cape of Good Hope. With this discovery in 1488, Bartolomeu Dias had opened up the prospect of an all-water passage to the orient, bypassing the monopoly-holding merchants on the old land routes through Persia, Arabia and Egypt. Oriental luxuries like spices, perfumes, silks, opium, gold and gems could now be acquired at a discount, and the Portuguese lost little time in taking advantage. Within a decade another countryman, Vasco de Gama, had reached India. Another ten years and Alfonso de Albuquerque, taking up his post as governor of Portugal's oriental possessions, captured Goa on India's west coast, then Aden at the south-western tip of Arabia. To these he added Malacca, on the Malayan peninsula, the centre of the eastern spice trade. From this one port alone, Albuquerque sent home riches worth $25 million in current values.[1]

While the Portuguese had established immensely profitable routes to the east, the Spaniards had elected to explore in a westerly direction. On the eve of their entry to Tenochtitlan, it still looked as if their choice had been a poor one. Although their transatlantic journeys had uncovered vast territories representing the greatest geographical discoveries by any European nation, for years the driving Spanish ambition was not to locate America, but to capture the same fabled oriental riches that had inspired their Portuguese rivals. Columbus, in his four lengthy journeys wandering the islands of the Caribbean or along the eastern shores of Central and South America, could never quite rid himself of the hope that he had found some outlying region in the empire of the Great Khan, China's fabled ruler. When it finally dawned on the Spaniards they they had not landed in Asia, but had uncovered two continents of whose existence Europe had not even dreamed, it seemed poor compensation.

By 1516 Portugal's rapidly expanding trade network embraced Africa's south-eastern littoral, as well as ports in India, the Malayan peninsula, the Celebes, the Moluccas, Thailand, southern Vietnam and even mainland China herself. The Spaniards, meanwhile, had located varied and richly self-sufficient communities amongst the archipelagos of the Caribbean and on the mainlands of both Americas. At each of these newly encountered localities, they had hoisted the flags of Castile and Aragon. In 1513 one of their explorers, Vasco Núñez de Balboa, hacking his way through the forests of modern-day Panama, had waded into the surf on its (as yet unnamed) Pacific shore and, brandishing his sword, claimed even the ocean in the name of his sovereigns. Despite such gestures, the Spaniards' genuine rewards for all their enterprise were few.

Gold ornaments had been found amongst the neolithic Arawak of the Caribbean, but the quantities were only moderate and rapidly exhausted. Certainly, Columbus' effusive claims of great mines of gold in these American islands, or his prophecy that most of the rivers would be found to flow with it, had proved hollow. During all his travels he had made little hard profit to justify even the capital spent on the first and most modest of his expeditions.

Yet in 1516 there were signs that the tide of fortune might have turned in Spain's direction. Expeditions sent out that year and the following winter, from Cuba to the North American mainland, brought back incontestable proof of cultures far more advanced than anything the Spaniards had previously known. Encountering first the Maya of the Yucatan peninsula and then the Totonacs, a coastal people within the political orbit of the Mexican empire, the explorers were deeply impressed with their large stone buildings, their temples, highly developed agriculture, fine cotton clothing. However, Spanish attention was particularly absorbed in other achievements of these Mesoamerican peoples – the abundance of their gold ornamentation and the high quality of its workmanship. The second expedition returned with precious metals valued at 16,000 pesos. At last Spain seemed to have found potential sources of wealth to rival those of the Portuguese and to justify their costly explorations.

In time, however, the Spanish encounter with the Mexican empire would have a significance far greater than these simple economic benefits. On a purely symbolic level it represented a point of intersection of two communities, whose parallel evolutions had continued in mutual ignorance for thousands of years. At the moment of their convergence, Spain and Mexico had achieved fresh heights in their independent development and were the dominant powers in their respective hemispheres. If it was not the first then it was the most significant confrontation of the Old with the New World.

For Europe to collide in this manner with any civilisation of such radically different orientation is virtually without parallel. In recent history one of the few encounters that bears any resemblance is the British forced entry in 1902 of the Tibetan capital, Lhasa, a place previously seen by only three Europeans. Yet this later meeting on the high plateau of Central Asia was the culmination of decades of intermittent communication. The surprise of final encounter was much more muted, and in the labyrinth of Asian politics the Tibetans were a marginal people. Their confrontation with Europe brought no immediate, radical transformation of Tibetan society. Nor did it initiate a major realignment in the world of human affairs.

In contrast, the wealth and power gained from Mexico – Europe's first major colonial conquest – would set Spain on a new, dazzling trajectory as the great European superpower of the sixteenth century. At a stroke the Spaniards had cancelled any initial economic lead established by Portugal in its nascent oriental empire. In the Americas, Mexico's discovery and seizure constituted a pivotal event, propelling the Spanish into a career of headlong conquest. Much of this outburst would be inspired by the fabulous riches that accrued to the new master of Mexico, Hernan Cortés. The gold and other sources of wealth gained by his victory would change him from a Castilian noble of negligible status into one of the richest princes in the Spanish empire. It was a transformation that captivated not just his compatriots, but the whole Christian world. As one commentator has noted, 'Cortés' success was the loadstone which drew to the Americas the iron might of Europe.'[2] Another historian suggested it had an even wider significance: that the manner of his conquest, relying as much on false promises and exploitation of tribal division as on force of arms, 'provides us with a model for all subsequent red/white relations in the New World'.[3]

Certainly, within just forty years of Cortés' personal triumph, the Spaniards would hold territories spanning thousands of kilometres on both continents. By 1560 they had explored the Pacific coast of North America to a point north of the current California/Oregon state borders. Other expeditions penetrated to the Grand Canyon and along the course of the Mississippi. Parts of Florida were settled. Mexico, most of modern-day Central America, large portions of the contemporary states of Venezuela, Colombia, Ecuador, Peru, Bolivia, Chile, Uruguay and Argentina were all within the Spanish domain. If it was not the largest European empire, it was one of the most rapidly established.

Spain's victory over the Mexica was the major catalyst for these historical developments, but today it retains a pre-eminence amongst all the examples of European conquest for other reasons. First, it raises, as it did at the time of the events themselves, major questions concerning the morality of such an invasion. In their previous victories in the Caribbean or parts of South America, the *conquistadores* had been fortified by the idea that they had subjugated rude savages barely one remove from the beasts of the jungle – people presumed to be lacking in the higher ideals of a developed religion, in legal and political organisation, in the arts, in technologies commonplace for Europeans; in fact, lacking in all the refinements of civilised existence.

However, Mexico was a completely different case. Here the Spaniards met a people who could trade with them almost blow for blow in technical and organisational ability. Although retaining some characteristics from their tribal antecedents, the Mexica had carried forward the flame of civilisation that had been burning in Mesoamerica for thousands of years. While Muslim forces had confined tenth-century Christian Spain to a mountainous strip along the northern coastline, the Mexican Valley, through which Cortés and his men were even now marching, had been home to a flourishing urban society celebrated for its religious innovation, its artistic and architectural achievement.

In November 1519, as the Spaniards advanced on Tenochtitlan's centre, they could appreciate that the capital's construction on a huge, brackish lake was immediate and powerful proof of Mexican capabilities. The complex of causeways connecting the city to the mainland, along which the Spanish horses could ride eight abreast, was an outstanding feat of engineering. So too was a sixteen-kilometre dyke that they had erected to prevent flooding. At the city's outskirts the Spaniards studied the agricultural innovations, especially the *chinampas*, the irrigated floating gardens – with their orchards, fishponds and intensively managed crops of maize, beans, squash, tomatoes – which ensured year-round produce for Tenochtitlan's population.

Other striking examples of organisational ability were the city's public steambaths and the system of ceramic pipes which supplied it with sweet-water fountains. More prosaic, perhaps, but no less impressive was the citywide network of latrines and the organised collection of waste and refuse, which constituted a sanitation system far superior to anything in Europe until the end of the eighteenth century. Even further in advance of any European equivalent were the frequent *telpuchcalli* and *calmecac*, the two school systems, which provided a universal education for Mexican children. Finally, at the end of the causeway along which the Spaniards tramped, they would eventually find themselves in a huge plaza – the city's administrative and cultural heart, holding no fewer than seventy-eight civic buildings, temples and palaces.

Despite the abundant evidence of a civilised existence comparable with the Spaniards' own, within eighteen months of that famous march the European newcomers had reduced Tenochtitlan's skyline and much additional evidence of Mexican sophistication to a platform of rubble. They had slaughtered probably half the population. They had reduced the most formidable military force in the Americas to a docile peasantry, notorious amongst Europe's later generations as the epitome of hopeless lassitude. Of all European confrontations with a tribal people, the Spanish destruction of the Mexica seemed the least morally defensible. Far from advancing the cause of humanity, they had accomplished its opposite, assassinating an entire civilisation in its prime.

Rather than confront the ethical questions that seem to haunt this tale of destruction, the Europeans who perpetrated the deed, and those who inherited its fruits, preferred a different line of inquiry. The question for them was not how such a thing could be justified, but how had it been physically accomplished. For the army that had inflicted such a massive defeat upon the millions of inhabitants of the Mexican empire had never numbered more than 1,500 Europeans at any one time. How could they have won such an impossible victory against such apparently overwhelming odds unless they had received the highest possible support?

Viewed from this angle, all the manifold evidence of Mexican achievement and power ceased to be a moral reproach upon the victors. It became the evidence for Spanish vindication. Like no other tale of imperial conquest, the lightning overthrow and capture of the Mexican empire seemed freighted with proofs of European greatness, the technological mastery and heroism of its soldiery, the pre-eminence of Christian civilisation. Cortés' achievement was passed on to subsequent generations of Spaniards, not as historical evidence for their rapacity, but as a myth substantiating their right to subdue and dispossess tribal society. For four centuries it was a received truth that victory in the teeth of such numerical superiority had been an act of divine justice. Even in our own time, while its theological implications have fallen from view, the conquest has remained evidence of Europe's invincible superiority. Cortés, the exemplar of that racial supremacy, was identified by one recent biographer as a Nietzschean Superman.[4] Another British author of a popular work on the *conquistadores* wrote that 'Cortés, a man who never faltered, never despaired even when the outlook was utterly hopeless, must rank as one of the greatest military leaders in history.'[5]

It is for all these reasons that the Spanish conquest of Mexico remains an event of perpetual fascination and controversy. As an example of Europe's clash with tribal society it also has one additional importance. Either because pre-Columbian Americans had no written language, or because the process of extermination was completed so quickly, there are few instances in the early European conquests where the events were recorded from the perspective of the defeated. However, in Mexico a number of sources describe the Spanish invasion as it appeared to the vanquished Americans. One of the most important of these was by the sixteenth-century Spanish cleric Bernardino de Sahagún, who learnt the Mexican language, Nahuatl, and transcribed native eyewitness accounts of the war and its immediate aftermath. Known as the *Florentine Codex*, it is one of the most important documents on the period, providing rare first-hand insights into how the bearers of European civilisation first appeared to their victims.

Sahagún's informants could recall the pervasive atmosphere of dread which oppressed Tenochtitlan as the small Spanish caravan made its way down from the slopes of Popocatépetl and through the Mexican Valley, before its entry through the capital's gates:

> Everyone was greatly terrified. There was terror, astonishment, expressions of distress, feelings of distress. There were consultations. There were formations of groups; there were assemblies of people. There was weeping – there was much weeping, there was weeping for others.[6]

Even then the large Mexican crowds lining each side, as the Spaniards breasted the main causeway of Tenochtitlan, could never have known that in that strange column pushing on relentlessly between them, many were confronted by their own assassins. Before their eyes was passing almost every one of the technological, cultural and biological advantages the Europeans possessed.

Most conspicuous in the Spanish procession were their magnificent horses. Originally brought to Spain by the Arabs of North Africa, these Barb–Arab mounts were then shipped out to the Caribbean where the English explorer, Walter Raleigh, later judged them as the best horses he had ever seen in his life. Cortés still had about thirteen when he entered the Mexican capital and they made an enormous impression, galloping back and forth, pawing the ground, mouths foaming, their flanks glistening with a sour sheen of sweat. The Spaniards also had huge dogs, wolfhounds or mastiffs, which slobbered and strained at the leash. Each was capable of dispatching a human and trained for the task. The only canid familiar to the residents of Tenochtitlan was a hairless miniature bred for the table, ancestor of the Chihuahua.

The Mexica were initially shocked and mystified by the Spanish cannon – ten culverins and four falconets – assembled from separate short bronze sections and dragged in on wheeled carts, the first wheels to touch American soil. The insistent staccato rhythms of the *Florentine Codex* capture perfectly their sense of bewilderment at the impact of these strange devices:

> . . . how it resounded as if it thundered when it went off. It indeed bereft one of strength; it shut off one's ears . . . Fire went showering forth; sparks went blazing forth. And its smoke smelled very foul; it had a fetid odor which verily wounded the head. And when [the shot] struck a mountain, it were as if it were destroyed, dissolved. And a tree was pulverised; it was as if it vanished; it was as if someone blew it away.[7]

Equally perplexing to the crowds, thirty-two of the Spanish infantrymen carried crossbows while twelve of them shouldered arquebuses, the sixteenth-century muskets whose impact on the Mexica would be as much psychological as physical. Then there was the whole shining panoply of metal weapons and equipment synonymous with European warfare: chainmail, helmets, armpieces, greaves, heavy steel-tipped lances, swords, daggers, knives. Foremost amongst the Spanish weapons were their solid-hilted Toledo swords, famous for their quality throughout Europe. It was a peculiar misfortune of the American people then scrutinising this military caravan that they had developed techniques for working the pliant ores of gold or silver to inflame Spanish greed, but they lacked the necessary metallurgical skill which would have empowered them to meet the steel weaponry of the Spaniards with steel of their own.

The formidable parade of European military technology finally came to a halt before the litter of the Mexican emperor. The two leaders then greeted one another. Cortés attempted to embrace Moctezuma, but was restrained by the Mexican attendants. Then he placed a necklace of pearls around Moctezuma's neck, and in return received a string of red shells, adorned with eight shrimps delicately fashioned from gold. When Moctezuma completed his speech of greeting, Cortés is reported to have said: 'Be assured [Moctezuma], have no fear. We love you greatly. Today our hearts are at peace.'[8]

2

The Kidnap

The Spaniards' campaign to defeat the Mexica can be divided roughly into three stages. The first eight months, occupied by the *conquistadores*' march to the capital from a base camp on the coast, was largely a period of political manoeuvring, as Cortés sought to discover the nature and potential of the American state and also to probe for possible weakness. The second eight-month period, covering the Spanish stay in Tenochtitlan, was marked by a breakdown in relations between the Europeans and the Americans and ended in a major military victory for the Mexica at the outskirts of their capital. The third, final phase was a period of all-out war and, following the Spaniards' recovery from initial disaster, saw their eventual triumph after a long and bitter siege.

If the first stage was initiated by Cortés' bold decision to march to the very heart of the Mexican power-base, then its climax was the even more audacious kidnap of the emperor. Using as a pretext a clash between a Mexican force and the Spaniards' rearguard at the coast, Cortés sought an audience with Moctezuma less than a week after his arrival in the capital. The emperor duly obliged his guests in his own throne room, only to find himself accused of treachery and surrounded by forty heavily armed men. Faced with increasingly violent threats, Moctezuma finally capitulated and returned under armed escort to the palace in which he had accommodated the *conquistadores*. While most Eurocentric historians have characterised it as a political master-stroke, today the world's media would describe the Spanish action as a terrorist *coup d'état*.

The seizure of their head of state momentarily paralysed effective

36

Mexican opposition. It also enabled the *conquistadores* to exact the formal submission of Moctezuma and a large number of his senior officials to the Spanish crown. When the Mexica finally attempted to evict their unwanted guests by force, the *conquistadores* claimed that the Mexican oaths of allegiance made them rebels and traitors to their Spanish overlord. The campaign of conquest was thus a legitimate restitution of acknowledged European authority. As a pretext for the destruction of the Mexican empire, such an argument now appears ludicrously flimsy. The emperor himself had been kidnapped at sword-point in an act of shocking illegality, while, only days before the formal ceremony of submission, many of the leading nobles had been in chains on Cortés' orders. Whether they would have sworn loyalty to the Spanish crown if they had been at liberty to choose is, to say the least, highly doubtful.

Yet Cortés' kidnap of Moctezuma and the subsequent coerced submission remain of enormous significance. Of the various Spanish manoeuvres, it was, as Hugh Thomas noted in *The Conquest of Mexico*, 'the critical one in the history of the expedition'.[1] It also assumed a later symbolic importance, the personal relationship between the Spanish leader and his imperial hostage almost coming to stand for the entire confrontation of the two hemispheres and their respective civilisations. The kidnap also dramatises, like few other events in the incessant conflict between Europe and tribal societies, the Christian oscillation between the exercise of ruthless power and an almost obsessive concern for dressing such action in technical legalities.

In subsequent episodes of Europe's war with tribal society, as in the case of the British in Tasmania or the Euro-Americans against the Apache, the tribal opponents were deemed so far outside the realms of ordered society that it was not necessary to provide the actions against them with this modicum of respectability. In the early sixteenth century, however, and the age of kings, one did not lightly kidnap an emperor and despoil his realm, even when the emperor was an American heathen. Equally, in the late nineteenth century, when faced with the indigenous communities in South West Africa, who were both Christian and often educated by missionaries, the German colonists felt it necessary to substantiate their claim to African territory with the necessary 'legal' documentation.

In the case of the Germans this meant acquiring title deeds to tribal land from chiefs too drunk to know what they were surrendering. And in the case of Columbus 400 years earlier, legitimising his

Caribbean annexations meant unfurling the Spanish royal standard and making formal announcement to a beach entirely deserted except for the necessary European legal witnesses. For subsequent Spaniards elsewhere in the Americas it was a case of reading the *Requerimiento*, a document incomprehensible to those it was meant to address. What all these performances had in common was that they completed a self-referential circle. They were not bilateral contracts between equal parties. They were rituals by Europeans for European audiences, unilateral declarations dressed in legal phraseology to fulfil contingent political requirements, and they were normally followed by, or excused the prior use of, force.

In an example like Moctezuma's submission to Cortés, where there was an appearance of mutual consent, such an agreement provided other opportunities. The tribal leader who became in some way contractually bound to Europeans often then became a strategic weakness for his people, a point of leverage his antagonists could use to prise apart tribal unity. Typically, Cortés soon demanded of the captive emperor that he summon for trial the Mexican officials responsible for attacking the Spanish rearguard – the event that had justified the initial kidnap. Following an inevitable European verdict, about twenty of Moctezuma's men were taken to the city's main square and burnt to death amidst a huge bonfire of Mexican wooden swords and arrows. For the silently assembled crowds it was a terrifying display of national impotence. For their emperor it was a symbolic defeat and a deeply public humiliation.

Moctezuma's capture was in many ways the culmination of a policy that the Spanish commander had pursued since leaving Cuba in November 1518. Simultaneously, it was a ploy as eloquent of its author's otherwise shadowy personality as any event in the history of the conquest. Throughout the period before the kidnap, Hernan Cortés had demonstrated a Machiavellian capacity to manipulate surface appearance, both to outwit Spanish rivals and to secure support from American allies. Even as he was setting sail for Mexico, for instance, he had offered quayside reassurances of loyalty to the Cuban governor, Diego Velázquez, the man nominally in charge of the departing expedition and the man Cortés betrayed immediately on arrival at the American mainland. In order to silence anyone with lingering loyalties to Velázquez, Cortés appealed directly to the Spanish throne to confirm his position as expedition commander. His next, extraordinary step was to break up nine of his twelve ships, thus impressing on the tiny army of 530 men that with their backs to the sea, their best hope lay in unity behind a single leader, Cortés the *Caudillo*.

Cortés' opening move to secure support from American allies revealed a similar political finesse. The Totonacs, a coastal people only recently drawn into the Mexican imperial orbit, were the first community that the Spaniards encountered. By chance the *conquistadores'* arrival in their capital coincided with the appearance of an official delegation from Tenochtitlan. Cortés, trading on Totonac resentment of Mexican control, urged them to arrest these officials, only for the Spanish commander to release them secretly at a later date. The double deceit was another master-stroke. For while the Totonac act of defiance against the sovereign power had fatally compromised them, Cortés, in liberating the delegation himself, had obscured his own aggressive intention towards their masters in Tenochtitlan.

The kidnap of Moctezuma was the ultimate expression of these methods – an attempt to rule Mexico through its emperor, a painless transmission of political authority from America to Europe backed, only if absolutely necessary, by ruthless military force. Small wonder, perhaps, that in the demonography of contemporary Mexico the Spanish *Caudillo* is portrayed not as a brutal warrior, but as a wheedling businessman.

If the emperor's kidnap throws the brightest spotlight on the style and temperament of the kidnapper-in-chief, by contrast, the personality of the victim himself seems, from the moment of capture, to recede into an increasing obscurity. In fact, even before his arrest Moctezuma appeared to suffer a strange character transformation. Right up until the Spanish arrival in his realm from his accession in 1502, he had been the model of a decisive and powerful ruler. In fulfilment of his Nahuatl name, meaning 'Angry Lord', he had pushed back the empire's southern frontier, personally leading his troops into several major battles. He was honoured as a prudent and astute statesman, particularly gifted in oratory. It was also during his rule that many of the works of art now considered typical of Mexican civilisation were completed. Towards the close of his reign, Moctezuma could look out across Tenochtitlan from his palace rooftop and survey a nation at the height of its military power and a civilisation in its very prime.

According to Jacques Soustelle, one of the most eloquent and compelling, if now somewhat dated, proponents of their achievement, the Mexica represented one of the high points, if not the pinnacle of pre-Columbian civilisation. 'Their culture . . .' he wrote in a characteristically impassioned conclusion to *The Daily Life of the Aztecs*, 'is one of those that humanity can be proud of having created . . . it must take its place among our precious treasures – precious because they are so rare.'[2] Such an affirmative judgement may well have been in honour of the fact that Mexican civilisation was as short-lived as it had been brilliant and dramatic.

Moctezuma's daily routine might include meals of dozens of finely prepared dishes, served on golden plates, accompanied by music or dance, while moments of imperial leisure could be spent amidst exquisite flower gardens or royal aviaries with collections of brilliantly coloured birds. Yet it was barely 300 years since his tribal ancestors had been rough and impoverished hunter-gatherers. These origins in the arid south-west of the North American continent were reflected in the tutelary deity of the Mexica, the bloodthirsty Huitzilopochtli. Translated somewhat innocuously as 'Hummingbird of the left', Huitzilopochtli was the god of war, of the sun, of the young warrior, of the chase.

About the middle of the twelfth century the oracle of this patron deity advised the Mexica to embark on a wandering journey southwards, which eventually brought them to the Mexican Valley. The rich volcanic soils and abundant water supply had made the region a focus of human settlement for almost 500 years, and it had seen the flowering of successive Mesoamerican civilisations. This cultural legacy was still evident throughout the region and, by its standards, the newly arrived Mexica were a crude people.

The dense population and their unwelcome reception elsewhere in the valley initially restricted the Mexica to the occupation of only two small islets near Lake Texcoco's western shore. It seemed an unlikely site for residence. But Huitzilopochtli had delivered an omen ordaining the location – an eagle perched on a prickly pear with a serpent clasped in its talons – and the god eventually proved worthy of his followers. Although at the outset they had lacked the arts of settled existence, the Mexica put to good use the tribe's one indisputable asset – their ruthless aggression. Firstly as hired mercenaries and then as conquerors in their own right, they established a steady hegemony over the other communities around the shoreline of the valley lakes. And as they expanded, so they absorbed, integrating with their own traditions the cultural legacy that had survived elsewhere in the valley.

In time they became skilled farmers, and with their *chinampas*, they created a vast garden out of Texcoco's unpromising marshland. As a consequence of these cultural changes another divine force slowly came to assume equal prominence alongside Huitzilopochtli. Tlaloc, god of rain, of cultivation and the harvest, sovereign power against drought or famine, was the second of the Mexica's two principal deities. Jacques Soustelle suggested that the dual presence of these gods at the head of the religious world consecrated 'the union of the two basic ideologies of Mexico . . . On the one hand the religion of the warlike nomad and on the other that of the settled peasants . . .'[3]

After they had embarked on their imperial career the Mexica, ashamed that they had once been considered outcasts by the city-states they now dominated, decided to destroy the historical records revealing their humble origins. In their place they fabricated a genealogy suggesting they were the direct heirs to the Toltecs, creators of the last great civilisation to flourish in the Mexican Valley. Inbuilt into this falsehood was the parvenus' reflex deference towards their legendary betters. Yet, in fact, their own artistic accomplishments had come to rival, even to surpass, those of their predecessors.

Some of the artistry in which Moctezuma could take especial pride was the Mexican gift for building – cutting, dressing and polishing stone, erecting monumental temples and palaces. Their capital was testament not only to the high level of skill attained by their architects, engineers and masons without the assistance of metal tools, the wheel or draught animals, but to an infinite artistic patience. Tenochtitlan had taken decades to build. When Cortés and his men first surveyed the place, noting the clean, sharp lines, the chiselled concision of its frescoes and the fresh brilliance of its stuccoed walls, they were admiring all the hallmarks of the slowly matured and newly completed artefact.

Amongst the many other elements of Tenochtitlan life which astounded the *conquistadores*, and which have been adduced by later commentators as evidence of indigenous America's firm grasp of civilised existence, was the Mexica's deep love of flowers and of formally laid gardens, crisscrossed with flowing channels and luxurious pools. Their reverence for cleanliness, so suspect to the dirty and unwashed Spaniards, was manifest in their fondness for bathing, in the construction of public steambaths and in the ubiquitous use of vegetable soaps. The Mexica were fascinated by the abundant flora and fauna which surrounded them. Their medical practices embraced the use of 1,200 different plants; their knowledge of animals had enabled the emperors to maintain large collections of the region's exquisitely beautiful birds, as well as a wide selection of Central America's mammal fauna.

The range and quality of other Mexican crafts were similarly impressive. Observing their paintwork on wooden carvings and sculptures, the veteran *conquistador* and chronicler Bernal Diaz wrote that some of these artists were so skilled that 'had they lived in the age of the Apelles of old, or of Michael Angelo [*sic*] or Berruguete in our own day, they would be counted in the same rank.'[4] Tragically, like Tenochtitlan itself, little of this work survived Spanish occupation.

One of the most vulnerable arts was the uniquely American feather craft, which involved the creation of elaborate mosaics entirely out of feathers harvested from wild and captive birds without killing them. These weavings were used to adorn ceremonial costume and items of religious ritual. The handful of examples spared by time, climate and the *conquistadores* confirm the highly refined aesthetic expressed in this fragile art. Even at the time of the conquest, Cortés was able to acknowledge the nature of their achievement; 'its like,' he wrote, 'is not to be seen in either wax or embroidery, it is so marvellously delicate.'[5]

Equally susceptible to European indifference was the work of both Mexican lapidaries and goldsmiths. Metallurgy was an innovation dating only from the late Toltec period, but the manufacture of delicate mosaics fashioned from fragments of precious stone, especially their favoured turquoise, had a much longer artistic pedigree. The Mexica's own examples of this craft, especially their death masks and skulls, represent some of the most powerful and haunting images in the art of pre-Columbian America.

Mexican gold work was the most inevitable casualty of Spanish greed, with only a small sample of the finest pieces being retained in an original form. As one authority noted, these surviving ornaments 'make one realize that the Spanish descriptions of Cortés' loot understated the rich ability of the Aztec goldsmiths.'[6] A contemporary European fully qualified to appreciate the nature of their achievement was the German artist Albrecht Dürer, himself a goldsmith's son. When he saw a sample of Mexican treasures on display in Brussels, he wrote: 'In all my life I have never seen anything that rejoiced my heart so much . . . I have been astonished by the subtle spirit of the men of these strange countries.'[7]

The sheer diversity of their cultural achievements spoke eloquently of a high degree of specialisation amongst the work force, and the surpluses of wealth and leisure enjoyed by the upper strata of Mexican society. However, these fundamental constituents of civilisation had largely been acquired at the expense of neighbours, and were the fruits of violent conquest. Although the national character had been softened by contact with urban life in the valley, the need to produce soldiers for war was an enduring coordinate of Mexican society. The emperor's own record as personal commander of his army reflected its central position in Mexican society. The state schools for the ruling and priestly classes, the *calmecac*, which Moctezuma himself had attended, imbued in their students a Spartan discipline and a constant yearning to excel in arms. For the Mexica, war was a holy rite and for the individual soldier success in arms meant social prestige and material opportunity, while death in battle conferred spiritual salvation.

By the time the Spaniards landed on the North American continent, the Mexica, nominally in alliance with two neighbouring cities, had imposed themselves on 371 client tribes in thirty-eight provinces from the Pacific to the Atlantic Oceans. The total area of the lands within their military orbit was about 325,000 square kilometres, and included much of present-day Mexico and a wide variety of peoples with many different languages and customs. In these subject provinces the Mexica established few recognisable institutions of formal empire. The principal burden inflicted upon inhabitants was a tax, in the form of produce, to be paid at regular intervals to Tenochtitlan.

Although some nations, like the recently conquered Totonacs, detested this imposition and readily allied themselves with Cortés in order to regain full independence, the tribute may have been less onerous than they suggested. One of the Spanish officials charged subsequently with an inquiry into Mexican fiscal arrangements wrote: 'In all this there was a great deal of regularity and of attentiveness to see that no one person was more heavily burdened than the rest. Each man paid little; and as there were many men it was possible to bring together great quantities [of goods] with little work and no vexation.'[8]

Despite this judgement, the massive volume of goods pouring into Tenochtitlan, which the Mexica recorded with meticulous care, makes extraordinary reading. Distributed amongst the columns of bearers arriving every eighty days were 33,680 bundles of feathers, 123,400 cloaks of cotton and other fibre, 11,200 tunics and skirts for women, 4,400 bales of cotton, 1,600 loads of chilli, 32,000 spear canes, 64,000 baskets of unrefined copal, 2,200 pots of honey, 16,000 balls of rubber, 32,000 reams of paper, 4,000 loaves of unrefined salt, 3,200 deerskins, 60 bowls of gold dust, two live eagles.[9] It was estimated that a million men were needed to carry the unending flow of products.[10]

By means of this enforced tribute the imperial power provided itself with many of the raw materials of Central America. From these, their labourers and craftsmen manufactured what had become the daily necessities of Mexican life, but they also utilised tribute goods and surplus home produce to manufacture export commodities. For the Mexica were a vigorous trading nation and those men conducting the commerce held a privileged position in their society. Long-distance merchants carried away from the capital cloth, rabbit-fur blankets, embroidered clothes, golden jewels, obsidian and copper earrings, obsidian knives, cochineal dye and medicinal herbs. With these they acquired further luxury merchandise for Tenochtitlan, such as emeralds, tortoiseshell, and exotic parrot and quetzal plumes from the coastal rainforests. The main system of exchange was barter, although a few trade items, such as the universally prized cocoa beans, as well as copper axes and gold dust poured into goose quills, had come to play the role of a primitive currency.

Markets were a ubiquitous feature of Mesoamerican life, with the largest and most impressive in a district of Tenochtitlan itself. Tlatelolco, originally a separate city-state with an independent administration and its own long-established commercial traditions, was immediately to the north of the Mexican capital and had been conquered in the late fifteenth century. By 1519 it had been all but incorporated by its more powerful neighbour. The great tiled square enclosed by covered arcades that had once housed the Tlatelolco market had eventually become the main commercial centre for both. It was the second great plaza of Tenochtitlan, and the largest trading outlet in the Americas. A docking area at one end gave access to the city's canals and then outwards to all the lake waters of the Mexican Valley, so that goods could pour in by canoe from all over the region.

Every few days as many as 60,000 people would congregate to meet, buy, sell and exchange. If, on the day of his arrival, Cortés and his column of soldiers had provided the Mexican crowds with a spectacular live exhibition of European civilisation, then Tlatelolco had served a similar purpose for the Spaniards. All the products of a particular type were concentrated in one of the market's fifty zones, and literally everything that Central American humanity had invented, used or cultivated was on display in these different sections.

Remarkably, given the massive state resources which surrounded the emperor, not to mention his own personal record of military conquest, Moctezuma reacted to the news of the Spanish arrival in a mood of abject despair. Following his preliminary intelligence-gathering missions, he then vacillated between a policy of appeasement – hoping to buy off the intruders with expensive gifts – and an attempt to find direction out of the crisis with the aid of state oracles and religious prophets. Possessed by gloomy premonitions as the *conquistadores* marched on his capital, he is alleged to have said: 'All of us will die at the hands of the new gods [the Spaniards] and those who survive will be their slaves and vassals. They are the ones to reign now, and I shall be the last ruler of this land.'[11]

This almost blank desolation at the Spanish advance, seemingly so disproportionate to the scale of the threat, was also deeply revealing. It brings into focus an element of the Mexican national character that seemed not to have been expressed in their roll-call of achievements. Equally, it provides an insight into Moctezuma's own personal background: in his earlier years, before his accession as seventh emperor, he had been a chief priest in the national religion.

Religious belief and religious duties were an all-pervasive aspect of Mexican society. Almost as a counterbalance to the aggressive, centrifugal energies which they had channelled into conquest and international trade, the Mexica held profoundly pessimistic views on the interpenetration of human conduct and cosmic order. Religious duty was for them not merely a practice enriching the human spirit, but an essential precondition of their existence. They believed that if their devotional rites were discontinued, then the smooth ordering of the cosmos would collapse, the sun would cease to rise, and death and destruction would befall the people.

An attachment to sacrifice was universal amongst Mesoamerican religions, rising in the most profound and dire circumstances – drought, famine or war, for example – to the ceremonial offering of human blood. Self-mutilation – by drawing obsidian blades or cactus spines through the limbs, the earlobes, the tongue and, in the case of priests, even the penis – was a commonplace practice. But higher sacrifice was also required. Although this had probably had modest origins in the early years of the empire, by the time of Cortés' arrival the ceremonial presentation of human hearts had assumed a central position in Mexican worship, and also served as powerful state propaganda concerning Mexican military and political might.

Different religious festivals required specific kinds of human victims, as well as alternative modes of sacrifice. The god of rain, Tlaloc, required that children be drowned in water. Female devotees of the earth goddesses danced in a frenzy, apparently unconscious of the priests who, stalking amongst them, would slice off their heads. The victims of the god Xipe Totec were first placed in a wicker frame, then shot with arrows by priests, when the skin was flayed from their bodies. For the god of fire, captives were first anaesthetised with hashish, then plunged into a blaze until scorched and barely alive, only to be plucked out with hooks to have their hearts ripped from their chests.[12]

Prisoners of war taken during combat with one of the many regional enemies of the Mexican state were amongst the most esteemed and also the most frequent victims. The rite most typically employed in their sacrifice required that the captive be held over a slightly convex stone with his arms and legs pinioned by four priests while a fifth, making a deep gash in the chest with an obsidian blade, tore out a still palpitating heart and plunged it into a burning brazier. The head would be cut off and held up, and the body, depending on the status of the victim, either slung or carried down the steps of the temple. Limbs might on occasions be ceremonially consumed by Mexican nobles and warriors, while the torso might go to feed the wild carnivores in the emperor's private zoo.[13]

Jacques Soustelle suggested that human sacrifice amongst pre-Columbian Americans was an act neither of cruelty nor hatred. Mesoamerican society in general accepted it as a necessary and sacred obligation. There was, moreover, in the build-up to sacrifice, a process of ritual identification between the captor and his victim. The Spanish chronicler Bernardino de Sahagún recorded that 'When a man took a prisoner he said, "Here is my well-beloved son." And the captive said, "Here is my revered father." '[14] Victims were often identified with the deity to whom they were dedicated. Eating their limbs thus symbolised the communion of men with the sacrificed god – the Christian ritual of the Eucharist, but with genuine flesh and blood.

Notwithstanding the sense of ceremony and of obligation attending these religious matters, the Mexica had carried human sacrifice to appalling extremes. A much-quoted example concerns the dedication of the great temple of Huitzilopochtli at the heart of Tenochtitlan.

When this ceremony took place in 1487 perhaps as many as 20,000 people were slaughtered over four days, the lines of victims converging on their place of extinction along the city's four main causeways.[15] Amongst the structures in the capital's main plaza was a huge rack on which the skulls of the sacrificed were collected. A Spanish eyewitness claimed that it held 136,000. Even when allowances are made for the fact that this probably more than doubled the true figure, the scale of the practice becomes apparent.[16]

Hugh Thomas surely speaks for all contemporary observers when he writes, 'one would have to have a strong stomach to accept with a purely anthropological judgement all the manifestations of human sacrifice.'[17] Indeed the practice remains a major barrier to an understanding of pre-Cortesian Mexico. There has been an increasing effort to place it in a context which, if not favourable, is less disturbing. A number of authors have challenged the earlier exaggerations which depicted Mexico as one 'vast human shambles', and which continue to distort the popular European image of Tenochtitlan society.[18] Soustelle, for instance, attempted to glean the kernel of religious meaning from the outer layers of blood and guts, and also pointed out that it consumed fewer human lives than the circuses of ancient Rome.[19]

Some contemporary historians deeply sympathetic to the Mexica, and wishing to counterbalance the pervasive over-emphasis on this one aspect of Mexican society, have ignored the issue almost completely. Ronald Wright in *Stolen Continents*, an account of America's conquest from the perspective of its indigenous people, cast doubt on ritual cannibalism and confined his commentary on human sacrifice to saying that it 'was . . . not the persistence of an old "savage" practice among civilized people who should have known better but rather a hypertrophy of sinister elements in their culture which in more gracious times had been kept in check.'[20]

Others, however, felt less constrained. Hammond Innes, for instance, author of *The Conquistadors*, called the Mexican religion 'a filthy one, their rites and practices abominable'.[21] A century earlier, William Prescott was even more precise:

How can a nation, where human sacrifices prevail, and especially when combined with cannibalism, further the march of civilisation? . . . men became familiar with scenes of horror and the most loathsome abominations . . . The heart was hardened, the manners were made ferocious, the feeble light of civilisation . . . was growing fainter and fainter, as thousands and thousands of miserable victims throughout the empire were yearly fattened in its cages, sacrificed on its altars, dressed and served at its banquets! The whole land was converted into a vast human shambles! The empire of the [Mexica] did not fall before its time.[22]

In short, human sacrifice justified the conquest, however much loss of life that might have entailed. In these lines Prescott sums up what has been for Europeans, for almost half a millennium, the essential moral lesson at the heart of the story of Mexico's conquest.

Moctezuma's sense of foreboding might have allowed the *conquistadores* to take the politico-military initiative. It may even have enabled them to capture his physical person and therefore stage-manage the oath of allegiance. This in turn may have provided the flimsy legal edifice that would protect them in the immediate aftermath of the conquest, deflecting awkward moral objections that jealous or conscience-stricken compatriots might raise. But the disgusting sacrificial practices conducted in the temples of Moctezuma's empire supplied the materials for Europe to construct an impregnable moral fortress around its actions. And in time Mexico's rituals of religious death converted their society's destruction into a morality tale, in which evil was banished and good triumphed. Even now in many European representations of pre-Cortesian Mexico, human sacrifice is depicted not just as a subordinate, if macabre and depressing, feature of their society, treated on a par with the circuses of ancient Rome or the Tyburn gallows of eighteenth-century England, but as something fundamental. Sacrificial victims lying prostrate on altar stones constitute *the* paradigmatic image of Mexican civilisation, as something evil, brutal and perverted, constantly reinforcing the idea that its destruction was a divine blessing.

The whole question of human sacrifice has crucial moral implications for the conquest. When they first encountered the phenomenon, the *conquistadores* were understandably appalled. Cortés wrote in his dispatches that those Europeans who had seen it said it was 'the most terrible and frightful thing that they have ever seen'.[23] Bernal Diaz, in his description of the exploratory expedition to the American mainland in 1518, recalled how, on visiting a temple and discovering for the first time the bodies of two freshly sacrificed boys, these battle-hardened *conquistadores* were 'all too upset by the sight . . . and too indignant at [the priests'] cruelty.'[24] They were as disgusted by the blood that caked the walls and floors of the temples, as they were terrorised later, during the battle for Tenochtitlan, by the screams of their compatriots captured and condemned to the obsidian blades of the Mexican priests. Small wonder that the practice was rapidly suppressed on completion of the conquest, or that it loomed large in their imaginations, holding a central place in their subsequent accounts of the events.

And yet the horrors of human mutilation hardly represented a phenomenon outside the scope of the *conquistadores'* New World experience. In a quarter of a century they had inflicted a holocaust of death and suffering on indigenous Caribbeans. Bartolomé de Las Casas described such men betting on whether they could slice their victim in two with a single stroke of an axe. He recounted incidents in which babies were swung by the feet, and their heads smashed open against rocks.[25] The Spaniards' armoured dogs were trained to run down and disembowel human quarry, and were reared on the flesh of their victims. Even one of their more lenient twentieth-century assessors described this portion of the Spanish conquests as 'one of the most dismal episodes in the history of exploitation'.[26] For Spaniards in America at that time, the sight of death and of the mutilation of indigenous inhabitants was almost a universal experience.

Clearly then, there were powerful reasons other than genuine shock or moral outrage for the deep preoccupation with human sacrifice. Most obviously the *conquistadores* recognised from the outset its huge propaganda potential in their enterprise of conquest. Who would condone an anthropophagous society, or condemn its dissolution when it violated one of Europe's cardinal taboos? In his dispatches Cortés turned the moral screw even tighter by falsely suggesting children were the usual victims of sacrifice.[27] On another occasion, to justify his slaughter and enslavement of one community, he pointed out in a letter to Charles V that 'they eat human flesh'; then added with sinister indifference, 'a fact so notorious that I send your Majesty no further proof of it'.[28]

In addition to its value as moral ammunition in the Spanish campaign there were other, less obvious factors at work in the European obsession. The Spaniards, on almost all their missions of American conquest and exploration, were relatively few in number and often deep in unknown, potentially hostile territory. They had no means of guidance. Their maps, if they possessed any, were not so much exercises in cartography as blotting paper for the medieval imagination, populated with a whole bestiary of freaks – beings with huge ears, with a single Cyclopean eye, with tails, without heads, with heads in the middle of their chests, people who lived off the smell of fruit, Amazons, sorcerers, devourers of human flesh. The *conquistadores'* willingness to confront these grotesques is one undeniable constituent in their legendary courage. But they were also haunted by such images, just as they were oppressed by fears of the eternal flames in an actual hell.

In the gruesome demon-gods and morbid practices of Mexican religion they seemed literally to have encountered the most forbidding aspects of their own internal landscape. It is hardly surprising that as the men of Cortés advanced deeper into the Mexican heartland, they were haunted by fears of being surrounded, engulfed by the dark and menacing realm of their own subconscious. Typical of this anxiety is Bernal Diaz's lurid nightmare vision before passing into the maw of Tenochtitlan itself. If Moctezuma were to attack them, he wrote,

> he would put an end to us in a single day, and he could then offer his sacrifices to [Huitzilopochtli] . . . and to Tezcatlipoca, the god of hell; and they could feast on our thighs, legs, and arms, and the snakes, serpents, and tigers that they kept in wooden cages . . . could gorge on our entrails and bodies and all that was left.[29]

In Mexico the pervasive European dread of being consumed by the unknown environment – which was surely, in part, a projection of their own violent intention – conjoined with the threat of being literally, physically devoured. Descriptions of human sacrifice and cannibalism, which are an overwhelming obsession of sixteenth-century Europeans in the Americas, became the single dominant trope through which this wider complex of subconscious urges and anxieties were expressed.

Not only were there factors which led the *conquistadores* to overstress this aspect of Mexican society, but they were far from consistent in their approach to the subject. Their own indigenous allies who joined a final alliance to destroy Tenochtitlan regularly sacrificed Mexican soldiers, and allegedly ate them. But Cortés turned a blind eye to this behaviour, allowing expediency to overrule any question of morality. It was evidently neither so terrifying nor so repugnant when there was a degree of identification not with the victim, but with the sacrificer.

Of equal significance is the way in which the Spaniards' own behaviour came remarkably close to the reviled Mexican habit. Bernal Diaz, for example, described how his compatriots repeatedly opened up enemy corpses for fat to seal their own wounds and those of their horses, detecting nothing exceptional or unwholesome in it.[30] While the Mexica's post-mortem dismemberment and use of human flesh, stripped of its religious and social context, appeared to European eyes as demonic barbarism, their own actions were comfortably sheathed in cultural rationalisation.

The opposing emotions of pity and anger, aroused by the sight of the two sacrificed boys, and so firmly expressed by Diaz in the passage quoted earlier on his first visit to a Mesoamerican temple, are to be seen not so much as expressions of an absolute moral code, as responses with social and political functions. Spanish pity for the victims buttressed the sense of moral mission, while their anger nourished common feelings of hatred towards the agents of such cruelty, the Mexica.

It was that same moral inconsistency that enabled them to invest their own actions with totally separate values from those attached to the specific act of human sacrifice. They were content to see accused Mexican commanders burnt alive, or to perpetrate acts of mutilation, to lop off hands, arms, ears, feet, noses, testicles. They were willing to torture and to inflict mass slaughter: in a single charge they claimed five times the number of Spanish dead for the whole siege; in one day during the siege they claimed 40,000 casualties.[31] Moreover, they clung to the underlying rationale that converted the uses of deliberate terror and unopposed massacre into perfectly acceptable and necessary components of military policy. Writers like Hammond Innes, so repelled by the work of the obsidian blade on the Mexican altar, could appreciate the argument for such cold-blooded use of Spanish steel. 'It only goes to prove,' he argued, 'that . . . the ruthless use of force induced respect, even admiration, rather than hatred.'[32]

Despite such judgements, one has to conclude that the issue of human sacrifice offers no genuine ground for differentiating between Mexican and Spanish standards. In the end it was simply a question of aesthetic and social conditioning that made slaughter on the field of battle seem so much more acceptable to Europeans than that delivered on the temple altar. Although today human sacrifice might still seem an act of appalling cruelty, so too does the practice of burning humans at the stake or throwing them to the lions. Human sacrifice neither justified the conquest, nor can it be the only criterion for assessing Mexican civilisation; in exactly the same way Iberian society cannot be considered solely on the basis of the horrors of the Spanish Inquisition. Both communities in the sixteenth century were capable of extreme brutality, but, locked within their own cultural systems, each viewed the actions of the other with incomprehension and repugnance.

When Bernal Diaz asserted that all their victories were the work of Jesus Christ he expressed not only the superiority of the Spanish deity as intended, but just how closely the violent fundamentalist ideology of the *conquistadores* – in fact, of many European Christians, from the Spaniards in the sixteenth century to the Germans in the twentieth – resembled the religion of the Mexica. Blood, sacrifice, death, conquest, power: these were the concerns of the gods of both nations. As Ronald Wright noted: 'Both believed they had a divine mission to rule the world. In more than one way, they deserved each other.'[33]

3
The Night of Sorrow

On the morning of 24 June 1520, eight months after the Spaniards' first triumphant procession into Tenochtitlan, Hernan Cortés was about to lead another military parade through the Mexican capital. He had just returned from a brief and successful journey to the coast, and this second entrance should have been even more spectacular than the first. Cortés had intended it to be exactly that – a grandiose victory march which would burn into the minds of the populace the idea that the Spaniards were the new, permanent and undisputed rulers of Mexico.

As he approached Tenochtitlan that June morning, Cortés' position had never seemed stronger. His Euro-American fighting force had been massively increased. At his back were thirteen hundred Spanish infantry, ninety-six horsemen, eighty musketeers, eighty crossbowmen and two thousand American allies. His army had almost tripled in size. It was the largest European force Cortés would ever lead during the conquest of Mexico.

Moreover, during the winter months the Spanish captain had enhanced his political position in Tenochtitlan, securing oaths of allegiance from the Mexicans and averting a possible armed challenge. He had also enriched himself beyond his wildest dreams with Mexican gold. Suggesting that Moctezuma should confirm his gestures of obedience to the Spanish crown with appropriate gifts, Cortés forced him into a massive asset-stripping exercise. Parties of Spaniards and Mexican officials travelled the country overseeing the collection of gold and other precious items.

By chance the Spaniards had also stumbled on a treasure room in the apartments where they had been housed. The building was the palace of Moctezuma's father, the former emperor Axayácatl, and a huge store of his most valuable possessions had been hastily concealed before the Spanish arrival. Once it had been uncovered Moctezuma acquiesced in its removal, his kidnappers melting much of the gold down into standard ingots for shipment to Europe. By the time of an official stock-take they had accounted for at least 235,000 pesos worth of gold, silver and jewellery, and this figure may have seriously under-stated the scale of Spanish extortion.[1]

Throughout his winter of 'protective custody', authority had con-tinued to ebb away from Moctezuma towards his Spanish gaoler, ful-filling the Cortesian ambition of conquest by stealth. In the spring, however, the balance of power between the two commanders received a sudden jolt with the dramatic arrival of a new unaligned force. In April 1520 a fleet of about eighteen ships had appeared off the Gulf of Mexico. The nine hundred soldiers who disembarked were all Spaniards, but they were led by Panfilo de Narváez, the man chosen by the Governor of Cuba, Diego Velázquez, to pursue the Cortesian expedition and capture and punish its renegade leader.

This third party seemed to open up equal prospects for the two other principal players in the drama. To Moctezuma, imprisoned in his own imperial capital, Narváez was a potential means of escape from the current predicament. For Cortés, on the other hand, the arrival of an army owing allegiance to Velázquez was a direct threat to his own position. However, if it could be won over, it might equally offer the possibility of reinforcement for his planned conquest of the Mexican empire.

In the ensuing manoeuvres for Narváez's support Moctezuma seemed to gain an initial advantage. The two leaders exchanged diplo-matic niceties and acknowledged their mutual interest in defeating Cortés, while the newly arrived Spaniards advanced on Cortés' base camp at Vera Cruz demanding its surrender. There then followed a series of diplomatic missions between the two Spanish sides, as the *Caudillo* hurried towards the coast with about 300 men. At this stage Cortés was heavily outnumbered. Even with his rearguard force at Vera Cruz of about a hundred – mainly the sick and injured – he was facing an army more than twice the size of his own. Yet Cortés exploited divisions in the ranks of his opponents, plying a good number of those deemed susceptible with captured gold and promises of further riches. By the time the two forces were within striking dis-

tance of one another, many in Narváez's camp had been convinced
that they would prosper whatever the outcome of any approaching
contest. On the opposite side, however, all were committed to outright victory. During the night of 28 May 1520 it was morale, not
numbers, which carried the day.

Having arranged his forces near the Totonac town of Cempoallan,
Narváez was incredulous of a scout's report that his Spanish enemy
was only an hour away, while many of his leading captains were discouraged by the torrential rainfall that evening. By the time the
Cortesian force attacked most of its opponents had retreated to the
town and were sleeping around its main temple. When the sentries
eventually sounded an alarm it was already too late. The first all-
European conflict on American soil was less a battle than a confused,
rain-soaked rout. The defenders' gunpowder was wet and failed to
ignite. Their cannon fired too high or were bunged with wax – the
result of a well-placed bribe. The girths on many horses had also been
cut, so that the cavalry slid off their charges even as they mounted.
Fifteen of the losing side paid with their lives for their leader's over-
confidence, while Narváez was himself a casualty, blinded in one eye.
His opponents had lost just two men. Prescott described it as a battle
'fought quite as much with gold as with steel'.[2] Whatever the
methods, Cortés had scored a stunning victory and he lost no time in
making it count.

Expansive descriptions of the surrounding country and the prospect
of riches offered by its conquest served to weld all the Spaniards into
a single force. It was this new, powerful army that Cortés had led back
to Tenochtitlan and which he had intended to display in military
parade through the city. Yet instead of encountering Mexican crowds
dazzled by the glitter of Spanish steel and panicked by the clattering
hooves of Spanish cavalry, Cortés passed along a causeway deserted
and silent. On one empty street the Spaniards stopped to ponder a
Mexican corpse swinging from an improvised gallows – a sinister
omen that seemed only to confirm their impression of inexplicable
menace. It was obvious that during his few weeks away at the
Mexican coast, affairs had gone seriously wrong in the capital. It
would, however, be several more hours before Cortés grasped completely the terrible danger to which he and his compatriots were now
exposed.

In his enforced absence, the Spanish leader had ceded overall com-

mand to one of his main officers, Pedro de Alvarado. While he had
served hitherto as the *Caudillo's* right-hand man and was a popular
captain amongst the troops, proving every bit as ruthless and bold in
combat as Cortés himself, Alvarado lacked his leader's icy self-control.
During his period of command in the capital he had become increasingly uneasy about the build-up to the Mexican feast of Toxcatl, one
of the main events in their religious calendar. Although he had given
permission for the festival preparations, which Cortés had granted
before his departure, Alvarado later claimed that Toxcatl was being
used as cover for a surprise attack upon the Spaniards.

To pre-empt this he divided his men into two units, one to guard
Moctezuma and his high-ranking attendants, another to cover the
crowd of Mexican nobility assembled to watch the ritual dances at the
foot of the great temple in the central plaza. A further group of
Spanish guards with support from American allies moved to block the
three gates giving access to the main square. As the festival moved to
its climax the dancers orbited in concentric circles around the drums,
while thousands of celebrants looked on, absorbed in the ecstatic spectacle. Alvarado then gave a signal for his men to strike. The *Florentine
Codex* records the ensuing horror in overwhelming detail:

> Thereupon they surrounded the dancers. Thereupon they went
> among the drums. Then they struck the drummer's arms; they sev-
> ered both his hands; then they struck his neck. Far off did his neck
> [and head] go to fall. They they all pierced the people with iron
> lances and they struck them each with iron swords. Of some they
> slashed open their backs; then their entrails gushed out. Of some
> they cut their heads to pieces; they absolutely pulverised their
> heads; their heads were absolutely pulverised. And some they struck
> on the shoulder; they split openings . . . of some they struck the
> belly; then their entrails gushed forth. And when in vain one would
> run, he would drag only his intestines like something raw as he
> tried to escape. Nowhere could he go.[3]

Then they attacked the crowd, maiming and slaughtering until the
great plaza eventually emptied of living victims and until the Spaniards
themselves were exhausted by the carnage or weighed down by the
spoils of their looting. None of the Mexica was armed. Amongst those
butchered were large numbers of the Mexican nobility. Even the captive royal relatives standing at Moctezuma's side were cut down. With

the assassination of so many national leaders in one action, its author had virtually decapitated the state. Of the two major English-language historians on the destruction of the Mexican empire – both of them Hispanophiles – one described the massacre at the feast of Toxcatl as an 'atrocious deed'; the other acknowledged that there was no evidence for a Mexican plot.[4]

Cortés omitted all mention of the incident in his dispatches to the Spanish monarch, and Alvarado claimed that the total number of casualties was between two and three thousand. He himself was one of the few Spaniards to receive an injury. With blood streaming from a head wound he rounded on Moctezuma in bitter accusation, 'See what your people have done to me.'[5]

If there had been no armed resistance before the festival of Toxcatl, there certainly was afterwards. The Mexica rallied in a spontaneous outburst of vengeance, driving their assailants back to the palace of Axayácatl. Massively outnumbered, Alvarado played the Spaniards' one remaining trump card. With a knife at his chest, the Mexican emperor was invited to go out onto the roof of the palace and placate his people. His presence eventually calmed the frenzied atmosphere and almost certainly saved the besieged Spaniards. However, the momentary peace had been achieved at great expense to Moctezuma himself. The role of appeaser had finally drained away his prestige with the Mexica, carrying with it any remaining hostage value to his European kidnappers.

When Cortés finally reached his besieged compatriots in the palace, he discovered that many of the veterans he had left in Tenochtitlan were wounded, hungry and exhausted. All food supplies for the Spanish garrison had been stopped and their only drinking supply was an improvised well of brackish water. Cortés tried to secure provisions by forcing the Mexica to reopen the suspended Tlatelolco market. But this tactic proved to be one of his few major errors of judgement. Moctezuma may have been a discredited leader, but in the eyes of his people he was still the emperor, and his living presence discouraged the election of any successor. However, when Cortés freed Cuitláhuac, the Mexican emperor's brother, to negotiate the resumption of trading at Tlatelolco, he liberated the heir apparent and a critical rallying point for the nation's forces. Cuitláhuac did return to the buildings around the palace of Axayácatl, but only to command the Mexican assault on his brother's captors.

Henceforth the Spaniards would meet with nothing but steely resistance from their Mexican hosts. The city's numerous drawbridges had been raised, all channels of supply were severed, while the streets and canals were made increasingly dangerous for any European force probing for a gap in the blockade. Even the palace itself had been set on fire and parts of the wall had been breached. The Spaniards were trapped in the very city they had intended to present to their own monarch as a great capital for New Spain, the richest and most recent addition to his American realms. Now Cortés' control was so reduced that he could not even get a messenger out to alert his base camp at Vera Cruz, while a force of over three hundred Spaniards had been beaten back with heavy casualties. The men of Narváez, freshly recruited to the Cortesian cause, were not introduced to the dazzling riches and easy pickings on display at Tlatelolco market, but to the bitter realities of Mexican warfare.

Two days after Cortés' re-entry into Tenochtitlan, Moctezuma, having been insulted and ignored by the *Caudillo*, made his last appearance in the Euro-American power-play. Walking out onto the palace roof, the emperor attempted to repeat his message of appeasement. This time it was futile. He was met by insults – reviled apparently as a 'whore of the Spaniards' – and by a hail of missiles. One of these struck him on the head and he died a few days later, possibly of his wounds. Once renowned amongst his opponents as a formidable warrior and feared even by the Mexica as a ruthless disciplinarian, Emperor Moctezuma II expired an impotent cipher disregarded by his enemies, and an embarrassment to the people he had ruled for eighteen years. His body, with those of the remaining Mexican nobles that the Spaniards had murdered on Cortés' instruction, was found dumped outside the palace gate.

It was increasingly obvious to Cortés that his fighting force of several thousand men, with its daily requirements running into tonnes of rations and its military advantages neutralised in the cramped street-fighting, would have to break out of Tenochtitlan if it was going to survive. It was decided, therefore, to make a bid for the mainland via the short western route on 1 July 1520, the Spaniards leaving at midnight to hide their departure.

In the initial stages all seemed to be going well. The column had been organised with a large force of Spanish foot in the lead. Then came Cortés and his entourage, with his treasure, prisoners, some ordnance and a mixed protective force of Spaniards and American allies. Finally came the rearguard largely made up of the new men formerly under Narváez. They had reached the outskirts of the city and their departure was still undetected.

On the narrow causeway, however, progress for the long column of several thousand could only be slow and nerve-racking, while constant drizzle made the going difficult. A portable bridge had to be hauled along to get over the canals, whose crossing points the Mexica had earlier sabotaged. And there was a further critical obstacle to speedy evacuation. Although large quantities of gold belonging either to Cortés or intended for the Spanish monarch had been loaded onto horses, much had been left behind. Rather than abandon it, many soldiers, especially the new arrivals, burdened themselves with the heavy ingots. On *la Noche Triste*, as the ensuing hours of darkness became known, possession of such breathtaking wealth would prove extremely costly.

As the Spaniards proceeded over the lake they were spotted. The alarm went up and within a short time huge numbers of Mexica arrived, exploiting the flat rooftops beside the causeway or firing from canoes. Other parties came ashore ahead of the Europeans, forcing them into desperate fighting, and the orderly retreat rapidly lost coherence. Gaps in the causeway where bridges had been lifted became a main target for the Mexica. Here the heavily burdened Spaniards, in their panic to get across, poured on top of their compatriots already floundering in the water. The wounded and dying eventually formed temporary pontoons for those trapped at the rear. One Spanish eyewitness recalled that 'no one at that moment was interested in anything except saving his own skin.'[6]

Few commentators give a clear picture of what happened in the hours before dawn. Even the principal participants contradicted one another. Nothing better illustrates the sense of total Spanish disorder than the wild discrepancies in their later casualty reports. Estimates of their own losses ranged from 150 to 1,170, while the casualties amongst their American allies were put at between 2,000 and 8,000.[7] The *Florentine Codex* spoke of corpses heaped 'like a mountain of men'.[8]

Such inconsistencies in the records were no doubt a reflection of the chaos unleashed on *la Noche Triste*. However, another key factor must have been the scale of the European defeat. It was poorly recorded precisely because few who took part wished to remember such an ignominious disaster. This much, however, was undisputed: it was the largest European defeat in their first quarter-century in the Americas. Thousands of the retreating army were killed, including half to three-quarters of the Spaniards. They lost most of the horses, the cannon, the muskets, the crossbows, while the disappearance of Moctezuma's treasure, as Hugh Thomas has pointed out, suggested one of the few other certainties of that night: 'those who set off with gold weighing them down were more likely to be killed than those who had no more than their cotton armour.'[9]

When an eerie calm returned to the streets of Tenochtitlan on the morning of 2 July 1520, it was clear that *la Noche Triste* had been a decisive moment in the fortunes of both sides. The Spaniards, on the one hand, appeared to be in a desperate plight. Cortés' dream of a peaceful transition of power from Moctezuma to himself – so close to realisation after his stunning victory over Narváez – had been swept away. Worse than this loss of political ascendancy was the massive depletion of European forces and equipment. Without these advantages, and given the blow inflicted on their reputation for military invincibility, Cortés' band faced total annihilation.

For the Mexica, by contrast, the morning of 2 July 1520 was the high point in their struggle with the European invader. To many in both camps it must have seemed only a matter of time before they would follow up this success, bringing to bear on the straggling rump of the enemy the overwhelming resources and numerical superiority at their control, and convert the Spanish nightmare into reality.

4

The Siege

The debacle known to the Spaniards as *la Noche Triste* was undoubtedly a key moment in the confrontation between Europe and America. However, it was not, as it might have seemed in its immediate aftermath, the prelude to a great American recovery. Certainly, it was the nadir in Spanish fortunes, and certainly it was the fulcrum on which the final outcome pivoted. But the issue turned in completely the other direction. The Spaniards' Night of Sorrow can be seen as the real starting point for their success, and it was they who would convert the story of the Mexican war into a tale of racial aggrandisement.

William Hickling Prescott, whose epic but deeply biased account, *The Conquest of Mexico*, has a legendary status to match the events it describes, exemplifies this attitude. Prescott claimed that the achievements of the Spaniards – 'a mere handful of indigent adventurers' – were 'little short of the miraculous, too startling for the probabilities demanded by fiction, and without a parallel in the pages of history.'[1] Elsewhere he wrote that the 'whole story has the air of fable rather than of history! a legend of romance, – a tale of the genii!'[2] For the American historian the Spanish victory was evidence of the Europeans' superhuman courage and intelligence and their divinely inspired sense of mission – a sixteenth-century equivalent of his own Christian nation's manifest destiny to defeat North America's red savages and wrest an empire from its wilderness. The almost insuperable odds against Spanish success served only to prove the point.

Certainly, of all the wars between a colonial power and a tribal people, the Spanish conflict with the Mexica was theoretically one that offered the least opportunity for European success. Of the four tribes whose conquest and dispossession are considered in this book, the citizens of Tenochtitlan were the closest to fully developed nationhood. Although the wider Mexican confederation was based on economic relationships and largely exploitative, it was nevertheless a coherent structure, giving potential access to the military and economic resources of at least nine million people, and possibly more than twenty million.[3] Moreover, the organisational ability of the Mexica, like their numerical superiority, was both colossal and indisputable.

The European forces, by contrast, were the smallest of any of the four conquering armies, totalling only about two thousand men. For these reasons Mexico should have provided the greatest resistance to Europe. Yet, of the four tribes considered in this work, their overthrow was most rapid. Only the later Spanish seizure of the Inca empire, a campaign inspired by the methods and the huge war profit of Cortés, presents an historical example which combines the same speed of collapse with such an apparently huge differential in respective forces.

What, then, enabled the Spaniards to overcome such apparently fantastic odds? Uncovering the real basis for the Spanish victory is of paramount importance. Firstly it enables us to banish completely transcendental notions such as Prescott's European superman and his preordained right to world supremacy. Equally, while some of the reasons behind the Spanish victory in Mexico were peculiar to this theatre, we also find a number of key factors that allowed Europeans to triumph so widely over tribal opponents.

Ironically, the best place to start such an analysis is with *la Noche Triste*. While it constituted Cortés' largest defeat, it demonstrates fully what led the Mexica to win that battle but lose the war. On that rain-blurred July evening the inhabitants of Tenochtitlan, without opportunity for preparation, had launched themselves at the fleeing Spanish army in an ambush of spontaneous vengeance. These surprise tactics had brought them overwhelming success, but they were far from their traditional approach to fighting.

To comprehend Mexican warfare it is important to grasp the extent to which their conduct was subordinated to the claims of religious ritual and also to the rigidly structured nature of Mexican social organisation. Almost from cradle to grave, everything about the citizen's life was predetermined by priestly rite and state law. Details even down to what an individual might wear or where he might live were governed by prescriptions that changed in accordance with his evolving social status. The penalties imposed for what seem today relatively minor infractions could be extremely severe. Theft on the highway, for example, was a capital offence, as were adultery, female premarital sex, and even drunkenness.

The social code stressed collective over private well-being, public responsibility over individual liberty, precedent over innovation. While it seems so progressive for its age, even the state-provided education was another means of ensuring that each generation of Mexica was stamped with the same cultural impress. And in the contrived Mexican genealogy, which falsely suggested their descent from the Toltecs, one finds a concern to stress social continuity and cultural harmony, rather than the capacity for independent action that had given power to the Mexica in the first place.

It was typical that such an obsessively structured society would apply the same sense of ritual to military affairs. Long before any conflict ever occurred between Mesoamerican contestants, the two sides made elaborate exchanges of gift-bearing ambassadors. If their diplomatic talks failed, there followed a bizarre custom in which each side provided the other with a number of weapons – 'so that it might never be said that they had been defeated by treachery.'[4] Several twenty-day periods were allowed to elapse in the hope of a negotiated settlement. If all these preliminaries failed, the two sides were then assumed to be at war. Even then, the period of actual combat was managed to accommodate the needs of religious festivals and the agricultural cycle. Most conflicts took place after crops had been harvested in autumn, and when state augury had divined a propitious date. The element of surprise was clearly not a tactic with enormous appeal for Mexican military strategists.

Finally, after battle had been joined, the pervasive concern for religion continued to influence Mexican military conduct. For rather than inflicting instant slaughter, each soldier had as a principal aim the seizure of an opponent so that he could be returned to Tenochtitlan, there to be sacrificed on the altar-stones of the temples. This live harvest of enemy numbers was a mutually recognised means of asserting dominance. At the same time, it provided the winning army with the sacrificial victims so essential for the fulfilment of religious duty.

When both sides were American, preserving the enemy for the

altar-stones was no handicap. But to the sixteenth-century *conquista-dores*, fighting on an unequivocal policy of maximum slaughter, the ritual niceties of Mesoamerican conflict meant absolutely nothing. The gulf between their respective military cultures left the rulers of Tenochtitlan at a crushing disadvantage. In attempting to capture their Spanish opponents, it was as if the Mexica had elected to fight with one hand tied. Worse, in fact, since the concern for capture affected more than simply the method of fighting. When slaughtering the enemy was not the primary objective there was no incentive for developing arms with a lethal capability.

The weaponry of sixteenth-century Mesoamericans was large in variety, but neolithic in quality. They included clubs, slings, bows and arrows, stone-headed wooden spears and darts. These last were hurled by means of a launcher which the soldier retained in his hand. Wooden shields and padded cotton armour provided the only defence – and a further clear index of war's limited risks. The most formidable of their weapons was a wooden sword with a double edge of obsidian blades glued into slots. Bernal Diaz recorded that they were often as long as a broad sword, and the blades 'so set that one could neither break them nor pull them out'.[5] The Spanish chronicler added that they could cut worse than a knife – a claim confirmed by a twentieth-century archae-ologist, who wrote that they 'can be used without retouching, since the edges of a freshly broken piece are as sharp as a razor'.[6]

Against Spanish steel, however, the obsidian shattered easily. Moreover, all the Spanish weapons were lethal. That, after all, was their purpose. Cortés had also ensured that his force possessed some of the most sophisticated military hardware available to any army. Primitive by modern standards, European artillery had been in devel-opment for 200 years and was among the best in the world by the end of the fifteenth century. Cortés' bronze cannon 'were the aristocrats of the artillery', capable of firing over a distance of 400 paces.[7] His arque-buses, an even more recent innovation, were an important addition to the Spanish arsenal, if only for the fear generated by their noise and smoke.

The most crucial advantage possessed by the Spaniards was also one of their most ancient weapons – the warhorse. 'Our whole safety,' wrote Cortés, 'lay (after God) in the horses.'[8] Initially the Mexica were terrified by the creatures, confusing the mount and rider as a single, formidable monster. The Spanish leader went to considerable lengths to maintain this psychological advantage, seeking opportunities for public display of their power and burying dead animals to disguise their mortality. His exertions were well rewarded. In a number of critical battles the use of horses was decisive. Small wonder perhaps that towards the close of the siege for Tenochtitlan, horses were changing hands for 800 to 1,000 pesos, a huge sum, equivalent to more than five years' income for a reasonably prosperous Spaniard.[9]

Almost as important as their offensive capability were the Spaniards' defensive measures. Only the wealthier soldiers could afford a full suit of armour, brilliantly hinged at the joints to ensure complete manoeuvrability but offering protection to the whole body. These conspicuous and intimidating outfits weighed as little as twenty-five kilogrammes. Yet in tropical temperatures many *conquistadores* preferred the lighter alternatives, such as chainmail or a double covering of leather. Eventually Cortés and his seasoned veterans came to realise that they could forgo armour altogether, safeguarding themselves with the cotton padding used by the Mexica.

Europe's superior arms technology, almost a constant in their conflicts with tribal society worldwide, was seldom by itself the decisive factor. During their early conquests in the Americas, however, the European advantages of the horse and of steel were of overwhelming importance. In Mexico particularly these weapons combined with devastating results for the defending nation, with their preference for seizure in battle rather than slaughter of the opponent. This impact was never more apparent than when the attempted capture involved Cortés himself. On two occasions – once during his escape from Tenochtitlan and later in the siege of the capital – Cortés was in danger of being overwhelmed. During the first of these he fell in the water and was being dragged away by Mexican soldiers, when two of his lieutenants came to the rescue. Had the Mexica been less bound by military custom, less anxious to take him alive and more willing to inflict the fatal blow there and then, the whole course of their history might have been different.

Notwithstanding this one critical lapse into tradition, the Mexica fought during *la Noche Triste* on lines radically different from their conventional battle plan. There was no chivalrous warning to the opponent, no elaborate preparation or massed formation in spectacular frontal assault. Instead the fight was a continuous skirmish, conducted without rules or mercy and catching the Spaniards on the run, when many were already encumbered by their share of eight tonnes of gold. Over-burdened and funnelled along a narrow linear space, they were least able to bring into play their important military advantages – their cannon, crossbows and arquebuses – while the all-important cavalry was hopelessly unwieldy. In these circumstances their infantry's legendary discipline collapsed into a suicidal stampede, panic often ensuring the demise of colleagues left behind and many of them simply drowning before they could even be captured.

La Noche Triste should have been an important military 'lesson for the Mexica, indicating what they could achieve when Europe's critical armoury was neutralised and its coordinated use of horse and foot frustrated. Yet they chose to ignore it. When they confronted the Spaniards a week later in a battle that was intended to deliver the final *coup de grâce*, they had returned to the more conventional Mexican strategy involving a massed frontal assault announced by spectacular displays of pageantry.

On the day that Cortés faced this force, he would certainly have recognised that his chances of success had been greatly increased by the Mexican choice of tactic and battle site. Although he had suffered major losses, he had also been driven to escape by the knowledge that once outside the city his army would enjoy important advantages. During the original march on Tenochtitlan in 1519, the Spanish commander had gained the full measure of his Mesoamerican opponents in open combat.

The most notable opportunity had been in his struggle with the Tlaxcalans, a community which occupied territories immediately west of Tenochtitlan. These people had been long-standing antagonists of the Mexica and eventually entered a critically important alliance with Cortés against their traditional enemy. It was they who had accompanied the Spaniards during their first triumphal entry and then helped perpetrate the massacre of Toxcatl, and who had finally suffered such losses on the city causeway. Despite this later record as willing ally, the Tlaxcalan state initially opposed the European progress and fought them in three engagements before making peace.

In each of the encounters the Spaniards were confronted by armies vastly greater than their own. While the *conquistadores* were disconcerted by this apparent imbalance, they later discovered that it brought unforeseen but valuable psychological and tactical benefits. For, once they had survived and triumphed in such an apparently unequal contest they were all the more buoyed by their success. Of the second of their battles with the Tlaxcalans, Bernal Diaz exclaimed, 'What an opportunity for fine writing the events of this most perilous and uncertain battle present!'[10] In the early sixteenth century Spanish military culture was deeply influenced by medieval works of romance such as *Amadis de Gaula* and stories of the legendary Spanish hero, El Cid. In these tales, lone Christian knights did battle and won through against an infidel foe of oceanic number and anonymity. In their own eyes, Mexico's conquerors believed they had done no less and it gave them enormous self-confidence to think they had equalled the deeds of their mythical heroes. Bernal Diaz wrote of the Spaniards, without any hint of insincerity or modesty, 'What men in all the world have shown such daring?'[11]

Cortés exploited this valuable psychological benefit at times of drooping morale, encouraging his army to think 'that God was on our side, and to Him nothing is impossible, which they might plainly see by the victories we had already won, in which so many of our enemies had fallen, but not a single one of ourselves.'[12] Moreover, the Spanish commander recognised that there were even practical advantages in their opponents' numerical strength, since this tended to work in tandem with enemy indiscipline to aggravate losses. Of one contest, for instance, he wrote that 'their numbers were so great that they got in each other's way and could neither fight nor fly.'[13]

While allowances must be made for the exceptional physical courage of the *conquistadores*, any objective examination of the statistics from the Tlaxcalan encounters must lead to conclusions more prosaic than Bernal Diaz's boast of incomparable daring. Even by his own account, the Spanish chronicler noted only three European fatalities in the trio of engagements, while the really significant loss was that of two horses. His American adversaries, meanwhile, fielding armies of thousands, suffered high totals of dead and wounded in each battle. With odds against them of hundreds, even thousands to one, it defies common sense to believe that so few Spaniards could ever have won had they suffered a steady haemorrhage of numbers. While many incurred wounds, few sustained fatal blows. Even fewer were captured. Indeed, how could Mesoamerican soldiers seize a man who could cut off their arms or their heads in a single blow? As *la Noche Triste* proved, the Spaniards were only vulnerable when their superior weaponry and greater discipline were neutralised.

Otherwise, Cortés had quickly grasped their situation. Why else, indeed, would 500 men have dared to embark on the conquest of millions? The fact was that fighting Mesoamericans was a relatively risk-free business. Typically Cortés wrote of one rout: 'I did them great damage, without suffering anything worse than the toil and weariness of long hours of fighting without food.'[14] In Mexico the *conquistadores* challenged an enemy of Lilliputian dimensions – great in number but negligible in impact. During the nineteenth century, tribal peoples in Africa and America, confronted by seemingly invincible European invaders, would resort to the powers of their spiritual leaders in the hope that certain medicines would confer immunity to Western bullets. In Mexico in the sixteenth century the *conquistadores* seemed to enjoy just such a miraculous invulnerability. In this case, however, it was not a triumph of magic, but of superior European technology in combination with indigenous America's extraordinary military culture.

Another factor favouring the Spaniards and often overlooked in accounts of the Mexican war was that they almost always fought alongside American allies. Against the Tlaxcalans, the *conquistadores* enjoyed the backing of the Totonacs, whom they had recruited on the coast. Later, it was the Tlaxcalans themselves who became their most important supporters. These larger formations of indigenous soldiers shielded the Europeans and also did much of the offensive fighting. However, their role has been largely ignored, either because the original written accounts were all by Spaniards, indisposed to acknowledge their debt, or because subsequent historians, viewing the *conquistadores* as the sole beneficiaries of victory, sought explanations entirely in terms of European factors. However, it was the lethal combination, a highly trained Spanish corps within the massed ranks of their American allies, which gave them such an important military edge. The European cavalry, crossbows, cannon and arquebuses could open up enemy formations, often from a safe distance, and leave them vulnerable to a combined assault by the Euro-American force.[15]

On 8 July 1520, merely a week after *la Noche Triste*, all these factors came into play in the battle near the town of Otumba. The Spaniards and Tlaxcalans had retreated in a wide north-easterly arc around the lakes of Tenochtitlan. When they first confronted the huge Mexican assembly, the Euro-Americans were overwhelmed by its sheer weight of numbers. But unlike the capital's causeway, where the Spanish horse had found no room for manoeuvre, the open plain at Otumba suited the cavalry perfectly and it was they who turned the battle. Cortés himself spotted the Mexican commanders decked in resplendent costume as a mark of their rank. With four other cavalrymen, he forced aside the protective cordon surrounding the Mexican general and ran him through at full charge. The sight of their defeated leader and, more importantly, their army's standard on the tip of Spanish lances had a devastating psychological impact on the Mexica, and they abandoned their positions in confusion.

The split second in which Cortés was seized by the idea of his dramatic gesture was perhaps the critical moment in the Spaniards' fortunes. Victory at Otumba shielded his men from further harrassment and on 9 July 1520 they reached the territories of their Tlaxcalan allies. There, the *Caudillo*, like all successful commanders, was blessed with good fortune. Firstly, the Tlaxcalan leaders, rather than finishing off the exhausted army, welcomed the Europeans, dressing their wounds and feeding them. Within three weeks they had been restored to fighting fitness, while Cortés received the support of other allies. Six small Spanish expeditions had arrived fortuitously off the Mexican coast, and each in turn was persuaded to join the *Caudillo*. These added 200 European troops, with a number of fresh horse and cannon, to his growing army of reconquest.

However, another unforeseen circumstance tipped the balance most decisively in favour of Cortés. This was the arrival of the smallpox virus, which had made its silent entry to the American continent, probably stowed away on one of Narváez's ships. The timely eruption of this epidemic in the aftermath of *la Noche Triste* had in part spared his forces from an immediate and conclusive Mexican blow. Within a very short time the disease, while seeming to spare the already resistant Europeans, took a devastating toll on the Spaniards' enemies and their allies. The American people, having lived in isolation from the virus for millennia, had no immunity and died in tens of thousands. As the corpses piled up in Tenochtitlan and the surrounding cities, the crops remained unharvested, and famine eventually added to Mexican hardships. Amongst the victims was the new emperor, Cuitláhuac, forcing the nation into the hasty appointment of a successor.

Their choice, Cuauhtémoc, although the son of a former emperor and cousin to Moctezuma, and thus well versed in imperial government, had been left an awesome task. The devastation in parts of Tenochtitlan served as an outward symbol of the less visible but more critical damage inflicted on the Mexican state. In undermining the nation's military reputation, the European invaders had irreparably weakened the network of relationships between the capital and its client populations. The unquestioning obedience of the subject states had been the foundation of Mexican power. But with the Spaniards looming and the Mexica *in extremis*, these former tributaries now held their support at a new premium. A measure of the changed political climate in the empire of late 1520 was that Cuitláhuac, before his death from smallpox, had failed in diplomatic overtures to his most important American neighbours.

Cortés, by contrast, had enjoyed considerable success, though his methods were anything but diplomatic. When the Tepeacans, neighbours of the Tlaxcalans, refused to recognise European authority, they were invaded by a Spanish force and defeated. Cortés then decreed that the Tepeacans, as tributaries of the Mexica, were themselves in turn subjects of Spain on the basis of Moctezuma's spurious vassalage. They had therefore rebelled directly against the Spanish crown. Punishment for such a crime was the indiscriminate slaughter of the male population, many being thrown to the dogs. Their dependants were branded on the face and sold into slavery. After this, city after city made alliance with Cortés, caving in to his terrifying methods.

With a new Euro-American military league in place, giving him the support of tens, possibly hundreds, of thousands of American allies, Cortés turned his attention to the overthrow of Tenochtitlan itself. Like so much of European behaviour his methods were totally alien to his adversaries. They were to be defeated, not through some crushing blow in open combat, but by the steady constriction of military blockade.

To complete his plans Cortés had authorised the construction of twelve brigantines. These were flat-bottomed, permitting free access over the shallow waters of the Mexican lakes. With their launch on 28 April 1521, each manned by twenty-five to thirty Spanish soldiers, Cortés had made a critical addition to the European arsenal of superior military technology. If, as one commentator has stated, the Spanish knight on an armoured horse functioned as the tank of his day, then in the curious amphibious battle for Tenochtitlan, the Spanish boats represented the equivalent advantage of modern air supremacy.[16] Their greater speed, strength and manoeuvrability made them all but impregnable, allowing them to cut off Mexican supplies being ferried to the capital by canoe, and to deliver superior firepower almost at will. Commanding the small fleet himself, the Spanish leader divided his other European forces into three companies, one each for the southern, western and eastern causeways. Only the road to the north lay open, and this was quickly sealed off in the first weeks of fighting.

Tenochtitlan was then an isolated if heavily defended prison.

In the ensuing months the Spaniards steadily intensified their grip. Each day they advanced along the causeways, burning and dismantling buildings, then retreating at dusk to their mainland headquarters. Each night the Mexica returned, attempting to make good the fortifications they had lost in the fighting. Although there seemed few dramatic advances, Spanish progress was as inexorable as it was hard-won. Eight weeks after the launch of the boats, the Euro-American forces were sallying into the heart of the city. As summer advanced to its height the Mexica were forced to abandon Tenochtitlan altogether, retreating to the precincts of Tlatelolco. There they made a final desperate stand.

In what was intended as the decisive phase of conquest, Cortés made a three-pronged assault on the Mexican stronghold in Tlatelolco. Each of his units converged on their defences, crossing as they did so gaps in the causeway engineered by the Americans. The Spaniards' allies were responsible for filling these flooded ditches, to avoid the Euro-American forces ever being stranded on the wrong side in the face of a fierce Mexican charge.

During the assault, however, one deep canal was re-opened, probably by a lightning strike of Mexican sappers, and the sheer ferocity of their planned counter-attack forced one of the Spanish units to retreat to this ditch. Cortés claimed that it was ten to twelve metres across and about six metres deep. Faced with such an obstacle, European discipline melted away in the panic to get back across. The Mexica took full advantage. Their canoes cut off any escape route and the trap closed. It was a repeat of *la Noche Triste*, but this time in only a minor key. Even so the besieging army lost between fifty and seventy Spaniards and possibly two thousand Americans. Seeing what numbers of men were falling, Cortés claimed he had decided 'to take my stand there and die fighting.'[17] At one point he was almost seized and killed. When they finally got back to safety the rest of the American allies slipped away overnight, raising hopes amongst the Mexica of an eleventh-hour delivery.

But in the war for New Spain there were to be no miracles. Beneath the elation of a sudden success was the unavoidable reality of impending defeat. Though European morale was shaken, it was not broken. Nor was the siege lifted. The *conquistadores* still controlled two-thirds of the city. Mexican resources, on the other hand, were almost completely exhausted. Everywhere lay evidence of their brutal

71

hardships. In the absence of food they had been reduced to eating roots and the bark of trees. 'Their excretions,' wrote Bernal Diaz in one of his typically graphic observations, 'were the sort of filth that swine pass which have been fed on nothing but grass.'[18]

While Tenochtitlan was virtually won, it was no longer the glorious metropolis which had dazzled and amazed the *conquistadores* only months earlier. It had become a wasteland of ruins littered with the debris of war. Diaz wrote that in Tlatelolco it was impossible to walk without stepping on the heads and bodies of dead Mexica.[19] The stench was appalling. So too had been the cost in human life. The minimum contemporary estimate was 100,000 Mexicans dead during the three-month siege. And their own sources suggested that 240,000 was the true total: 2,400 for each of the Spaniards slain – a further compelling indication of the war's one-sided nature. A Spanish chronicler recorded that when the end finally came, 40,000 inhabitants drowned themselves, choking the canals with corpses.[20]

The emperor Cuauhtémoc was caught, according to European sources as he tried to escape by canoe, according to the Mexica as he came to negotiate surrender. Whatever the truth, his captors squabbled bitterly over the anticipated reward, while the fever for gold and loot consumed the entire European force. They searched everywhere and everyone – in their ears, between women's breasts, up their noses, up their skirts – but little was ever found and frustration led first to anger, then violence. Cortés, who had initially received Cuauhtémoc with the exaggerated courtesy befitting such a valiant opponent, then acquiesced in his torture. The emperor and a relative were bound to a pole and their feet doused in oil, which was ignited. As the flesh melted away Cuauhtémoc's companion, unable to bear the pain, cried out in agony. Cuauhtémoc replied, 'And me? Do you think I'm lying here on a bed of roses?'[21] Cortés claimed this treatment of his imperial prisoner weighed heavily on his conscience but three years later he hanged him on a charge of rebellion.

In this story of Mexico's last emperor one finds in miniature the key elements in Spain's first fifty years of New World dominion: the stubborn patriot vulnerable in defeat, his captors working anxiously upon him with the instruments of coercion; behind, the ineffectual or indifferent voice of Spanish officialdom, and impelling the whole onslaught an unrelenting appetite for riches which the prone and exposed American body could never quite fulfil.

5

The Besieging

In the immediate aftermath of Tenochtitlan's fall, the Spaniards decided to stage an event to commemorate their great success. On this occasion it would not be a triumphal march through the capital's streets, since there was now no audience to witness such a parade, but a banquet.

It is valuable to summarise exactly what the Spanish success represented to them. The two-year war had been the *conquistadores'* most important confrontation in the New World – not a one-sided rout of Caribbean 'savages' but a great clash of civilisations. For Europe as a whole, it represented the most valuable colonial acquisition by a single nation – a territory larger than the European parent state. For the individual nation which had made the conquest, it confirmed its status as a major power both in Europe and even on a world stage. Spain's victory in Mexico launched her on a career of imperial expansion that embraced both American continents and beyond.

As we have seen, it had been possession of the war horse and important European technologies – especially the military application of steel and advantages in ship construction – working in concert with the Mexica's bizarre military culture, that had played a major part in securing victory. Yet, while these material factors tell us much about *how* the Spaniards had managed to win, they do little to explain *why* they were so motivated for outright destruction. A major question that remains unanswered, haunting their drunken celebrations in Tenochtitlan, is how the *conquistadores* could look upon the corpse-choked waterways and stinking ruins around them and drink toasts to their achievement? What enabled them to see the ruthless dismemberment of one civilisation as somehow the fulfilment of their own? And what had first propelled them to seek such an outcome? After all, their European contemporaries in Africa or Asia had encountered many new societies and done no more than establish trade or diplomatic relations. Why had military conquest been such an overriding imperative in Central America?

One obvious answer immediately presents itself. Profit. The instant material rewards of military success, in the form of gold, precious stones, land and slaves, had driven the Spaniards to conquest after conquest during their first quarter-century in the New World. The prospect of further riches, either genuine or simply imagined, is a motivation whose impact on indigenous Americans we will consider later. However, cupidity is not by itself sufficient to explain the extraordinary character of Spain's conquests. In order to understand the forces that shaped their actions in sixteenth-century America, we need to explore the underlying character of the people from which the *conquistadores* were recruited.

Many of the distinctive qualities of Renaissance Spain were deeply embedded in the country's long history of religious warfare. Since the early Middle Ages the Christians had fought a relentless crusade against the Islamic kingdoms of the Iberian peninsula. Known as the *Reconquista*, these wars spanned 700 years – a century for each year of the original campaign that had delivered Spain to the forces of Allah. However, by 1469 the process of Christian unification was nearing completion and had received symbolic expression in the marriage of Ferdinand and Isabella, respectively heirs to the thrones of Aragon and Castile. By 1492, the year of Columbus' first transatlantic voyage, the peninsula's full restoration to Christendom became political reality with the Muslim surrender outside Granada, the capital of their last enclave in Andalusia.

Yet the fact that King Louis XIV of France could sneer in the late seventeenth century that Europe ended at the Pyrenees, suggests Islam's enduring impact on Spanish culture despite the accomplishment of Christian political unity.[1] In the early sixteenth century the most visible element of this non-European heritage was a sizeable Muslim population. Another immediate reminder of Spain's Moorish past was the presence of a large Jewish community. Jews had once been welcome during the more enlightened years of the Caliphate in Cordoba, and had made a major contribution to the life of Moorish

Spain. Even after the Christian *Reconquista*, the Jews remained an almost indispensable educated élite. However, from the fourteenth century jealousy of their wealth and social prominence intensified, erupting in violent anti-Semitic riots and discriminatory legislation. Rather than face the perils of persecution, many Jews were baptised, forming an important community known as *conversos*. It is a measure of the deeply rooted nature of Spanish prejudice that another name for them was *marranos* – pigs.[2]

In 1482, to ensure purity of faith amongst her Catholic subjects, Queen Isabella had given royal consent to the formation of the Spanish Inquisition. By the beginning of the sixteenth century, under the guidance of the first inquisitor-general, Tomas de Torquemada, it had overseen the torture and execution of thousands of suspected heretics hunted down from amongst Spain's crypto-Jews, its *conversos* and other recent converts from Islam. In 1492, three months after the surrender of Granada, the two monarchs brought the Jewish 'problem' to a final dramatic conclusion. They put their signature to an edict banishing from their realms within four months all who clung to the Hebraic faith. Before the deadline expired Columbus had set sail for the New World and 150,000 Spanish Jews had fled into exile. Europe's career in the Americas had hardly begun in a spirit of racial and religious tolerance.

This triple process, the completion of internal unification, the violent purging of minority populations and the beginning of overseas empire, had their origins in that same growth towards full national self-identity. The historian J.H. Elliott had suggested that in 'a country so totally devoid of political unity as the new Spain, a common faith served as a substitute, binding together Castilians, Aragonese, and Catalans.'[3] The Christianity of the people, however, tempered by centuries of defeat and sharpened on the stone of Islamic resistance, was a double-edged tool in the business of Spain's national reconstruction. While their all-embracing religion was a source of massive cohesion and of absolute certainty, as the sense of unity intensified, so paradoxically did a deep intolerance of any unorthodoxy. The fanatic's militant convictions seemed to grow in parallel with his self-doubt, expressing itself in ever more ruthless violence towards the perceived alien or outsider. Typical was the siege of Moorish Malaga in 1487. It was a campaign financed in part by heavy taxes upon the Jewish community. The Spanish forces took no prisoners and ignored the wounded. At its capitulation, the town's entire Muslim population –

15,000 men, women and children – was sold into slavery.

In addition to this central ideological contradiction there was another fundamental paradox in Spanish society. While the joint monarchs had acquired title through the house of Aragon to the Balearic Islands, Sardinia, Sicily and the kingdom of Naples, and while Machiavelli described Ferdinand as having 'been transformed from a small and weak king into the greatest monarch in Christendom', there was an altogether less confident, more desperate side to Spain's national life. About ten per cent of the country was bare rock, another thirty-five per cent was poor or unproductive.[4] And of all the Spanish lands, ninety-eight per cent was owned by the clergy and the aristocracy. Yet these upper classes constituted only two per cent of the total population. By the turn of the fifteenth century the vast majority of Spain's 8,000,000 population, more than four-fifths, were landless rural poor. In fact, the Jewish expulsions may have been a knee-jerk response to the severe problems of over-population. Working from Spanish data, the French historian Fernand Braudel speculated that in the whole Mediterranean region one in five – twelve to fourteen million – lived near the starvation level.[5]

Mass death as a consequence of famine and plague was commonplace in Spain, as it was throughout Europe. According to one source, an early sixteenth-century pandemic carried off nine-tenths of all the inhabitants of Rome and Naples. A later outbreak left Marseilles with only 5,000 citizens.[6] Indifference to such losses of life ran all the way to the highest levels of society. Told once of the demise of 7,000 indigenous children on Hispaniola in only twelve weeks, the Bishop Fonseca of Burgos, the prelate invested with supreme authority over Spain's colonial affairs, inquired, 'And how does that concern me?'[7]

It was inevitable with such widespread hardship at home that the American colonies, with their promise of easy riches, attracted recruits from the most impoverished regions. Extremadura, the high, stony, arid plateau of the southern Spanish interior, was a case in point. A large number of Cortés' men, including the *Caudillo* himself, were from this area. So too were the Pizarro brothers, leaders in the conquest of the Incan empire. However, while many took passage to seek their fortune, few were destined to find it. Often all they discovered was more intense hardship: the dangers of disease, of warfare, starvation and shipwreck. Braudel described one galleon returning to Europe with gold worth a million pesos and only sixteen of the original three hundred crew still alive. Another treasure ship sailed into

Mexico's pacific port of Acapulco with not a living soul left on board.[8] Given the great risks, it is hardly surprising that the *conquistadores'* lives were often desperately short, their methods violent, their outlook cynical and uncaring. The Spanish novelist Cervantes described the New World as 'the refuge and protection of all the *desperados* of Spain, the church of rebels and sanctuary of murderers'.[9]

Once they arrived in the New World, the behaviour of these Spanish adventurers was rooted in the same contradictions that had been so powerfully expressed in their European past. The fanatical certainties of their Christian faith would function side by side with a deep intolerance and suspicion of any form of ideological difference. As much as they pushed outwards on the wave of confidence radiating from Spain's new-found strength, they were driven to escape by remembrance of its desperate past.

It is a telling expression of the seamless continuities which a man like Columbus expected to find between his European experience and his New World discoveries, that he carried with him a copy of the Old Testament, believing it would prove an indispensable travel guide. It was equally apparent that he viewed his transatlantic journey very much in the context of Old World crusades – he constantly dreamed of pioneering a route which would allow Christendom to take Jerusalem in the rear from the forces of the Ottoman Turks.

In fact, all the *conquistadores* looked upon their American ventures as imbued with the religious spirit of their Old World conquests. Like crusaders, Cortés' men were presented with papal bulls giving remission of sins committed during battle. At moments of intense fighting they would claim, as did their medieval forebears in the Holy Land, visions of the blessed apostles, St James and St Peter, riding out to assist them.[10] Even the words to describe Mexican religious elements were taken from a vocabulary for their Islamic equivalents. Thus the word used constantly by Cortés to describe the Mesoamerican temples was 'mosque'.[11]

Just as the *Reconquista* had been a war of faiths, so in the Americas the Spaniards saw the conversion of the heathen savage as an explicit goal of their crusading enterprise. In his written instructions to Cortés, for instance, the Cuban governor Diego Velázquez had insisted that the 'first motive which you and your company have to carry with you is to serve our Lord God and increase the dimension of our holy

Catholic faith.'[12]

The Spanish methods of achieving this were often brutally direct. In the town of Cempoallan, the capital of the Totonacs, Cortés bound its inhabitants to his cause and accepted their military support, then inflicted on them a final ritual of submission before departing for Tlaxcala. The Totonac idols – 'fearsome dragons as big as calves, and others half-man half-dog and hideously ugly' – were rolled out of the temples and smashed or burnt.[13] Totonac protests were silenced with threats of instant violence, the temples were stripped and white-washed, while four priests were forcibly shorn and placed in charge of the new Christian altar. Hugh Thomas suggested that it was 'surely one of the most remarkable events in the history of Cortés' life'.[14]

It was certainly remarkable for its insensitivity to an ally. But its real significance was far wider and more sinister. For Cortés' actions embodied an almost complete negation of meaning in the Americans' lives. It was as if, through the lens of their militant Christianity, the *conquistadores* could only recognise an inverted image of the other's reality. Mesoamerican belief was a gross falsehood, the orientation of Totonac society a monumental delusion. Their very gods, the symbols of what was most valued in their world, were not images of the divine, but of the devil, hideously ugly and unspeakably evil – in the words of Bernal Diaz, 'abominations which would bring their souls to hell.'[15] The priests matted locks and lacerated earlobes were not out-ward signs of submission to the sacred, but examples of conduct that was both meaningless and disgusting. Even the fastidious cleanliness habitual amongst Mesoamericans could not be acknowledged as a laudable refinement. It was reviled by the unwashed Spaniards, who found in it an echo of Islam's hated ritual ablutions.

Just as the *conquistadores'* mirror-like distortions denied meaning to American society, so did it reverse the moral content implicit in their own actions. Thus, for them to allow such a society to continue in tranquillity was to permit a kind of hell on earth. War, on the other hand, became a divinely inspired process of redemption. To enslave was to liberate. To conquer was to pacify. To destroy their world would be to create afresh, an expression of charity, a benign harvest-ing of souls for their Christian god.

This contorted moral schema had obvious antecedents in Spain's millennium-long confrontation with its own dark shadow: the equally advanced, equally dynamic, but opposing forces of Islam. Muslim armies had tested the utmost resources of Christian Europe, most completely in Iberia. It had been the defining ordeal. Out of it had evolved a set of perceptions of foreign society which Tzvetan Todorov has succinctly defined in his consideration of Columbus' initial response to the Arawak of the Antilles. In this, he wrote, 'We can distinguish . . . two component parts, which we shall find . . . in practice, down to our own day in every colonist in his relations to the colonized.'

> Either he conceives the Indians . . . as human beings altogether, having the same rights as himself; but then he sees them not only as equals but also as identical, and this behavior leads to assimilationism, the projection of his own values on the others. Or else he starts from the difference, but the latter is immediately translated into terms of superiority and inferiority (in his case, obviously, it is the Indians who are inferior). What is denied is the existence of a human substance truly other, something capable of being not merely an imperfect state of oneself.[16]

It followed naturally that what was imperfect, since it diminished and threatened the Christian ideal, was also evil. The one overriding demand of the encounter was the destruction of the other.

However crude they might have been, such ideas provided the expansionist communities of Christian Europe with a conceptual framework and a language for confronting another civilisation. For the *conquistadores*, it meant that when faced with indigenous America, they at least had a tradition of discourse with a radically alternative society, which cushioned them against the possibility of surprise or confusion at the moment of impact. From this prior acquaintance with the other stemmed a number of advantages.

One of these was the traditional value placed on translators and interpreters as mediators between distinct cultures. Spanish knowledge of Arabic had been an essential tool in their penetration of Moorish society, and Cortés was well aware of the importance of an interpreter to his own enterprise. Even before leaving Cuba he had availed himself of the enforced services of a Mayan fisherman kidnapped in Yucatan expressly for this purpose. Although this man later escaped, the *Caudillo* was fortunate in replacing him with a far more willing interpreter, a Spaniard called Gerónimo de Aguilar. In 1511 this man had been shipwrecked near Jamaica and swept by currents to the

Yucatan peninsula, where he was eventually enslaved by a local leader. On hearing of Aguilar's existence and whereabouts, Cortés sought him out and took the castaway with him for the rest of the expedition. Aguilar, however, had learnt only the Mayan language, not the Nahuatl spoken by the inhabitants of Tenochtitlan. It was another, more important interpreter who offered Cortés a final linguistic bridge into the very heart of Mexican thought and society.

This was a young and apparently beautiful girl, the daughter of minor nobility from the southern edge of the empire. On the death of her father she had been sold into slavery, passing into Mayan owner-ship before they had finally offered her to the *conquistadores*. The gift could not have been more valuable. La Malinche, as she was known to her fellow Americans, or Doña Marina as she became to the Spaniards, was a gifted linguist speaking both Nahuatl and Mayan. Moreover, her background of parental exploitation made her ripe material for conversion to the foreigners' cause.

Initially Cortés required a chain of translation involving Aguilar and Marina to communicate with the Mexica – firstly from Spanish to Mayan, then Nahuatl, and the answer back again in reverse order. However, Marina quickly acquired an understanding of Castilian, and served thereafter as the single critical mediator between the Europeans and Americans. She was a central figure in the Spanish conquest. For the duration of the war she was constantly at Cortés' side, even sharing his bed and bearing his child, before she was given in marriage to one of the Spanish knights. During all the critical negotiations she combined with her master in a formidable duet that exhibited many qualities of a modern, hard-man soft-man interrogation team. As Hugh Thomas put it, they mixed 'eloquence with subtlety, piety with menace, sophistication with brutality'.[17]

It is difficult to overstate the importance of these interpreters. They gave Cortés a permanent insight into the mindset of his adversaries. They helped shape his policies. In fact his hold over the Mexica's lan-guage and thought processes was a linguistic corollary and precondi-tion of his final physical mastery of the empire itself. With astonishing perception, Bernal Diaz described the discovery of Aguilar and Marina as 'the great beginning of our conquests'.[18]

Critical as Cortés' control of language was, perhaps the most crucial advantage resulting from Spain's long intercourse with its great Islamic antagonist was the Spaniards' radical enmity towards any other society. It meant that there was never any question about their moral response to another civilisation, nor did they doubt their ultimate objective. A collective cultural background programmed them to pursue one end: the overthrow of Mexican power. The fanatical strain to their Christian faith gave to that common ambition a powerful moral impetus. Shared experiences of poverty and hardship had stamped them all with a formidable mental and physical toughness, as well as a powerful, even desperate, appetite for material riches.

And just as in the differences of military culture, where the weaknesses of one side seemed to dovetail with the advantages of the other, so did the Spaniards' total commitment to Mexican overthrow operate in tandem with a profound confusion amongst Tenochtitlan's high command, as well as a deep tribal disunity amongst the wider Mexican confederation. The appearance of the Spanish fleet off the coastline triggered nothing short of an intellectual crisis for its American inhabitants. While the Mexica had a history of contact with uncivilised 'barbarians' – the nomadic tribes that roamed the northern periphery of the empire – these sea-borne newcomers were in an entirely different category.

Alien in dress and physiognomy, bizarrely equipped and transported, of a single age group and sex (mainly men in their military prime, bar a handful of Spanish women), and heralded only by inflated rumour that had travelled the Caribbean shorelines for almost two decades, the Spaniards offered little frame of reference to Moctezuma and his advisors. In the absence of any precedent, the high command scoured Mexican oral history and legend for an identity to match the radical otherness of the strangers. To this deeply religious people it seemed possible that they were not dealing with humans like themselves at all. Their initial name for Cortés' men was *Teules*. Gods.

Moctezuma in particular was mesmerised by the coincidence linking the Spaniards to one of the Mexican gods and mythical culture-heroes, Quetzalcoatl. In the story of this deity one date had magical significance. He had been born and died in a year which, according to Mexican astronomical calculation, was known as One Reed. This was also the year in which he had vowed to return after he had been exiled by a divine rival. In their cyclically arranged calendar, this prophesied date of Quetzalcoatl's reappearance recurred every fifty-two years. By sheer chance, 1519 was One Reed. As Ronald Wright put it: 'Cortés's timing was perfect: without knowing it, he had gained a psychological advantage at odds of fifty-two to one.'[19] Moctezuma took this coincidence, in conjunction with other omens, as a sign of impending disaster. Immobilised by doubt, he handed the initiative squarely to the invaders.

While the notion of the Spaniards' divine identity was eventually laid to rest by their murderous behaviour and obvious mortality, the Mexica never truly recovered from their inaccurate assessment. The initial failure to divine the strangers' inimical intentions gave the Spaniards time to consolidate a physical and diplomatic beachhead. Yet at no point after that time did Tenochtitlan's masters seek to recover their position even by availing themselves, as their opponents had done, of the other's language.

Cortés was further able to exploit indigenous America's uncertain grasp of the European identity by presenting himself as a potential ally and friend to the tribute states in the Mexican empire. Bernal Diaz was eloquent on the *Caudillo*'s mastery of diplomatic camouflage. 'He displayed much affection', 'with many flattering protestations', 'won over . . . with kindly words', 'with a great show of affection and flattery', 'comforted them with kind words, which he did not find difficult' – all these phrases testify to the mimetic dimension in Cortesian diplomacy.[20] Another *conquistador*, one of his most trusted lieutenants, said his master had 'no more conscience than a dog'.[21] Such a judgement meshes perfectly with Cortés' trail of political manipulation which eased his journey to Mexican control.

However, his smooth words could hardly have been so persuasive had they not made an appeal to concerns of central importance for the Mesoamerican tribes. To people like the Totonacs and Tlaxcalans the Spaniards loomed as a potent but vaguely comprehended force, a timely *deus ex machina*, whom they simply shaped to fit their own limited and, as it proved, short-sighted schema – the overthrow of Mexican control. Not that this objective was without justification. The repeated Mesoamerican complaint about the behaviour of the imperial power cannot have been the invention of Spanish chroniclers. 'If their hosts were inattentive or indifferent,' wrote one contemporary historian, 'the [Mexica] pillaged and sacked the villages, despoiled and dishonoured them; they destroyed the harvests and inflicted a thousand injuries and damages upon them. The whole country trembled before them.'[22]

The main plank of the *conquistadores*' diplomatic offensive in Mexico was to pander to these regional grievances, while Cortés' promise of redress initiated the fault-lines that eventually tore the empire apart. In a dispatch written in October 1520, long before Tenochtitlan's fall, Cortés described to the Spanish king the divisive and improvisatory nature of his methods during negotiations with the Tlaxcalans and their neighbours, the Cholulans, respectively the enemy and ally of Tenochtitlan:

> I was not a little pleased to see such discord between the two, since it seemed highly propitious to my plan, and I should thus in all probability discover a means to subject them more swiftly . . . Accordingly I continued to treat with both one and the other, thanking each in secret for the advice he gave me, and professing to regard each with greater friendship than the other.[23]

In his *Mexico and the Spanish Conquest*, Ross Hassig warns against an over-simplified interpretation of the Euro-American diplomacy that credits Cortés as an all-seeing architect of the triumphant alliance. The *Caudillo* was himself, according to Hassig, as much used by his American allies as he used them. The Euro-American conquest of Tenochtitlan:

> required a thorough understanding of the political organization of Mesoamerican states and empires, the nature of rule and patterns of royal succession, and the individuals and factions involved. Cortés had some grasp of the situation, but not the detailed knowledge or understanding necessary to determine which faction to attack and which to support: only the Indians had this knowledge. The political manipulations that funnelled men and material to the Spaniards was engineered by the Indians in furtherance of their own factional interests . . . The Conquest was not primarily a conflict between Mexico and Spain, but between the Aztecs and the various Mesoamerican groups supporting Cortés. The clash was centred on issues internal to Mesoamerica . . .[24]

While European historiography has traditionally under-recorded the American contribution to Tenochtitlan's downfall, and correspondingly over-emphasised the Spaniards' more advantageous politico-intellectual background, it remains true that no tribe party to Mexico's destruction fully grasped Cortés' opposition to all independent American society. Certainly, no American group secured the benefits they expected from victory. Cortesian diplomacy outflanked them all, leaving the Spaniards alone the true conquerors. So completely did the peoples of Central America fulfil Spanish objectives that it would be almost true to say that the Mexican empire conquered itself on Europe's behalf. Cortés estimated his American forces in the siege of Tenochtitlan at anywhere between seventy-five and a hundred and fifty thousand men – an army large enough by itself to neutralise the defenders' total military strength.[25]

The readiness of these indigenous allies to complete the invaders' task reveals a fundamental difference between the political culture of European society and that obtaining amongst tribal societies. Christian peoples, on the one hand, had an extraordinary potential for spontaneous fission, giving rise to new replica bodies – roving groups like Cortés' expedition – willing to travel far from the parent organism and function in apparent independence. Yet they also showed a comparable capacity to reunite at critical moments and to retain loyalty towards and then call upon the greater resources of their original European source.

Tribal societies, by contrast, seldom enjoyed the same shared inheritance of culture and ideology from which sprang the Europeans' overarching unity. An infinite capacity for disunity (illustrated by the tens of thousands of Americans fighting in the Cortesian army) is almost a defining element of tribal society. Indigenous communities were invariably guilty of a type of collective myopia, a deep failure to see the European threat in anything but a local context. And it was this lack of a wider horizon, itself part of the very foundation and cement of tribal identity, as much as any technological or numerical deficiency, that often sealed their fate worldwide. Divide and rule thus became a central principle of European supremacy for four hundred years.

Recognition of this tribal myopia, and misidentification of the European invader, also helps us to understand more fully the *how* of Spanish success in Mexico. For it was the highly fissiparous character of the Mexican empire and the ease with which Cortés prised it apart that constituted, with the deeply ritualised nature of their warfare and the inefficacy of their weapons, the three key American deficiencies in the face of the European assault. Together they operated in an inexorable synergy of self-destruction.

It was this, in a sense, that justified the Spaniards at their victory celebrations as they drank toasts to Tenochtitlan's tragic desolation.

For they could argue with some conviction that the American tribes had inflicted the chaos on their own, and that the *conquistadores* had served merely as catalysts to the whole process.

As regards the charge that they had celebrated the destruction of one civilisation as somehow the fulfilment of their own, the Spaniards and their proponents had had few doubts. William Prescott typified the Eurocentric perspective when he wrote of Cortés, 'If he desolated the land and broke up its existing institutions, he . . . [introduced] there a more improved culture and a higher civilisation.'[26] The ruin of indigenous Mexico was euphemised as a kind of foundation dig, upon which the Spanish leader was shown building 'a more magnificent capital', and 'employing his efforts to detect the latent resources of the country and to stimulate it to its highest power of production'.[27] But just exactly how much of that production was intended for the benefit of Mexico and the Mexica themselves? This was not a question that Prescott had troubled to ask.

6

Gold – The Castration of the Sun

In the months and years after Tenochtitlan's fall, both victors and vanquished experienced a blending of cultures which, for the indigenes especially, was nothing short of a revolution. The introduction of Old World metallurgical techniques, of the wheel and a written script helped transform American lives beyond recognition. Equally important was the exchange of biological riches, by which the Mexica acquired a range of European staples. Crops like wheat, barley, sugar cane, vines and other fruits – apples, oranges, lemons – as well as the full complement of European domesticated animals – cattle, horses, donkeys, sheep, pigs, goats, chickens – arrived for the first time in the New World. Simultaneously a number of household items of pre-Columbian America, including maize, tomatoes, haricot beans, turkeys and even tobacco, all travelled back across the Atlantic to become popular and economically important in Europe.

If this mutually beneficial trade in resources was a critical by-product of the Euro-American collision, it had played little or no part in initiating the encounter. The search for material resources had been a primary motivating force for Spaniards in America, but this drive had been focused on a single commodity – gold.

Gold ran in a continuous seam through the events of the conquest. The early discovery of fabulous Mexican ornaments had been one of the inspirations for the march on Tenochtitlan. Gold had then helped define the character of the Spaniards' most important military defeat, their burden of treasure being a chief reason for such massive loss of life during *la Noche Triste*. Equally, once they had re-entered the capital as victors, a principal concern of the Spaniards was the recovery of their vanished eight tonnes of gold.

The theme of gold and its pursuit by the Spaniards remains a key element in the history of their American conquests for decades, even centuries. Rich in extraordinary tales of adventure and extremes of behaviour, it is a theme that repays further examination. For it also reveals patterns of exploitation and attitudes towards colonised peoples that are not just specific to this one nation and its particular period of expansion. In many ways the Spanish quest for gold is representative of Europe's wider imperial enterprise, taking us to the very heart of the relationship with tribal society.

In an age of computerised credit facilities and instant currency transfer, it is hard to recapture fully the extraordinary power of gold. For the developing cash economies of Renaissance Europe no other currency represented such immediate and incontestable wealth, none retained such stability, none had the same near-universal appeal as a trade commodity. The historians Frank Spooner and Fernand Braudel estimated the total quantity of gold in Europe before 1492 at 5,000 tonnes.[1] However, it was gold that had unlocked for European consumption the luxury products of the orient, such as silk, spice and ceramics, and the insistence of Eastern merchants on payment in gold had seriously depleted European coffers. This in turn fuelled the search for alternative supplies and provided a powerful incentive for maritime exploration. West Africa, the most important medieval source of European gold, became the focus for Portuguese adventurers operating along its Atlantic coastline, where in the twenty years before the fall of Mexico they had taken an annual haul of about 700 kilos.[2]

By the time the Spaniards sailed for America, gold had assumed a status which was more than simply economic. Its magical and untarnishing colour gave it deep associations with the source of all life, the sun, and it was believed to be most abundant precisely where sunshine was greatest – on the equator. The medical connotations of the word 'sovereign' also express something of the life-giving properties widely believed to be attached to it. Gold was, in short, the *summum bonum* of Europe's material civilisation, and it was typical that Cortés, when attempting to give expression to the achievement of indigenous American culture, singled out neither the scale of Mexican architecture, nor their outstanding capacity for urban planning, nor their universal education system. 'What could there be more astonishing,' he wrote to Charles V, 'than that a barbarous monarch such as he should

87

have reproductions made in gold, silver, precious stones, and feathers of all things to be found in his land, and so perfectly reproduced that there is no goldsmith or silversmith in the world who could better them.'[3]

The Spanish hopes of booty in Mexico were extraordinarily high. A sign of their expectation was given on arrival at the Totonac town of Cempoallan, where a Spanish vanguard mistook the brilliant stucco work on some buildings for a complete covering of silver plate.[4] 'To our mind it is probable,' Cortés wrote as he advanced on the capital, 'that this land contains as many riches as that from which Solomon is said to have obtained the gold for the temple.'[5] In stark contrast, however, to this burning desire for Mexican gold, was the indigenes' deep revulsion at the European obsession. The *Florentine Codex* describes the Spaniards seizing upon the gold 'as if they were monkeys': 'It was as if their hearts were satisfied, brightened, calmed. For in truth they thirsted mightily for gold; they stuffed themselves with it; they starved for it; they lusted for it like pigs.'[6]

The final post-conquest division of treasure and the whirlwind of rumour rising up in its aftermath, which swept through the Caribbean and on across the Atlantic, illustrates the almost constant gap between Spanish ambition and the realities of the American gold hunt. There was little doubt that the Spanish treasure represented a fantastic haul, far in excess of anything previously found in the New World, and estimated at somewhere between 185,000 and 200,000 pesos.

The share of the treasure kept by Cortés himself has remained a matter of controversy. As expedition commander he was entitled to extract 29,600 pesos of gold from the final official total. David Stannard has estimated his total profit in the region of $10 million at current values.[7] However, it was widely alleged by the ordinary soldiers that he had secretly salted away far more. Bernal Diaz recalled a disgruntled colleague complaining that they should call themselves 'not the conquerors of New Spain but the victims of Hernando Cortés'.[8]

In view of the fact that a single gift which he sent to Charles V – a solid silver cannon weighing over 1,200 kilos – apparently cost him 27,500 gold pesos and was almost equal to the value of his entire official share, this seemed a reasonable contention.[9] It was certainly the case that the *Caudillo*'s personal booty was spectacularly greater than the 80 pesos apiece dished out to the horsemen, or the 50 or 60 pesos offered to the ordinary foot soldiers. Small wonder that many of his men refused the payment and accused their leader of cheating.

Notwithstanding these allegations and the widespread discontent amongst those actually present in Tenochtitlan, the news of its conquest, inflated in a firestorm of hearsay, detonated America's prototype goldrush. Perhaps more than anything else it was the example of Cortés himself and his extraordinary social elevation that spoke most eloquently of gold's almost miraculous transformative power. Mexican treasure had made him one the richest men in the world, and others flocked to emulate his success in the Americas.

Even those who had benefited most from the Mexican conquest, like Cortés and Pedro de Alvarado, themselves could not resist the lure of further campaigning. Once the war had ended, there seemed to develop in these becalmed soldiers of fortune an irresistible momentum towards greater power and more wealth. Thus, one finds that both embarked on new missions, Cortés disastrously into modern-day Honduras, Alvarado as the brutal conqueror of one of the most tragic and oppressed countries in modern-day Central America, Guatemala.

Even after he had been rewarded with the governorship of this newly-won province, Alvarado did not give up hope of one final, great success. In 1534, with an expedition larger than that assembled by Cortés for Mexico, he set out in pursuit of the treasures of the northern Incan empire, newly discovered and now disintegrating under the Spanish onslaught. However, Alvarado's army chose the wrong route through modern-day Ecuador. Their armour rusted in the steaming rainforest. On some of the Andes' highest passes many of the indigenous porters froze to death. Other locals were fed to the dogs or tortured to reveal the route. When they finally emerged on the high Andean plains almost all the enslaved porters were dead. The Spaniards, meanwhile, found themselves thwarted by a rival Spanish force and Alvarado was bought off for 100,000 pesos.

His final throw of the dice came six years later. The mythical seven cities of Cibola, each spectacularly constructed from solid gold, were widely believed to lie in north-western Mexico. Alvarado's expedition set out in 1541, stopping en route to suppress a local rebellion. During a cavalry charge the leader's horse fell on top of him. He died eleven days later from his wounds. He was about forty-six.

While Alvarado had failed in his quest for the ultimate treasure trove, others would be more successful. In 1524, while Cortés was busying himself with the expedition into Honduras, a triumvirate of ageing gold-hunters in the port of Panama City were cementing a devil's pact to explore southwards along the Pacific coastlines of modern-day Colombia and Ecuador. One of these men was Francisco Pizarro. It was long a part of his rags-to-riches legend that as an infant he had been suckled by pigs. In fact Pizarro, like Cortés, was the son of minor nobility. In the New World he had risen steadily if unspectacularly to become a prominent citizen of Panama City. He was both illiterate and illegitimate, and in 1524 he was already approaching fifty. His principal partner, Diego de Almagro, was even older. Neither had much time to spare.

In the initial stages their plans hardly seemed to prosper. It was four years and three arduous voyages of exploration before they brought back conclusive proof of a highly advanced civilisation based in the Andean mountains beyond a coastal fringe of sterile desert and dripping forests. The project then demanded that Pizarro return to Spain to secure the financial backing and recruits for an expedition, as well as the royal licence which would sanction it. Finally, in January 1531, seven years after that first agreement in Panama City, Pizarro and a small army of only 180 men set sail for their destination. The delay, however, would soon be justified. For what he and his compatriots had stumbled into during their earlier voyages was the largest political structure ever established by indigenous Americans – the empire of the Incas. Eighteen months later its conquest would make Pizarro wealthier even than Hernan Cortés.

In the space of only 300 years, spanning the reigns of eight semi-mythical and three historical rulers, the Inca had expanded from a tribal base in the region of their capital city of Cuzco to command a territory covering almost a million square kilometres. At the time of Pizarro's invasion it stretched for 5,000 kilometres, from its southern border in central Chile to a northern frontier in modern-day Colombia. As John Hemming noted, this was greater than the distance from the east to the west coasts of the USA, or from Europe's Atlantic shoreline to the Caspian.[10]

Like the Mesoamericans, the Inca had erected an imperial structure without the benefit of many fundamental constituents of European civilisation. They had no written language, not even the pictographs and ideograms of the Mexica. Their architecture was without the arch. Domesticated animals were few. Guinea pigs formed an important source of protein. Llamas and alpacas, derived from a wild Andean camelid, the guanaco, were another source of meat, but more especially of exceptionally fine wool. They were also beasts of burden ideally suited to the high-altitude conditions. Yet the Inca had no wheeled vehicles. They also lacked any form of currency, an advanced trade system and the highly developed tradition of markets which was such a dazzling feature of pre-Cortesian Mexico.

However, the Inca more than compensated for any technical shortcomings by the brilliance of their organisational abilities. The smooth administration of their Andean empire was conducted by a large bureaucracy – calculated at 1,331 officials for every 10,000 head of the population. Arranged in a pyramid, this hierarchy culminated in the sacred person of the Inca himself, and oversaw almost every detail of Andean life, which was based, unlike the urban orientation of Mesoamerican society, on the rural village. For the Inca, farming was the most esteemed profession, the source of all the agricultural surpluses that made the entire imperial project possible. It has been estimated that more types of food and medicinal plant were cultivated by the Inca than in any other comparably sized area of the world.[11] Maize, with a yield almost twice that of wheat, was the principal crop of the coastal plains and the lower valleys. In the high Andean paramo, up to altitudes of almost 5,000 metres, the other Incan staple was the potato, of which there were an incredible 240 varieties.

In order to overcome the steepness of the Andean slopes, the people cooperated in the construction of terracing and irrigation projects of breathtaking complexity. It is a measure of their engineering skills that, following the firestorm of Spanish destruction, the region never recovered pre-Hispanic levels of agricultural production, not even today. The empire's communication network involved possibly 40,000 kilometres of roads. The main route ran for 5,000 kilometres north–south through the Andes and was longer than the Roman road between Jerusalem and the empire's northern frontier on England's Hadrian's Wall. At set intervals along this highway were east–west link roads joining up with a 4,200-kilometre coastal route that ran in parallel. A regular system of resthouses supported a relay postal service that could transmit imperial messages at a daily rate of 230 kilometres. 'Can anything comparable be said of . . . any of the mighty kings who ruled the world,' wrote one sixteenth-century Spaniard, 'that they built such a road, or provided the supplies to be found on this one!'[12]

Certainly Europe would have nothing equivalent for three centuries. As Paul Valéry noted, 'Napoleon moved no faster than Julius Caesar.'[13]

There is no more enduring testimony to the Incan achievement than the immense structures which constituted the empire's principal military, civic and religious buildings. The capital, Cuzco, built on a gridiron system with four districts representative of the four quarters of the empire itself, still holds the most impressive palaces and forts. In Incan architecture it was not the intricacy of design, but the sheer massive bulk and the technical precision of their construction that overwhelmed both the historical and modern spectator. According to Victor von Hagen, it 'has never been duplicated anywhere in the world'. He pointed out that at the fort of Sacsahuamán, overlooking the city, there is a single stone in the wall whose weight is calculated at 200 tonnes.

Somehow the Inca engineers, with only stone hammers and axes, bronze chisels, sand abrasives and wooden crowbars and rollers, managed to quarry these monsters, shape them, transport them distances ranging from nine to twenty miles, and finally place them exactly in position, lifting and setting them down a hundred times until they fitted perfectly on all their sides. No mortar is used, yet there is not a crack for the thinnest blade to be inserted.[14]

Pedro de Cieza de Léon, one of the more enlightened sixteenth-century Spaniards to see the Incan capital, felt that 'those who founded it must have been people of great worth'.[15] Yet this was hardly the official Spanish line once their conquest had been completed. Early European chroniclers were keen to stress that the Inca were recent and tyrannical usurpers, imposing themselves by ruthless violence on the other Andean peoples. Another element in the European self-justification was the inevitable litany of alleged American practices – human sacrifice, cannibalism, sodomy, royal polygamy, 'the abominable use of beasts', and other 'wicked and accursed customs' – all of which, officially, ended after Spanish rule had been established.[16]

In the twentieth century, proponents of Spanish conquest have articulated criticism of the Incan empire in terms of contemporary political conditions. Hammond Innes, for instance, perceives, in the absence of an Andean market economy, the collectivist methods of the population and the rigidly hierarchical central bureaucracy, an indigenous American version of the Soviet state. The Inca empire was the original repressive regime, its administrators prototype *apparatchiks*, its emperor the Josef Stalin of pre-Columbian America. The Spaniards, by implication, were the champions of individual liberty and the free world.

Other commentators, however, favourably disposed towards the Incan system of government, have tended to emphasise the more benign aspects of its civil project. They have pointed out that while Andean farmers were obliged to work on state lands or state engineering projects and yielded the surpluses to support the large numbers of administrators, in return the government addressed many of the needs of the populace, ensuring an equitable distribution of land, administering stores of surplus produce for public consumption and providing a welfare system to support the poor and elderly. Pedro de Cieza de Léon was unstinting in his praise of the Incan administrative methods. 'One of the things most to be envied these rulers,' he wrote,

> is how well they knew to conquer such vast lands and, with their foresight, bring them to the flourishing state in which the Spaniards found them when they discovered this new kingdom . . . In a word, the Incas did not make their conquests any way just for the sake of being served and collecting tribute. In this respect they were ahead of us, for with the order they introduced the people throve and multiplied, and arid regions were made fertile and bountiful.[17]

According to the American historian of Andean civilisation Philip Means, 'The Empire ruled by this most rational of systems was one whose people were as fortunate, in a material way, as any who have ever lived. It is safe to say that a high proportion of the architectural and technological constructions built in the Incaic period . . . was dedicated to the direct or indirect benefit of the people rather than to the selfish vanity of the rulers.'[18] Means, while praising the 'matchlessly logical administrative hierarchy', was also able to identify with hindsight its one key strategic weakness. In the great mountain empire of South America there was, to a degree greater even than in Mexico, a focus of absolute power in the central figure of the Inca himself, who was identified with the sun god, Viracocha. 'Thus, to capture the person of the ruler was . . . to capture all the authority of the empire.'[19]

★

At the time of Pizarro's fateful landfall on the edge of the Inca empire in May 1532, such thoughts were hardly uppermost in the minds of its 9,000,000 inhabitants. By then they had been consumed and exhausted by almost a decade of national tragedies. Even before the ageing Spanish adventurer had made his first tentative moves, the smallpox epidemic that had previously devastated the Mexica had travelled overland via the Maya kingdoms of Central America, along the isthmus of Panama, into continental South America and finally over the Andes. In about 1523 this initially Spanish-borne pathogen constituted the Incas' first European encounter. Silent and unseen, its impact was no less catastrophic than the later human onslaught. Although the epidemic is poorly documented, some historians have suggested it precipitated a fifty per cent decline in the Andean population.[20] What remains beyond dispute is that the emperor Huayna Capac and his principal heir were both early victims.

The consequences of these premature deaths were almost as serious as the epidemic itself, causing a bitter dynastic dispute between the emperor's two surviving senior sons, Atahualpa and Huascar. By the time of Pizarro's appearance in 1532, the younger of the half-brothers, Atahualpa, had finally emerged triumphant from the civil war. However, the empire was exhausted in its aftermath, while the violent rivalry which had driven the conflict was still close to the surface. Like the conqueror of New Spain before him, Pizarro could not have shown better timing. And the ageing *conquistador* was soon to cap Cortés' luck with Cortés' methods.

Forging inland, the Spaniards encountered the newly victorious Atahualpa and his entourage in November 1532, taking the waters at the hot springs of Cajamarca. Although the emperor was surrounded by as many as 80,000 men, Pizarro, whose physical courage 'was his one outstanding virtue', then planned an operation which, for reckless daring, outstripped even that of Pedro de Alvarado. Philip Means describes it as an act of 'sublime audacity'.[21] It was agreed during their initial negotiations that Atahualpa would descend from his camp to visit the Europeans, whom he had billeted in Cajamarca itself. The Spaniards waited until the emperor had taken his place in a three-sided courtyard, surrounded by a large number of unarmed royal attendants. A Spanish priest came forward to engage him in a discussion on religion to distract his attention. Then at a given signal, invoking the names of their holy saints, firing their cannon, the Spaniards launched themselves at the Incan delegation.

The unprovoked assault on American towns and villages was by 1532 a well-established tactic of the Spanish troops. So too was the sudden massacre of American forces and their leaders, lured in under the pretext of negotiations. However, on 15 November 1532 in the plaza of Cajamarca, the Spaniards' gift for treachery and for wholesale slaughter was to achieve its apotheosis. Faced with this unexpected attack, many unarmed Inca attendants rushed towards Atahualpa's litter in order to protect their emperor, only to be cut down or trampled underfoot. Others, refusing to abandon him, had their hands and arms lopped off as they held him aloft. In an act of sublime futility they then struggled to support the royal person with their bleeding stumps. In only an hour and a half, a crowd of between five and ten thousand was almost completely annihilated. Perhaps only two hundred escaped the carnage. One eyewitness noted that 'During all this no Indian raised a weapon against a Spaniard.'[22] It is without question one of the most notorious incidents in the history of Spanish imperialism.

And world-famous slaughter was soon to achieve its world-famous reward. The captured Atahualpa, recognising the Spaniards' greed for precious metals, offered to buy his freedom with a spectacular ransom of gold. Over a period of seven months gold and silver were collected throughout the empire and brought to the Spanish camp. A room more than six and a half metres long and five metres wide was filled with gold to a line beyond the reach of the tallest European. Two further rooms were stacked with silver. Many of the art treasures of an entire civilisation were then consigned to the smelting furnaces and reduced to standard ingots – an act of cultural destruction commensurate with the earlier crime of human massacre. The total haul included more than six tonnes of 22.5 carat gold and almost twelve tonnes of silver. Pizarro's personal share was 285 kilos of gold and more than half a tonne of silver. The emperor's conversion to Christianity spared him being burnt at the stake. When he had laid his hands on the ransom, Pizarro had Atahualpa garrotted. Charles Lummis, a popular American writer in the nineteenth century, described the Spanish general as 'one of the greatest of self-made men'.[23]

The death of Atahualpa unleashed once more the powerful centrifugal forces which had only just ripped the empire apart. As in Mexico, the Spaniards took full political advantage, harnessing to their cause the factions that had previously supported Atahualpa's rival, Huascar. The invaders also selected an imperial successor, Manco, another younger son of the former emperor, Huayna Capac. While he retained something of the Inca's traditional godlike aura amongst his own subjects, to the Europeans Manco was nothing more than a puppet. On reaching the capital, Cuzco, they raped the women of his royal household and stabled their horses in the imperial temples.

The supporters of Atahualpa mustered what military opposition they could to the invaders, but they were badly organised. The foremost imperial general, the one leader who might have reunited the shattered Inca forces, was lured into Spanish captivity at an early stage, then burnt alive. What elements of resistance remained, fighting as an undisciplined mob and armed with an arsenal hardly more advanced that that of the Mexica, had no answer to European steel or European horses. Although the forces of Pizarro and Almagro were far smaller than those of Cortés they quickly swept aside the indigenous armies attempting to bar their 1,250 kilometre journey to Cuzco. One Spanish captain boasted: 'I took no more notice of a hundred armed Indians than I would have of a handful of flies.'[24]

The Spanish arrival at the capital triggered another frenzied treasure hunt. Much of the gold had already been seized for Atahualpa's ransom, including 700 solid gold plates which had covered the exterior walls of the main sun temple. In the second operation they found only half as much gold as that taken to Cajamarca. However, there were four times the amount of silver, and overall the official division yielded slightly greater quantities of booty. Amongst the finds were some of the most spectacular and varied examples of Incan goldwork: huge altars and fountains, statues, religious images, life-sized modes of llamas, of former emperors, of women and armed sentries. Amongst the smaller items were cups, salvers, vases, vessels sculptured with birds, insects and lizards, life-sized images of lobsters, a miniature garden including clods of earth and cornfields with tiny leaves, stalks and corncobs all fashioned in meticulous detail from precious metals.

When news filtered out of the great Incan treasures seized in Peru, exceeding even the haul made in Mexico almost a generation earlier, it was met with incredulity. In the words of the Spanish governor of Panama, it was 'like something from a dream'.[25] The immediate consequence was a dramatic influx of adventurers from the Caribbean and the other Spanish colonies. This was welcomed at first as a source of reinforcements. However, as in the earlier goldrush triggered by Cortés' victory, the exodus from the other territories left some seriously depopulated. On Puerto Rico the problem was so alarming that one official wrote, 'there will not be a single citizen left unless they are tied down.' In the event, the governor found a more effective method of detaining them. Would-be absentees were whipped and their feet were chopped off.[26]

In Peru itself the violence was far worse, and focused on the indigenous inhabitants. Desperate to share in the incomparable prizes seized by the first wave of Spanish conquerors, the newcomers subordinated all considerations to the discovery of gold. 'The greed of Spaniards of all classes,' wrote one observer, 'is so great as to be insatiable: the more the native chiefs give, the more the Spaniards try to persuade their own captains and governors to kill or torture them to give more.'[27] In the eyes of Pedro de Cieza de Léon, such violent measures were also deeply counter-productive. 'If, when the Spaniards entered, they had behaved differently,' he argued, 'and had not so quickly displayed their cruelty by putting Atahualpa to death, I do not know how many ships would have been needed to carry to Spain the vast treasures lost in the bowels of the earth, where they will remain, for those who buried them are now dead.'[28]

It was a judgement that was both deeply prophetic and deeply flawed. Beneath the lands of the former Inca empire there would indeed prove to be silver deposits of incomparable size and value. However, the existence of further, as yet undiscovered, Inca treasure was another matter. The possession of precious metals and gems had been restricted to an extremely narrow band of Andean society: members of the extended imperial families. The whereabouts of most of their hoard had already been uncovered. In fact, in the whole of the Spaniards' American territories the instant cornucopia of gold already mined and worked was rapidly diminishing. By 1534 they had located and asset-stripped the three major American civilisations – the Mexica, the Maya and the Inca. There remained only one more important gold-working culture to locate. And it was on a much smaller scale.

The conquest of the Muisca, the Andean inhabitants from what is now central Colombia, would prove to be merely a dark, glittering coda to the greater Spanish symphony of gold-inspired madness and violence. By the time Francisco Pizarro was entering Cuzco as master of the Andes, other European parties were already on the threshold of its discovery.

From 1530 the Caribbean shorelines of modern-day Colombia and

Venezuela were the starting point for a number of expeditions attempting to penetrate southwards into the South American interior. Most of them were launched from the recently established colony of Coro, on the eastern edge of the Gulf of Venezuela. Although a Spanish possession, the town had been granted as part of a concession to the Welser, the German banking house that had provided important financial support to Spain's Hapsburg monarchy. These Coro-based forces were therefore German-led, and the troops, while predominantly Spanish, were often multinational in character. Whatever their background, all the Europeans were united by massive resilience and common ambitions. 'We all believe,' wrote one participant, 'in good fortune and great wealth . . . for we already know very well here that the land in the interior is full of gold.'[29] While few would prove the conviction to have been well-founded, many would die trying.

Each of the expeditions was enormously costly in terms of European lives. Disease and extreme hardship were constant dangers. So too, given European methods, was the threat of attack by local inhabitants. Despite their neolithic arms technology, some of the tribes made formidable use of poisoned arrows. Struck by these missiles, the only American weapon the *conquistadores* truly feared, they would cut chunks from their own flesh or attempt to cauterise the wound with red-hot brands before they collapsed into agonising convulsions and delirium. 'In the end,' wrote one eyewitness, 'they die in such a desperate state that the living are often prompted to kill them themselves rather than await such a death.'[30]

Of two parties leaving Coro between 1530 and 1533 led by a young German merchant, Ambrosius Dalfinger, the first lost 100 men in eight months, the second lost almost all of its 170 Europeans, including Dalfinger himself. The fourth Coro-based expedition, setting out in 1535, lost 240 of an original force of 400. However, the expedition incurring the greatest number of casualties was led by a Spanish lawyer, Gonzalo Jiménez de Quesada. It was both the largest and the first party actually to reach Muisca territory and seize the instant bonanza of gold. At the start of this mission in April 1536, 800 men left Santa Marta, a Spanish colony to the west of Coro. A year later barely 200 survived.

If European losses were great, the destruction inflicted on the indigenous Americans through whose lands the *conquistadores* moved was incomparably greater. Large expeditions, often lasting several years, required massive quantities of food and supplies, as well as the labour to transport them. If these were not forthcoming from compliant hosts, the Spaniards simply took them by force. A common tactic was to exploit local tribal conflict to curry favour with one community and then use them as allies to despoil another. This often produced a double harvest of voluntary and captured resources.

The enslaved porters were then subjected to grotesque cruelties. Shackled together and fed on a minimum diet, they were expected to carry heavy loads, often until they dropped. The lame and the sick were then often beheaded to avoid the irksome delay involved in unlocking their chains. Pedro de Alvarado, as in most affairs of the *conquistadores*, set the example. His expedition into Guatemala wasted the lives of thousands of the Mexica from his newly acquired estates in New Spain. In the Andes he employed the same brutal methods. And where he led others followed. Dalfinger, for instance, on one freezing high-altitude pass, allowed 120 Indian porters to die of exposure in a single night.[31] It was hardly surprising, as one chronicler noted, that the people 'preferred to die than be subjected or dominated by [the Spaniards], because they received excessive, intolerable abuse to themselves and their children, wives and property.'[32]

However, those who did fight the Europeans had little answer to the depredations in terms of either tactics or weapons. The fate of one tribe, the Guaicari of Venezuela, will serve to illustrate the wider military consequences of European/American conflict. Confronting one of the Coro-based expeditions led by another young German officer, Nicolaus Federmann, the Guaicari allowed themselves to be lured into negotiation. While Federmann engaged them in peace talks, he ordered his mounted troops to surround the 800 warriors. After an initial cavalry charge, the foot soldiers followed up and 'slaughtered [them] like pigs', while the horses ran down those who attempted to escape. Some of the Guaicari then hid amongst the tall grass or beneath the corpses of their fellows, 'but these were found and many of them beheaded'.[33] Federmann, described by his contemporaries as 'a man of exceptional intelligence', claimed 500 Guaicari were killed. His methods demonstrated that there was nothing peculiarly Spanish about the tactic of ruthless deception and wanton slaughter.

Federmann eventually led three expeditions out of Coro between 1530 and 1536, more than any other of the key protagonists in the quest for the Muisca treasure. In his case, however, persistence was unrewarded. By the time he located the Muisca territory, Federmann found that Jiménez de Quesada, with the rump of his original 800, had got there before him. The Muisca lands, although only a fraction the size of the Inca empire, were intensively cultivated with cotton, maize, potatoes and other crops. As many as a million people lived in substantial wooden structures with conical thatch roofs grouped together in large towns. They were also vigorous traders, specialising in the manufacture of salt, which they obtained from mines and then exchanged, significantly, for gold. For the Muisca had no gold sources of their own, although they did mine emeralds – the only supply in the Americas – and traded as far away as Tenochtitlan.

Instant booty was the prime concern of Quesada's forces and led to the familiar trail of bleak and monotonous destruction. For once, however, it was not a European campaign distinguished by high competence, or the customary cynical flair for manipulation. Lacking adequate interpreters, they failed to discover or exploit the major rivalries between the three principal rulers of the Muisca. When the most important of these, the Zipa of Bogotá, initially eluded capture, the Spaniards pushed on to the territories of one of his rivals. There they found a magnificent temple full of gold. In their eagerness to loot it, the *conquistadores* set it on fire by mistake and burnt it to the ground. When they finally returned to capture the Zipa of Bogotá, they killed the man in a night attack on his camp, thus silencing their key informant on the whereabouts of gold. Despite such blunders, they were consoled by the final division of spoils. In June 1538 the meltdown of Muisca treasure yielded about 750 kilos of gold – most of it of high quality – and more than 1,800 emeralds.

In 1538, with the destruction of the Muisca, the Spanish quest for the golden treasures of the New World should have drawn to its tragic and violent close. In less than twenty years they had found and overwhelmed all the higher cultures on the two continents. The flame of human inventiveness that had shone for almost 5,000 years among indigenous Americans, had been doused by the Spaniards in a single generation. Yet the passing of these brilliant societies was not accompanied by any parallel loss of appetite on the part of the colonists. On the contrary, the *conquistadores'* urge for gold had developed its own independent momentum, an almost maniacal desire feeding solely upon itself. The final destruction of American civilisation simply heralded the beginning of a new, frenzied phase of European searching which would drag on beyond the end of century and consume the lives of tens, if not hundreds, of thousands. Its central and non-existent focus was the legend of El Dorado.

El Dorado holds resonances deeper even than the genuine riches of Mexico or Peru, certainly more than the little-known treasures of the Muisca, and rather than any of these historical localities it has remained the classic metaphor for the possibility of instant and fabulous wealth. Yet the precise constituents of the legend have long been a matter for conjecture.

One enduring theory is that it derived from a Muisca investiture ceremony for the Zipa of Bogotá. At the side of a lake called Guatavita, which had been formed in the mountains by a falling meteor, the Muisca gathered to anoint the body of their future ruler with a mixture of gold-dust and gum. When this golden man, or El Dorado, performed his ritual ablutions in the lake the glorious coating was washed away, accompanied by further offerings of precious stones and metals. The Spaniards of New Granada, their title for the Muisca lands, heard about the ceremonies and made Guatavita a focus for further brutal gold hunts. Later still, futile attempts were made to drain the steep-sided lake to reach the sunken treasures.

More typically, however, El Dorado was a place rather than an individual. The British historian John Hemming, following the Venezuelan writer Demetrio Ramos Pérez, has argued that the myth's origins were in Quito in late 1540, and that they had nothing to do with a gold-encrusted Zipa on Lake Guatavita.[34] For the earliest seekers of El Dorado it referred to a province somewhere to the north-east of Quito and beyond the Andean highlands. Yet, almost with each failed attempt to find it, El Dorado withdrew eastwards in direct proportion to the advance of Spanish geographical knowledge.

The destinations of the various expeditions included the lowland rainforests of Ecuador and Peru, the flooded grasslands of eastern Colombia, then the headwaters of the Orinoco in Venezuela. By the end of the sixteenth century it had little to do with the Andean highlands around Bogotá. Typically, the avatar of El Dorado recorded in *The Shorter Oxford English Dictionary* is on the other side of the continent: 'A fictitious country (or city) abounding in gold, believed by the Spaniards to exist upon the Amazon within the province of Guiana.'

Any attempt to adjudicate between these rival versions, which sent Europeans across millions of square kilometres of South America, and to establish a single contender as the one genuine article, is really to miss the point. The key constituent of El Dorado is the lack of any fixed coordinate. That the details are so enormously elastic is the clearest indication that a belief in its existence was rooted, not so much in any empirical evidence, but in a burning need that it *should* exist. The Spaniards' genuine treasure seizures were the obvious ground out of which such a fantasy emerged. But rather than allowing these real hauls to serve as an anchor against further inflated speculation, the *conquistadores* tended to make the last discovery the basis for ever larger invention. No matter what fellow-Europeans had already achieved in the Americas, the new generation would soon outstrip it.

Heading off up the Orinoco, one persistent hopeful declared in 1534: 'I think that in a short time I will do for your Majesty more service than any man has done in these parts.'[35] It was a boast that no amount of time seemed able to diminish. The British adventurer Walter Raleigh, almost sixty years after the destruction of the Muisca, claimed of his particular El Dorado objective:

> Guiana is a country that hath yet her maidenhood. The face of the earth hath not been torn, the graves have not yet been opened for gold. It hath never been entered by any army of strength and never conquered by a Christian prince. Men shall find here more gold than either Cortés found in Mexico or Pizarro in Peru, and the shining glory of this conquest will eclipse all those of the Spanish nation.[36]

The inexorable movement towards an ever brighter horizon could only culminate in a realm of pure fantasy – a dream-place never to be discredited because it was beyond the reach of any contradictory reality. El Dorado was that inevitable terminus. What makes it such a powerful metaphor for Europe's unfulfilled desire in the New World is that, no matter the scale of the *conquistadores'* tortured efforts, they were irrevocably doomed to failure. However, El Dorado is more than this, for it was in a sense a recapitulation of all the gold legends and gold stampedes that had motivated Europeans since their arrival in the Americas. It serves as a microcosm for much of the Spanish imperial adventure, and provides major insights into their behaviour and attitudes towards the New World and its inhabitants.

One of the few common ingredients in all the various El Dorados is that it was a location where gold was present in an exquisite super-fluity. One had only to pull up the grass and the gold-dust would fall sparkling from its roots. The notion that this utopia was the ultimate

New World destination, transcending all previous conquests, gave the vision an almost eschatological quality. However, there was something deeply radical about the offer of heaven held out by El Dorado. Its exaltation was on a purely physical plane, rooted in an infinity of material wealth, but the immortality it could confer was that of unparalleled social fame and status.

El Dorado represented in the most heightened form that new and unprecedented opportunity which in some sense beckoned all European colonists to the Americas, the chance for self-recreation and social elevation. As Bartolomé de Las Casas noted, this affected the very lowest class amongst the colonial recruits, who sought, 'with a staff in their hands, to be persecutors of the tame and humble Indians, and to command'.[37] Men like Cortés and Pizarro were the acme and model of that possible transformation: born to the gilded poverty of the Spanish hidalgo, they had been transfigured into great Euro-American princes.

Perhaps the most resonant example of the way in which El Dorado both captivated and expressed a new age is the obsession displayed by the Elizabethan courtier Walter Raleigh. By virtue of personal gifts and the queen's patronage, Raleigh rose to be the darling of the nation with near-royal status. When he suffered the classic fall from power because of monarchic disapproval, he sought to re-establish himself through 'the shining glory' of Guiana's conquest. Here was the late Renaissance figure, whose meteoric career serves as an emblem for his era, aspiring to the ultimate possibility of social ascendancy, the treasures of El Dorado.

As Tzvetan Todorov has noted, there was nothing specifically modern about the European desire for gold.

> What is new is the subordination of all other values to this one . . .
> it has become quite clear . . . that everything can be obtained by
> money, that money is not only the universal equivalent of all
> material values, but also the possibility of acquiring all spiritual
> values . . . This homogenization of values by money is a new
> phenomenon and it heralds the modern mentality, egalitarian and
> economic.[38]

This deeply modern dimension to El Dorado makes it a symbol of relevance even to our own age, expressing something about much later European colonisation in America: an enterprise deeply involved with fantasies of wealth, of personal escape and social transformation, where spiritual values have become inextricably fused, if not made subservient, to a vision of material aggrandisement. El Dorado was the prototype American dream.

Like its Protestant equivalent, it was a fantasy in which no genuine American was ever invited to share. El Dorado mirrored the *conquistadores'* ludicrous legal document, the *Requerimiento*, which demanded of New World inhabitants their instant capitulation to Christian supremacy. Both involved a self-referential circle, fictions by Europeans for Europeans, which bypassed and denied the human substance of the people they were addressing. If El Dorado was envisioned by its seekers as a fabulous province shining in the jungle, then it was, in that classic colonial phrase, an 'empty land'. Otherwise it was occupied but somehow unowned, a city ready-built but whose actual builders simply awaited, with heads bowed and hats doffed, the European arrival and possession. What was implicit but never illustrated in any version of the legend was the absolute denial of any prior right of its presumed American creators.

One of the things that is so riveting and appalling about the El Dorado legend is the chasm between the almost heavenly vision it represented to its seekers, and the hellish crimes they perpetrated in its name. For the American peoples who seemed either to offer the promise of El Dorado's discovery or to hinder access, the dream permitting all European desire was a nightmare that unleashed all human depravity. It was, in fact, a monster's charter. The relentless Spanish columns involved in its discovery engaged in a process of breaking down entire American communities, then consuming them in a manner no less destructive or terrifying than if they had physically eaten them. On some occasions, of course, they actually did. But in truth they were far worse than genuine cannibals, because it was behaviour untouched by constraining ritual. Spanish methods were random, profligate, purposefully wasteful. 'If they wanted one pig,' wrote Pedro de Cieza de Léon, 'they killed twenty; if four Indians were wanted, they took a dozen . . . Were one ordered to renumerate [*sic*] the great evils, injuries, robberies, oppression and ill treatment inflicted on the Indios during these operations, there would be no end of it.'[39]

Even to make a start is to recount behaviour that carries one to the very limits of human brutality. This embraces not just the remorseless enslavement and deliberate exhaustion of slave-porters, nor the massacre of opponents, as described earlier, but an infinite elaboration of cruelties: the torching of villages and incineration of whole tribes, the cutting off of women's breasts or the seizure of uncooperative guides who were then cut into quarters, as examples to others, the impaling of victims with a stake through the anus, rammed home till it emerged at the mouth (because, its Spanish advocates pleaded, it was the only form of death the Muisca really feared).[40] There was also a whole catalogue of atrocities involving children – the rape of seven-year-olds, the severance of their hands or noses, their disembowelment for dog-feed, or suckling infants skewered to their mothers with a single thrust.

Amongst the more obvious implications, such unrestrained behaviour reflected the way in which El Dorado and the places believed to lie in its path comprised a landscape of inherent transience for Europeans. Each member of the gold-seeking caravans was the quintessential asset-stripping raider without any longer-term objective. Since he sought no relationship, nor intended any investment in it, the surrounding environment was reduced to a moral vacuum requiring no constraint. Such deep alienation simply completed within each *conquistador* a self-perpetuating syndrome of violence that allowed him to subordinate all consideration to the goal of instant plunder.

Although the methods characterising the search for New World gold seem to represent a desperate nadir beneath which no conduct could possibly sink, they were by no means confined either to the Spaniards or to South America. In the Belgian Congo of central Africa at the end of the nineteenth century, one finds another colonial power exhibiting the same chilling inhumanity and employing the same macabre atrocities to harvest a product that was known, significantly, as 'black gold'. Rubber had assumed a central economic importance in Europe because of its growing commercial application, especially in the nascent automobile industry. With most of the Congo's vast territory under his personal control, the Belgian King Leopold II sought to capitalise on this boom by exploiting the colony's huge potential for rubber production. In the interest of maximum profit, African tribes people were forced into the rainforests, without pay and with threatened violence as their chief incentive, to collect the raw latex from wild trees.

On their return they often suffered punishment from African soldiers on a scale calibrated to the victim's shortfall in the quota. Being beaten with a hippo-hide whip – 'trimmed like a corkscrew, with edges like knife blades and as hard as wood' – was one of the most frequent and lenient of the penalties for such an infraction.[41] Mutilation was another, the hands sometimes being smashed off with a rifle butt. Eventually diligent soldiers would bring in basketfuls of severed hands to their approving European superiors, as proof of their bag and evidence they had not wasted ammunition.[42] The murder and mutilation involved in this system of economic terror eventually depopulated large regions of the colony, and has been described as 'the most blatant system of exploitation the world has seen since the Ancient World.'[43] The commentator was wrong in one detail: we had received glimmers of Leopold's Congo just three centuries earlier in South America.

Although the behaviour unleashed in the Congo and the search for El Dorado appears to be deeply aberrant, nonetheless it is in many ways representative of the wider culture of exploitation from which it so monstrously evolved. Thus one finds throughout much of their New World empire for the first fifty and, in some areas, the first hundred years of Spanish rule, something of the same nihilistic disregard for American humanity that is associated with El Dorado.

After their various conquests, and once any portable wealth had been pillaged and transported, the Spaniards introduced a formal system of colonial administration to the newly conquered territories. Central to the control of resources was the institution, inaugurated by Columbus and adopted thereafter, of the *encomienda*. This was a temporary and non-hereditary grant to individual Spaniards of lordship over a specified number of inhabitants. The *encomendero* had rights to tribute in both money and goods and also to the labour of his allotted community. In return, he was charged with the care of his new wards and with ensuring their Christian instruction. His *encomienda* conferred on him no title to the land itself. Native ownership was to be formally respected.

In practice, however, the system was often indistinguishable from slavery, and Spaniards approached its opportunities with the same mentality that characterised their hunt for treasure.[44] In fact, Bartolomé de Las Casas noted that, in the absence of actual precious metals, 'the gold [the *conquistadores*] came to seek consisted in grants of Indians'.[45] Charles Gibson, author of a classic study of post-conquest Mexico, *The Aztecs Under Spanish Rule*, summed up its early years of operation in that country:

The record of the first *encomienda* generation, in the [Mexican] Valley as elsewhere, is one of generalized abuse and particular atrocities . . . They overtaxed and overworked them. They jailed them, beat them and set their dogs on them. They seized their goods, destroyed their agriculture, and took their women. They used them as beasts of burden. They took tribute from them and sold it back under compulsion at exorbitant prices. Coercion and ill-treatment were the daily practices of their overseers . . . The first *encomenderos*, without known exception, understood Spanish authority as provision for unlimited personal opportunism.[46]

Gibson described in detail the conditions on one *encomienda*, under Gonzalo de Salazar, the factor in the post-conquest administration of Cortés, and a man with whom the *Caudillo* would eventually quarrel bitterly. Salazar's *encomienda* of Tepetlaoztoca, previously under Cortés' personal control, had been accustomed to the captain-general's demands for gold, cloth, food, fuel, servants and labour. However, under its new lord the demands intensified and when Salazar made a visit to Spain, hundreds of Tepetlaoztoca's citizens died carrying the extorted booty to the Mexican port of Vera Cruz. With his eventual return the exploitation increased even further. Salazar seized communal land for his own use and herded his stock on privately owned properties. Traditional Mexican leaders were beaten, or deposed and expelled. He commandeered the inhabitants' assembly building and converted it to a mill using enforced local labour. He then diverted to it the town's water supply. By violent intimidation he silenced their legal requests for drought relief and it was not until the 1550s that the town received water, for half a day per week.[47]

Although the *encomienda* system provided the colonist with easy access to free labour, conventional slavery never completely lost its appeal. Typically, Nuño de Guzman, rather than plough the furrow of long-term extortion like his compatriot Salazar, preferred the benefits of immediate profit, selling outright 10,000 of the 25,000 inhabitants under his control.[48] The standard practice was to burn into the slave's face the initials of their owner. Often these unfortunates changed hands so regularly that their foreheads and cheeks were transformed into a type of parchment bearing an illegible screed of multiple brand marks.[49]

The discovery of immensely rich silver mines in both Mexico and

Peru presented the Spaniards with new challenges in the organisation of native labour. In Peru, the authorities found one answer in a system known as the *mita* – a period of conscripted, waged labour whereby the inhabitants could earn money necessary to pay their obligatory cash tributes. In order to supply workers for Potosi, a silver deposit discovered in 1546 in modern-day southern Bolivia and described as 'one of the most famous mines in the history of the world', workers were drawn from as far as Cuzco, 1,000 kilometres away.[50] For Europeans, Potosi was 'throughout the centuries a synonym of great wealth'.[51] For the *mitayos*, the indigenous conscripts forced to work there, it was a stark and bitterly cold wasteland at an altitude of more than 4,000 metres and bereft even of vegetable life.[52]

The workers' ordeal began even during recruitment in the home village. The local Inca leaders, the *curacas*, the stratum of indigenous society benefiting most from collaboration with the colonial authorities, were charged with assembling the district's quota of men. No doubt they took advantage of the standard colonial policy forcing Andean people to grow their hair long, which then 'served as a convenient rope for dragging them about'.[53] The more fortunate amongst the selected workforce were able to buy their way out of the ordeal with payments to the *curaca*. Those equally unwilling but unable to find the money often simply ran away, abandoning homes and families – a problem that eventually led to Peru's high levels of vagrancy. The unlucky ones, however, had to walk to the mine – often two months there and two months back – carrying as large a food supply as they could, and often with other family members, to avoid Potosi's exorbitant prices and the inevitable consequences of debt.

Once at Potosi, the workers were consigned to four-month stints, while a week's shift eventually became exactly that – 168 hours underground. At the bottom, reached by means of leather ladders that descended for almost 230 metres, the miner toiled amongst a labyrinth of hot, airless narrow tunnels. The only light was the single candle fixed to his thumb on Monday. If it expired before the end of the week, he worked in total darkness. Ventilation was non-existent and the thick black candle smoke made asphyxiation a real danger. So too, given the lack of shaft props, was the collapse of walls and ceilings. The quota was almost six tonnes of ore a week. If it was not met, the miner was fined. The ore was carried up to the surface on his back in 45-kilo baskets. Each load had to be lugged the 230 metres to the surface (more than half the height of Manhattan's Empire State Building)

on ladders that were often worn and frayed and whose steps were half
a metre apart. Accidents were frequent.[54]

Conditions at Potosi were dreadful, but at the Huancavelica mine
they were worse. Huancavelica was Potosi's monstrous twin sister, the
source of the mercury crucial to the amalgamation process that
extracted the pure silver from the ore. Since the dangers of mercury
were so appalling there was no voluntary labour supply for this mine.
The *mita* system, however, ensured a steady flow of victims, who were
expected to produce more than five tonnes of mercury ore a week. As
they broke up the hard dry rocks the miners were enveloped in clouds
of noxious dust which contained four poisons, including sulphide of
mercury and arsenic. Inevitably, many workers contracted mercury
sickness, a slow debilitating illness that left the respiratory tract
ulcerated, the blood and bones infected with mercury, and induced
bouts of trembling, fever and paralysis. Death was often a longed-for
release.[55]

Enforced labour of this kind, widespread throughout the Spanish
colonies, not only killed many of the indigenous labourers, but also
removed the most productive members of society, broke down family
relationships and local communities, and ruptured agricultural cycles,
which in turn exposed Americans to the risks of malnutrition, debt
and wider family misfortune. In the sixteen provinces forced to supply
labour for Potosi, for example, deaths in the mines, combined with
disease and the exodus of unwilling workers, had reduced the population by over three-quarters by the mid-seventeenth century. Yet the
remaining inhabitants were still forced to provide the same quota of
miners.[56]

As in the case of El Dorado one finds a staggering disjunction
between what these mines represented to their owners and what they
represented to most of the Andean peoples who performed all the
hard labour. For the Spaniards it meant nothing less than the possession of El Dorado itself, dwarfing the spoils of any of the military conquests. Between 1 January 1556 and 31 December 1783 the mines
yielded 820,513,893 pesos. In addition were 151,722,647 pesos in tax
for the Spanish crown. The fabulous riches pouring out from that desolate mountainside soon conjured into existence a ramshackle settlement, which eventually became the largest city in the Americas with
14 dance halls and 36 gambling houses. Its prosperous European
citizens lacked none of the world's luxury commodities: silks from
Granada, precious stones from India, perfumes from Arabia, Malayan

spices, Turkish rugs, white porcelain from China, negro slaves from Angola, pearls from Panama.[57]

In the early period of the mines' operation, many Andean peoples also became wealthy. They were usually voluntary workers, operating on a daily or contract basis. By 1603 they represented the vast majority of the 58,800 labourers at Potosi, while the *mitayos* made up less than ten per cent. However, a report in the same year indicated that not a single free worker opted for the back-breaking and dangerous work of lugging the ore to the surface. By contrast, four-fifths of the *mitayos* were put to this task.[58] For these men – in effect, the mine-owners' unwilling slaves – whose lives were often ended in the airless tunnels, or whose health was broken by accident and over-exertion, or whose families were shattered by the remorseless demands of the *mita*, Potosi was, in the words of one Spanish cleric, 'a mouth of Hell' – a place where one community of human beings looked on their fellows as 'animals without masters'.[59]

Once excavated and processed, most of the massive riches from Potosi and the other New World mines were shipped home to Europe in bullion fleets. Yet on arrival in Spain the treasure hardly had the beneficial impact that was expected. The seemingly inexhaustible wealth lured the Hapsburg monarchy into a mire of exorbitantly expensive foreign wars to further their own imperial ambitions and, in continuation of the old Hispanic crusading ethic, to defend the Catholic world against both Muslim enemies and the new Protestant threat. Their total impact was disastrous. Charles V bequeathed a royal debt of 700,000,000 ducats, while his son, Philip II, left a situation in which two-thirds of crown income went on the interest payments alone.[60] Most New World windfalls were instantly re-exported to the monarchy's principal creditors, like the banking houses of Antwerp and Genoa. A report from the Spanish parliament, the Cortes, complained that the country simply 'served as a bridge over which the products of our mines pass to foreign hands, at times even to our worst enemies.'[61]

For the Spanish people in general, the effects were not much more positive. The huge increase in the supply of silver currency helped to force prices upwards – there was a fourfold increase in the sixteenth century – and to make Spain's nascent industries uncompetitive compared with other European rivals. Simultaneously, the monarchy, to meet its spiralling debts, imposed higher and higher taxes upon the population. And since one of the privileges of the aristocracy was exemption from tax, the burden fell most heavily on those least able to pay.

If New World resources failed to benefit the home nation as completely as its citizens had dreamed, for the colonised of America the ruthless methods of their extortion formed part of a downward spiral in fortunes that was nothing short of a cataclysm. The key factor in this was Old World diseases, like smallpox, typhus, measles, influenza, whooping cough and mumps, which swept through the dense, unresistant populations in successive and devastating waves.

Quite how devastating has been a point for protracted controversy. For while the Spaniards and their admirers prefer small pre-Columbian population totals for the Americas, to minimise the negative impact of empire, others, especially those critical of Spanish methods, have opted for much higher figures. However, even the most conservative estimates now suggest totals of twelve and nine million for Mexico and Peru respectively. Moreover, few disagree that by the end of the sixteenth century Mexico's population stood at just over a million, while in Peru by 1620 there were just 600,000.[62] These figures indicate a demographic collapse of over ninety per cent.

Far from seeing colonial abuses as a contributory factor in these huge population losses, many colonial Spaniards could not even accept or regret their part in the tragic, if blameless, spread of the diseases that so afflicted Americans. On the contrary, the epidemics too were invested with moral force. Just as the Christian deity had been harnessed as a supernatural agent in the initial conquest, so the American population slump was an expression of divine retribution.[63] One seventeenth-century author, writing of the post-conquest holocaust, attributed it to Mexican 'vices, drunkenness, earthquakes, illnesses, and recurring epidemics of smallpox and other diseases with which God in His mysterious wisdom has seen fit to reduce their numbers'.[64] And if there had been any 'evil done by a few' colonists, conceded a sixteenth-century Spanish author, it had been done 'with divine permission because of the enormous sins committed by those people.'[65] European violence and greed had thus been co-opted by God as officers of His justice.

While few contest the idea that most American losses were a result of their complete lack of resistance to long-established Old Word pathogens, disease was not the sole culprit. The devastating if vaguely comprehended effects of the epidemics were embraced by colonial

Spaniards as an outcome which confirmed and reinforced their view of indigenous Americans as both morally deficient beings and as abundant and readily expendable resources – literally, as 'animals without masters'. In turn those attitudes resulted in a pattern of colonial action and policies that bore down on Americans in a spiral of destruction. European disease was simply one element in that larger, brutal matrix.

Faced with the initial European conquest, then the violence of European colonial methods, inflicting death on so many relatives, friends, compatriots, even upon their gods and idols, and shattering their way of life and the 'very foundations of their mental universe', many of the colonised peoples of the New World were plunged – in the words of Nathan Wachtel – 'into a world both tragic and absurd'.[66] It is not difficult to understand why, in attempting to articulate the significance of these events, Americans strove for an imagery that expressed a violation and denial of all that they had held sacred. For the Inca, Europe's advent in the New World represented the castration of the sun.

Part II

The British in Tasmania

'The natives had become . . . nothing better than a horde of lazy, filthy, drunken, listless barbarians.'

BRITISH TASMANIA

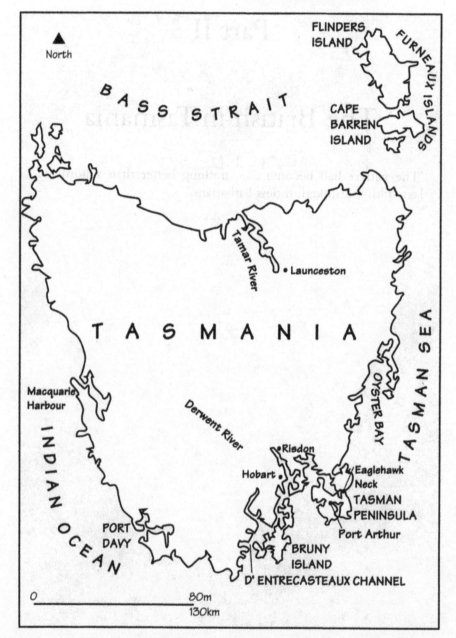

7

The Bones of King Billy

It was not really the stuff from which a classic Victorian deathbed scene could be made. On 3 March 1869 William Lanney died of chronic diarrhoea in the Dog and Partridge, a public house in the town of Hobart, capital of the British colony of Tasmania.[1] Despite the prosaic manner of his passing, the news of this 34-year-old sailor's death was heralded as an event of great local importance. Lanney had been amongst the only surviving, pure-bred representatives of the Aboriginal people of Tasmania: in fact, the last male of the race, and his loss now signified its certain extinction.

Recognising his unique position even as he had walked their streets, the European inhabitants of Hobart had grown accustomed to William's celebrity status. Around the town he was a well-known character, a fashionable attraction at colonial functions, while amongst the ageing all-female remnant of his people, his sense of fun and his round, handsome, full-bearded face made him a great favourite. He was also a popular workmate, well respected by his whaling companions who, like the rest of the Hobart community, had crowned his acknowledged rarity with a royal title. Only the year before his death, William Lanney had been introduced to the son of Queen Victoria, Prince Alfred, Duke of Edinburgh and of Saxe-Coburg-Gotha, as the King of the Tasmanians.

Despite the exaggerated reverence with which they had surrounded the living person, once Lanney was dead the citizens of Hobart were soon to reveal more traditional European attitudes towards Tasmania's indigenous people. As the last male representative, he had long been coveted by British scientists as their final chance for a good Tasmanian skeleton. Lanney's death precipitated a scramble by two august rival organisations – London's Royal College of Surgeons and the Royal Society of Tasmania – for the prize of his physical remains, and it was the former who gained the initial advantage.

With her urgent invitation to tea, the wife of Dr William Crowther managed to lure the house surgeon away from the mortuary in which Lanney's body had been deposited. She had thus provided her husband, who was acting as unofficial agent for the London institute, with a golden opportunity to seize the honours. Crowther and his son gained entry to the locked morgue and were watched through the keyhole by an intimidated gatekeeper as they attended the body. Later it was revealed that Lanney had been decapitated and his skull had been removed, while that of a recently deceased European schoolmaster had been rammed crudely into the skin peeled off Lanney's head. Returning a short while later, the house surgeon, Dr Stokell, realised he had been the victim of a gruesome plot and, seeking to thwart further attempts on the remaining trophies, himself removed the hands and feet for the learned body with which *he* was associated, the Royal Society of Tasmania.

Lanney's funeral service had been planned for the following day, but rumours of mutilation had already begun to circulate in Hobart. Eventually these precipitated a public inspection of the coffin interior, where the body's severed head and missing limbs bore macabre testimony to the performances of the night before. Despite the gasps of horror, however, it was decided that nothing could now be done, and in a final act of British betrayal, a Union Jack was draped over Lanney's coffin as 120 mourners gathered to ponder his tragic end.

Unfortunately, not everyone that day had seen enough of the violated cadaver of poor King Billy. On the evening after the funeral, two rival bodies of learned gentlemen gathered to plan a final assault on the grave. This time the savants of the Royal Society got to the cemetery first, disinterred the coffin and then removed the body to complete a third session of butchery. By the time Crowther and his cronies had realised the grave was empty and had smashed down the morgue door with an axe, there were only a few scraps of flesh left. Amongst the body parts which had been taken to advance biological knowledge were William's nose, his ears and a part of his arm, while Dr Stokell had secured a further piece of skin to press into scientific service – as his personal tobacco pouch.[2] Crowther's defeat was almost total. For although he had bagged the ultimate body part in the skull, he was soon to be undone by the laws of physical decay. When he shipped out his prize to London wrapped in a seal skin, the smell from the whole rotting mess became so appalling it was eventually tossed overboard.[3]

With that act of final rejection, the penultimate episode in Tasmanian extinction draws to its close. Yet this point is both an end and a return to our story's beginning. To consider the factors that had marooned William Lanney in a homeland of white-skinned aliens, we must first travel back all the way across the Atlantic to the lands that we have, as it were, just left. The tragic sequence of events that led to his people's extinction has its earliest recognisable beginnings in Europe's American colonies.

Although, for the first half-century after Columbus' landfall, the Spaniards and Portuguese enjoyed a near monopoly in American conquest, two other European nations with Atlantic seaboards were eager to capture a share in the New World bonanza. Dazzled in particular by the gold and silver pouring across the Atlantic, a whole generation of British privateers had set sail throughout the late sixteenth century for Spain's Caribbean ports and her tempting bullion fleets. On board the departing ships were some of those the British have considered their greatest and most adventurous seamen. To their opponents they were amongst her most infamous buccaneers – men like Francis Drake, John Hawkins, Humphrey Gilbert and Walter Raleigh.

Despite a growing British expertise in Atlantic navigation, and increased familiarity with America's coastal geography, it was not until the seventeenth century that the nation finally secured a permanent toehold on mainland North America. In 1607 a group of settlers established a colony on the shores of Chesapeake Bay in modern-day Virginia. After an uncertain start, the colony quickly flourished, prospering on the cultivation of an American plant now enormously popular in Europe, tobacco. By the 1620s the British planters of Virginia were shipping home an average of 65,000 lbs annually. By the end of the 1630s it had risen to over 1,000,000 lbs.[4] However, New World producers were confronted with an ever-pressing demand for labour to work the expanding acreage, and the colonial farmers, merchants and government authorities sought to address the problem in one of two ways.

Almost half a century before the Virginian settlement had been conjured into existence, John Hawkins had scouted the commercial opportunities in African slaves, capturing an initial 300 in 1562, whom he later sold at enormous profit on Hispaniola. There, the Spanish producers of another intensely labour-dependent crop – sugar – quickly absorbed all the living cargo that the slavers could transport and Hawkins' speculation in human lives blossomed into a full-blown slave trade. But the colonists of the North American mainland were slow to exploit the opportunities initiated by this labour source. By 1660 in Virginia and in the neighbouring colony of Maryland there were still only 1,700 black slaves, compared with almost 50,000 in the British Caribbean by 1670.[5]

Until around that date, the North American planters had mainly found their labour from British sources. In particular, they had been beneficiaries of an Elizabethan law – 'An Acte for Punyshment of Rogues, Vagabonds and sturdy Beggars' passed in 1597 – which stated that persistent offenders and idlers could be banished from the British Isles to a foreign land, unable to return except on pain of death. From this statute evolved a form of commuted sentence, whereby convicted felons were shipped across the Atlantic and made to work for a fixed term – often seven or fourteen years – before earning a right to join colonial society as a free person. Despite this final, theoretical opportunity, the system known as indentured labour was often no more than a form of white slavery. And it was this that had helped build the nascent American state and which, for decades, had filled the gentlemen's pipe-bowls in the coffee-houses and drawing-rooms of England. From 1630 onwards the annual average number of transportees to North America was 1,500 and although this figure declined, a steady flow continued until the eve of the American War of Independence in 1775.[6]

It was this shattering blow to Britain's American empire that brought the transatlantic flow of convicts to an abrupt halt. For the new republic, keen to impress upon the world its moral credentials, declared itself unwilling to be a dumping-ground for George III's social rejects. High-sounding and principled though it may have seemed, the American refusal of white slaves was little more than hypocrisy. For by the time of independence, American capitalists had long recognised that the convicts eventually worked their terms and then troubled the authorities with demands for land of their own. The planters' wishes, on the other hand, were for a labour force even more subservient to their economic objectives, and they had steadily exchanged their temporary white slaves for permanently owned black ones. By 1775 there were already 331,000 Africans in British North America. A further 47,000 were arriving on the continent every year. White labour was now simply an expensive irrelevance.

However, if British felons had become surplus to requirements in America, they were hardly more welcome at home. Shipping convicts out from the mother country had addressed more than simply the labour needs of her colonial offspring. In the developed capitalist ethos of eighteenth-century Britain, one of the most important relationships ordering the pyramidal structure of society was the bond between an individual and his accumulated physical possessions. Since many of the offences for which indentured labour had been convicted were crimes against property, transportation was seen as one of the most effective means of safeguarding public stability. The Atlantic had served British hitherto as its social cloaca, carrying off its most offensive human waste, its criminal classes. But with the sewer now blocked up by an independent America, British prisons were soon at bursting-point with unwanted prisoners.

A temporary expedient had been found in the prison hulks, old Royal Navy transport ships anchored and rotting in many British ports. In 1785 Newgate prison, recently rebuilt and already over-crowded, had disgorged 300 of its inmates to be incarcerated on a hulk in Portsmouth harbour. But even these floating hell-holes were soon full to overflowing. Epidemics were rife and in March 1786 riots on one hulk left eight dead and thirty-six wounded. Political pressure was rapidly pushing the Conservative government of Prime Minister William Pitt towards a drastic solution. And the germ for this was located in the hare-brained proposal of a military engineer to transport convicts to Australia.

Technically, there were few places better calculated to absorb Britain's surplus criminals. Ignoring completely the country's Aboriginal popu-lation, the British cabinet could see only vast areas of open country, ripe for settlement and cultivation. Almost 8,000,000 square kilometres in extent, Australia was twenty-six times the size of Britain and Ireland – an area greater even than all the territories of Europe, Greenland, Iceland and Turkey combined. However, the scheme had one over-whelming problem: Australia's remoteness. The continent was halfway round the planet, 24,500 kilometres away if one took the eastern route via the Cape of Good Hope, or just slightly less if one sailed via Cape Horn. Either way it was at least an eight-month journey.

Running the problem of Australia's inaccessibility a close second was the scale of geographical ignorance amongst the scheme's sponsors. Although Portuguese explorers may have visited it as early as 1523, amongst Europeans it was the Dutch who had first definitely found the southern continent at the turn of the seventeenth century. By the 1660s their navigators had extensively mapped its northern and western coastlines. In fact, even as Pitt and his ministers contemplated their new penal colony, they still referred to the place as New Holland. But in 1786 only two British ships had ever anchored off Australian shores, both under the captaincy of James Cook.

Towards the end of his first Pacific expedition and on his way back from New Zealand, Cook had stopped briefly on the as yet unmapped and – to Europeans – totally unknown south-eastern coastline. With a team of naturalists and artists he had gone ashore at a natural inlet, bounded by wooded hills and teeming with exotically coloured birds and marine life. In honour of the numerous plant specimens his men had collected on that April morning of 1770, Cook named the promising-looking spot Botany Bay. Little more than a week later he noted a natural harbour further to the north, which he called Port Jackson, but this time the explorer declined to investigate further, having already set his course for home.

It was on the basis of this fleeting visit sixteen years earlier that Pitt's cabinet now took its decision about the future of British penal policy. Just how large a leap into the antipodean darkness their plans involved was revealed almost before the first fleet got under way from British waters. Typhus was reported on one of the stinking, overcrowded ships and all the loaded convicts had to be disembarked. Eventually the outbreak was contained, but not before sixteen men and a woman had died. By 13 May 1787 all was finally deemed to be ready once more. The 8 ships setting sail from Portsmouth carried two years' supplies for a crew of over 400 men, 211 marines, 50 women and children of the officers' families, the future governor of the colony and his 9 staff, with an additional cargo of 750 convicts.

It was not just the threat of instant death for any attempted escape that kept this first consignment of Britain's criminal population, in the words of one officer, 'humble, submissive and regular'.[7] Amongst these hundreds of felons there was not one person convicted of either rape or murder, although violence had featured in some of their charges. More typically, however, the offences deemed so dangerous to the realm as to warrant their authors' exile, were crimes against property. One woman, for instance, had been caught taking twelve pounds of Gloucester cheese. Another transported thief had got seven years for pinching chickens – 639 days for each of the four pennies at which the birds were valued. An unemployed Norfolk woman, Elizabeth Powley, could perhaps count herself more fortunate. She had been apprehended lifting several shillings' worth of groceries. Lying in her allotted space of under two square metres for most of the 252-day passage, Elizabeth Powley must surely have reflected that the 'down under' she was soon to experience was preferable to the one on offer in England: for her, transportation to Australia had been an alternative to the gallows.[8]

Once they had arrived at Botany Bay on 20 January 1788, this miscellany of felons was intended to bring into existence a microcosm of the parent society. Unfortunately, conditions were not quite as Cook had depicted them or as the British cabinet had imagined. The soils were poor for cultivation, the hardwood trees blunted their axes, there was little stone for construction and their tents kept out neither the oppressive heat nor the torrential rains. The governor, Captain Arthur Phillip, quickly recognised that Botany Bay was a poor location for the future colony and moved everything, lock, stock and barrel, up the coast to Cook's natural harbour at Port Jackson. Renaming the spot Sydney Cove, Phillip could hardly have realised that when his men assembled a few canvas and wooden shacks over the next few days they had selected the site for the largest city on the continent.

By rights Britain's first Australian colony should have ended in initial disappointment, and had its governor been a cleverer or more ambitiously gifted man, it might easily have done so. But Phillip, in the words of one historian 'a middle-aged nonentity', who only a few months earlier had been retired on half pay, seeing out his days as a modest gentleman farmer, was blessed with the patience and thoroughness to steer the settlement through the initial years of hardship.[9]

His problems were varied and intractable. His men, for instance, could find few local products to supplement their salted beef and hard tack rations. Nor could Phillip call on many of the talents of his charges to help build the new society. Although the waters of Sydney Cove were teeming with fish, amongst the 700 or so convicts there was but a single fisherman. While the governor's needs were for simple tradesmen, builders, carpenters, farmers and blacksmiths, he had to make do with the intricate repertoire of the pickpocket, the forger or the cattle rustler. As the months wore on, food became the all-consuming priority. By September 1789, while his superiors in London fretted over the French Revolution and the latest convulsion in Paris, Phillip's thoughts were on butter. He had just run out. Within a few weeks everybody in the colony was on two-thirds rations of all foods.[10]

The governor's final response to the threat of starvation was to ship out 300 of his convicts with half the marines to Norfolk Island, a pin-prick in the South Pacific that had been chosen as the site for a further British penal colony, 2,000 kilometres from Phillip's base at Sydney. There at least, he calculated, they would have the benefits of the island's fertile soils and teeming wildlife. Afterwards the ship carrying them, the *Sirius*, was to sail on to the Cape of Good Hope for fresh provisions. But two months later *Sirius'* tender appeared in Sydney with the news that the parent ship had gone down off Norfolk Island, and while all those aboard had scrambled ashore they were now cut off. In desperation the Norfolk Island castaways turned to a species of shearwater they called the muttonbird, to see them through. In one three-month period they harvested 170,000 – a pattern of exhaustive consumption typical of European colonial society, which eventually drove the bird into local extinction.[11]

On the mainland, however, there was no such source of manna. The best Phillip could do was to eke out the rate at which they were starving. Punishment for pilfering stores was merciless. One man received 1,000 lashes for taking three pounds of potatoes, while those who informed on thieves were as extravagantly rewarded. A convict apprehending a raid on garden vegetables received sixty pounds of flour – an incentive, in the words of one officer, 'more tempting than the ore of Peru or Potosi'.[12]

The tide of misery finally turned with the arrival of a second fleet in June 1790, by which date even a third had been dispatched. Although these fresh arrivals meant many more mouths to feed, the additional supplies on board tided over the whole population at Sydney, which rose to over 3,000 by the time Governor Phillip left in 1792. By that date the colony was becoming self-sufficient in food, with some 600 hectares under cultivation and a harvest of 5,000 bushels of wheat. Sydney Cove was also evolving into an embryo port, sheltering or sending out ships to trade with England, Ireland, Calcutta, Batavia, China and the United States of America.

Almost before this initial beachhead had been fully consolidated, another governor was working on sites for fresh colonisation. The motive for the expansion was similar to that which had launched

Britain's southern Pacific empire in the first place. Philip Gidley King had been appointed Lieutenant-Governor of the New South Wales colony in 1800, and was soon keen to find some suitable spot away from Sydney in which to quarantine his own mischief-makers – in effect, to create a penal colony at the service of his wider convict society. In Van Diemen's Land he seemed to have located the perfect antipodean dungeon.

Covering half the area of New York State and roughly the same size as the republic of Eire, this land of lakes and forested mountains had first entered the European consciousness almost 160 years earlier. The explorer Abel Tasman had landed on its shores and named them in honour of the Dutch governor-general who had commissioned his expedition. However, for more than a century it had remained on the map as an uncharted bulge at the continent's south-eastern extremity, and neither of the first two British explorers to visit the spot (James Cook in 1777 and William Bligh in 1788) managed to correct Tasman's initial misconception that Van Diemen's Land was attached to New Holland. Yet by the time King had taken up his appointment, the British were well aware that it was, in fact, severed from the main-land by a 200-kilometre-wide strip of water known as the Bass Strait.

Accessible but not too close, Van Diemen's Land, or Tasmania, as we shall call it here (although the official name did not change until 1856), was perfect for the governor's purposes. Moreover, King had other reasons for wanting to push ahead quickly with the island's settlement. Only recently it had been visited by a French scientific vessel exploring along Australia's south-eastern coast. King recognised that technically there was nothing to prevent the ship's captain from hoisting the *tricolore* on Tasmanian soil and claiming it for France, a nation with whom Britain had only recently been at war.

In order to forestall such a possibility, King dispatched a Lieutenant Robbins to overhaul his putative Gallic rival in the Bass Strait, to land on the island and to run up a Union Jack as fast as he could. Thus Robbins, coming ashore on its eastern coast and echoing Columbus' Caribbean solemnities of three centuries before, declared to the time-less cadence of Tasmania's Pacific surf that the land was now in the possession of His Majesty King George III.

By February 1804 the business of Tasmanian settlement was well underway and centred on the River Derwent that ran into a deep bay in the southern third of the island's east coast. Despite its name's comforting associations with the English Midlands, the Derwent of Tasmania flowed through a land of rich unfamiliarity for any British settler. When parties of woodcutters ventured into the dense forest they sent up great rainbow flocks of unaccustomed birds, parrots, rosellas and cockatoos, whose eerie cries mingled with the new, alien sound of steel on wood. Stranger still were the flocks of woolly-plumaged emus – birds the size of sheep but lacking in a bird's most characteristic ability, the power of flight. While around the colony settlers found open grassy slopes reminiscent of the English downs, these abounded with Australasia's strange, primitive marsupial fauna: wallabies, kangaroos and wombats.

As the first settlers attempted to grapple with the elusive and unnerving strangeness of Tasmania's physical environment, as well as the pervasive uncertainty of their colony's future, they were to initiate a crisis that brings this chapter back full circle, close to its starting point and the grotesque pantomime of William Lanney's funeral. The event occurred at Risdon on the east bank of the Derwent, where British settlement was approaching its first anniversary. On Thursday 3 May 1804, at 11 a.m., a large group of about 300 Aboriginal Tasmanians emerged from the trees in pursuit of kangaroos and wallabies grazing on the grassy slopes. The members of the party, men, women and children of all ages, were shouting and waving their wooden clubs as they drove the game into their enclosing circular formations.

All the settlers were aware that the island was inhabited by naked savages, but few had seen anything more than mere signs of the Aborigines, and the sudden appearance of such large numbers closing on the European colony caused considerable amazement. Nonetheless, Edward White, the first man to spot them and report their presence, later recorded his lack of any fear and his belief that they had no other objective during their approach on Risdon than the kangaroos crowding ahead of them. Moreover, the tenor of his wonderfully quaint construction – 'They looked at me with all their eyes' – indicates that they were as amazed by their first glimpses of the British as White himself was by them.[13] Certainly, neither of these pieces of his testimony, nor the presence of their women, children and elders, suggested that the Aborigines had planned any violence.

Yet the officer in charge at Risdon on that occasion, Lieutenant William Moore, subsequently claimed that the Tasmanians were organising an attack upon the camp. He also reported that he had been forced to respond to the urgent pleas for protection from a settler whose house and family had been physically threatened. This particular claim was flatly contradicted by White on oath, who said that the Aborigines had never been less than 200 metres from the farmstead in question. Whatever the truth of this, the most likely cause of violence at Risdon that morning was the alcohol Moore was alleged to have consumed, and his desire for a few minutes' rifle practice with the added entertainment of a live and moving target – or as he himself put it, his wish 'to see the Niggers run'.[14] On this issue Moore certainly got his way, especially after he had been persuaded by his colleague, Jacob Mountgarrett, that the best way to open British relations with the Tasmanian Aborigines was with grapeshot and cannon.

The number of casualties caused when this murderous fusillade was loosed into the naked crowd has remained a matter of unsatisfactory dispute, although it is now certain that the oft-repeated figure of fifty Tasmanians dead was a major exaggeration. Over the issue of who was to blame there was less disagreement, even though J.E. Calder, in his book *The Native Tribes of Tasmania*, wrote that 'in balancing the evidence, the blacks seem to have been the aggressors'.[15] While Calder is a valuable source for nineteenth-century prejudice against the Aborigines, his opinion on this occasion seems out of step with the judgement implicit in the title – the Risdon Massacre – which colonists soon gave to the events of that May morning.

The slaughter at Risdon was later said to be a catalyst for all the ensuing hostilities between the island's indigenous population and the British colonists. Although it cannot be made to bear that heavy burden, it was without question the opening act in the drama of Tasmanian extermination. Moreover, while separated from it by sixty-five years and seemingly so different in character, the Risdon Massacre bore a number of similarities to that tragedy's penultimate scene, the battle for William Lanney's bones.

In Lieutenant Moore's drunken desire, for instance, 'to see the Niggers run' there was that element of whimsy contained in Dr Stokell's wish for his Tasmanian souvenir – his tobacco pouch – flayed from William's degraded body. Another striking coincidence was the fact that Surgeon Mountgarrett, the man who had urged the use of cannon and grapeshot on the Tasmanians, shared the same caring profession of both Stokell and Crowther. He even displayed that serious concern for science of those two later good doctors, when he started to collect the bones of his Tasmanian victims, salting them down in casks to be sent to Sydney.[16]

In fact, the Risdon Massacre, like William Lanney's dismemberment, touches on something that characterises almost all of British
relations with the Aborigines and which we should highlight before
considering that tragic process: that somehow these strange, dark,
unpredictable beings of Tasmania must be converted into something
much more recognisable and controllable, and preferably, as in the
case of William, into a physical object that could be readily possessed.
In many ways that urge for possession of the original inhabitants was
closely involved in the very fact of British settlement in Tasmania,
which itself had been driven by that society's deeply metaphysical
attachment to the notion of ownership.

The convict colonies of the South Pacific had evolved out of the
anxieties of eighteenth-century Britain to protect physical property,
and that society's determination to convert those who transgressed
against that sacred relationship into property themselves. The transport
ships also expressed Georgian England's belief that social ills were best
treated by social amputation and physical removal of the infected part.
During the early history of British Tasmania these two urges are dominant forces in the colony's development. In the course of the
colonists' confrontation with the island's indigenous people, that
deeply proprietorial concern to change humans into property returns,
like Tasmania's Pacific surf, time after time, after time, after time.

8

The Black Crows

As opponents of European invasion, it is difficult to imagine a people more distinct from the metropolis-building, god-beguiled Mexica of Central America than the original inhabitants of Tasmania. When the British first encountered them, they were considered amongst the most primitive humans on earth. 'In every respect,' wrote one observer, 'the most destitute and wretched portion of the human family.'[1] It was even conventional to look upon them as a completely separate species. One of the things propelling the dog-fight for William Lanney's bones was the belief that he represented a last living link between man and ape.[2] More typically, the nineteenth-century Europeans settling in their island referred to them as 'crows' or 'black crows' or 'black vermin' – dehumanising terms reminiscent of the 'dink' and 'gook' labels applied in our own century by US servicemen to the Communist Vietnamese.

Though undeniably primitive, Tasmanian culture was also amongst the most distinctive and puzzling of any in Australasia. They lacked, for example, some of the technology characteristic of mainland Aborigines, such as the boomerang and spear-thrower, as well as the biological advantage of the Aborigines' hunting dog, the dingo. They also showed very little of the rich artistic traditions that so distinguish communities on the continent. Yet it was the absence of these elements that offered some insight into the origins of this unique lifestyle and the circumstances by which their ancestors had come to occupy Tasmania.

Like the Mexica, they had originally migrated away from an earlier base far to the north, and were amongst the first waves of human migrants to utilise the land bridges once linking Australasia with southern Asia. Setting out at least 40,000 years ago, these prototype Aborigines gradually worked their way down the continent's eastern coast, finally arriving in Tasmania, which was then attached to the mainland. Much later, in about 8000 BC, warmer conditions in the post-glacial period melted the polar ice-caps and caused sea-levels to rise dramatically. The Bass Strait was a product of these climatic changes and severed Tasmania's umbilical cord to its continental parent. The island's human occupants, unable to regain the mainland on their rudimentary bark canoes, were thus completely cut off. Yet they had survived intact with their Pleistocene technology until the European arrival 10,000 years later.

Those millennia of isolation accounted for what was considered the Tasmanians' extreme backwardness, but they also spoke eloquently of a perfect adaptation to the island environment. Although Tasmania lies on a comparable latitude in the southern hemisphere to Mediterranean France in the north, it experiences a damp, temperate climate of mild winters and cool summers. The heavy precipitation deposited by the easterly-moving Roaring Forties leads to an annual rainfall in parts of Tasmania's mountainous west of over 380 centimetres. This in turn provides conditions for some of the world's last great temperate rainforest. Elsewhere, in the island's central, eastern and south-eastern portions are mountainous plateaux, forested at lower elevations and pocked throughout with lakes. In the north-eastern section of the central plateau alone, for instance, there are at least 4,000 separate bodies of water.

The best estimates of Tasmania's Aboriginal population at the time of the British arrival suggest a total of 3,000 to 4,000 spread throughout the island in nine distinct political groupings. These tribes were in turn divided into from six to fifteen separate bands, which comprised a number of different families and formed the basic social unit of the whole people. The best estimate for the total number of bands is about fifty.[3] Each band moved around within its own particular territory, following seasonal availability of its most important foods, which included a wide range of items, from fungi, ferns and bracken to ants' eggs, swans' eggs and penguins. Primary sources of protein included Tasmania's marsupials, the various species of kangaroo and wallaby, bandicoots, possums and wombats.

Bands also moved down into coastal areas to harvest seals from the many breeding rookeries, and marine plants, such as kelp. Curiously, given the abundance around the Tasmanian shores, the Aborigines observed a strict taboo on all scaled fish. This may help explain the rudimentary nature of their boat technology, although their flimsy bark and reed rafts did enable them to travel to outlying islands and along the rocky coasts to gather seabirds and their eggs, as well as crayfish, oysters and other shellfish.

In view of Tasmania's cool, wet climate, it is remarkable that the Aborigines had adopted little in the way of protective dress. Although women occasionally wrapped themselves in a kangaroo skin, both sexes normally went completely naked, relying on thick layers of ochre and animal grease to insulate them against wind and rain. Their only other means of shelter from the elements were crude windbreaks made of bark, or sometimes a roughly constructed hut, but most of the time they relied on the hearth fire for any additional warmth.

In most other aspects of their culture Tasmanians displayed a similar concern for utilitarian simplicity. Oyster shells served as water vessels. The women set out on gathering forays with little more than a sharpened stick for digging, or a flattened wooden spatula for prising shells off rocks. The men had two basic weapons for the hunt – their waddies or throwing clubs, a length of hardwood of substantial thickness, or their extraordinary wooden spears, which could be anything up to five metres in length. Fire-hardened at the tip, spun in flight and thrown with exceptional accuracy, these javelins were highly effective at bringing down game. (Later they would prove formidable weapons of war.) An assortment of stone or bone axes, scrapers and borers, lengths of grass rope to assist in tree-climbing, bags made of rushes or skin to carry offspring and the rest of their portable possessions, encompassed almost the full range of Tasmanian material technology.

However, the Tasmanians offset these apparent limitations with a profound knowledge of their physical environment, through their great skill as hunters, including the use of fire to flush quarry, and also with their remarkably acute senses. A compelling illustration of their powers of vision was once offered by a British settler who recorded an occasion when his Tasmanian companions spotted a boat with the naked eye and named its owner, before he could even see the vessel with his telescope.[4]

In combination, these accomplishments secured them a more than tolerable existence. What one commentator has noted about mainland Australians could easily be extended to the original inhabitants of Tasmania:

If we specify the main ingredients of a good standard of living as food, health, shelter and warmth, the average Aboriginal was probably as well off as the average European in 1800 . . . Aboriginals of course could not match the comfort and security of the upper classes of Europe, of the wealthiest one-tenth of the population, but they were probably much better off than the poorest one-tenth. In the eastern half of Europe the comparison favours the Aboriginals, and they probably lived in more comfort than the nine-tenths of the population of eastern Europe.[5]

Yet, like all hunter-gatherer communities they did experience periods of shortage and had developed a capacity to exploit food surpluses when opportunity arose. One woman, for instance, was observed once to eat fifty muttonbird eggs at a single sitting, while an eight-month-old infant devoured in one go a whole rat-kangaroo, a marsupial similar in size to a rabbit.[6]

The most serious threat to their physical security probably originated in their frequent practice of bride-kidnap, which reduced inbreeding amongst the polygamous tribes, but often led to rivalry and even warfare, sometimes involving the deaths of the principal combatants. However, inter-tribal fighting, whether as a consequence of this abduction or other disputes over access to food sources, was normally a highly ritualised affair with limited bloodshed. Equally, the maintenance of internal order for a band or tribe was usually achieved, in the absence of any pronounced hierarchy of authority, through collective humiliation of the offending individual.

Their other social requirements, such as the need to relieve collective tensions, or to reaffirm family and group bonds, or for simple recreation, were usually met by the multi-purpose Aboriginal ceremony, the *corroboree*, a mixture of dance, rhythmic music, re-enactment and song. These assemblies were regularly observed during the colonial period, but further evidence for a Tasmanian aesthetic was limited to a few petroglyphs of abstract design and some bark drawings. The one significant form of decoration was body scarification, the pattern of raised weals on the back and chest often serving a social as well as artistic function by distinguishing the male members of one band from another.

The data concerning the Tasmanians' spiritual life are even more fragmentary. However, they did disclose to European settlers their belief in the existence of good and bad spirits – respectively known as 'Parledee' and 'Wrageowrapper'. Further supernatural forces were associated with creation, with fires, rivers, trees and other natural phenomena, and, as a defence against malign spirits, individuals some-times wore amulets incorporating the bones of dead relatives or loved ones. Occasionally these charms included the whole skull of a favourite lost infant.[7]

On the death of a family or band member, the different Tasmanian tribes followed a variety of rituals, either burying or cremating the body or placing it in a tree. However, all of them observed a taboo against mentioning the deceased's name, and confirmed to Europeans their belief that after death a spirit living within the left breast went to live elsewhere.[8] Later this tradition of an afterlife mingled with their perception of the white-skinned European colonists as the returned ghosts of lost relatives and, as on mainland Australia, they came to assume that England was a final resting place for their own dead.[9]

Since so little was ever discovered about the true nature of the Tasmanians' religious life, it was customary amongst the colonists simply to assume that it was as primitive as their stone-age tools. Yet in the first half of the nineteenth century, the period when Tasmanians were undergoing the crisis of invasion and extirpation, British settlers on continental Australia believed much the same of the natives there. It was only in the twentieth century that Europeans came to appreciate how completely the creative energies of mainland Aborigines had been invested in the spiritual, intellectual and social aspects of life, rather than in any material technology. The degree to which the extinct Aborigines of Tasmania might have shared the lat-ter's vision of the Dreamtime, with its complex and deeply spiritual attachment to the natural landscape, will now never be known.

However, it was certainly the case that when they were later forced into exile from their island home, a number of Tasmanians responded to that experience in a manner suggestive of deep spiritual crisis. And a British doctor responsible for their medical care could account for a number of deaths only in terms of the victims' overwhelming but unfulfilled desire to return to the lost country.[10]

Sadly, the eighteenth-century explorers who saw Tasmania before European colonisation, and who provided the earliest accounts of its inhabitants, were not particularly interested in the scope of any native religion. They were much more engrossed in immediate appearances: the men's blackened bodies patterned with lacerations, their grim shoulder-length dreadlocks smeared in grease and stained with ochre, the women's shaven heads and unabashed nakedness, the Aborigines' neolithic tools, the manner in which all gathered round the fire for a meal – a seal or kangaroo pitched into the flames and plucked out barely cooked – consuming the whole mess, gristle, bone, fat and all, like animals at a kill.

Based on evidence like this, most agreed that 'they may be justly placed in the very lowest scale of barbarism' or, more primitive still, that they formed 'the connecting link between man and the monkey tribes'.[11] In 1777 Captain Cook's assessment was slightly less pejorative, registering the Tasmanians' fine teeth and eyes, and the fact that their other features were far from disagreeable, although in a final summary he thought them 'altogether an ignorant wretched race of mortals'. Ominously for the Aborigines, he went on to note that they inhabited 'a country capable of producing every necessity of life, with a climate the finest in the world'.[12]

It is instructive, at this stage, to pause and consider how these early portraits of Aboriginal primitiveness operated within Britain's overall justification of Tasmanian settlement, and also how they contrasted with arguments advanced by the Spaniards to sanction their conquests in Central America. In the sixteenth century the *conquistadores* noted the abundant evidence of cultural achievement but exploited it as a subtle means to evade the moral challenge to their destruction of Mexico. For while they were prepared to acknowledge material and technological progress in Mesoamerica, they could not extend the same sympathetic approach to the nation's moral and spiritual life. The Mexican gods, as we have seen, were reviled as 'abominations which would bring their souls to hell'.

They therefore concluded that the sparkling streams of technical ingenuity and cultural sophistication, that should have been so laudable, ultimately flowed towards a spiritual dead end – the appalling pools of blood and gore that gathered on the floor of the temple altar. Mexico's religion of human sacrifice made their civilisation an inversion of Christian Europe, in fact, a type of anti-civilisation, socially bankrupt, morally decadent and spiritually perverted. Christian conquest could thus be dramatised as the purification of an evil empire.

In the South Pacific, by contrast, the British conquistadors of the eighteenth and nineteenth centuries viewed themselves as confronted by the opposite problem. In the Aborigines they faced beings who had barely managed to initiate any cultural improvement, let alone a civilisation. Just as Australasia was geographically remote from the planet's presumed European centre, so were its inhabitants caught in a developmental backwater. Without the essential machinery of creative reason they had been unable to break through into the refreshing streams of human progress. Unless Europeans offered them that opportunity, the Tasmanians would be mired forever in a dumb, benighted wasteland of brute nature.

As tribal victims of the colonial enterprise, the Mexica and Tasmanians represent opposite poles in that singular process. Yet in each case the European ideology of conquest adjusted itself to the radically different circumstances to advance a moral basis for invasion and dispossession. And despite the chasm that existed between the Spanish and British portraits of their respective victims, one common feature was obvious. Both the Mexican and Tasmanian were inadequate forms of society when measured against the one true model of human normality – Christian Europe. For the colonists it was an ideological case of heads I win, tails you lose. No matter what stage of development their opponents enjoyed – cultured sophisticate or undeveloped primitive – Europeans had an all-embracing remedy for their social inadequacies: dispossession and replacement.

Like the Spaniards, the British in Tasmania found quasi-legal arguments to buttress the wider ideology of invasion. They reasoned in particular that the Aborigines' complete lack of permanent dwellings or any form of land cultivation raised fundamental questions about their relationship with the island they seemed to inhabit. Since their notion of place and location was so rudimentary, and their presence upon the land so transient, could they really be said to be in occupation of it? And if not, how could it be a crime for the British to take possession? In *The Road to Botany Bay* Paul Carter has suggested that the fundamental differences in their respective approaches to land and its usage meant that, in a sense, the settler took possession of a country of which the Aborigine was unaware. For to 'talk of contracts and boundaries to an Aborigine,' Carter argued, 'was to talk a foreign language. Logically then, possession could go ahead without consultation.'[13]

These unilateral inroads into Tasmanian resources took two distinct forms, both of which led eventually to conflict with the indigenous people. The first of these was focused on the island's northern coast and the smaller satellite islands in the Bass Strait, where European seal-ing and whaling vessels had been in operation even before the Derwent settlements had been established. By 1802 there were about 200 sealers of various nationalities in the region, and by 1803 Governor King in Sydney had already expressed concern about the scale of their harvest. In a single month, for instance, the crew of one brig brought in 4,300 seal skins and the hides of 600 elephant seals. During the first six years of the nineteenth century these rates of exploitation yielded a total of 100,000 skins, pushing the seals towards local extinction. Yet as the population fell and demand came to out-strip production, so seal skin prices rose from £1 a piece in 1816 to 27 shillings by 1825.[14] In the following year there were still 20 sealers operating in the area.

For the Aboriginal communities living along Tasmania's northern shores, the presence of these economic pioneers was catastrophic. The sealers not only depleted traditional Aboriginal food sources but in time triggered a total dislocation of indigenous social life. In the early years they managed to get hold of Tasmanian women, taking advan-tage of the men's callous treatment of their own females as little more than physical and sexual chattels. Since the sealers looked upon the woman's indigenous position as little better than slavery, they consid-ered their own acquisition of them as no more than a continuation of native practice, if not actually a kind of liberation. Moreover, although they initially bargained for the women by giving food, skins and dogs to the rest of the band, they were often either ignorant of or dismissed the Aboriginal understanding of these exchanges. Yet, to the Tasmanians, the sharing of women in this manner drew the two par-ties into intimate relations. As Henry Reynolds has written, 'the randy womanless white man was not only encircled in warm flesh: he was also enmeshed in an intricate web of kinship' and 'in expectations of reciprocity, and what was more, continuing reciprocity.'[15]

Skilled in the techniques of seal-catching, the Aboriginal women were eventually regarded by the sealers as an essential part of their operation. One boat's captain acknowledged in 1816 that it was cus-tomary for each of his men to have between two and five females, who doubled up as temporary sexual partners in the remote offshore loca-tions.[16] Violence, sometimes of the most brutal kind, became endemic in their relations. A group of sealers, for example, was recorded to have punished one runaway female by tying her to a tree, cutting off her ear and the flesh from one thigh and then forcing her to eat them.[17]

Atrocities of this kind gradually caused the supply of voluntary labour to cease. And although one Tasmanian group regularly kidnapped the women of another band and used these to barter for European products, direct and violent seizure eventually became the sealers' most frequent means of securing fresh recruits. Moreover, their relationship with the Aboriginal men became one of open conflict. Eyewitnesses reported that along the island's north-east coast, the shores were littered with Tasmanian skeletons, the skulls bearing wounds inflicted by the sealers' musket fire. The demographic collapse inflicted by this outright slaughter was further exacerbated by the loss of most of the Tasmanian women of reproductive age. By 1830, of seventy-five natives living close to the north-east coast, seventy-two were men, and there was not a single child amongst them.[18]

In time the coercive relations between European sealers and Tasmanian women gave rise to a relatively stable population of mixed race. However, the initial female partners were often deeply ambivalent about the offspring from these unions, regularly seeking to abort the foetus or destroy the child after it was born.[19] A further compelling indication of their history of abuse was offered in a dance performed by some of the Tasmanian women living with sealers. In this they acted out their enforced coupling with a devil and their evil delivery of its offspring.[20] Considered obscene by later Victorian witnesses, the dance expressed the manner in which Tasmanian women both acknowledged and strove to record the tragic experience of their people, then sought to accommodate the resulting trauma.

In addition to the onslaught along the northern coast, Tasmanians were soon forced to cope with environmental damage inflicted elsewhere. This disruption arose initially out of the British failure to provide for themselves in the first years after arrival. As on the mainland, where Governor Phillip's colony had suffered a period of near-starvation, the settlers in Hobart, the colony's capital on the Derwent, and at Launceston, the main town on the north coast, were unable to cultivate enough food to keep pace with their expanding population. Their response was to exploit the local fauna to see them through the period of shortage, and kangaroo meat was soon a mainstay of the whole colony. The official ration was set at over 3.5 kilos per week per person and in one three-month period in 1805, Hobart's population consumed 7,740 kilos, turning the skins into everything from shoes to hats and jackets.[21] By 1808 kangaroos were a scarce commodity and the hunters were forced to go further and further into the Tasmanian outback to find unexploited populations.

The business of hunting kangaroos had fallen to a relatively small number of individuals experienced in field craft, known as bushrangers. Many of the most successful were convicts who had escaped from their masters, equipped themselves with stolen arms, and were profiting from their sale of meat and skins to other colonists. At one stage, in fact, His Majesty's authorities were in the deeply anomalous position of depending for the survival of their convict colony upon the efforts of these escaped felons. Even worse, the bushrangers acquired a taste for the free life of the Tasmanian bush and began to return to their former trade, robbing and terrorising other settlers almost at will.

Their threat to the indigenous population was even more sinister. They competed directly for Aboriginal food resources, while their hunting forays brought them into direct contact with a number of Tasmanian bands. Recruited from the toughest categories amongst the convict community, these kangaroo hunters were hardly calculated to make the best ambassadors for European society. However, they did make one significant contribution to indigenous culture. The Aborigines quickly recognised the value of hunting-dogs and readily traded for them with the whites. This one inadvertent benefit aside, the bushrangers, the lowest of the low in colonial society, took a malicious pleasure in victimising a people even more despised than themselves.

An index of their endemic hatred and casual violence towards the Aborigines was provided by one of their number, who told a Tasmanian historian that he 'liked to kill a black fellow better than smoke a pipe,' adding 'and I am a rare one at that, too.'[22] Another confessed that he would 'as leave shoot them as so many sparrows'. Despite his innocent-sounding name, a man called Lemon was accustomed to use them as target practice, while others confessed to feeding their dogs on Aborigines shot specifically for that purpose.[23] Their relish for murdering the men was more than equalled by their sexual appetite for the women, and a bushranger called Carrot found a way of satisfying both urges almost simultaneously. After slaughtering a Tasmanian man, he then abducted and raped his widow and forced her to carry her husband's severed head around her neck 'as a plaything'.[24]

The most infamous of all bushrangers was a Yorkshireman transported for highway robbery in 1812, called Michael Howe. Styling himself 'Lieutenant-Governor of the Woods', Howe was a ruthless murderer, who kept a diary of kangaroo parchment where he recorded his bad dreams in blood. Having taken an Aboriginal partner, known as Black Mary, Howe had picked up much of his bushcraft directly from her people and ran a daring convict gang which pillaged remote farmsteads all the way from Hobart to Launceston. However, he was not averse to turning his native skills back upon Black Mary's own race. One favourite Aboriginal ruse he admired was their ability to approach seemingly unarmed while dragging a spear behind them between their toes. Howe apparently adapted the technique so that he could lay a gun at his feet, make friendly gestures towards approaching Tasmanians and then shoot them, working the trigger with his toes.[25]

Although they had initially benefited from the supplies of kangaroo meat, the British authorities in Tasmania deplored the presence of the bushrangers and took vigorous measures to stamp them out. Typically, Michael Howe was eventually caught and decapitated, his head exhibited on a spike in Hobart in 1818, by which date even his devoted Black Mary had disowned him, after he had shot and abandoned her during an exchange with government forces.[26] While such official action against their worst persecutors was an undoubted benefit to the Tasmanians and while the British authorities publicly denounced bushranger depredations upon the indigenous population, they had certainly not been motivated by any concern for Aborigines.

For although the convicts languished at the ill-favoured margin of Britain's own complex system of tribal identity, the native people of Tasmania lay way beyond even this periphery. It is hardly surprising, therefore, that no one was ever committed for trial, let alone convicted, for murdering an Aborigine. Punishment, if administered at all, was normally restricted to the convicts and even these penalties need to be placed in context. For example, one man received a beating after showing off the little finger he had sliced from an Aborigine to use as a tobacco stopper. Another was flogged for the ears and other parts he had cut from the living body of a Tasmanian boy, while two men received twenty-five lashes each for their violence against native women.[27] Although these last crimes were denounced as 'indescribable brutalities' – the nature of which we can probably surmise – they were nevertheless deemed to be only half as serious as those of a convict cook, who was given fifty lashes for smiling at his mistress' orders.[28]

The truth was that while the colonial authorities had automatically made the indigenous Tasmanians answerable to British laws, they had never dreamed of bestowing on them the privileges of British citizens. And since they had ascribed to the Aborigines no prior right of occupancy, any attempt on their part to defend their land was automatically defined by the colonial government as a criminal offence. The settlers' vision of the Tasmanian as an angry savage beyond the pale was, in fact, a self-fulfilling prophecy inbuilt into the nature of their judicial framework.

As the scope of British settlement increased, so did the risk of violent confrontation between the two peoples, and yet throughout the first decades, colonists continued to record positive contacts with Aborigines. One farmer, for instance, faced with a bush fire across his land, was helped for several hours by a band of Tasmanians as they battled to stop the blaze engulfing his crops. Even as late as 1825, when relations were reaching crisis point, a settler recorded an occasion when he chanced upon a hunting party in the forest. 'We found them broiling an opossum,' he wrote,

> which when cooked they partook of with good appetites, and invited us by motions to join them. After the meal they began a kind of dance, all hands repeating the word 'corobory'. We remained among them till towards daylight, during all which time they continued their revelry. They appeared to us an harmless people, though since they have proved very dangerous neighbours.[29]

By the date of the opossum feast British settlement had mushroomed since the precarious days on the banks of the Derwent. In the previous year, the number of Europeans in the colony had risen to 12,643, while the indigenous population had probably already fallen to half its original total. Barely more than twenty years after the first British landing, Aborigines were outnumbered on their native Tasmania by more than six to one.

It was not just the human population that posed such a threat. Environmental changes wrought by European livestock were equally disruptive. Sheep in particular were having a huge impact on the natural grazing available to the island's native marsupials. Between 1816 and 1823 the settlers' flocks almost quadrupled to 200,000, and within five years they had virtually tripled again. By the end of the 1820s this voracious trampling army stood at a million – 1,000 sheep for every single surviving Aborigine in Tasmania.

Even by this date the colony was still largely concentrated on the north and south coasts and between the two major towns of Hobart and Launceston. Equally there remained vast upland areas of forest untouched by settlement, especially in the west. Yet there were now no Tasmanians unaffected by the British presence. Their best hunting grounds had been absorbed for agriculture or sheep grazing and they and their principal prey species were slowly squeezed out. Nor could those areas least visited by Europeans sustain the Aborigines indefinitely and they were forced increasingly to travel close to or through settled districts to find their traditional foods. This brought with it the attendant dangers of direct contact with antagonistic settler communities.

By 1825 the confrontation between the island's indigenous people and the British was rapidly reaching its climax in a five-year period known generally as the Black War. By that date, the sealers on the north coast had largely destroyed the source of their own harvests, while the British authorities had succeeded in eliminating most of the bushrangers. It now fell to a third group of Europeans, the colony's growing population of farmers, stock-keepers and farm-hands, to pick up the baton of genocide.

9
The Black War

Although the administration in Hobart repeatedly called for restraint in the settlers' dealings with the indigenous people, those who manned the farms in the Tasmanian outback were remote from the impact of government. Moreover, many of them were convicts working tickets of leave, hostile towards any form of authority and especially resentful of policies that might seem to favour mere savages. To these despised outcasts of colonial society the Aborigines were the ultimate underdogs, over whom even they could pull social rank, and towards whom they displayed all the malign creativity of the psychotic. In fact, it is a credit to European historiography in Tasmania that so much evidence of their hidden deeds has reached the light of day. That many of the stockmen openly boasted of their actions is also a powerful indication of the extraordinary values of their time and place.

Typically, they were indifferent to the edicts of Hobart vetoing the use of poisoned flour, which had been sanctioned in New South Wales to stop Aborigines from stealing settlers' supplies. In Tasmania, the natives had the contaminated product actively urged upon them, sometimes even before any theft had been attempted. Another tactic was to gun them down while pretending to hand out food, one stock-keeper hitting nineteen with a swivel gun loaded with nails. Another managed to rip open an Aborigine's stomach while seeming to offer bread at the end of a knife.[1] One farmer, obedient to the ban on poison, found an equally effective deterrent for Aboriginal theft. When the Tasmanian band, which was accustomed to stop and shelter in his outhouse, arrived one day, the farmer watched to see the results of his alternative measure. After a short time he had his first volunteer, the Aborigine immediately leaping back in terror from the tempting flour cask, his hand snapped off in the jaws of a concealed gin trap.[2]

Another landowner proved that casual brutality was by no means the preserve of Tasmania's criminal underclass. Encountering a lone Aborigine on his land, the farmer started to fool around, holding an unloaded pistol to his own temple and pulling the trigger, laughing at the click of each empty chamber. Once he had demonstrated the game, he then encouraged his companion to join in. This time he handed over a fully loaded weapon, and the Aborigine held it to his ear and blew his own brains out.[3]

Inevitably, the all-male work-force on isolated Tasmanian farms became as lonely as the sealers in the Bass Strait, and stockmen regularly kidnapped Aboriginal females in order to work off their frustrations. The standard practice was to chain them up and then turn on the charm, one suitor thrusting a burning stick into the skin of his would-be partner until she succumbed to his advances. The commonest form of foreplay, however, was a good beating with a bull whip. It is worth noting that *having* these women expressed a sexual dimension to the pervasive settler concern to possess and occupy Tasmania's Aborigines. Ownership of the living object could, of course, eventually pall. Two stockmen, bored of their *ménage à trois*, took the shared third party and pegged her out spread-eagled on the ground, then left her to die.[4]

Sometimes the liaisons were the product of chance encounter, like the two Britons out hunting birds who happened upon an Aboriginal party. Although the Tasmanians fled in panic, one of their number was a heavily pregnant woman and she was forced to drop behind and hide up a tree. The bird hunters found her and shot her down, the trauma of which caused her to miscarry. Finally the dying woman dragged herself off to a creek and buried her head completely in mud, while the sportsmen looked on in amusement.[5]

Occasionally, things did not go as the stockmen had hoped. One individual chained up his female prize, flogged her with a bull whip and raped her, only to find himself surrounded by the rest of her group at a later date, who then speared him to death.[6] Another notorious incident occurred out on the island's north-westernmost extremity, the appropriately named Cape Grim, where in 1827 shepherds attempted to lure the females of a Tasmanian band into their huts. The Aboriginal men objected to the shepherds' advances and in the ensuing quarrel one of each party was wounded. In retaliation the band later attacked the shepherds' stock, 118 sheep being speared to death or driven over the Cape Grim cliffs. Six weeks later this dispute reached its weary and gruesome climax, when the shepherds gained final revenge. Thirty Aborigines were alleged to have been slain that day, then thrown off the sixty-metre-high cliffs, although the shepherds' foreman later wrote to the colonial secretary and tried to suggest that the real number of dead was probably only four.[7]

With hindsight it is easy to conclude that the Aboriginal position was always hopeless. On all sides they were assailed by an overwhelming European deluge which swept away the animals that had traditionally sustained them, swamped their island ecosystem with alien fauna, or which gnawed incessantly at their numbers in direct violence or kidnap or the introduction of new and, for the indigenes, irresistible diseases like influenza and tuberculosis. Yet the Tasmanian people fought back in a desperate and violent attempt both to stem the European invasion and to assuage their swelling desire for revenge. Their tactics inflicted considerable damage across the island and gave rise to a mixture of responses from the colonists.

On the one hand, settlers experienced a sense of expectations fulfilled, as Tasmanians indulged in that savagery so ingrained in the European image of them. Sometimes their strikes appeared indiscriminate, targeting those who had no direct involvement in the settlers' own atrocities, and even some who had been friends to their race. Such 'motiveless' brutality led one British magistrate to speak of 'the cold malignity of a wicked spirit', while J.E. Calder called it the 'wrath of the savage . . . so inextinguishable and deeply rooted'.[8] Even the government's own Aborigines Committee, set up to inquire into the causes of the Black War, deplored the 'wanton and savage spirit inherent in them'.[9]

Mingled with this gloomy resignation, however, was deep British shock and outrage that mere brutes of the forests, armed literally with sticks and stones, had succeeded in inflicting these losses. The Tasmanians often raided remote farmsteads at will, burning outbuildings and crops, spearing livestock and plundering the stores of flour and sugar, often as replacements for traditional Aboriginal foods so depleted by the effects of settlement. Sometimes the European occupants became the victims of cleverly orchestrated attacks. A raiding party might keep watch on a building for hours and even days to catch the owners off guard. Colonists also recorded the ploy, so admired by bushranger Michael Howe, in which the Tasmanians would approach hands on head, as if unarmed, and then slaughter an unsuspecting colonist with a spear or club which they had dragged along between their toes.

In a mixture of horror and frustrated anger, colonists also noted the Tasmanians' propensity to attack in overwhelming number, their ability to creep undetected to within metres of an intended victim and, most despicable of all, their revolting mutilation of the fallen corpse. One such murdered stockman was found to have thirty-seven spear wounds, while the head had been smashed to a pulp. Some victims were castrated and had the testicles pushed into their gaping mouths. Yet when pursued themselves the Aborigines had a gift for disappearing completely as if swallowed up by the ground itself. 'And though you may see them at a short distance,' wrote one thwarted combatant, 'and run up to the place where they are, not a vestige of them will be found.'[10] Although men like Calder railed at the Tasmanian reluctance for the 'fair and open fight', at their 'uniform disposition to treachery' and 'mischievous craft', they also acknowledged the capabilities of such a 'subtle enemy'.[11]

As a measure of their fighting skills, Calder pointed out that in the official inquests into settler–Aboriginal conflicts between 1826 and 1831, the deaths of ninety-nine whites were recorded, as opposed to nineteen Tasmanians. According to the author, the statistics for the wounded were even more one-sided: sixty-nine Europeans for only a couple of Aborigines.[12] These figures undoubtedly presented a highly partial view of the Black War, taking no account, as Calder himself acknowledged, of the far greater incidence of British attacks on Tasmanians that went completely unrecorded. Yet the overall figure of 176 British settlers adjudged to have died at Aboriginal hands does suggest a degree of brutal effectiveness in their methods. In fact, although it lacked the dramatic unities of time and place of the Mexican war of resistance, the Tasmanians' piecemeal counter-offensive was of much greater duration and, in terms of lives lost, almost as costly to the European invaders. The Spanish casualties in the siege of Tenochtitlan were only about half those of the British during the Black War of Tasmania. And if one takes into account the colossal disparities in both manpower and resources available to the tribal peoples in each of the colonial theatres, then the scale of Tasmanian success appears all the more remarkable.

To account for these differences one must look in part to the widely differing economic and social organisations of the two tribal peoples. The Mexica's urban-based concentration, their highly centralised military culture and agrarian lifestyle channelled them towards fighting an all-out and decisive war. In fact, there are very few colonial conflicts where the outcome so conclusively turned on one campaign. Such tactics played directly into Spanish hands.

It was those tribes with a diffuse population spread and fluid social structures that proved the most awkward opponents for Europeans, whose preference was for the decisive knock-out victory. On Tasmania the loose nature of tribal organisation combined with the difficulties of the island's rugged mountainous terrain and dense forests to make such a campaign impracticable. As we shall see, on the one occasion when the British attempted such once-and-for-all measures, they were a tactical failure, more significant now as a diversionary note of farce in the otherwise bleak tale of Tasmanian extermination.

Although the different Tasmanian bands never managed to operate in concert, the attacks of the independent groups seemed so carefully coordinated and executed that, as Calder noted, amongst the settlers there was 'a universal belief that a man of our own race was living with the blacks . . . as the active abettor of, and instructor in their hostile operations.'[13] Equally striking is the fact that when intelligent planning became a feature of Aboriginal resistance to European settlement on the Australian mainland, the colonists there adopted a similar myth about a white leader.[14]

It is worth pausing to note that these legends were part of a wider and more dogged misconception amongst Christian imperialists that any display of ability or achievement on the part of their despised opponents had to have a European or, at least, Old World origin. It was similar assumptions about tribal incompetence that led the seventeenth-century Spanish propagandist Pedro Sarmiento de Gamboa to propose the Greeks as the originators of Mexican civilisation, the Jews as the creators of Muiscan culture and the 'primeval Mesopotamians' as the source of Incan achievement.[15] Equally, in the nineteenth century, when Europeans in southern Africa were confronted with the dry-stone citadels at Great Zimbabwe, they resorted to some forgotten tribe of Phoenicians or Arabs to explain such monumental structures.

It was not just the Aborigines' military competence that so aggrieved the British in Tasmania. They were equally affronted by the idea that the indigenous people entertained notions of the island's

Diego Rivera's recreation of the Mexican emperor in the market
plaza of Tlatelolco, which presented the *conquistadores* with a great
showcase of Mesoamerican civilisation.

Hernan Cortés in an eighteenth-century engraving as the great conqueror of New Spain.

Cortés as the vile extortionist by the twentieth-century artist, Diego Rivera.

(*Facing page*)
Moctezuma's attempt to halt the Mexican attack on the *conquistadores* was the final act in his debasement.

The Spanish massacre of Mexican nobles at the religious festival of Toxcatl.

The chilling beauty of Mexican skull mosaics drew on an artistic tradition
stretching back a thousand years.

The acculturated Aboriginal couple, Mary Ann and Walter George Arthur.

William Lanney,
the King of the Tasmanians.

Until the end Truganini's face
suggested her fierce personal resistance
to the fate of her people.

'The race is fast falling away
and its utter extinction will
be hardly regretted' – the last
Tasmanians at Oyster Cove.

The lives of the mixed-race
community of Cape Barren
Island embraced many old
Aboriginal traditions.

Sir George Arthur,
Lieutenant-Governor of
Tasmania (1784–1854).

George Robinson,
the Conciliator to the
Tasmanian Aborigines.

ownership which preceded those of the world's foremost maritime power. Typically, the secretary of state for the colonies, Sir George Murray, lamented 'the extremely difficult task of inducing ignorant beings . . . to acknowledg[e] any authority . . . particularly when possessed with the idea which they appear to entertain in regard to their own rights over the country in comparison with those of the colonists.'[16] Similarly galling was the notion that the Tasmanians had spurned the generous hand of civilisation. As one settler put it, the British had co-existed with the island's indigenous people for a quarter of a century yet the Aborigines 'had not advanced one step towards a state of improvement'.[17]

For this man the way to deal with such useless and ungrateful material was its complete elimination from the island, a view widely shared amongst the colonists. When the government's Aborigines Committee called settlers before it in order to formulate official policy, almost to a man they advocated ruthless measures. These included employing Maoris to hunt them down and then the enslavement of any Tasmanian captives in New Zealand. Others proposed using dogs or the old favourite – decoy huts containing bags of flour and sugar laced with poison.[18]

At a further public meeting at the Hobart courthouse, the call was for similar actions. 'If there is an imperative necessity to destroy the blacks,' announced one speaker, 'then I say we are bound to use the measures that Providence has placed in our hands for that purpose.' When another of those present questioned whether violence would achieve the desired result, a Dr Turnbull disagreed, arguing that 'extermination had been adopted in New South Wales with the greatest success.'[19]

To their credit the two men who served as governors of Tasmania during the period of greatest violence, Colonel William Sorrell (1817–24) and Colonel George Arthur (1824–36), repeatedly condemned the excesses of the settlers. Even when Aboriginal reprisals had reached their most intense and bloody phase, the latter of these officials clung to the notion that the Tasmanians were a race more sinned against than sinning. When asked to declare martial law in response to the depredations, Governor Arthur wrote in reply:

Notwithstanding the clamour and urgent appeals which are now made to me for the adoption of harsh measures, I cannot divest myself of the consideration that all aggression originated with the white inhabitants and that therefore much ought to be endured in return before the blacks are treated as an open and accredited enemy by the government.[20]

For all their good intentions, however, such expressions of official concern need to be measured against the policies ultimately adopted by officials like Arthur. Equally they need to be placed in the context of the Tasmanian governor's role as master of a penal colony. Both Sorrell and Arthur presided over an island fortress planned from the outset as the terminal destination for Britain's transported convicts. But within Tasmania itself, both men intended that their joint project, a prison settlement at Macquarie Harbour on the island's isolated west coast, should be the *ne plus ultra* of criminal punishment.

The Australian historian Robert Hughes has identified Macquarie during its ten years of operation as 'the worst spot in the English-speaking world'.[21] To its inmates it was known more simply as 'Hell's Gates', and whatever vestiges of human dignity might have endured in the miserable incorrigibles passing through its portals, the regime seemed designed to strip away completely. The inmates were moved relentlessly between filthy, overcrowded, verminous quarters to work sites felling timber or sawing logs for twelve to sixteen hours a day. The only relief was a diet of watery gruel and lumps of two- or three-year-old brine-soaked pork or beef. Otherwise there was the daily diversion of punishment beatings – floggings so meticulously recorded in prison ledgers that we know exactly 33,723 lashes fell between 1822 and 1826: one for almost each time the clock struck the hour.[22]

There is no more compelling evidence of Macquarie's hellish ethos than the details of the inmates' attempted escapes. Sometimes convicts were so morally defeated they played a 'game' in which participants drew lots to see who would be murderer and who the victim. Then in full view of guards the deed would be carried out, ensuring the assailant's execution and a diverting trip to Hobart for witnesses to the crime. This might then provide the opportunity for a breakout, although this too was a serious gamble. Of the 112 who tried, it is known that more than half died in the attempt.

The most notorious of these failures was a man called Pierce. He and seven others fled the prison at Macquarie and attempted to head east through the dense bush for the settlements on the Derwent. Gradually, however, their food supplies, including their own kangaroo-hide jackets, were exhausted and in the absence of other fare the group started to eat each other. Having once crossed this moral threshold, these desperadoes pursued the relentless and gruesome logic of their cannibalism until just one man, Pierce, was left alive. He managed to reach the Derwent and join up with a band of bushrangers, only to suffer the humiliation of recapture within a matter of days.

On return to Macquarie, Pierce demonstrated that his desire for liberty had not been quenched by this setback, and with just a single companion called Cox he escaped again. However, equally undiminished, it seems, was his appetite for human flesh. Pierce is alleged to have eaten Cox in preference to his supplies of bread, pork and fish, and then on his second recapture to have sung the praises of his erstwhile colleague for the excellence of his flavour. Pierce finally succeeded in escaping the horrors of Macquarie when he was transported back to the jail in Hobart Town and hanged for murder in 1822.[23]

Although one of the most macabre of stories to emerge from Tasmania's penal colony, it indicates the desperate brutalities to which inmates were subjected and to which they eventually became inured. In turn, it suggests the causative background for the convicts' psychopathic treatment of Aborigines and also the wider climate of violence that made such atrocities acceptable to large swathes of the colony's population. Finally, it reveals something of the Janus-faced nature of the governor's policy towards Aborigines. On the one hand officials like George Arthur condemned the behaviour of white scum like the bushrangers and stockmen, but then oversaw institutions that were a forcing-house of men stripped almost completely of moral qualities.

It is similarly instructive to consider the government's response to the recommendations made by its own Committee for Aboriginal Affairs. Once it had taken evidence from a wide range of sources, the committee proposed five measures to tackle the problem of racial conflict: there should be no indiscriminate murder or ill-treatment of Aborigines; no killing of their principal prey, the kangaroo; the introduction of a bounty system for the capture of natives; an increase in field police, and the presence of mounted police at district police stations.[24] As the *Hobart Times* pointed out, the government never instituted any legal proceedings to enforce the first two of these measures.[25] And to the last three proposals it objected on the grounds of cost, refusing either an increase in police or mounted police, while any bounties paid for capture were to be provided by settlers themselves. The one measure the secretary of state for the colonies, Sir George Murray, would countenance concerned the number of convicts used to guard farms and farm property. Thus the only step adopted by government to reduce racial conflict involved an increase in that class of people all agreed to have been the most brutal in their dealings with Tasmania's Aborigines.[26]

Hypocrisy it might have been, but it was inexpensive and it was perfectly in line with the mood of extermination prevailing in Tasmania by the late 1820s. At that time the colonists had adopted a tactic of roving parties of militia who patrolled in search of Aboriginal bands, often attacking them regardless of evidence of their involvement in any violence. Typically, a member of one roving party recorded an occasion when a group of Tasmanians was found cooking round a fire. The soldiers surrounded them, opened fire and rushed in with fixed bayonets to finish off any wounded. One infant found by its dying mother was bayoneted and pitched straight into the flames. Another individual openly boasted of having pushed an old Tasmanian woman into her own fire and having watched her roast to death.[27]

It is worth returning momentarily to sixteenth-century America to consider one of the parallels between the *conquistadores'* behaviour and that of the British in Tasmania. Bartolomé de Las Casas, the famous Spanish defender of indigenous Americans, is one of the principal sources on his countrymen's atrocities. He recorded occasions when men took bets to see if they could slice Americans in two or sever the head from the body at a single stroke.[28] When he brought such deeds to the attention of fellow Spaniards the response was complete disbelief: de Las Casas was branded as an infernal liar and at best as an impassioned and over-credulous defender of indigenous interests.

Yet the ludic dimension to European atrocities is almost a leitmotif of their 400-year conquest of indigenous peoples. In Tasmania there are records of a prosperous colonist being seated at dinner with neighbours, when his convict stockman came in announcing cheerily, 'Well Master! I've shot three more crows today'; of another man who kept a pickle tub to preserve his trophy collection of Tasmanian ears; of occasions when colonists went abroad *en famille* with food hampers so they could combine a country picnic with a spot of 'crow' hunting.[29] (Nor was this European right to treat the black man literally as fair game lightly abandoned. In 1926, a full century after the Tasmanian incidents described above, when policemen from Alice Springs were involved in slaying seventeen Australian Aborigines, settlers wrote to the press during the subsequent inquiry complaining that it 'would be a dangerous state of affairs if a policeman could not shoot an Aboriginal'.[30] Even as late as 1972 in southern Colombia, a party of hunters were acquitted of gunning down Amerindians when they pleaded in their defence that it was sport and not a punishable offence.)[31]

Although the British authorities were either unable or unwilling to do so, other witnesses to the Tasmanian saga grasped the deeper continuities between the settlers' actions against the Aborigines and those of European colonists elsewhere in the world. The English 'have committed upon the Tasmanian Race (and that in the nineteenth century),' wrote one outraged French ethnologist, 'execrable atrocities a hundred times less excusable than the hitherto unrivalled crimes of which the Spaniards were guilty in the sixteenth century in the Antilles.'[32] But by 1828 Governor Arthur was less concerned with defining the historical background to the Tasmanian conflict, than with bringing it to an end, or at least calling a halt to the colonists' recriminations against his government's inaction.

In November 1828 martial law was finally declared. In the twenty-four months from its introduction, roving parties were known to have killed sixty Aborigines and taken about another twenty alive.[33] To increase the number captured, bounties of £5 were offered for adults and £2 for children. 'Black catching' was now as profitable as it was entertaining and the number of roving parties, official and private, rose to nine by the winter of 1829. There were also 100 soldiers patrolling the main areas of settlement. In combination these measures were devastating Aboriginal numbers, and despite Governor Arthur's figure of 2,000 Tasmanians in the settled districts, by 1829 the stragglers present in that area probably totalled no more than 100.

Yet one of the factors behind the governor's over-estimate was that Aboriginal aggression had continued at a furious level. Two bands, known as the Big River and the Oyster Bay people, launched an unprecedented series of attacks. In the first eight months of 1830 what remained of the Big River tribe – and it had probably lost as many as 240 people in the previous six years – killed twenty Europeans. Lone shepherds were clubbed to death or isolated farms attacked, their occupants, often just women and children, falling victim to well-aimed stones or the Tasmanians' lethal spears. In the ensuing inquests and newspaper reports, the recurring names of the British settlements – places like Abyssinia, Jerusalem, Jericho, Bethlehem, Lake Tiberias,

Bagdad, the River Jordan – suggest less a modern colonial conflict, than some mythic clash between the forces of good and evil, or the triumph of the Israelites over the heathen Philistine hordes.

In the austral spring of 1830, Arthur, appalled by the constant news of bloodshed and murder, summoned his entire colony for one final, supreme effort to end the hostilities. The governor had struck upon the brilliant idea of a massive game drive which would push the notorious Oyster Bay and Big River tribes out of their strongholds on the east coast and into the central lakeland district to the south of Launceston. The cordon would then press its quarry inexorably southwards into a natural funnel to the east of Hobart known as the Tasman Peninsula. Its isolation and the easily guarded neck of land connecting this peninsula to Tasmania proper had already qualified it as a perfect site for one of Arthur's remote penal settlements. Now the isthmus, like a crooked finger or hook in shape, would be an ideal spot at which to bring the Black War to its close.

For a distance as the crow flies of about 150 kilometres and from a third of the way down the east coast to Lake Echo, at almost the island's dead centre, men were to be spaced at intervals of fifty metres and organised in parties of ten with a leader and guide. In total the Black Line, as it was eventually known, included 2,000 soldiers, special constables, settlers, convicts and volunteers. It was the largest force ever summoned to combat Australian Aborigines and equalled the total number of troops employed by Cortés to subdue Mexico, while Francisco Pizarro had destroyed the Inca with a tenth of Arthur's men. But the governor was leaving nothing to chance. He personally planned everything down to the minutest detail. The men's rations, fixed with proper military exactitude, included three ounces of sugar, a half-ounce of tea, two pounds of flour, a pound and a half of meat, a quarter-pound of tobacco and half an ounce of soap. At a central headquarters close to Lake Echo, 1,000 muskets, 30,000 rounds of ammunition and 300 pairs of handcuffs were assembled – the arms deemed essential to ensnare 200–500 ferocious savages, which was at best a fourfold exaggeration of their number. Temporary defensive huts were erected, and fires prepared on strategic hilltops to guide the line in its awesome sweep of Tasmania's south-eastern quarter.

By 7 October all was deemed ready. The men, each ordered to bring two pairs of boots, were hurried into position. On the Sunday before its departure, the line was blessed in every church on the island, while a special plea was offered up for the Tasmanians' speedy conversion from heathenism to Christian worship.[33]

A government proclamation also spelt out the blend of educational and punitive objectives for the Aborigines, once the great drive had done its work: to capture and to raise them in the scale of civilisation, by placing them under the immediate control of a competent establishment, from whence they would not have it in their power to escape and therefore to molest the white inhabitants of the country.[34]

It required only that the eleven drummers roll out their stirring tattoo and the historic campaign began.

The Black Line was a scheme as bold in its conception as it was ludicrous in its execution. Few of those involved in the organisation, least of all Arthur himself, seemed to have considered the nature of the country over which they were casting their human drag-net. The line of march so beautifully worked out on paper now disintegrated in a world of impenetrable bush, precipitous ravines and rugged mountains. The shortcomings in the survey department's maps were soon exposed, while thorny scrub shredded the men's clothes, and jagged rocks wore out both their boots and any initial enthusiasm. Many deserted. Others mistook a possum hunt for the sounds of battle or fired at a tree stump, believing it the enemy. At night they huddled around camp fires, discharging weapons at the leaping shadows or preparing for attack from non-existent hordes. Four or five British soldiers were killed in accidents.

Still Arthur remained hopeful, firing off daily dispatches to all sections of the line and awaiting his operational commanders' signed receipts to confirm they had seen his instructions. Otherwise he rode out personally, inspecting conditions, ordering fresh equipment for the troops, urging them on to success. On one occasion they came close to achieving it. A group of about fifty Tasmanians was discovered bedding down just before nightfall, but instead of watching in silence and awaiting a large body of reinforcements, the small British contingent led by a buffoon called Walpole charged in, guns blazing. The Aborigines fled in panic, leaving two dead and two others to be captured – a token victory instead of the conclusive round-up the assailants had anticipated.

Towards the end of November, as the Black Line closed in on its final destination, Arthur called for a palisade of sharpened stakes to be erected as a further means of controlling Aboriginal movements, while settlers living in the vicinity of the Tasman Peninsula were asked to keep indoors lest they frighten the hostile tribes as they stampeded into the trap. 'The providence of God will, I trust, crown the measure with success,' wrote the governor as he looked for one last divine blessing.[36] Others also found their leader's sense of optimism catching and even the most cynical of its critics started to speculate on the size of the bag. As the men congealed into a last triumphant procession, they rushed to their terminal point at Eaglehawk Neck, the spot where the peninsula joined the mainland, to survey a landscape devoid of human movement. They had trapped not a single Aborigine.

To explain the failure the colonists fell back on their old favourite, the conspiracy theory. The Black Line had been infiltrated by white traitors who had assisted the Tasmanians in making a cunning escape. What few would recognise was that during the seven weeks the cordon had blundered its way across thousands of square kilometres of impossible terrain, blazing away at stray livestock or kangaroos, the Tasmanians had simply melted into the densest thickets and slipped back through.

Yet perhaps not all had been in vain, for many of those involved seemed to get their just deserts. For example, one of the two Aborigines captured during the operation later managed to make his escape, leaving just a single boy in British hands. Walpole, meanwhile, the man who had led the abortive raid upon the sleeping band of Aborigines, began to lark around after the march, urging one of those with captured weapons to try his hand at spear throwing. The novice duly obliged and hit his target, Walpole himself, full in the knee. Arthur also, although appropriately evasive in his concluding dispatch to London on the campaign's achievements, had shown the colony the depth of his concern for their plight, while the £30,000 (some put it as high as £70,000) spent on the operation amounted to a life-saving injection into the economy of the island's interior. Moreover, the Black Line had enjoyed some success, the whole of the settled areas of the colony having now been cleared of the remaining aggressive bands.[37]

In fact, Arthur's great game drive marked the beginning of the end of hostilities throughout the whole of the island. For the indigenous people of Tasmania, their war of resistance had run its natural course, and was now becoming almost impossible to maintain in the face of their wider demographic collapse. For the colonists, too, the period of all-out aggression was coming to a close. Although for many settlers the path of violent extermination had never lost its irresistible appeal, their governor was looking for a radically different answer to the 'black problem'. Even as his intended military solution reached its farcical anti-climax at Eaglehawk Neck, the agent of this alternative approach was already at work.

His name was George Augustus Robinson, a hard-working and public-spirited soul of humble background. Of a deeply religious temperament, he was a strict Calvinist and predestinarian, who shared with his patron, Arthur, a conviction that in his efforts for the Tasmanians he had been divinely inspired. 'I have reason to know,' he once wrote in his voluminous diaries, 'that the work in which I am engaged is the work of God.'[38] Robinson is one of the few Europeans in the brief but tragic period of their contact with indigenous Tasmanians who genuinely cared for them and strove for their well-being. An individual more distant from the maniacal violence of bushranger and convict stockman it is hard to imagine. And yet this much, ironically, he shared with the worst of them: all his efforts, however well intentioned they may have been, moved the Aborigines of Tasmania inexorably closer to the abyss of extinction.

10

The Conciliator

A t first glance George Robinson didn't seem the material from which heroes are generally made. A London builder by trade, in 1830 he was forty-two years old, although it is symptomatic of his obscure background that the date of his birth was recorded with only approximate accuracy. It is known, however, that the Robinsons had docked in Hobart in January 1824, after a nineteen-week passage from Scotland. A family of seven on arrival, they were blessed with two further additions shortly thereafter, and during six years' residence in the island's capital, the head of the household established himself firmly within the solid, unglamorous world of its lower middle class, becoming secretary of the Van Diemen's Land Seaman's Friend and Bethel Union Society, a committee member of the Auxiliary Bible Society and a founder and first chair of the Van Diemen's Land Mechanics' Institute.

His career as a prominent figure in the island's early history started in 1829, when Governor Arthur appointed him as the guardian of a small group of already captive Aborigines. This band of about twenty-five lived on Bruny, the long island that snakes around Tasmania's southern shore and which forms, with the Tasman Peninsula opposite, the two jaws either side of the gaping inlet leading towards Hobart Harbour. It was Robinson's initial project to bring the word of God to this dwindling remnant. However, he took the step, exceptional for his time and place, of finding out as much as he could about the island's original inhabitants. After several months acquiring the rudiments of their language and their customs, Robinson realised what had previously been glimpsed only by the first European visitors to

Tasmania and was now long obliterated by years of bloody conflict.

The Aborigines, far from warranting the 'black demon' image general amongst British settlers, were by and large a peaceful people, even intelligent and capable of extraordinary adaptation. Like very few of his fellow countrymen at that time, Robinson could also see the fundamental links between the atrocities committed by his own nation in the nineteenth century and those inflicted by the *conquistadores* on indigenous Americans of the sixteenth: 'The cruelties exercised upon them beggars all description,' Robinson wrote of his Aboriginal charges, 'and their sufferings have been far greater than those of the Indians at the hands of the Spaniards.'[1]

During his period on Bruny, Robinson also recorded touching scenes of family affection amongst the Tasmanians, their loving care for their children, and their deep sense of mourning as relatives and spouses succumbed to the European illnesses decimating their number. 'They resemble,' he noted in his diary, 'the gem in its rough unfashioned state which requires only the artisan's skill to develop its true lustre and expose to light the rich qualities with which it abounds.'[2]

In that sentence its author revealed many of the personal attributes which distinguish his work for the Tasmanian Aborigines. On the one hand, Robinson was the most important advocate for and sympathetic champion of their rights, doing more to change settler attitudes towards them and to improve their position than any other individual. He also acquired a greater understanding of their culture and lifestyle, and it is to his facile if prolix pen that we owe much of our limited knowledge of the island's original inhabitants.

Yet the sentence also offers us a glimpse of that egotism and self-righteousness that could make Robinson so irritating to his contemporaries, and rendered his work for the Tasmanians of such ambiguous value. For when he spoke of that artisan whose skill would reveal the Aborigines' fine lustre, Robinson was thinking largely of himself. On another occasion, when confronted by a settler who maintained that Tasmanians were incapable of cultural improvement, he fumed, 'Fine sophistry truly! Will a soil, however rich, produce its grain without the aid of a husbandman?'[3] Elsewhere he confirmed the implied identities of both artisan and husbandman. 'It is no small honour conferred on me,' he wrote, 'that I should be the individual appointed to ameliorate the conditions of this hapless race and to emancipate them from bondage.'[4] During his Bruny period, Robinson developed an image of himself leading these poor benighted souls Moses-like out of the wilderness and into the bosom of European civilisation and the light of God's love. In fact, this is what he eventually managed to accomplish. Yet once they were under his control, the predestinarian's assurance of 'certain certainties' made him obsessively stubborn in his treatment of them and blind to their most obvious needs.

Tasmania's governor, however, of similar religious convictions to Robinson, could see the obvious merit in his employee's enlarged scheme to bring in all the remaining Tasmanians. In 1830 Arthur appointed him 'Conciliator' to the Aborigines. In October of that year, as the Black Line stumbled towards its final destination, Robinson completed the first of his epic journeys across the island in search of the remaining bands. Accompanied by a dozen Aborigines, including some of his most faithful from the Bruny community, and six convicts, he trekked for ten months across much of western Tasmania.

Although on this occasion he did not manage to bring any of the tribes back with him to Hobart, Robinson was perfecting his art of gentle persuasion. He contacted many of the groups, learnt of their movements, their numbers, of their appalling treatment at the hands of stockmen and sealers – in fact, his diaries are a vital source on many of the atrocities. He also recognised the need to develop the confidence of these suspicious people by advancing into their midst completely unarmed and without any other European companions. Once amongst them he would play his flute to soothe their troubled minds. At times this trusting approach was tested to the limits, and on one occasion he was forced to flee for his life.

It is a measure of the man's extraordinary faith and indefatigable energy that having returned from his first long period of exploration in October 1830, within a matter of days Robinson turned around and marched back into the Tasmanian bush. This time he was away for a whole twelve months. The conditions were appalling. On occasions his supplies failed completely and he and his Aboriginal helpers were forced to live for days off shellfish. As well as their food, Robinson shared the Aborigines' lice and fleas, while his body was covered with boils from a debilitating skin infection.

The ground they covered was often uncharted. At times he was forced to wade through half a metre of snow and at others he complained of travelling 'for days through the impervious forest, worn out with fatigue in scrambling over rocks and dead timber'. Razor-sharp grasses entwined his body like ropes, and the endless stretches of brambles and vines entangled his legs.[5] These conditions quickly shredded his clothes so that often his only garments were the empty sacks used to carry their supplies.

But Robinson, with his flute and his Bruny friends and his unshakeable conviction, was starting to succeed where the Black Line's thousands had failed. By 1831 he had persuaded fifty-four Tasmanians to accept the hospitality of the British authorities. Within twelve months this figure had more than doubled. Throughout 1833 and 1834 he continued his long treks in the outback, and on each occasion he was accompanied home by a handful of the final holdouts. The regular arrival of these processions in Hobart were often the moments when many of the gathered settlers obtained their first glimpse of these dark enemies of civilisation. Yet rather than occasions for fear and suspicion, the mood often seemed celebratory. Like prize exhibits the Aborigines were asked to show their skill with a spear or a waddy, or the island's journalists crowded around for an interview, and the procession's historical importance was commemorated in scraps of doggerel:

> They came; sad remnant of a bygone race,
> Surviving Mourners of a Nation's dead.
> Proscribed inheritors of rights which trace
> Their claims coeval with the world! They tread
> Upon their nation's tomb![6]

By 1835 the sad remnant that Robinson had tracked and then brought under British control totalled 195. This was all that remained of the several thousands who had been living when Europeans first landed on Tasmanian shores. As many as 700 are thought to have died violent deaths during the Black War – four Aborigines for each of the settlers killed. The rest had succumbed to introduced disease, and to the wider consequences of European settlement – the loss of their traditional diet, the impact of eviction, the dislocation of tribal life, and the strains of a fugitive existence. More than 230 women and children had been abducted, often by settlers for use as domestic slaves. And apart from some of these surviving captives and the females and their mixed-race children living with sealers in the Bass Strait, not a single indigenous Tasmanian remained at large throughout the island. The Conciliator had completed his task.

★

Before going on to examine the consequences of Robinson's efforts and their impact upon the people he so wished to help, it is valuable to step back from the specific details of his career to consider the conciliator in a more general sense, as a recurrent figure in Europe's 500-year confrontation with tribal society. Relations between these communities have often been profoundly influenced by outstanding figures who managed somehow to bridge their two worlds. In each of the four historical settings treated in the present book there are individuals bearing some relationship to Robinson.

In the story of the Apache's dispossession, General George Crook and his more scholarly subordinate, Captain John Bourke, were the two men who probably did more than any other to defeat the tribe militarily. Yet, paradoxically, they were also the individuals who showed most understanding of the Apache, who later championed their cause and earned the respect of the tribe. Equally, in the history of Germany's subjugation of South West African tribes, the roles of military conqueror and political mediator combined once again, if to a lesser degree, in the person of the colonial governor, Major Theodor Leutwein. These three Europeans, as a consequence of long association with tribal peoples, and through seeking the detailed racial information to fulfil their European military and political objectives, actually developed a level of sympathy for the old enemy.

However, none of these men combined that rich empathy for indigenous people and impassioned criticism of European behaviour that were so powerfully expressed by the sixteenth-century Spanish cleric, Bartolomé de Las Casas. Known as 'the Apostle of the Indians', Las Casas is inseparable from the image of the tribal champion. If that figure is a recurrent archetype in Europe's confrontation with pre-industrial societies, then Las Casas is its ideal Platonic form. Even Robinson, with all his ineradicable pacifism and Christian charity towards Aborigines, is only a pale version of his Spanish predecessor.

Born in Seville in 1474, Las Casas was immersed from childhood in the ethos of Spain's New World adventure. He had originally gone out to Hispaniola in 1502 and after being ordained as a priest had participated in the conquest of Cuba with Cortés' erstwhile friend and employee, Diego Velázquez. For his services Las Casas had received a number of the island's indigenous inhabitants and for a time lived as an *encomendero*. However, in 1514 the prosperous priest and landowner underwent a Damascene conversion on the issue of Spain's American empire, and until his death in 1566 Las Casas remained a vigorous champion of indigenous people. His publications, such as *A Short Account of the Destruction of The Indies*, constituted a devastating exposé of Spanish methods and were controversial bestsellers throughout Europe in the sixteenth and seventeenth centuries.

While Las Casas is the foremost example, there are also a number of other well known historical figures who, though peripheral to the four histories treated here, may help clarify the characteristics of this European model. One good candidate and a close parallel to George Robinson and his earlier work for Tasmanian Aborigines was the Anglo-Irish woman Daisy Bates. In the first decades of this century, Bates worked tirelessly amongst the indigenous people on the Australian continent, evangelising and offering basic medical care at a time when these communities were widely believed to be as doomed as the Tasmanians.

An even better known figure is David Livingstone, whose career in nineteenth-century Africa exhibits many of the characteristics of the tribal champion. Another name that might be included is the Anglo-Irish consular official Roger Casement, who was central to the exposure of the nineteenth-century atrocities in the Belgian Congo and of similar twentieth-century scandals in the Amazonian forests of Peru. In our own period, individuals like the British explorer Wilfred Thesiger and the American writer and traveller Peter Matthiessen have been powerful moral advocates for tribal peoples.

All of these individuals reflect a cluster of distinctive qualities that are recurrent in the conciliator. One essential characteristic (visible in all with perhaps the sole exception of Matthiessen) is their ultimate loyalty to the parent rather than their adopted culture. Thus, despite genuine and often heartfelt efforts to understand and defend tribal communities, they seldom doubted the moral superiority of the civilisation of which they themselves were often glowing examples. Even Las Casas, although intent on justice, worked within the overall European framework of tribal dispossession and ethnocide. Typically, while he abhorred the cruelties inflicted by his fellow countrymen, he never questioned the Spanish right to possession of the Americas. Nor did he challenge the orthodox Christian view that the conversion of native Americans was a necessary and laudable objective. In his struggle to alleviate the sufferings of enslaved Indians, Las Casas also countenanced the importation and use of black Africans as a morally acceptable alternative, suggesting the narrow basis of his tribal sympathies.

Similarly, Robinson, although he had wished to spare the

Tasmanians the violence and inhumanity of the outback colonists, in the end had done no less than the very worst of them. For while some of these torturers had used Aboriginal body parts as personal trinkets, Robinson had converted the entire remnant of the Tasmanian people into a possession to be controlled and directed at the whim of colonial officialdom.

Sometimes their well-intentioned efforts were simply subverted by more hard-line superiors. Thus, once they had defeated sections of the Apache, Crook and Bourke instituted an enlightened regime on the Indian reservations of partial self-administration and economic self-sufficiency, but these policies were systematically undermined by corrupt Indian Agency staff bent on personal profit. Similarly in South West Africa, where hostilities eventually broke out between the Germans and the black African tribes, Theodor Leutwein found himself and his patient policies of basic co-existence replaced by one of the most odious figures in colonial Africa, General von Trotha, whose fundamentalist approach to racial issues prefigured the ethos of the Third Reich.

Often the very fact of a particular conciliator's involvement in conflict resolution and his renown as a proponent of humane measures could lend a degree of acceptability to a European policy whose overall intention was far more sinister. What has been written of Bartolomé de Las Casas – 'for many, both in Spain and beyond, his presence seems, somehow, to redeem the inescapable complicity of all Europe in the Spanish conquests' – could be extended to a number of the figures named above.[7] Often the individual's reputation and his relationship with his own European community became more important than anything actually achieved on behalf of the tribal people he so publicly championed.

This fame is itself worthy of further scrutiny. Typically, the conciliator figure who associated with tribespeople and became conversant with their lifestyle provided his own community with their own version of the 'savage' and gave them vicarious access to the untrammelled power of the primitive's world. However, a European audience's fascination with this type of savage manqué was an emotion very distinct from any genuine sympathy for the true primitive. John Bourke expressed these ideas perfectly when he wrote of his superior:

He became skilled in the language of 'signs' and trails and so perfectly conversant with all that is concealed in the great book of

Nature that, in the mountains at least, he might readily take rank as being as much an Indian as the Indian himself . . . But while General Crook was admitted [as such] even by the Indians, [he] never ceased to be a gentleman. Much as he might live among savages, he never lost the right to claim for himself the best that civilisation and enlightenment had to bestow.[8]

Bourke required his readers to see his hero as more Indian than the Indians, reassuring them simultaneously that Crook was always a Christian gentleman. The idea that one of their own could go native, embrace all the elemental hardships and primitive skills of the savage, and then return, is a notion of perennial appeal to Europeans, in part because it fulfils their expectations of inherent superiority. In the same way, the audiences for the books and films of British tribesman Wilfred Thesiger are awed by his capacity to overcome the terrors of Arabia's Empty Quarter, like the nomadic Bedu, or to endure the discomforts of his Samburu mud shack, but then find subtle comfort in his exchange of all these trials for the Victorian elegance of his Chelsea flat. Thesiger, like Crook, is the aborigine fit to be a member of the gentleman's club.

In order to explain the heroic status often accorded to the conciliator archetype we touch upon an issue fundamental to Western representations of their clash with barbarism ever since the time of the ancient Greeks. Europe had always seen itself as a small star of moral light surrounded by an unfathomed universe of darkness. Or it was akin to the ego, a vulnerable core of rational faculties, beset by the tumultuous urges of the unconscious. The imbalance of forces implicit in this form of representation was critical to Europe's self image. It meant that it was always waging a war, not of offence, but of justifiable and honourable defence. European efforts were constantly outnumbered and against the odds: an heroic last stand of colonial pioneers, a small laager of Christians, a settlers' wagon train encircled against the Indian war party or the African impi.

It is this paradigmatic image, incidentally, that explains so much about Europe's vocabulary for tribal society – 'mobs', 'hordes', 'multitudes', 'infesting', 'marauding' and 'swarming', to give just a sample – which connote the ideas of formlessness and uncontrollability. It also tells us much about the endless appeal for Europeans of Cortés' exploits in Mexico. The *Caudillo*'s minuscule conquering army is the military example par excellence of this paradigm.

However, the conciliator is its most potent moral or spiritual version. By going literally as a solitary figure amongst the heathen horde, he epitomises Europe's heroic relationship to tribal society. Some of them, especially figures like Daisy Bates, Livingstone, and Las Casas, have been represented as saintly, Franciscan individuals selflessly devoted to the moral uplift of lesser beings. A description of Bates' work will serve as representative of these wider attitudes towards the conciliator:

> The race on the fringe of the [Australian] continent has been there about a hundred years, and stands for Civilization; the race in the interior has been there no man knows how long, and stands for Barbarism. Between them a woman has lived in a little white tent for more than twenty years, watching over these people for the sake of the Flag, a woman alone, the solitary spectator of a vanishing race. She is Daisy Bates, one of the least known and one of the most romantic figures in the British Empire.
>
> . . . She has given her life and her heart to this dying race . . . She has done it for the love of humanity and for England.[9]

An island of Christian civilisation engulfed by barbarism, the conciliator represented an inversion of Kurtz in Joseph Conrad's *The Heart of Darkness* (which, significantly, was inspired in part by Roger Casement and his career in the Belgian Congo). Instead of being absorbed by the darkness like the novelist's fictional character, the moral light of the saintly European radiated outwards to illuminate the heathen.

Before returning fully to consider Robinson's work for the Tasmanian Aborigines, we should consider one last important aspect of the conciliator figure. Invariably, as a man like Robinson or Crook or Leutwein travelled outwards to explore primitive society, he often encountered his own tribal counterparts journeying inwards to fathom the encroaching colonial culture.

These tribal figures, just as much pioneers and bridge-builders, frequently have a status even more ambiguous than their European equivalent. For their collaboration with the colonists often hastened the disintegration of tribal order and its assimilation into the imperial structure. They were part betrayer, part culture hero. And just as the

Spaniards' early conquests in America have thrown up the classic example of the European conciliator in Las Casas, so has it given us the model for the tribal go-between, in La Malinche or Doña Marina. This remarkable woman, who served as the Spaniards' interpreter, was so completely identified with Cortés, and he with her, that the *Caudillo* was known to the Mexica as Malinche.

Moreover, the cross-cultural double act that they performed so brilliantly in Mexico is a partnership replicated in each of this book's quartet of histories. In Apacheria, Crook and Bourke enjoyed the vital services of a number of Native American guides, most notably an individual Apache called Tsoe or 'Peaches', without whom they would never have discovered the tribe's inaccessible retreats in the Mexican Sierra Madre. In South West Africa, Theodor Leutwein exploited the Christian upbringing and European leanings of the Herero's paramount chief, Samuel Maharero, to exert a devastating leverage upon his tribe. And finally, in Tasmania Robinson was able to influence the remnant tribes of the island's Aborigines only because of the presence of his Bruny aides, one of the most important of whom was Truganini.

Truganini is the most famous of all the Tasmanians, largely for her reputation as the last full-blooded member. She also had a personal history befitting her representative status. As a girl she had seen her own mother stabbed to death by settlers, then as a young woman had herself been raped and forced to witness the murder of her betrothed. They and a third Tasmanian had accepted a boat ride out to Bruny Island offered by some sealers. During the course of the journey these men threw the two Aboriginal males overboard and when her intended partner attempted to climb back in, they chopped off his hands and left him to drown.

Remarkably, given such experiences, Truganini in her prime had a reputation as a vivacious and attractive member of Robinson's Bruny troupe, and was known to other Europeans as Princess Lalla Rookh in honour of her good looks. In fact, it was widely rumoured that the Conciliator had himself had a sexual relationship with her. More certain was the report that when a band of Tasmanians had physically attacked Robinson, she had helped save his life.

The fact that Truganini had already adapted to captivity and to aspects of European culture singled her out as a key member in the brave new world Robinson now planned for his Tasmanian remnant. The

Conciliator's programme centred on the Aborigines' complete separation from the worst effects of white settlement and then their exposure to a regime that would prepare them intellectually and spiritually for Tasmania's settler society. Although the idea of a mainland reserve had been floated, it was soon exchanged for a plan to confine them to one of the smaller offshore islands. Even Robinson, who had gained the fullest insight into their lifestyle and their deep bond with Tasmania's physical environment, had no objection to this kind of exile. As early as 1831 the Committee for Aboriginal Affairs had reported his opinion that if they were located on one of the Bass Strait islands

> they would not feel themselves imprisoned there, or pine away in consequence of the restraint, nor would they wish to return to the mainland, or regret their inability to hunt and roam about in the manner they had previously done on this island. They would be able to fish, dance, sing and throw spears and amuse themselves in their usual way.[10]

That final sentence, which reduced the hunter-gatherer life of the Aborigines to a series of meaningless frivolities, is symptomatic of Robinson's paternalistic vision of his Tasmanians as essentially child-like and helpless. However, even more incredible, in view of his wide experience of the Tasmanian lifestyle, was his willingness to support a scheme recommended by the Committee. In February 1831 they were unanimous in the opinion that Gun Carriage, an island not even three kilometres by two, would be a suitable repository for the entire Aboriginal population, and this was at a time when their assumed number was possibly as high as 700.[11]

Fortunately, the eventual choice for Robinson's scheme was Flinders Island, almost seventy kilometres long and between twenty and thirty kilometres wide. For the Tasmanians its size was its one main asset, the game populations allowing for a partial resumption of their traditional lifestyle. For the British, Flinders' one unimpeachable virtue was its distance from the mainland: the Tasmanians were now completely exiled from the island they had occupied for thousands of years.

But Robinson intended to distract his wards from their banishment with constant activity. They were requested, for example, to participate in the assembly of nine communal huts that formed the heart of the Flinders establishment. These nine dormitories had to hold only

123 Aborigines, the rest having already succumbed to what Robinson termed 'the soft hand of civilisation'. Many of their children had also been separated out and sent to a boarding school in Hobart, where their rates of mortality were as high as their parents' on Flinders. Aboriginal deaths in both institutions meant that few families were ever reunited.

As preparation for European society, the Aborigines underwent baptism and christening and were each given a new European name. Many of these were so absurd – Alexander, Ajax, Columbus, Achilles, Bonaparte, Romeo, Princess Cleopatra, Queen Elizabeth and Juliet are just a sample – that they might easily be misconstrued as symptoms of a deep cynicism underlying the Flinders project, had Robinson's Christian sincerity not been so well established and the renaming been so popular with the Tasmanians themselves.[12] For all these grandiose titles, Robinson's social ambition for his charges was far more modest. Now known as the Commandant rather than the Conciliator, he imposed a regime of regular lessons in the scriptures, arithmetic, geography, needlework and cooking and of regular inspections of their clothes, underwear, bedding and sleeping quarters.

All of this stressed a desire to convert the neolithic hunter-gatherers into good *petit bourgeois* Victorians. The Tasmanians even had a police force, a regular market, a communal fund derived from their harvest of bird and mammal skins, and their own newspaper. Half a sheet of foolscap, twopence a copy and its proceeds divided between the editors, the *Flinders Island Weekly Chronicle*, like the other measures, was meant to reinforce the habits of civilised life, of industry and an interest in the acquisition of property. Most of the time, however, it informed its readership of the achievements of the Commandant. 'Now my friends,' ran one article,

> you see that the Commandant is so kind to you he gives you everything that you want when you were in the bush the Commandant had to leave his friends and go into the bush and he brought you out of the bush because he felt for you he knowed the white man was shooting you and now he has brought you to Flinders Island where you get every things and when you are ill tell the Doctor immediately and you get relief.[13]

More accurately, the Tasmanians had everything except decent water, adequate provisions, sanitary quarters, good health and the will to live.

Doctor Barnes, who ministered to their every need, admitted that they 'pine away, not from any positive disease, but from a disease that they call "homesickness". They die from a disease of the stomach too, which comes on entirely from a desire to return to their own country.'[14] There were also other problems. The lashing winds of the Bass Strait whipped the sand into their eyes, causing frequent opthalmia. Worse still, the Aborigines, accustomed previously to going naked, were now obliged to adopt European dress in conformity with the Commandant's notions of propriety. Unfortunately these cast-offs often got soaking wet in the course of their outdoor lifestyle and they frequently neglected to remove them. The drenched garments then increased their susceptibility to pulmonary infection, European colds and influenza.

The truth was that Flinders was a death trap, inflicting losses upon them no less severe than the Black War. Governor Arthur sensed that this was the case, but now mortality rates were exclusively black and, even more satisfactory, the dying was well away from view. 'Even if the Aborigines pine away,' he admitted, 'it is better that they should meet with their deaths in that way, whilst every kindness is manifested towards them, than that they should fall a sacrifice to the inevitable consequence of their continued acts of outrage upon the white inhabitants.'[15] It was classic British humbug. For Arthur, the key problem was not the fact of their deaths, nor was it a question of seeking to stem the mortality. What was important was *how* they died. Falling victim to well-meaning British ignorance, rather than the settlers' mindless violence, meant that His Majesty's imperial officers were absolved of any complicity.

To their eternal credit, some British settlers recognised this sanctimonious hypocrisy for what it was. Visiting the establishment in 1836, Major Thomas Ryan, the Commandant at Launceston, thought the Aborigines were being deliberately exterminated:

> If it is the wish of the Government to propagate the species it is our bounden duty to provide all means that are in our possession for the accomplishment of so desirable an end – if not, I tremble for the consequences, the race of Tasmania, like the last of the Mohicans will pine away and be extinct in a quarter of a century. [They live in] an artificial society where most of their traditional food sources have been hunted out, and living in damp, poorly ventilated huts with impure water and inadequate provisions.[16]

*

166

Even Robinson, in words that mingled a perverse optimism with sub-lime understatement, admitted that 'The only drawback in the estab-lishment was the great mortality among them. But those who did survive,' he added, 'were now happy, contented and useful members of society.'[17] By 1839, only five years after the Tasmanians' arrival on Flinders, fifty-nine of them had died.

Nor were they the only ones to abandon hope. In the previous year Robinson had been offered the post of Aboriginal Protector on the Australian mainland at £500 a year, double his salary as Tasmania's Conciliator. When he accepted the appointment he imagined he would be able to persuade the authorities to let him remove all the Tasmanians with him. Unfortunately, the proposal caused deep appre-hension on the mainland and the request was refused. However, the Commandant was allowed before leaving to select fifteen of his favourite Aborigines, including Truganini, to accompany him to mainland Australia, thereby robbing the Flinders establishment of its most articulate and acculturated champions. In exchange he left one final inadvertent gift. The Spanish influenza he brought with him on the occasion of his last visit killed a further eight Tasmanians. Only sixty now remained.[18]

The Commandant's personal departure saw the end of his highly structured regime on Flinders and in the more relaxed atmosphere introduced by his successor, the Tasmanians were able to resume aspects of their own culture, such as hunting, the use of ochre and ceremonial dances. But none of this compensated the Aborigines for the loss of their true home.

As early as 1837 the *Flinders Island Weekly Chronicle* had carried an article that read: 'The bible says some or all shall be saved but I am much afraid none of us will be alive by and by and then as nothing but sick men amongst us. Why don't the blackfellows pray to the King to get us away from this place.'[19] British visitors to Flinders recorded how, on clear days, a number of the women would climb up and sit on a suitable promontory and gaze longingly across the water towards Tasmania. In 1838 they had petitioned for their return to that distant land blurred by the sea haze. But the whites who now occupied their island shuddered at the thought of black savages once more in their midst. Having captured and neutered the wildest, most threatening predator in the Tasmanian environment, they were determined never to let it go free again.

Despite their unyielding stance on this issue, five peaceful years of

Aboriginal exile had done much to alter the mood amongst the settlers. Gone was the earlier sense of relief and gratitude and their willingness to see the Tasmanians removed at any price. A new penny-pinching attitude had now set in amongst the colony and a board of inquiry on the Flinders establishment imposed a fifty per cent reduction in expenditure. The slovenly good-for-nothing inmates were to be made to work for the charity so generously bestowed upon them, while the staff were reduced from an original forty-three to just sixteen. And yet, ironically, the presence of the families of these official personnel ensured that Europeans still outnumbered the decaying rump of Tasmania's indigenous inhabitants, even on their windswept, tear-stained island-prison.

11

The Last Tasmanian

lthough British missionaries had initially refused to work amongst the Tasmanians when they had been seen as godless savages in the wilderness, by the time they were reduced to the condition of domestic pets, the colonial church establishment had come to patronise Robinson's work on Flinders as an expression of Christian charity in action. The Bishop of Tasmania had himself gone to visit the island to comfort the natives in their exile. However, on the occasion of one of his last journeys in the Bass Strait, the bishop found the Flinders establishment much altered since his previous trip. 'Nearly eleven years have passed,' he wrote, 'since I landed on the selfsame rocks . . .'

> Then, the beach was covered with the aborigines, who greeted their kind and beloved benefactor with yells of delight; capering and gesticulating with movements of exuberant wild joy. . . Now all this is still. It was painful to witness the scene of ruin in the once neat and well-ordered settlement. Desolation stared me in the face, wherever the eye was turned: the comfortable house of the super-intendent, for instance, was rapidly falling into decay; the gardens well nigh rooted up; the range of buildings in which the aborigines were formerly hutted, untenanted, broken and tumbling down.[1]

In 1847, seven years before the prelate's melancholy visit, the Tasmanian government had acceded to Aboriginal demands to be returned to the mainland. Provision had finally been made for a settle-ment in Oyster Cove, just forty kilometres outside Hobart. The event had initially brought blood-curdling prophecies from some quarters on the consequence of re-releasing such savage beasts amongst them. However the diminished band that completed the journey to the mainland was such a pitiful spectacle that these anxieties were soon laid to rest. By 1847, only forty-seven had survived the years of exile – fifteen men, twenty-two women and ten children, with an average age of forty-two. Most suffered from chronic respiratory complaints, four were enormously obese, one was senile, one blind and another disabled by acute arthritis.[2]

Initially the Tasmanians themselves had looked towards the return as a moment for renewal and approached the event in a spirit of high optimism. But these hopes were to be short-lived. In reality the scenes of desolation witnessed by the bishop at the abandoned Flinders settlement were quickly reconstituted at the new Oyster Cove site. The place had originally been an old convict colony, but even that had been removed on the grounds of its swampy and insanitary conditions, and the Aborigines were soon infected by its melancholy atmosphere. Their garden plots fell into disuse, while the wooden huts that had been built for them were steadily trashed, as their inmates abandoned them one by one to the elements, the damp, their fleas and other vermin.

The Tasmanians had resumed aspects of their traditional culture and their dancing was initially a big attraction for the surrounding communities of woodcutters and settlers. But in time the men, bored by the institutionalised existence, preferred to abscond into nearby Hobart to drink in its taverns. The women also, wearied by the superintendent's attempts at Christian instruction or his wife's routine inspections for cleanliness, began to sell their clothes or bedding to the surrounding Europeans in exchange for other forms of stimulation, like alcohol and tobacco. Eventually some of the old women had only their dogs to keep them warm at nights. When they ran out of possessions completely, they got their booze by selling themselves.

Oyster Cove's one major advance over Flinders was the opportunity for the authorities to make even larger reductions in the budget. But its atmosphere of gradual moral decay brought sharp retribution from British officialdom. Whereas initially both the colony's governor and bishop had been accustomed to call at the site, these dignitaries, disgusted at Aboriginal ingratitude, sent proxies or ceased to visit altogether. By the time J.E. Calder saw the establishment, its inmates had become 'nothing better than a horde of lazy, filthy, drunken, listless barbarians; and in everything except the practice of theft,' he added in a fresh access of racism, 'a good deal the inferior of the gypsy.'[3]

Inexorably, the Tasmanian population continued to fall. By 1851 there was an ageing community of just thirty left at Oyster Cove, and no one seemed exempt from its pervasive mood of hopelessness. First the wife of the kindly superintendent died, then Robert Clark himself, robbing the Tasmanians of their last link with the era of George Robinson. For Clark had been Robinson's catechist on Flinders and had retained the Commandant's genuine concern to help and bring civilisation to the Aborigines. However, with his departure, Oyster Cove became no more than a ration depot for the last dregs. 'There are five old men,' ran one report, 'and nine old women living at the Oyster Cove Station – uncleanly, unsober, unvirtuous, unenergetic, and irreligious, with a past character for treachery, and no record of one *noble* action, the race is fast falling away and its utter extinction will be hardly regretted.'[4]

By the time the island had become a self-governing colony and officially changed its name from Van Diemen's Land to Tasmania, its indigenous people had been so reduced that their history had become a matter of individual biographies. Two of these cameos illustrate the blend of misdirected kindness and overt prejudice that had shaped British attitudes towards the captured Aborigines and now helped steer their final remnants into oblivion.

The first concerned Walter George Arthur, who provided a rare flicker of genuine hope for his people. At ten years old, this child of the stone-age had been placed in the orphan school in Hobart. There he had quickly grasped the conquerors' language, developed as a scholar in their exotic spheres of learning and then made incredible adaptations to the alien society. However, what would have been in his own culture a perfectly natural relationship with his eventual spouse, Mary Ann, was viewed as moral turpitude by his European masters. This ended Walter's chances of becoming a catechist like Robert Clark and he went firstly to Flinders, then on to the mainland with George Robinson, where he acquired experience as a stockman and drover. On his return with Mary Ann in 1842, the acculturated couple became leading members of the Flinders community, speaking out against poor rations and the lack of wages for Aboriginal labour.

At Oyster Cove, Walter and Mary Ann eschewed the hovels occupied by their compatriots and erected a three-roomed cottage, furnished and carpeted with donations from well-wishers. A British writer visiting the couple noted the large family bible that had pride of place in the modest, well-scrubbed dwelling. The master of the house was known to keep himself informed on colonial affairs with a regular newspaper. The couple also bought and managed a small-holding of three acres, to which they added a further eight through a government grant. All of this signalled their desire to be accepted by white society. If ever there were a need to rebut the widespread settlers' belief that Tasmanians were trapped in a developmental backwater, incapable of intellectual progress, then Walter and Mary Ann's extraordinary odyssey, out of a neolithic existence into a nineteenth-century European lifestyle, provides compelling evidence.

Equally, if one wished to expose how far colonial Europe, despite its violent insistence on cultural assimilation by tribal society, remained in essence a closed system, then Walter's ultimate fate is similarly instructive. European imperialists had always force-fed defeated tribals like Walter on a diet of their own higher Christian civilisation. But whenever such converts attempted to journey deeper into that vaunted superiority, as Walter and Mary Ann had done with their modest application to the government for a convict servant, they invariably ran into that impermeable membrane which held them at the insignificant outskirts of colonial society. The idea of a couple of Aborigines lording it over a white serf, no matter how degraded that servant might have been in the white tribal hierarchy, was too much for the Tasmanian government to bear and Walter's request was rejected.

His eventual failure to win acceptance by his adopted culture bore heavily on Walter's personality. On the Australian mainland he had acquired another European trait: a taste for alcohol. In 1861, after one heavy bout of drinking, which had become his refuge from the divisions within and prejudices without, Walter and an Aboriginal friend, Jackey Allen, overturned their boat and drowned without trace.[5]

If anything the brief life story of the young Tasmanian girl called Mathinna is even more tragic. As an act of Christian charity, she had been plucked from the desperate milieu of her race by Sir John and Lady Franklin, the island's new governor and his wife. Years of private education gradually wore away the girl's Aboriginal antecedents, exposing an attractive, witty young lady who comfortably held her own in matters of social grace, dancing and singing. Gradually she metamorphosed into a spirited and intelligent debutante identical to her white counterparts in everything, except perhaps the dark colour of her skin and the depressed configuration of her nose. So when the Franklins prepared to return to England at the end of Sir John's years of office and were obliged to abandon the girl they looked upon almost as their own daughter, Mathinna was marooned in a social and racial no-man's-land.

Without her high-society guardians she retained no valid claim to residence at the governor's palace. Nor, however, could she easily adjust to the dilapidated shacks that housed the dwindling remnant of her people, without performing a massive U-turn. For a while her schizoid personality was given refuge in a convict orphan school, but eventually her physical health gave way under the inner strain and she was forced to return to the swampy, verminous comforts of Oyster Cove. There she rapidly became the darling of the sawyers, splitters, slaughtermen, sealers and convicts, selling her formerly pampered body for the few hours' release of an alcoholic stupor. The inevitable end was not long in coming. Mathinna, the former toast of Hobart society, was finally discovered, inebriated and drowned, in a small creek in the bush.[6]

As the Tasmanian race trod the seemingly ineluctable path towards total extinction, their going was flanked by a number of dominant European myths that continued to gain in size and strength long after the moment of oblivion. One of these centred on the idea that the Tasmanians' fate had always been inevitable. One of the reasons contemporary missionaries had been unwilling to work amongst them was a belief that their dwindling number signified 'the wrath of God'. Another Australian cleric declared their disappearance to be by the 'general appointment of Divine Providence'.[7] J.E. Calder, always an accurate barometer of contemporary opinion, spoke of the 'days of their decay' or 'their declension', as if it were a natural process like the law of organic degeneration.[8] Calder also claimed that, far more than the violence of the settlers, it had been internal tribal conflict that had contributed to their decline.[9]

The idea of blaming Aborigines for their own demise also appealed to a correspondent in a Sydney newspaper. In the southern hemisphere, argued this particular authority,

it is discerned that unless the propagation of the species be limited by destruction and abominable customs, their natural indolence must in process of time have reduced them to the horrible necessity of existing as cannibals, as nature is wholly unassisted, and increase of the herb and the animal alike neglected.[10]

In short, it would have been disastrous to have left the hunter-gatherer Aborigine to his own devices: he would simply have ended up eating himself.

In 1914 a more enlightened commentator raised the one issue that would almost certainly have guaranteed Tasmanian survival – inviolate territorial rights over part of the island – but he raised it only to confirm the general thesis of inevitable extinction. 'If they could have been left in possession of a portion of their ancient hunting-grounds,' he wrote, '. . . they might have lived healthily and even happily for a long period of years, though even that would not have averted the final doom.'[11] Even as late as 1968, the author of *The Tasmanians: The Story of a Doomed Race* thought it a 'reasonable assumption that if the island had remained undiscovered and European settlement not attempted until the present day the aborigines of Tasmania would have already become extinct.'[12]

One might think, in view of the Tasmanians' ultimate fate, that this long-held European belief concerning their extinction had some validity. Yet, significantly, exactly the same myth of inevitable extinction has been applied almost worldwide by Europeans to tribal peoples who, in many cases, rudely refused to comply with the fallacy. That same cluster of ideas – mortality through morally neutral factors or the tribe's own inadequacies, leading inexorably to complete disappearance – recurs constantly. William Prescott, for example, writing of both the historical Mexica and the Native Americans in his own nineteenth century, suggested that 'The American Indian has something peculiarly sensitive in his nature.'

He shrinks instinctively from the rude touch of a foreign hand. Even when this foreign influence comes in the form of civilisation, he seems to sink and pine away beneath it. It has been so with the Mexicans. Under the Spanish domination, their numbers have silently melted away. Their energies are broken . . . In their faltering step, and meek and melancholy aspect, we read the sad character of the conquered race.[13]

★

174

In Daisy Bates' elegiac lament for the inhabitants of mainland Australia, *The Passing of the Aborigines*, the very title indicates her core thesis: that these 'Children of the woodland' could 'withstand all the reverses of nature, fiendish droughts and sweeping flood . . . but [they] cannot withstand civilization.' She recounted a stream of personal anecdotes that constantly underlined how Christian kindness 'killed as surely and swiftly as cruelty would have done'.[14] In the works of both Prescott and Bates the vocabulary expressing tribal losses – sink, pine, melt, wither, succumb, fade, waste and pass away – excludes all notions of violence, exploitation or dispossession, as if the process had no more human agency or moral content than the movement of a glacier in response to the forces of gravity.

In a passage by Theodor Leutwein, German governor in South West Africa, one finds all the same classic ingredients of the myth of tribal extinction. The excerpt concerns the death in battle of Hendrik Witbooi, an African leader in the colonial period (and survivor of the Hornkranz massacre described in the opening pages of this book):

> The little Chief had . . . immortalised his name in the history of the South-West African Protectorate. First his obstinate resistance of the mighty power of the German Empire, at the head of a small band of warlike but nevertheless tired and impoverished people; then his loyal support of our [the German] cause for ten years; and, eventually the change and the rebellion – these have bound his name inseparably with the history of the country . . . He was the last national hero of a dying race.[15]

As in the expressions of regret quoted earlier, Leutwein's death-bed lament achieved a more subtle purpose. By showing sympathy for Witbooi's tragic end, Leutwein seemed to embody that spirit of Christian generosity to whose touch tribal society had proved so vulnerable. Yet, at the same time as he appeared to show genuine concern, he managed to reaffirm the myth of unavoidable extinction: 'the last national hero of a dying race'. In so doing, such passages achieved their most important function. Since extinction was pre-ordained by higher forces, Leutwein's European readers could feel absolved from any responsibility for the tribal fate. Moreover, since the tribe had already disappeared, or was doomed shortly to do so, the reader was also excused from ever having to respond further.

From all these passages, we can begin to see the myth's critical importance for Europeans. They could exonerate themselves of any blame for tribal disintegration. They could show Christian concern for this tragic situation, fulfilling a key tenet of their own higher civilisation. And by strategic repetition of the myth they undercut the very basis for any kind of remedial action. The myth of inevitable extinction thus conspired in the fulfilment of its own prophecies.

Lyndall Ryan, in a penetrating study entitled *The Aboriginal Tasmanians*, has argued that for the wider European community in Australia, the extinction of Tasmania's indigenes had an additional value. The island soon became legendary as the one location where Aboriginal extermination was complete. Since this isolated case of genocide was so well known, colonists elsewhere on the continent presumed that white–black relations closer to home had been far more benign. According to Ryan, though, the reverse was the case. 'Tasmania never experienced the levels of poisoning, trappings, ambushes, and massacres that occurred in other parts of Australia.'[16] But the greater notoriety of events in Tasmania served to cover up and deflect attention from the dispossession and slaughter in these other areas, especially in western Victoria, western New South Wales, and most of Queensland.

Notwithstanding Ryan's judgement on the island's role as scapegoat, it is valuable briefly to widen our focus in the southern Pacific, to see how far Tasmania's individual history was in fact representative of the larger pattern of racial conflict in the region.

In Australia itself, Britain's relentless convoys of unwanted humanity – 160,000 criminals were transported in the eighty years after that first armada of 1788 – quickly ensured the colony's expansion. Although there was a steady landward penetration from the original Sydney beachhead, satellite communities also started to appear long distances from the parent colony. Typically, in the late 1820s the townships of Perth, Fremantle and Albany sprang up thousands of kilometres away, on the continent's far south-western shore. Less distant were the settlements established on the south coast, at Melbourne in 1835 and Adelaide a year later. At first these communities also hugged the coasts, then gradually expanded towards Australia's great unfathomed centre. By the 1890s large populations were concentrated in a broad, continuously settled belt between Victoria, New South Wales and southern Queensland. Other pioneers, ever hungry for new cattle and sheep ranges, journeyed and established themselves in the continent's arid heartland.

Throughout all these advances, white settlers had encountered the country's original inhabitants. Yet, like the Tasmanians, mainland Aborigines, for all their millennia of occupation and despite a social, cultural and spiritual life that was inextricably tied to the Australian landscape, seemed oblivious of any notion of land ownership. Since they seemed not to care for these juridical niceties, the white invaders cared on their behalf. In 1836 a New South Wales court decreed that the Aborigines were too few and too disorganised to be considered the owners of the land.[17] Not that the pioneer settlers, many of them freed convicts, were too concerned about Aboriginal legal rights. They wanted land too, and they simply took it. And were they ever required to fight the Aborigines for it, they did.

Throughout the nineteenth century and the early part of the twentieth a low-level frontier war persisted between blacks and whites across most of Australia. The white casualties of this conflict have been estimated at 2,000–2,500. The total number of Aborigines killed is put at 20,000, although this is widely acknowledged as a best-guess figure.[18] The problems involved in any accurate assessment were clearly explained by a nineteenth-century police magistrate, who wrote: 'A murder committed by the blacks is paraded in the papers, and everybody is shocked; but there have been hundreds of cold-blooded murders, perpetrated by the whites on the outskirts of the Colony, which we have never heard of.'[19]

Even if the figure of 20,000 dead understates the true total, acts of direct violence accounted for a relatively small proportion of the pre-1788 Aboriginal population, which is now put at 1,000,000 at least.[20] However, the wider impact of European settlement was catastrophic, inflicting losses on a scale familiar in areas of Spanish-controlled America. Much of this decline was caused by a battery of Western infections – smallpox, influenza, tuberculosis, whooping-cough, measles, even the common cold – that swept in waves through indigenous communities. Venereal disease was another introduced scourge, although the settlers preferred to call it 'black pox', exemplifying the way in which its moral stigma was projected back onto the Aborigines themselves. It was apparently not uncommon for white frontiersmen, should they suspect themselves of being infected by Aboriginal partners of the night before, to shoot the women dead the following morning.[21]

Although diseases were a critical cause of Aboriginal disintegration, as in South America, they also operated within a broader matrix of forces that bore down with cumulative impact. Whites ousted the first Australians from the most productive land, cut them off from access to water resources, slaughtered their main food species, disrupted patterns of migration and pushed them back into the most marginal territory. It was the sheer remoteness of these last sanctuaries that spared them the kind of total collapse witnessed on Tasmania.

Even so, after a hundred years of white contacts, mainland Aborigines numbered as few as 50,000, and slumped again to a final nadir of 30,000 in the 1920s, indicating a ninety-seven per cent decline. The nineteenth-century novelist Anthony Trollope reflected conventional British attitudes throughout most of this demographic catastrophe, when he wrote in the 1870s: 'an increasing number of aborigines in the land, – were it possible that the race should increase, – would be a curse rather than a blessing . . . their doom is to be exterminated; and the sooner that their doom be accomplished, – so that there be no cruelty, – the better will it be for civilization.'[22]

When Trollope travelled in New Zealand later on his Pacific tour he found little evidence there to modify either his belief in aboriginal worthlessness or in their imminent extinction. Writing of the islands' lighter-skinned Polynesian inhabitants, the Maori, whose culture had formerly combined ritual cannibalism with sophisticated agriculture, the English novelist suggested that 'There is scope for poetry in their past history. There is room for philanthropy as to their present condition. But in regard to their future – there is hardly a place for hope.'[23] By the date of Trollope's visit British colonists already heavily outnumbered the original inhabitants. And given the pervasive white conviction that the Maoris' complete demise was pending – the population fell from a pre-contact total of around 240,000 to just 40,000 by 1896 – they actually felt little need to exercise the Victorian novelist's proposed philanthropy.

Despite treaties that had confirmed the Maori in possession of New Zealand's most fertile lands, smooth-talking British officials, grog-sellers and crooked land speculators had whittled away these vast territorial holdings. Wars in the 1860s, partly provoked by British land seizures, gave the pretext for further confiscations once the bitter campaigns had been won. However, some of those punished with loss of territory were not the tribes that had opposed the victors, but those who held the most attractive country. By 1900 in New Zealand's North Island, the Maori estate had been reduced from over 11,000,000 hectares to less than 3,000,000. During the twentieth century, with the 'liberalisation' of trade in Maori property, this was halved again.[24] 'You taught us to pray,' complained their demoralised spokesmen, 'and while we looked up to Heaven you stole our land.'[25]

Land was a major source of antagonism between French colonists and the Kanaks, the indigenous inhabitants of New Caledonia, which will have to stand as our sole example of European methods in the Pacific archipelagos of Micronesia and Melanesia. About 1,700 kilometres north of New Zealand, the main island of New Caledonia, Grande Terre, is part of the latter group and one of the largest islands in the Pacific, almost equal in size to Wales and twice that of Jamaica.

Annexed by the French in 1853, Grande Terre, like Tasmania, was used as a penal colony and governed by a military regime. The indigenous Kanaks, in continuous occupation since about 4000 BC, were soon subjected to repressive legislation that underpinned wholesale alienation of their land and a policy of 'cantonnement', which meant removing and concentrating communities in artificial villages. This social and cultural dislocation had a grievous impact on Kanak numbers, as did Western imports of guns, alcohol and disease. By the 1920s, seventy years after the advent of Christian civilisation, indigenous numbers had fallen to 27,000, less than half the original population.

'When we will have done our task of kind civilized people towards the weak,' spouted a propaganda pamphlet for French imperialism,

> we will then just have to bend to the irreversible natural law which suppresses the population ill-adapted to the struggle for life, and then exploit the lands freed by the extinction of our subjects of black race . . . If the natives keep on leading their careless life they will leave their place to the more energetic races from Europe.[26]

To save the Kanaks from the ill effects of their careless lives, the French imposed forced labour on public works. Another 'kind civilized' measure was the institution of a capitation tax in 1900. Either the native population had to earn the currency to meet their fiscal obligations, or in cases of non-payment they were forced to labour in lieu of money. All of this dovetailed nicely with the discovery of large deposits of nickel. The French mine-owners required a cheap labour force and the landless, poll-taxed Kanaks were primed to supply their demand.[27]

Even towards the end of the twentieth century, the Kanaks remain a minority and an underclass in their own country, with fewer opportunities for work, education or health-care than the largely French expatriate population. Land also divides the black from the white of New Caledonia. Just 1,000 French landowners possess two-thirds of the ground suitable for agriculture, while a tiny élite, representing just five per cent of landowners, own half of all farmland.[28] However, neither the country's land nor its nickel deposits (though they are the third largest in the world) explain the French determination to cling to its South Pacific territories. The principal reasons for their continued imperial presence are strategic.[29]

Like two of the other nuclear powers, the British and the Americans, the French have traditionally used the vast spaces of the Pacific Ocean for the critically important military purpose of testing and observing the effects of their nuclear arsenal. Though it seems a form of exploitation far removed from that which banished the Tasmanians from their island home, the impact of nuclear tests on indigenous Pacific communities has imposed levels of largely unacknowledged suffering and powerlessness comparable to those endured by the Aborigines of Van Diemen's Land.

At Mururoa atoll in French Polynesia, the military authorities have tested more than 150 atomic weapons, 44 of them above ground. These surface explosions were only discontinued in 1975, after international pressure was brought to bear by the white governments of New Zealand and Australia, over 3,000 kilometres away.[30] Indigenous complaints far closer to the explosions were, however, much easier to silence. The dearth of information on the environmental and health effects of its nuclear programme is just one part of the smokescreen of secrecy maintained by the French government. Official data, for instance, on cancer deaths have been unavailable on Tahiti since 1963. Cancer victims are often flown to France for treatment, sometimes as many as fifty on one military plane. Reports indicate that most of the patients are under thirty-five and suffer from brain tumours related to test exposure when they were just ten to twenty years old.[31]

The other nuclear powers have no better record on the issue of information provision or consideration for local people. In fact the most notorious nuclear incident involved a US test in 1954 in the Marshall Islands. It has been suspected that the weapon was actually exploded with the knowledge that fall-out could contaminate neighbouring islands, but the intention was for its inhabitants to become a subsequent basis for research into the nuclear aftermath.

Following the blast, radioactive ash showered the nearby island of Rongelap to a depth of five centimetres and turned its water blackish-yellow. The inhabitants' immediate symptoms included extreme lethargy and severe itching and by the third day they were all evacuated by a US destroyer. Since 1958 the rates of stillbirths and miscarriages had become double those amongst unaffected Marshallese women. Some of the deformities invoke a Dantesque nightmare, such as those known as 'jellyfish babies' – beings born without faces or bones. Growth retardation amongst children, premature ageing of the old, physical and mental deformity have all increased over the years and by 1985, seventy-seven per cent of the exposed community had developed tumours requiring surgery.[32]

In his excellent book, *Black War: The Extermination of the Tasmanian Aborigines*, Clive Turnbull argues that part of the problem for that island's indigenous people was 'the fact that Tasmania was settled in the early part of the nineteenth century, before the humanitarian movement had gathered momentum.'[33] However, the evidence from these other islands exposes the fallacy that there has ever been a good time for the peoples of the Pacific to be subjected to the rigours of European contact. From the very beginnings of colonisation, there has been a continuum of European exploitation, just as the history of indigenous suffering has gone on almost unbroken. Moreover, their woes have been comparable, if not identical, in nature to those inflicted on the islanders' more plentiful and better-known continental neighbours. It is only the relative smallness of their number, their helpless isolation and, if anything, the greater ease with which their protests have been silenced that distinguishes their particular plight. The fate of the Tasmanians, far from being remote in time and isolated in circumstance from events elsewhere, continues to hold deep resonances for contemporary political conditions in the Pacific region.

Finally, we should now return to the ultimate myth associated with the disappearance of Tasmania's Aborigines, which was the fallacy of extinction itself. Contrary to the celebrated story, the Tasmanians did not, in fact, completely vanish. Like many of the subjects for the myth of extinction, they actually survived. By 1871 and the death of Mary Ann, Walter Arthur's wife, there was just one full-blooded representative left from the original Flinders community – Truganini. Photographs taken of this 'Last Tasmanian', as she became known, in her early sixties depict a diminutive, bewhiskered, grey-haired woman almost comically drowned by her voluminous Victorian dresses. Yet to the end, her face retained a natural dignity, her firm-set mouth and intense stare suggesting a fierce personal resistance to the fate of her people.

During her last years she became increasingly concerned that after death she would suffer the same degrading mutilation as that inflicted on William Lanney's corpse. Despite official reassurances, events following her funeral on 11 May 1876 proved the accuracy of her sad foreboding. Her body was soon exhumed and the Royal Society of Tasmania, the scientific institute so callously cheated of William Lanney's skull, now acquired her prize skeleton, strung it together on wires and put it on public display, where it remained until 1947.

Truganini's death marked the melancholy end of all those Aborigines originally taken into possession by Conciliator Robinson and then incarcerated, firstly at Flinders, then Oyster Cove. Yet there had always been a small community of Tasmanian women living with the sealers out in the islands of the Bass Strait. While their captive compatriots learnt to exchange the ways of the neolithic for the *petit bourgeois* of the nineteenth century, and to praise their Commandant in the *Flinders Island Weekly Chronicle*, these female sealers were gradually creating the basis of a new Aboriginal community.

Although European in dress, and increasingly in physical appearance, by the 1850s the group still included at least seven full-blooded Aboriginal women and as a whole the community retained characteristics of its Tasmanian antecedents.[34] Based on the Furneaux Islands to the south of Flinders, the group followed the traditional harvest patterns of the original hunter–gatherers, taking seals, muttonbirds and kangaroos during periods of seasonal abundance. They also kept pigs and goats and tended small plots of wheat or potatoes around their wooden dwellings, but their lifestyle was an obvious blend of the two cultures. Collecting and threading shells to make traditional necklaces was, for example, a time-consuming and important ritual in their yearly cycle of activity. So too were their communal gatherings and dances, especially after the main muttonbird season. They were, in short, an Aboriginal community very similar to the many surviving on mainland Australia and, indeed, to many post-colonial tribal communities throughout the world.

Partly acculturated to the dominant settler society, but isolated from its more destructive influences, like disease, alcohol and the attrition of race prejudice, the islanders were far better equipped than their pure-bred Aboriginal relatives to hold their own. By 1872 there were thirty-two adults and fifty-two children on just one island, Cape Barren. Although the group clung doggedly to aspects of their Tasmanian past and were clearly distinct from other settlers, whom they often deeply disliked, the colonial government was at a loss to know how to respond to them.

On the one hand, to have accepted the Bass Strait group as Aborigines would have made a nonsense of the myth of extinction. At the same time, to have recognised them simply as a racially mixed community, distinct but of equal status to mainstream settlers – as indeed the Bass Strait people wished themselves to be seen – was almost as difficult. For one of their key distinctions from whites was their collective lifestyle, their sharing of resources and their communal approach to their hunter–gatherer tasks. The fact that they had not taken on board in its entirety the individualism and economic self-interest of the dominant culture was an unacceptable slight to Tasmania's white government. Worse, to have conceded the notion that these hybrids could prefer anything of their savage past to the ways of modern society would have been an affront to Christian Europe's superiority. Therefore, while the precise taxonomy of the Bass Strait group could not be fixed, two things were beyond dispute: neither their status as Aborigines, nor their distinct lifestyle could be accepted.

For almost a century the islander community persisted in a legal and administrative no-man's-land, as the authorities moved from one set of prescriptive measures to another. Central to these was a desire to bleed out their Tasmanian heritage and to oblige them to adopt European patterns of social and economic behaviour. It is only in the last quarter of the twentieth century that the policies of coercive assimilation were truly abandoned and the islanders allowed to claim in full their Aboriginal identity. In 1976, the number of people openly asserting this status was 2,942, while in the 1990s the figure has risen again to over 8,500.

After almost two centuries, the Tasmanians' resistance – still so powerfully expressed by that glare of invincible opposition in Truganini's photographs – had at last prevailed. And in a sense the 'Last Tasmanian' continued to be central to that protest and to symbolise her people's survival. For in 1976 her skeleton ceased to be a physical object on display for European curiosity. In the centenary of her passing she was finally reclaimed by her people and her physical remains were accorded the dignity befitting her human status. Ironically, in that act of restitution – when the bones of the 'Last Tasmanian' were cremated and her ashes scattered on the waters of her ancestral home – Aboriginal Tasmania had also finally consigned to the flames the myth of its own extinction.

Part III

The Dispossession of the Apache

'The kind of war needed is steady, unrelenting, hopeless and undiscriminating war, slaying men, women and children, until every valley and crest and crag and fastness shall send to high heaven the grateful incense of festering and rotting Chiricahuas.'

APACHERIA

ARIZONA

NEW MEXICO

San Carlos
Reservation

Fort Thomas

San Carlos

Camp
Grant

TUCSON

Tombstone

Dragoon
Mountains

Skeleton Canyon

Canon de
los Embudos

The Black
Range Mountains

Warm Springs

San Andreas Mountains

Silver
City

Mimbres
Mountains

Chiricahua
Mountains

Tres
Castillos

TEXAS

SONORA

Sierra Madre Mountains

CHIHUAHUA

Rio Grande

PACIFIC OCEAN

▲
North

0 ——— 100m
160km

12

The Tiger of the Human
Species

According to one associate, Sugarfoot Jack was the handsomest devil he had ever met. In an age and location not short of desperadoes, he was also considered an adventurer with few equals – 'brave, reckless and cruel to the last extent'.[1] Although his largest reputation was achieved in the American Southwest, Sugarfoot's exploits were truly international. English by birth, he was an escaped convict transported to Tasmania while still only in his teens, probably for larceny. Another acquaintance later recalled that he was a notorious thief and that his enlistment in the California Volunteers was followed promptly by his discharge for stealing. A second account of the event had him court-martialled for striking his colonel with a bludgeon.[2] Whichever version was true, both were consistent with Sugarfoot's short and violent life.

The most unforgettable of his deeds occurred in Arizona in the early 1860s, during an organised raid on a band of Apaches. The posse of about a hundred attackers stumbled upon a large settlement and although their approach was detected, the Apaches had been unable to evacuate safely with all of their family members. While Sugarfoot was wandering amongst the wicker and straw shelters, he came upon a baby abandoned outside one of the dwellings.

Still only in his early twenties, Sugarfoot was too young to have taken part in operations against the Aborigines of Tasmania. By the time he arrived in the antipodes they had been reduced to the harmless vestige at Oyster Bay or a forgotten few in the Bass Strait. Yet it is striking how a European familiar with this earlier theatre of tribal conflict seemed to carry forward into his new American setting the excessive temper of his island prison. Perhaps he had listened to the old hands who had fought in the Black War, for his exploits that day in Arizona seemed to express a wish to emulate, even to outstrip, the atrocities of that crime-tormented South Pacific land. Without hesitation or thought, Sugarfoot took the abandoned Apache child and slung it into one of their burning shelters, waited for a few moments to watch the results, then moved on.

Seeing what had taken place, some of his party tried to retrieve the infant from the flames, but each time they touched the tiny body, now curled to a posture of foetal helplessness, its blackened skin peeled away in their hands. Even amongst a band of death-hardened pioneers such behaviour was enough to mark Sugarfoot Jack as a man apart. However, if a number of them had found his first act unforgivable, his second was demonic.

Finding another abandoned child, he proceeded to dandle this infant on his knee as he sat on a large stone, tickling it under the chin 'in the manner of a playful mother'. Then, at the moment both he and the baby looked to be enjoying themselves, he drew his heavy pistol, placed it to the youngster's head and, in defiance of those who had protested at his earlier cruelty, pulled the trigger. When the smoke cleared his companions, outraged to the point of murder, could see once more the youthful, handsome face, now dripping with the brains of its victim.[3]

It is not its notoriety that makes the story of Sugarfoot Jack so instructive an incident in the Euro-American conflict with the Apache. Rather, it is the episode's 'lost' quality, its status as no more than a marginal footnote in the larger history, which speaks so forcefully of the ingrained hatreds and reflex brutality accepted almost casually on both sides. Other components that seem representative of the wider campaign are the disproportion of power, white to Native American, and the way the blameless – in this case the absolute innocence of the child – were indiscriminately punished on both sides for the deeds of others. Finally, there is the nature of the murder itself: not just unthinking slaughter, but violence imbued with the elaborate structure of a game, or a joke.

It was this sadist's combination of complexity and pathological cruelty that formed the basis of frequent European condemnation of the Apache. The more honest critics, however, were willing to acknowledge that it did not arise from the exclusive temperament of the Indians. It was a product of their fatal clash with the representatives of Christian civilisation, like Sugarfoot Jack himself. 'Naturally ferocious, warlike, revengeful and treacherous as were the aborigines of America,' wrote one commentator, 'we have educated them to a pitch of refinement in cruelty, deceit and villainy far beyond their normal standard.'[4]

More than almost any other group of Indians, the Apache had had time to acquaint themselves with the vices of Europe. By the time of Sugarfoot Jack's brutal movement in the Southwest, their confrontation with the colonists went back over 300 years to the very beginning of the white invasion of the North American mainland. Even during the lifetime of Cortés, Spanish expeditions, like that under Francisco Vázquez de Coronado in 1540, came back with tales of wild desert nomads living on the fringe of their American territories.

It was the implacable hostility of these savages that helped shape the northern limits of the Spanish empire. For the Apaches' capacity to improvise, and to borrow from their enemy's arsenal of advantage, eventually enabled them to turn the tables completely and force the expansionist Europeans into a defensive posture. Foremost of the Indians' cultural grafts were steel for war lances and for knives, the horse for both transport and food, a taste for other European livestock, a knowledge of the Spanish language and, finally, of gunpowder and the repeating rifle. In the hands of these natural guerrilla fighters such weapons became the basis of a new era of predatory raids, the Apaches harvesting the resources of northern Mexico as if these communities were their own specially cultivated crop.

In time, the blending of Hispano-Mexican and indigenous cultural elements made them in the eyes of their European opponents a uniquely formidable enemy. 'It is proverbially true,' wrote one commentator, 'that from this mixture of races arises the most bloody, cruel and revengeful of American savages.'[5] In a sense their qualities represented a menacing distillation of the two stereotypes which Europeans had attached earlier to the Mexica and Tasmanians. The brute force and unthinking vengeance of the Aborigines combined with the refined cruelties and decaying malice of Tenochtitlan's inhabitants.

At once primitive and sophisticated, the Apaches were for Euro-Americans the ultimate tribal stereotype, the savage's savage. Even today, after several generations of this classic Western fiction, the word 'Apache' retains a detonative quality matched only by those for the standard demons of the natural world, like the wolf, the tiger, the shark.

That they had encountered, in the masters of Apacheria, the continent's supreme fighters was an idea that occurred to many of those involved in their conquest. 'Ten Apaches,' wrote one of these grudging admirers, 'will undertake a venture which will stagger the courage and nerve of a hundred Yumas, Pimoes or Navajoes.'[6] John Clum, charged with managing an Apache reservation, called them a 'race of supermen', while another contemporary described them as the 'shrewdest and most ferocious of all the tribes . . . within the present limits of the United States'.[7] Woodrow Clum, editing the diary of his famous father long after the war had been won, soared off into overstatement: 'Military men have said that Apache warriors were the greatest fighting men who ever lived, in any period of history.'[8] General Crook, however, one of those military men most responsible for their subjugation, could not be so generous. His old enemies, the great soldier wrote, were 'the tigers of the human species'.[9]

Not only were the Apaches the most formidable opponents of European encroachment and amongst the first tribes to resist it, they were also the last. In North America, the events at Wounded Knee in South Dakota are often portrayed as the final act in the tragedy of Indian military resistance. On a snowy December morning in 1890, the US Seventh Cavalry faced 350 Hunkpapa and Miniconjou Lakota, two-thirds of whom were women and children. Most of their weapons had been taken from them. Their mild-mannered chief, Big Foot, was already dying of pneumonia. When the US forces turned their Hotchkiss guns on his cold, weary people it was less a battle than an unopposed massacre.

Real Lakota resistance had, in fact, been broken years earlier, their great military strategist, Crazy Horse, having been killed in September 1877. In that same year the other focus of Lakota resistance, Sitting Bull, went into exile in Canada. As the Apache war in the American Southwest was reaching its celebrated climax almost a decade later, this Hunkpapa chief had become a star performer in Buffalo Bill's Wild West Show.

When the Apache wars were, in turn, brought to a close in 1886 they had thrown up an Indian war shaman, whose name became a byword for savage determination across America and even Europe and beyond. It is perhaps as much a measure of the militant values so prized by the Christian world, as the qualities of the man himself, that nearly a century after his death, Geronimo is still, with the two great Lakota leaders (and now also, perhaps, Pocahontas), the Indian best known amongst the non-Native American world. Before he died he was put on parade as a living totem of the nation's wild frontier past. Thereafter, his name and reputation were co-opted by his military conquerors, the US paratroopers of the Second World War regularly invoking his indomitable spirit as they hurled themselves into infinity.

If the white citizens of the United States thought the Apaches the most terrifying of all America's native people, then Geronimo was the apotheosis of these perfect savages. 'The greatest singlehanded murderer in American history' is a superlative typical of the hyperbole, luxuriant and hydra-headed, which continues to entwine his name.[10] Whilst he led, according to John Clum, the troublemakers of all the Apache tribes, he himself was cast as the most vicious, dishonest, treacherous and cruel of them all. In fact, he was only one of a number of the tribe's outstanding tacticians (his exploits were matched, if not bettered, by figures like Cochise, Victorio and Nana), but by the close of Apache resistance almost any blood-curdling exploit could be credited automatically to his legendary account.

In Mexico the mere mention of his name was enough to strike terror into the hearts of village women, who believed him the devil incarnate sent to punish them for their sins.[11] During his captivity in Oklahoma in the 1890s it was claimed that in pacing the endless perimeter of his cell, this human tiger had worn a trench two inches deep. It is also symptomatic of the legend of exquisite cruelty that at nights he was said to sleep with a blanket made from the scalps of murdered white women.[12] Even beyond the grave, the shaman's powers continue to conjure fantasy and myth. It is sometimes alleged, for example, that Geronimo was disinterred after death and his skull stolen, the unique talisman eventually finding its way to Yale University, where it forms the ritual centrepiece for a secret rightwing society (that boasts former president George Bush amongst its membership).

If a single Indian and his people had to stand for all Native Americans then there are few more fitting candidates than Geronimo and his Apaches. The tribe's resistance returns us to the very era of Hernan Cortés, then propels us forward to a time when the USA emerged as a world superpower. It seems both a reprise of much of the European conquest in America, and a burning intensification of its dominant element – military conflict. Finally, it reveals in detail the key Euro-

American policies towards tribal people, from outright genocide and territorial dispossession to their physical concentration upon reservations and forced acculturation.

Geronimo's individual life overarches much of this entire process, not just in the context of the Apache, but also for many of the other Indian tribes in America. If the 270-year story of white transcontinental expansion can be characterised as a plot with a long, sustained introduction, a shorter middle phase of consolidation, and a final extraordinary convulsion of drama and adventure, then Geronimo stands in closest relationship to this terminal climax. Yet he was born just shortly after the end of the first period, as white pioneers finally secured control over America's eastern states. He grew to manhood during the second phase, while settlers entrenched themselves on the Mississippi. And he was at the height of his powers in the third, as the 'Wild West' of the dime novels and Western movies was finally being won.

Yet he also outlasted the period of outright conquest. Unlike many of the other key tribal leaders he did not die in open conflict nor its violent aftermath. His endurance, initially in prison and then on a reservation in Oklahoma, symbolises the manner in which Indians ultimately survived the myth of their inevitable extinction. For all of these reasons Geronimo is a compelling witness to the experience of Native America.

Before exploring the background to his individual life and struggle, we should first recapitulate something of their context and the wider history of European–tribal relations in America. It now seems remarkable to think that in the time of Geronimo's parents, most Apaches had never heard of the United States of America. Equally, for the white population of that period, the 'Wild West' did not conjure the desert spaces, nor the canyons and soaring mesas of Apacheria, but the cool, forested slopes of Appalachia, 3,000 kilometres away to the east.

This long, sinuous range of moderately elevated mountains runs in close parallel to the eastern seaboard, yet it had acted as a critical psychological and physical barrier for European settlers since the early seventeenth century. By the time of Geronimo's birth, however, uncertainly dated in the early 1820s, emigrants had already breached this barrier and were pressing on towards the continent's great aorta, the Mississippi. In completing this westward expansion they had also destroyed key tribal alliances both east and west of the range.

The Tiger of the Human Species

Before American independence in 1776, the vast woodland tract spreading down from the Great Lakes, through today's New York State and the Appalachians as far south as Kentucky, had been dominated by the six nations of the Iroquois Confederacy – the Mohawk, Oneida, Onondaga, Cayuga, Seneca and Tuscarora. These warlike tribes had long managed to pool and harmonise their political interests through the rituals of their famous grand council, which was a prototype of New World democracy and a key inspiration for the fledgling American republic. They had also been largely successful in protecting their lands with a policy of neutrality amongst the competing European forces, especially the British and French.

However, when resident white settlers sought to break the sovereignty of the English crown, the Iroquois Confederacy was lured away from its unaligned posture and its tradition of consensual politics. Rifts within the grand council eventually mirrored the larger divisions between whites; and when the royal armies of the English king were finally ousted by American forces, those Indians who had placed their trust in the word and the red coats of the British were similarly exiled. Yet, as with so many tribal peoples, the sections of the Iroquois siding with the victorious settlers soon discovered that choosing a European ally was, in fact, no choice at all.

From the time of Columbus, Europeans had performed their self-referential rituals to confirm themselves in the path of conquest. At the Treaty of Paris in 1783, the British, preoccupied now by European rivalries and indifferent to the fate of their old Indian supporters, made 'generous' territorial concessions to the independent and victorious Americans. The new republic's boundaries were pushed west to the banks of the Mississippi and north to the Great Lakes. As far as the Americans were concerned the Appalachians and beyond were now theirs by right of both conquest and treaty, and they too set about negotiating their former Indian allies off their lands, almost as completely as if they had lost them on the field of battle.

Simultaneously, the Paris treaty underpinned settlers' advances beyond the Appalachians and into the rich alluvial lands of the Mississippi's main eastern tributary, the Ohio. In the process the focus of conflict overstepped the territory of the six nations and came to centre on a new frontier, the Northwest Territory, that now forms the states of Ohio, Indiana and Illinois. For the Indian tribes that had always lived and hunted over the region – the Delaware, Fox, Miami,

Kickapoo, Ottawa, Potawatomi, Sauk, Shawnee and others – the grandiose deliberations of white men in a distant land rang as hollow as the original Columbian decrees on a vacant Caribbean shore. But the fact of American encroachment could not be ignored. Compliant chiefs in the region had already been bribed and forced into releasing swathes of their old hunting-grounds for white occupation. By the beginning of the nineteenth century many tribes had also fought and lost to American forces.

Yet in 1805 their struggle of resistance found renewed hope in the eloquent speeches of a young Shawnee warrior leader, Tecumseh, who preached a return to their own traditional values and a rejection of European imports like Christianity, metal tools, woven cloth and alcohol, on all of which much of indigenous America had come to depend. In tandem with his cultural atavism, the Shawnee leader's programme involved a radical vision of Indian unity in the fact of white aggression. Constantly travelling up and down the frontier from Alabama to Illinois, Tecumseh pressed home a message of resistance through his compelling oratory.

White American leaders, recognising the threats implicit in his ideas, sought to pre-empt the creation of any fully fledged alliance and attacked Tecumseh's power-base in Northern Indiana. In 1811 the Shawnee leader gathered Indian forces from a range of disaffected tribes and then forged a new pact with the British in Canada. However, like the Iroquois before him, and despite initial military gains, he had finally to reckon with the shifting politics of a European power. The British, cut off from their supply bases further east, decided to withdraw across Canada and leave the Indians to face a powerful American army largely by themselves. In 1813 at the Thames River, just east of Detroit, Tecumseh's life, his dream of Indian nationhood and resistance to Euro-American expansion north-east of the Mississippi, were all finally extinguished. In just a single generation the white frontier had been consolidated 500 kilometres closer to the Apache strongholds of the Southwest.

Notwithstanding this shrinking margin, Geronimo claimed in later life that during his own childhood his people had still never seen a white man.[13] The great warrior was born at a location probably close to the modern town of Clifton in southern Arizona, and was known by a name far more mild than the one he would later acquire. As a child, this tiger of the human race was called Goyahkla, 'One Who Yawns'.

It is, in some ways, symptomatic of the manner in which his historical image has been defined and controlled by Euro-Americans that it was Mexican soldiers who gave him the name Geronimo. Another unexpected feature in his early life, given that raids into Mexico had long been central to the Apache economy and culture, was his recollection of a childhood of relative tranquillity.

Until the age of five or six Goyahkla, like other Apache children, accompanied his mother and the other women in search of natural food plants, or to tend small plots of beans, squash and corn, which they grew whenever settled conditions allowed. Thereafter boys and girls were separated to prepare them for the roles allotted to each in Apache society. As a future warrior and defender of his people, Geronimo was to be given a rigorous training in the arts of survival and war.

Apache boys were made to run long distances, often to the tops of mountains and back, with their mouths full of water to ensure they breathed only through the nose. A daily plunge in the river was another character-building test, especially in winter when a sheet of ice might have to be broken beforehand. They also learnt to make weapons or to tend and handle horses. Elders introduced them to the arts of camouflage and concealment, of reading signs and tracks. From the age of eight to ten they were allowed to follow the chase, or practised with bows and arrows stalking small game of their own. One activity involved running down turkeys or rabbits on the back of a pony. Such was their horsemanship that they could lean over to catch the creatures with their bare hands, or strike them with wooden clubs.[14] This whole repertoire of physical skills, which every Apache male was expected to master, was the background to their status as America's greatest guerrilla fighters.

In the 1830s, as Geronimo faced the challenges of adolescence, his Native American contemporaries, living mainly to the east of the southern third of the Mississippi River, were undergoing ordeals of a different kind. The Cherokee, with their four near-neighbours – the Creek, Seminole, Chickasaw and Choctaw – were known collectively as the 'Five Civilised Tribes'. For centuries they had dominated a large belt of territory across the eastern half of the continent, from Florida in the south and as far as Kentucky in the north. Like the Iroquois Confederacy, they had long been exposed to the presence of conflicting European powers, including the French, the British and the

Spaniards, who had colonised parts of Florida and Louisiana as long ago as the mid-sixteenth century.

This complex, multicultural milieu threw up familiar patterns of behaviour amongst the Indians and tribal peoples in other regions. Typically, they sought to offset one potential European aggressor through alliance with others. As with the Iroquois, the policy of neutrality backed by the threat of force served the interests of Indian independence well, but wherever this diplomatic balancing act broke down Native Americans seldom gained in conditions of open conflict. The fate of the Creek people exemplifies this wider failure.

In 1812, in the Anglo-American war that had triggered Tecumseh's military alliance with the British, a powerful section within the Creek nation made common cause against the United States. Although they experienced some successes, like the Shawnee leader to the north, the Creek soon reaped the inevitable rewards of tribal division. In 1814, the future US president and tough Irish-American commander, Andrew Jackson, backed by a large force of tribal auxiliaries, completely routed his Creek opponents at the battle of Horseshoe Bend in Alabama. Many from the defeated section of the tribe fled to their Seminole neighbours in Florida, while those Creek elements that had fought alongside Jackson were forced to cede 8,000,000 acres, about two-thirds the territory of their entire nation, to their American allies. The Cherokee, further accomplices in Jackson's great victory, were relieved of 2,000,000 acres.[15]

Realising the futility of armed struggle, many Indians began to accept the presence of whites as a *fait accompli*, and sought survival through cultural adaptation. In fact, their reputation as the Five Civilised Tribes honoured the manner in which they had taken on characteristics of European society. No tribe had been more successful in this assimilation than the Cherokee. Some had converted to Christianity, while marriage between Europeans and Indians often made good relations between the two races a matter of family politics.

The Cherokee had long been an agricultural society, but a number now embraced European methods and geared production to a market economy. The conventional symbols of prosperity in the American south – large plantation houses, fine clothes and black slaves – were all eagerly adopted by the more 'progressive' elements. However, none of this outward display of Western manners is half as impressive as the Cherokee achievements in the fields of education and internal administration. By the early 1830s the tribe had its own written language, newspapers, expanding literacy amongst its population and a political process based on that of white America, with a bicameral chamber and a court system.

Despite the Cherokees' extraordinary adjustments, large sections of Georgia's white population were hardly flattered by their imitation of settler culture. In fact, they were discovering that an Indian dressed in Western clothes, conversant with the white man's ways and laws, was a far more awkward opponent than a tomahawk-wielding savage in breech-clout and moccasins. Even more unwilling to stand and applaud the Indian march towards civilisation were Georgia's growing numbers of poor white immigrants, who gazed towards the Indians' prime farming country with increasingly hungry eyes. The eventual response of many of these squatters, further inflamed by gold strikes on Indian land, was to violate treaties with the Cherokee and seize their property while state officials winked at the theft.

The solution, meanwhile, for America's federal government was found in one of those classic agreements by which one set of Europeans had given to their fellows large tracts of country actually belonging to somebody else. In the case of the deal known as the Louisiana Purchase, concluded in 1804 with the French Emperor Napoleon, the US government had acquired the whole of the region between the Rocky Mountains and the Mississippi for the sum of $15 million. Not since the Treaty of Tordesillas in 1494, when the dazzlingly depraved Pope Alexander VI had divided the Americas between Spain and Portugal, had so much been given by so few for so little.

With the title to this vast wilderness estate, which doubled the size of the country, US officials began to translate into national policy an outrageous scheme to get the Indians to give up their centuries-old relationship to their lands in the east, in exchange for new territories beyond the Mississippi. Eventually passing into law as the Removal Act of 1830, this act of ethnic cleansing was presented by men like President Andrew Jackson as a gesture of altruism, offering the Indians lands more fertile than those they currently held and sparing them the pernicious consequences as whites crowded them out in the east.

It was certainly true, as Jackson indicated, that the Civilised Tribes had been subjected to some extraordinary treatment. In one period of conflict in Alabama, and in reply to the Indians' own earlier cruelty, dead Creek warriors had been skinned to make bridle reins for US cavalry, while other corpses had been stripped from the hips down for boot leather. On another occasion, soldiers had burnt down a house containing forty-six warriors, then eaten potatoes from its cellar basted in human fat.[16] What was doubly significant about these actions, however, was that they had been perpetrated by troops under Jackson's command.

The real reason for removal was, of course, the 33,000,000 acres occupied by the 50,000 members of the five tribes. Some sections of the Cherokee and Creek were sufficiently realistic to leave voluntarily. But most were simply rounded up off their farms and coerced into exile at gunpoint. The entire operation, largely concentrated in the ten years between 1828–38, involved not just the Five Civilised Tribes but a whole host of groups from further north and east, including the Shawnee, Miami, Sauk, Fox and Potawatomi. Yet the treatment of nations like the Cherokee, who had done everything to adapt to the invaders' culture, seems doubly treacherous. As Ronald Wright has suggested, it 'still casts a shadow today, for it was a betrayal of white America's own ideals.'[17]

The crime of removal was compounded by the appalling conditions to which the tribes were subjected during their march into exile. It has been estimated that as many as 10,000 Creek, 4,000 Cherokee and a similar number of Choctaw died from disease, exhaustion, hunger and accidents on what became known as the Trail of Tears.

After the complete annexation of trans-Appalachia, with its accompanying defeat firstly of the Iroquois Confederacy then Tecumseh's Shawnee alliance, the Indian removals of the 1830s and 40s are viewed as the terminal point for the second major cycle in Indian–white relations. They implied uncontested Euro-American control of the eastern third of the continent. They also seemed to mark a natural caesura in the adventure of white dominion. Certainly after 1840, American Indian history was located largely beyond the west bank of the Mississippi. It was this region that provided the setting for the most dramatic phase of the war, involving its best-known tribal stereotype – the horse-riding, buffalo-hunting Native Americans of the Great Plains such as the Sioux, Cheyenne, Arapaho and Comanche.

However, while it is convenient to break down white–tribal conflicts to correspond with settler advances to natural geographical features, like the Appalachians, Mississippi and Rockies, it was, inevitably, a more complex continuum. Thus, one finds that even during the 1820s and before Civilised Tribes like the Choctaw had even left their traditional lands east of the Mississippi, they had already been asked to cede for white settlement parts of their allotted Arkansas territory to the west of the great river.[18]

By the 1820s trans-Mississippian settlement was already an established fact. In the far north-west, the Pacific region of Oregon had attracted only an initial trickle of pioneers, but Texas in the south, despite forming no part of the Louisiana Purchase, had become a key destination for westering settlers. However, the Anglo-Saxon sense of racial destiny was by no means an exclusive march over the inhabitants of tribal America. Texan whites were equally resentful of the political control exercised initially by the Spanish and then by independent Mexican authorities, and in 1836 they proclaimed a self-governing republic.

When Mexican soldiers completely annihilated these secessionist forces at the Alamo and martyred a number of legends of the American West, like Davy Crockett and Jim Bowie, they converted the aspirations of white Texans into a national priority. Only weeks later, US forces achieved a sweeping revenge for their lost heroes, declared Texas an independent republic and elected the victorious General Sam Houston as its first president.

A decade after its declared independence, Texas became the flashpoint for further international discord. Border clashes proved the spark for a wider US–Mexican war, from which the southern nation emerged once again as the loser. In 1848, in a repeat of the arrangements by which it had first claimed the trans-Mississippian region, the US government secured legal title to the Mexican territories north of the Rio Grande. These included California, Nevada, Utah, Arizona and parts of New Mexico and Colorado. A purchase price of $15 million had given them an additional 3,000,000 square kilometres. The continent was now a white possession from coast to coast.

This agreement, known as the Treaty of Guadalupe Hidalgo, was followed in just five years by the Gadsden Purchase, which completed the exchange of Apacheria from Mexican to US hands. Between them the two documents had radically reshaped the political landscape of the Southwest, and converted the old Mexican problem of Apache raids into an American dilemma. In just three generations the white–tribal frontier had shifted 3,000 kilometres. Geronimo and his people were now on the frontline.

Not that the young Goyahkla was even then too preoccupied with these developments. Although his forty-year personal history of war-fare had already begun, the warrior's deepest feelings of hostility were not initially directed at the agents of Anglo-Saxon expansion. Nor, in fact, were they ever. One of the few things that he shared with his eventual enemy was an abiding racial contempt for Mexicans.

The genesis of this hatred was his experiences of 1851–2 (which he himself assigned to the summer of 1858). Despite this chronological confusion there is no doubting the event's importance in shaping the course of his adult life. Possibly as early as 1840 Geronimo had been admitted to the council of warriors, a step that allowed him to take his teenage bride, Alope. By the time of the young couple's participation in a trading expedition to the Mexican state of Chihuahua, she and Geronimo had three children. While Alope remained in camp with the family and her mother-in-law, Geronimo accompanied the other men into the town of Janos to trade hides for cloth, knives and ornaments.

During this absence, a Mexican army from neighbouring Sonora, in violation of an agreed peace between the Apache and Chihuahua state authorities, assaulted the family base camp, capturing fifty or sixty women and children and murdering a further twenty-five. All of Geronimo's family were among the slain. His sense of devastation when he saw what had happened was total. Half a century later, while dictating his memoirs, he recalled his feelings. Neither the passage of time nor the process of translation from Apache to English could diminish his sense of loss: 'I stood . . . hardly knowing what I would do . . . I did not pray, nor did I resolve to do anything in particular, for I had no purpose left . . . I spoke to no one and no one spoke to me – there was nothing to say . . . none had lost as I had, for I had lost all.'[19]

Within twelve months a large Indian force returned to the Sonoran town of Arispe to seek retribution. Geronimo himself stated that in recognition of his appalling personal loss and his burning desire for vengeance, he was allowed to lead the Apache attack.[20] It was also said that in honour of the mad-dog courage with which he charged their positions, the Mexican soldiers cried out at this wildest of young war-riors the name of their patron saint – Hieronimo. So was the legend born.

His intense loathing of Mexicans, which remained with him into extreme old age, is one of the leitmotifs of Geronimo's career. In fact, his tribe's constant struggle with those who occupied the land of the old Mexica is a further reason why the story of Apache resistance resonates well beyond its historical and geographical limits. For instead of a two-way, white–tribal confrontation, the war for Apacheria was a multilayered clash involving white Anglo-Saxons, a nation of largely acculturated Christian Indians and a traditional tribal society.

This complex arena threw up a number of facts which sit uncomfortably with any over-simplified thesis of European aggression towards innocent tribespeople. The most obvious was that of Apache attacks which devastated the Indian settlements of northern Mexico far more than any white American community. In 1835, one Mexican official calculated that in the previous fifteen-year period, 100 haciendas, ranchos and mines had been ruined, involving the loss of 5,000 lives.[21] During the wars that culminated in Geronimo's last stand, while Apache and American casualties were recorded with some accuracy, the statistics for Mexican losses were often presented like incidental extras and usually ran into thousands. It is hardly surprising that even today Mexicans from the state of Chihuahua will admit to being terrified of the Apache.[22]

Nor should it then surprise us that these deep-rooted fears spawned an equally violent response. In fact, it was not the racist ideology of white Anglo-Saxons that gave rise to a doctrine of outright extermination of the Apache. It was the Mexican authorities in Sonora and Chihuahua who, with their payments for the scalps of every Apache man, woman and child, pursued de facto policies of genocide. In 1849 alone, these bounty offers of 200 pesos per male scalp and 150 pesos per captured female or infant attracted claims totalling 17,896 pesos.[23]

Another striking element was the deep contempt shared by both Apache and the US military for the largely Indian conscripts of the Mexican army. Geronimo once boasted that he could defeat such rabble with mere rocks, while the US army scorned the idea that Mexicans might deal effectively with renegade Apache, and frequently crossed the border in pursuit of their quarry.[24] Equally the racial assumptions that shaped American policy towards the traditional Apache were hardly distinguishable from those that informed relations with their weaker southern neighbour, over whom they had come to hold the position of dominance once enjoyed by the Spaniards. (By the end of the nineteenth century capitalists from the USA and northern Europe had extracted more precious metals than during the whole of the Spanish colonial period. By 1904, three-quarters of Mexico's mines and half her oil-fields were owned by just seven American companies.[25])

Yet it was exactly these derided Mexican conscripts who inflicted the two major military defeats in the decade before the final Apache surrender. One of these was in 1880, when a key leader, Victorio, died with about eighty others, while a similar number were seized. Two years later, Geronimo himself was shepherding a large number of his people into Mexico when they ran into a devastating ambush that left over a hundred killed or captured. In the same period the US army never brought to bay such a large Apache force, nor scored such an outright victory over the tribe. Probably the largest single encounter on American soil with high numbers of casualties was the Camp Grant Massacre of 1871, a slaughter inflicted mainly on unarmed women and children living peacefully in reservation conditions. And most of the killing was actually done by a force of Papago Indians and Mexicans.

The habitual, centuries-old pattern of warfare between the Mexicans and the Apache partly explains why the initial contacts between American settlers and the tribe were relatively amicable. However, Geronimo and his people quickly grasped the deeper threats underlying the appearance of the first white pioneers. And although the American Civil War (1861–65) delayed the full impact of western expansion, it did not halt the process.

Inspired in part by Columbus' old dream of a 'passage to India' and the China trade, American railway companies were carving their routes through the Great Plains by the early 1860s.[26] Indeed, at the very moment that William Lanney slumped into terminal decline half a world away in the Dog and Partridge in Hobart, line gangs were hammering their steel rails into place to link up with those thrusting towards them from the Pacific. On 10 May 1869 at Promontory, Utah, when the last male Tasmanian was a scattering of hewn body parts, US capital and labour had cut the American West clean in half. The Union Pacific and the Central Pacific Railways had become one.

Such massive technological achievements now opened the Great Plains to industrial exploitation. Between the 1840s and 60s, while westward migration had been a matter of wagon convoys nosing through the oceans of grass, the plains Indians like the Lakota and Cheyenne had held their own. But huge gold rushes – the El Dorados of the North American continent – to California in 1849, to Denver in 1858 and then to the Black Hills of Dakota in 1874, turned the trickle of pioneers into a stream, then a flood.

Despite the achievements of the Lakota statesman Red Cloud, who had defeated the US forces in war, then wrung binding treaties confirming the tribe's territorial possessions, he could not better King Canute. The tide of white settlement ripped across the northern plains, drowning the final sparks of resistance centred on Red Cloud's compatriots, Crazy Horse and Sitting Bull. 'The white man made us many promises,' sighed the elderly Lakota in a famous address, 'more than I can remember, but they never kept but one; they promised to take our land, and they took it.'

Nor was the land all that they took. The conflict with the Indians seemed only part of a deeper and more complex need for bloodletting in white American society. In words that would have held deep meaning for the original inhabitants of Tenochtitlan at the zenith of their power, one US newspaper editor, William Simms, had written, 'War is the great element of civilization and our destiny is conquest. Indeed the moment a nation ceases to extend its sway it falls a prey to an inferior but more energetic neighbour.'[27] In order to pre-empt such a possibility, white America now seemed to declare war on the whole world of nature.

The most famous victim was the 25,000,000-strong population of American bison whose slaughter was a model of environmental holocaust. In just three years (1872–74) white hunters decimated the herds of the southern plains, killing an estimated 4,375,000 beasts. The new railroads freighted out the skins to make factory belts or the bones for industrial glue, while the rotting carcasses fertilised the plains on which they fell. 'As an example of the profligate waste of an abundant natural resource,' one authority has written, 'the story of the near extermination of the bison probably stands unsurpassed in recorded history.'[28]

If it is, then it was run a close second by the extermination of the passenger pigeon. This bird was once found across the eastern two-thirds of the continent from the Canadian Rockies to the swamps of Florida, and was a strong contender for the world's most numerous land bird. A single flock could obliterate the noon sun like an eclipse and move in continuous passage for over three days. To drive such vast populations into total extinction by 1914 required an unrelenting orgy of destruction. However, a complex blend of American farming, industrial and hunting interests rose to the challenge. A hint of the prodigious killing involved is given by one sports competition, in which entrants required a bag of 30,000 birds to claim a prize. Farmers fertilised the ground or fed their hogs on squabs battered from nests, while a single commercial dealer handled three million birds in just one year.

Arizona and New Mexico, because of their extreme westerly location and their burning aridity – ninety per cent of the land is unsuitable for cultivation - were among the last places to be consumed by the white American crusade: the two territories did not officially join the Union as the forty-seventh and forty-eighth states until 1912. But despite the distance, the heat, the dust, the Apache, white America still wanted them.

They wanted the silver, and they wanted the copper that ran in numerous rich seams through the mountains. Although it was small in quantity, they wanted also what the ancient Indians had called the 'Dung of the Gods' – gold. They wanted the green valleys for grazing cattle and the rivers for dams. They wanted coal to power the biggest economy on the planet. To acquire these products they needed, more than anything else, the land that the Southwest Indians had enjoyed for centuries. And in time – in fact, just sixty years after Geronimo had been railroaded out of his homeland into exile – they found a need even for the wind-slurred stillness of Apacheria. They wanted a place of cactus and silent desert on which to unleash the roaring mushroom cloud of the world's first nuclear explosion.

13

The Enemy
and the People

The twelve months between June 1876 and June 1877 were not a good period for American Indians. On the twenty-fifth day of that first month, on the bluffs above the Little Bighorn River in modern-day Montana, General George Armstrong Custer and 255 men of the US Seventh Cavalry were wiped out by Lakota and Cheyenne warriors in a fierce skirmish – 'lasting only the time it takes for a grown man to eat his dinner.'

Peter Matthiessen has described the battle on the Little Bighorn as 'the last great Indian triumph in American history'.[1] It remains, unquestionably, the most famous clash ever between white and Native Americans, if not between European and tribal forces anywhere in the world. Largely because American writers and artists, immediately afterwards, began working on the details to invest them with a symbolic importance wholly distinct from their prima facie meaning.

Even more than Cortés' compact army of *conquistadores*, that encircled band of US cavalry came to epitomise Europe's ancient self-image as bright star beleaguered by a galaxy of darkness. 'Custer's Last Stand', as it was immediately named, with its central character bearing a resemblance to Christendom's most sublime hero, was transfigured as a myth exalting the pioneer spirit of the West, which was willing to make the ultimate sacrifice for progress. In a world of symbols defeat was eventually transformed into triumph: Custer had died so that Christian civilisation might prevail.[2]

In the world of political realities, however, Little Bighorn had a different kind of significance. For the Indians of the plains it was undoubtedly a great psychological coup to have defeated the most glamorous US soldier of his generation, but as a military feat it resembled *la Noche Triste*, a short-lived victory that the losing side would eventually turn into final conquest. News of the disaster travelled with almost malevolent timing, bursting upon the American public as it geared itself for the Fourth of July celebrations. In 1876 that anniversary carried even deeper national resonances since it marked the centenary of American independence.

Eleven years earlier, after a disastrous brush with the Lakota known to the defeated as the Fetterman Massacre, in which eighty soldiers were killed, General William Sherman had written, 'We must act with vindictive earnestness against the Sioux . . . even to their extermination, men, women and children.'[3] The mood after the deeper trauma of Custer's death turned quickly from one of national mourning into a burning desire for indiscriminate revenge. Only twelve days after Little Bighorn, high officers in the War Department were advocating a policy of Indian genocide, 'the speedier the better'.[4] The US army thus scoured the northern plains throughout the autumn and winter of 1876–7 in a relentless search-and-destroy operation. By February, Sitting Bull was in Canadian exile. By May Crazy Horse had fallen into US custody on Red Cloud's Lakota reservation. Four months later he was bayonetted to death by his gaolers.

Native Americans everywhere bore the brunt of white vengeance. Even in the Southwest, the Apaches were to pay for Custer's reckless downfall. In the days just before Little Bighorn, a short, fiery 25-year-old American from New York State, called John Clum, had set out for an Indian reservation just east of the Arizonan town of Tombstone. Straddled between two rugged mountain ranges, this was the homeland of a group of the Chiricahua, the Apache band most fiercely resistant to white encroachment. For their defiance they had been branded 'the worst band of Indians in America'.[5] Yet in 1872 their famous leader, Cochise, had negotiated with the US government and secured the area as a permanent homeland for his people.

Then, just two years after Cochise's death and three weeks before Custer's own, Washington decided it wanted the lands back, using as a pretext an outbreak of violence between some Apaches and a station-keeper. Clum had thus set out to close the Chiricahua sanctuary and to take the Indians with him to an Apache reservation 150 kilometres to the north called San Carlos, on which Clum himself was the agent. Given their history of resistance, it was hardly surprising that he managed to secure the transfer of only 325 of the Chiricahua, while two-thirds of the group fled to escape removal. Amongst these 'renegades' was a warrior rapidly emerging as a champion of Apache independence: Geronimo.

Clum's failure to secure the troublemaker and, as he saw it, Geronimo's flagrant deception of him – he had promised to collect his band and go with the agent to San Carlos, and had then immediately bolted – turned this individual Indian into Clum's obsession. 'From that time on,' suggests Geronimo's biographer, 'he became the elusive warrior's nemesis':

> In [Clum's] lively writings he attributed every raid before and after his meeting to Geronimo. His solution to the whole Apache problem was simple: hang Geronimo . . . Other Southwesterners adopted the same simplistic interpretation. Thus, Geronimo acquired a fame – or notoriety – far out of proportion to his deeds or misdeeds.[6]

The agent's growing *idée fixe* meshed neatly with the US government's new hardline policy after Custer's defeat, and when Clum was ordered to make a second attempt to arrest Geronimo, he readily accepted the challenge.

The Apache leader had resurfaced on another Chiricahua reservation known as Warm Springs, to the north of Silver City in New Mexico and about 160 kilometres north-east of the old domain of Cochise and his people. Realising that to capture a large body of well-armed renegades would be a dangerous business, even the cocky Clum requested back-up from the US army. But in the event the San Carlos agent, with a private militia of Apache police from his own reservation, arrived two days earlier than the regular troops, and Clum decided to spring a trap of his own for his *bête noire*.

Asking Geronimo and his colleagues to come in for a conference, the young agent then stationed most of his hundred-strong police corps in the reservation's storerooms before the meeting. When Geronimo and his fellow leaders approached the rendezvous they were under the impression that the white man's total support was the twenty or so police he had lined along the parade ground. Not expecting any trouble, they had thus appeared with their wives and children. Then as the discussions began to get heated, Clum gave a pre-arranged signal and his entire force rushed from its hiding place and surrounded Geronimo's party, trapping it in a potentially fatal crossfire.

Clum, later the proprietor and editor of the Tombstone *Epitaph*, had a fine line in melodramatic prose. 'I have seen many looks of hate in my long life,' he wrote later of his adversary, 'but never one so vicious, so vengeful.'

Geronimo leaped to his feet; another picture one could never forget. Forty-five years old, erect as a lodge-pole pine, every outline of his symmetrical form indicating strength, endurance, arrogance. Abundant black hair draping his shoulders, stern, paint-smeared features, those vindictive eyes, the livid scar. Geronimo, the renegade, strategist, trickster, killer of pale-faces.[7]

The great warrior was caught by a white man for the one and only time in his life, as the author of the ruse never failed to point out. He was clapped in leg irons and taken as a prisoner with the other so-called renegades, Clum hoping that he would see his arch-enemy hang as soon as he returned. He then rounded up the rest of the Warm Springs Apaches, whose reservation was now also closed on the basis that they had harboured Geronimo and the other Chiricahua runaways. On 20 May 1877 the agent arrived back at San Carlos with the 110 of Geronimo's people and 343 of the Warm Springs group led by Victorio.

The agent had thus completed a massive round-up of Apaches, leaving just one other large reservation functioning in central New Mexico. He now had between 4,500 and 5,000 Indians under his control, almost certainly the largest gathering of Geronimo's people in their entire history. The US policy of concentration at San Carlos was a close parallel to the Tasmanian government's employment of Robinson the Conciliator and the Aborigines' confinement on Flinders. However, the American reservation was no conveniently isolated island, nor were the Apaches about to submit meekly, dying out as the race theories of their white masters blithely predicted.

Although Clum oversaw an unusually sympathetic regime, which he flattered himself to believe had created one big happy family at San Carlos, and although the agent himself was undeniably honest, imaginative and efficient, the US policy of concentration was, in fact, a gross betrayal of the Apache and exemplified much that was wrong with white America's treatment of Indians in the Southwest and throughout the continent.

For exactly the same reasons, the policy would prove as disastrous as it was immoral – especially after Clum resigned later in 1877, when he failed to obtain the increased salary he believed his additional Indian charges warranted. It would cause a further decade of conflict, costing thousands of lives. It would also launch the Apache raids that would confirm Geronimo's place in the history of the Southwest. Finally, it would squander promising and valuable peace arrangements that had been agreed only after an earlier ten years of unprecedented violence. To comprehend exactly why it was such a betrayal of the Apache, and also of those US soldiers who had campaigned to subdue them, we need first to explore something of the nature of Apache society and their initial years of contact with white America.

The most obvious problem arising from any reservation system for the Apache, let alone one based exclusively on San Carlos, was the deep restriction this placed on the tribe's customary mobility. The area gazetted for their occupation was only a minute fraction of the region the tribe had been accustomed to roam. Their range had originally embraced an area south of the Grand Canyon, involving two-thirds of modern Arizona and then across the southern third of New Mexico as far east as parts of western Kansas and Texas. In Mexico proper their hunting-grounds ranged southwards through the Sierra Madre Mountains to a latitude parallel with the state capital of Chihuahua. In total, Apacheria was an area greater than modern France, a statistic that speaks forcefully of the tribe's nomadic traditions.

Anthropological evidence suggests that, following a migratory pattern comparable to that of the Mexica, the proto-Apaches had come into the Southwest region from northern Canada between AD 900 and 1200. A number of these immigrant groups eventually acquired techniques of crop cultivation and had become highly proficient in methods of irrigation – skills they learnt from the other Indians resident in the region, like the pueblo-dwelling Zuni and Hopi. However, the tribe's economy had never been based exclusively on agriculture. The cultural traditions that the early Apaches had brought with them from the north were those of a hunter–gatherer people and, once rooted in the Southwest, they developed an intimate understanding of its many natural products, both vegetable and animal.

Not surprisingly for a people so renowned in the skills of war, they were also outstanding hunters. Almost all of the large edible game within their geographic range was taken by the tribe, with the notable exception of the bear, whose flesh was taboo. To approach their quarry unsuspected they could hide within an antelope or deer skin then mimic the animal's actions and, when in range, an Apache could fire off seven arrows before the first struck its target.[8] Another skilful technique involved floating gourds across a lake towards geese until the birds had grown accustomed to the sight.[9] Then, placing a hollowed gourd over his own head for disguise, an Apache moved amongst the unsuspecting birds, pulling them under by the feet one after the other, until his submerged bag was full.

The Apache were also exceptional botanists and harvested hundreds of different plant species for medicine and the pot. One of the most important of their food sources was the agave or mescal cactus, and the borders of Apacheria have been shown to coincide closely with the distribution of these desert-adapted plants. The flowers, roots and white fleshy stalks were all utilised, the latter especially important once baked in large heated pits. A dried, cake form of mescal, together with other preserved meats, flours and skins, was regularly cached in caves and other secret locations to serve as a critical standby in times of shortage.[10]

In order not to exhaust their territory's various natural resources Apache bands had to be highly mobile, shifting to take account of local and seasonal abundances. Thus, to root them in one spot as at San Carlos, despite its original extent of 18,000 square kilometres, involved a fundamental denial of this cultural pattern. And while on paper this may have seemed a generous territory to accommodate just 6,000 to 8,000 Indians – the suggested population for the Apache in the latter part of the nineteenth century – it takes no account of the principles on which the US authorities were accustomed to choose reservations.[11]

A typical area was the Bosque Redondo, gazetted as a Navaho reservation in the mid-1860s. Here the ground was later pronounced by the government's own inspector as too alkaline for grain production. Drought and insects devastated the tribe's crops. Their official rations were a third short of their requirements and consisted of products condemned for army consumption. What water they could find was black, brackish and disease-bearing. Before Bosque Redondo was closed in 1868 a quarter of the Navaho had died.

The choice of San Carlos reflected a selection procedure whose main criterion was finding land worthless for immediate white purposes. And as soon as anything valuable was discovered, Americans usually sought an amendment to the original terms of cession. A classic case was their seizure of the Black Hills in South Dakota. These had been guaranteed in perpetuity to the Lakota as the most sacred land in the tribe's territory. Two years after gold had been struck and just two months after Custer's death, the US government took the land back, exemplifying the way in which the Little Bighorn became an almost universal justification for Indian mistreatment.

Even San Carlos suffered reduction. Today it is about a third of its original extent. The reservation's principal deficiency, however, was not size, but a combination of heat and sterility. Typically, the troops stationed there judged its military base, Fort Thomas, as 'the worst army post in the domains of Uncle Sam', while Fort San Carlos was known as 'Hell's Forty Acres'. 'Dry hot dust- and gravel-laden winds swept the plain,' ran one description, 'denuding it of every vestige of vegetation. In summer a temperature of 100° in the shade was cool weather. At all other times of the year flies, gnats, unnamable [sic] bugs . . . swarmed in millions.'[12] Another commentator asked his readers to imagine 'stones and ashes and thorns, with some scorpions and rattle-snakes thrown in, dump the outfit on stones, heat the stones red hot, set the United States Army after the Apache, and you have San Carlos.'[13]

Their concentration in such a desolate, malarial spot was more than just an assault upon the tribe's nomadic traditions. It also forced a whole range of different Apache communities into an unhealthy and uncharacteristic association. Those speaking the Apachean language had never been accustomed to prolonged contact. Following their migrations into the Southwest and long before white Americans had arrived in the region, they had divided into seven groups with their own core territories. It is not necessary here to master the complex divisions and subdivisions of these bands, nor their specific geographical attachments, but a brief profile of two of these communities will indicate the tribe's schismatic tendency.

The Navaho, although part of the Apachean-speaking population, had eventually become so distinct they were considered a separate people. Based in the north-eastern quarter of Arizona, they had absorbed over the centuries the agricultural methods of pueblo Indians and Spanish techniques of animal husbandry, especially sheep-rearing. This blend of traditions formed the basis of a deeply rooted cultural identity and enabled them to resist the later onslaught from white America. Today they have the largest population of any Indian group in the USA and retain a reservation about the size of the state of West Virginia. However, in the late 1860s when they were originally exiled to the Bosque Redondo reservation with another group of Apache, such was the antagonism between the two closely related ethnic groups that they fought regular pitched battles.

Another of the seven branches of the Apache people were the Chiricahua, who ranged across the southernmost portions of Apacheria, including the Sierra Madre Mountains of Mexico proper. Over time these Indians had splintered into a number of smaller groups and bands, like the community led by Cochise and normally identified by his name, or the Bedonkohé, who were Geronimo's own particular people. Although the Chiricahua retained some capacity for collective action, such as the assault on the Mexican garrison in which Geronimo had acquired his legendary name, their political inclinations were at best democratic and consensual, and at worst deeply fissiparous.

The Chiricahua may have offered the most prolonged resistance to white domination, but they were also the Apache group that best dramatised the classic failure of tribal society. Individual Chiricahua like Jason Betzinez, a witness and participant in their final struggles, recognised the destructive impact of their internal disputes. 'A common subject of discussion among the[m],' he wrote, 'was the fact that the Apache were never able to form a strong confederation, on account of indifference and selfishness on the part of the different chiefs.'[14] Another damaging by-product of these rifts was the ease with which their white opponents were able to recruit Apache warriors to act as scouts and auxiliaries for their campaigns of pursuit. The reservation militia that helped Clum catch Geronimo was a typical example of an Apache force used against other Apaches. Without these aides the US forces would never have been so successful.

Later, following the defeat and submission of the 'renegades', their divisiveness had equally deleterious consequences. At San Carlos, the Chiricahua were often the worst offenders, at times even kidnapping and fighting their own people. However, they were by no means the only culprits. The reservation became a hot-bed of inter- and intra-tribal rivalries and while the Apaches could take a good measure of blame for these troubles, the government's scheme to corral them all into one place cut right across their traditional methods of avoiding dispute.

Another Apache custom that was severely affected by reservation life and which, indeed, the US policy of concentration was intended to curb, was their practice of raiding. Violent and socially disruptive it may have been, but raiding was a measure of the opportunist approach to resources adopted by the hunter–gatherer. Equally, evidence for its long pedigree in Apache culture appears even in their name. For the title by which the tribe is now universally recognised was not one originally used by them. Their own word to identify themselves was *Diné*, or *Indeh*, meaning simply 'the Living' or 'the People'. 'Apache', by contrast, derived from the language of the Zuni, to whom it denoted the 'enemy'.[15]

The whole issue of raiding was closely bound up with the consensual and democratic nature of Apache society. A chief could exert only limited authority over his people and an individual's participation in any collective enterprise, even defence of the tribe, was undertaken only on a voluntary basis. Conversely, each warrior could attempt independent operations without sanction from his chief. Geronimo's own career well illustrates this aspect of Apache society. Following the murder of his family he pursued a reckless and indiscriminate vendetta against Mexicans, making repeated sorties across the border. Some of these ventures cost the lives of men he had persuaded to join him, while Geronimo was himself almost killed on at least one occasion.

On the other hand, private raiding ventures did function as a proving-ground for young warriors like Geronimo – a test of their courage and resourcefulness – and success could confer tribal prestige on the lucky participant. Raids also brought material benefits in terms of stolen booty, and they were an important channel by which both individual Apache and whole bands could acquire wealth. Generosity, a cardinal virtue within Apache society, was given full rein once a successful mission brought an influx of bounty. Thus, by the time of white America's arrival in the Southwest, Apache attacks upon neighbouring communities were an integral element of the social and economic life of the Chiricahua.

Yet it is impossible to overlook the deeply destructive impact of raiding. It created a tradition of ineradicable hostility amongst all their neighbours, Indian, Mexican and white, and it was bound to lead to conflict, especially with the latter, who were as aggressive and predatory as themselves. This was even more the case when Apache attacks involved those extremes of behaviour that had given rise to their reputation for merciless savagery. One such incident involved an attack by 200 Apaches on a Mexican wagon train bound for

California. The Indians duped the eight well-armed families into surrendering half their wagons and mules and their weapons, then strapped the men to the wheels, lit fires beneath their upturned heads and roasted their brains, while the women and children were all taken into captivity.[16]

This was the kind of monstrous offence that launched the careers of corresponding white psychopaths such as Sugarfoot Jack. Yet the US war with the Apache was not simply a downward corkscrew of revenge atrocities, triggered by Indian violence. Although a self-perpetuating vendetta did play its part, the conflict with white America had its roots in a deeper and wider syndrome, for which the latter must take a full measure of responsibility.

While predatory raids were an inbuilt reflex of the Apache's warrior society and while raids directed at white settlers were bound to provoke a retaliatory response, it was equally the case that the Euro-Americans' incursion into tribal lands took absolutely no account of Indian occupancy and undermined their economy by destroying game and other natural harvests. Moreover, Apache raids were not initially targeted at white Americans, but focused on the traditional Mexican enemy.

It was only as whites moved deeper into Apacheria that raids became more likely, both because of the increased proximity of the two communities and because the Apache sought compensation for their wider ecological losses. By the time they had been stripped of their traditional lands – with all the natural products that had provided an alternative livelihood – and then marooned on only a desolate fragment like San Carlos, those Apaches attempting to maintain their independence had become virtually dependent on raiding as an economic necessity. As in the case of the British with the Tasmanians, white America's vision of the Apache as raiding savages was largely a self-fulfilling prophecy.

It was this cycle of cultural incompatibility and misunderstanding that formed a background to the first period of violence between the *Indeh* and whites in 1861. However, its more immediate trigger was a ruthless episode of kidnap, murder and atrocity, although on this occasion they were not exclusively Indian deeds. The first Apache war is now widely recognised to have originated in the blunders of US army personnel.

The incident began with the abduction of a young Irish-Mexican boy by an Apache raiding party. When his parents applied to the US army for his return, an inexperienced second lieutenant called George Bascom was sent with over fifty troops into the Chiricahua stronghold to arrange a meeting with Cochise. The unsuspecting leader duly obliged, only to find himself held to account for the actions of an Indian band totally outside his control or his knowledge. Although Cochise offered to retrieve the boy and find the offenders, he and his family were made victims of the same kind of trap that had ensnared Geronimo. However, the Chiricahua leader had not earned his reputation amongst white Americans as 'an uncompromising enemy to all mankind' for meekness and timidity.[17] Finding himself under arrest, Cochise whipped out a knife, slashed the tent wall and escaped amidst a hail of bullets.

By the time Cochise had seized his own set of hostages no white official troubled himself to consider how they had arrived at this stand-off. Like the original kidnap of the boy, the round of revenge killings that ensued were all to be set down to Cochise's account. When the army refused to release the chief's relatives, he slaughtered a number of his captives, at which point Bascom hung his six Apache prisoners at the site of the whites' remains. And so it escalated. Within days, fighting was general. Within three months the Apaches had killed 150 Americans.

The army then seemed to enjoy a stroke of better fortune. Along with Cochise, the other key Chiricahua leader was his father-in-law, Mangas Colorado. By 1863 he was about seventy, yet even in old age he retained the physical presence and natural authority that had led one commentator to suggest Mangas was 'beyond all comparison the most famous Apache warrior and statesman', who 'exercised an influence never equalled by any savage of our time'.[18] He had initially attempted friendly relations with the white settlers, but after being seized during a visit to a mining settlement and horsewhipped he had readily participated in Cochise's campaign of attacks.

Then the old chief, despite his sage reputation and his years, made a second diplomatic mission to a white camp. Invited in under a flag of truce, Mangas quickly found himself placed under arrest once more. This time he would not pay so lightly for his trust. The commanding officer told the chief's guard: 'I want him dead or alive tomorrow morning, do you understand, I want him dead.'[19] During the night the two pickets duly obliged, heating their bayonets over an open fire and sticking them on the prisoner's bare feet and legs. When at last the chief responded, they shot him six times through the head and torso. His body was rifled for souvenirs, while his corpse was later scalped and dismembered, the massive head being cut off and boiled down to the skull in a big pot.[20]

Geronimo called this 'Perhaps the greatest wrong ever done to the Indians', while one contemporary Apache has described Mangas' murder, along with Bascom's arrest of Cochise and his family, as 'his people's "Pearl Harbor"'.[21] For the tribe the decapitation of their great chief meant that he was doomed to wander headless through eternity. A number of them suggested that their own post-mortem mutilation of American victims was in response to this piece of white savagery.[22] Although this causative relationship is disputed, there is little doubt that the two assaults on the Chiricahua chiefs helped launch a decade of warfare. The fighting would cost the lives of 5,000 whites.[23] In one single seven-kilometre stretch of road, 400 were reputed to have died in only five years. In response, the US army between 1862 and 1871 expended $38 million on a campaign that resulted in the deaths of just 100 Apaches, including old men, women and children.[24]

By the early 1870s the US government, searching for a solution to the intractable Apache 'problem', adopted tactics that involved a mixture of carrot and stick. While the Chiricahua remained undefeated and susceptible only to the first, in the form of territorial guarantees, the second was used with greater impact elsewhere in Apacheria. The soldier wielding the cudgel was one Lieutenant-Colonel George Crook, a warrior just a little younger than Geronimo himself, and with a military reputation equal to the Apache's own.

According to President Grant and General Sherman, commander of the US army, Crook was the greatest Indian fighter in American history. Yet this brilliant career had started in unpromising fashion, the young cadet having passed out of West Point thirty-eighth in a class of forty-four. However, as Joseph Porter has suggested, the taciturn, somewhat gruff demeanour 'veiled the soul of an innovative and aggressive officer'.[25] Firstly in Oregon, Idaho and California, then later in the Southwest, Crook built up an enormous experience of Indian cultures and of wilderness lore, becoming himself a passionate hunter. He also developed a corresponding aversion to the ignorance and alcoholic habits of many time-serving fellow officers. Unconventional in his attitudes to discipline and dress, he hardly ever wore military uniform in the field. Yet, with Crook's eccentricities came a deeply innovative approach to military tactics which entirely transformed the campaign in Apacheria.

His most inspired policy was to employ 'tame' Indians in pursuit of their compatriots – although the widespread use of the adjective 'tame' to describe his Apache scouts understates Crook's originality. For his preference was for the recruitment of the wildest Indians available, who, he recognised, made the most skilful and toughest guides. His other great innovation was to detach his fighting force from its dependence on lengthy, cumbersome and unreliable supply wagons and replace them in part with compact, efficiently managed mule trains. These he often supervised down to the smallest detail, exercising a meticulous eye for organisation, for the quality of his equipment and the worth of his subordinates.

Crook's other great asset was his aide-de-camp, Lieutenant John Gregory Bourke. In the words of his biographer, the Irish-American Bourke became 'adviser, confidant, amanuensis, and henchman to the silent, austere' colonel, although any image of him as merely Crook's second fiddle would be a radical injustice.[26] During the late nineteenth century Bourke was one of the most talented officers serving in the US army, an ethnologist with a distinguished reputation and a gifted author, whose book *On The Border with Crook* is a classic of Western literature. The many talents of the aide-de-camp were highly complementary to those of his superior. Where Crook was taciturn and uncommunicative, Bourke was highly sociable and possessed of a devastating wit, which he used to powerful effect in his own writings and in presenting Crook's campaigns to a wider audience.

Of widely differing temperament, the two men also had many qualities in common, such as their intellectual honesty, their sense of fairness and their deep contempt for the corruption rooted in US policies towards Indians. Asked once if it was not hard to set off on yet another campaign against the savage, Crook replied: 'Yes, it is hard. But, sir, the hardest thing is to go and fight those whom you know are in the right.'[27] Although Bourke's early career was marked by a crudity common to many in the army – he had framed a pair of Indian ears and used a scalp as a lamp mat – he was soon to bury his human souvenirs and embark on a long intellectual and spiritual journey towards the first people of the American continent. To a degree greater even than his distinguished master, Bourke developed deep personal ties with and political sympathies for his Indian opponents. Later still he became a vigorous champion of the Chiricahua, vehemently denouncing their mistreatment and exile in the American east.

Charity and sympathy, however, did not seem to form part of Crook and Bourke's programme for the Apache in the winter of 1872. In November of that year the colonel unleashed his hammer-blow against a large group known collectively as the Western Apache. These Indians occupied a region of Arizona to the west and north of San Carlos, including an area known as the Tonto Basin. Bourke called this stronghold of soaring crags and impassable defiles 'one of the roughest spots on the globe'.[28] However, having divided his forces into a number of compact, highly mobile columns, each with a unit of Indian scouts, Crook was confident that he could comb the area incessantly until his enemy was either overtaken and destroyed, or forced to surrender through sheer attrition.

In the event, it took five months of relentless campaigning, but Crook's plan proved its worth. So too had his Apache scouts, who, for courage and physical resilience, had outstripped any of the other Indian tribes employed, while their tracking skills were acknowledged by Bourke as crucial to the whole arduous enterprise.[29] The aide-de-camp calculated that one of the commands in its 147 days of patrols covered 2,000 kilometres and killed 500 Apaches. However, there were few pitched battles of any great significance. The most famous of the engagements, in which Bourke was a participant, was known as the Battle of Salt River Cave. Apache men, women and children had been surprised and trapped inside their own secret stronghold. But by firing at its roof and making the bullets ricochet down beyond the cavern's throat, the soldiers killed almost all those inside. Bourke counted seventy-three casualties.[30]

Ruthless as his campaign had been, the newly promoted Crook now showed that humanity which subsequently led his fellow general, Philip Sheridan, to declare him soft on Indians. The honesty and genuine concern that Crook blended with his policy of firmness constituted one of the few true rays of light in the gloomy tale of tribal–white war in the Southwest. Guided by the humane ideas of his aide-de-camp, Crook sought to equip the reservation Apaches with the necessary economic and social stability to withstand the oncoming tide of white settlement. As far as possible Apaches were to manage their own affairs, while Crook arranged for the army to buy Apache harvests in order to create the market essential to their self-sufficiency. He also knew the importance of protecting them from corrupt whites.

'Bad as Indians often are,' he once wrote, 'I have never yet seen one so demoralized that he was not an example in honor and nobility to the wretches who enrich themselves by plundering him of the little our Government appropriates for him.'[31]

By 1875 the prospects for racial harmony in the Southwest had never been better. In central Arizona there were three reservations based on the US military posts at Camp Verde, Fort Apache and San Carlos. In the far south, peace had even come to the Chiricahua. Much against Crook's better judgement he was keen to prove himself a military match even for the great Cochise – they had been confirmed in possession of their old haunts between the Dragoon and Chiricahua Ranges. On their eastern flank, Victorio's people, the Warm Springs Indians, over whom Mangas Colorado had once presided so skilfully, settled down on a reservation in their beloved homeland in south-western New Mexico. Further east still were two other reservations for additional discrete communities within the Apache nation.

There remained undoubted problems, some of them serious, such as the Apache raids. The Chiricahua of Cochise, for instance, continued to penetrate deep into Mexico with impunity and despite their chief's disapproval. However, the foundations of a lasting settlement were in place. The various Apache tribes had been confirmed in at least a portion of their favoured territories. Crook had implemented a viable programme for the reservations, and although it reflected the conventional views of the age – that of the savage doomed inexorably either to the white man's path or to extinction – the general himself was both honest and well-meaning. 'Crook was a true friend of ours,' recalled Jason Betzinez. 'He was a hard fighter . . . But he played fair with us afterwards and did what he could to protect the Indians. We actually loved General Crook, and even today think of him, and talk of him, with genuine affection.'[32] The process of mutual trust that he had initiated could have carried white–red relations forward into a period of co-existence.

Tragically, amongst the region's wider American community the desire for a just settlement of the Indian–white conflict had never taken root. As soon as Crook and Bourke were removed from the scene in 1875 (to the northern plains, where they would help subdue the gathering Lakota storm), the ancient pattern of European behaviour towards tribal people resumed. The keenest exponents of these methods were the leading merchants of the Southwest, known generically as 'The Tucson Ring', who had grown accustomed to the fat profits produced from their army contracts. Inevitably, they had little to gain from peace. Hostile Indians were their bread and butter. Nor did they have much enthusiasm for Crook's project of Apache self-sufficiency, as Bourke noted with characteristically biting sarcasm:

> Had the Apaches had a little more sense they would have perceived that the whole scheme of Caucasian contact with the American aborigines – at least the Anglo-Saxon part of it – has been based upon that fundamental maxim of politics so beautifully and so tersely enunciated by the New York alderman – 'The boys are in it for the stuff.' The 'Tucson Ring' was determined that no Apache should be put to the embarrassment of working for his own living; once let the Apache become self-supporting, and what would become of 'the boys'?[33]

The Tucson Ring was not the only group profiteering. A number of agents on the reservations were swindling both their government and the Apache. Crook alleged that one of these officials had left Arizona having made $50,000 in only a short time, while on some reservations they had so reduced rations it had actually caused starvation amongst the inmates.[34] Writing specifically of the San Carlos agency, Bourke believed that the corruption 'extended all the way to Washington, and infolded in its meshes officials of high rank'.[35] Although he worked on the reservation during a later period, Britton Davis, a scrupulously honest military officer, described the kinds of manoeuvres he unearthed. Checking the meat rations delivered to his Indians, Davis found that a fraudulent set of scales meant a contractor was being paid each week for 680 kilos of beef that he never delivered.[36]

The Apache were deeply aware of this exploitation, and their sense of grievance only exacerbated the festering atmosphere of discontent on the reservations. Yet the mixture of hatred and contempt for Indians that underpinned white abuses also made it extremely difficult for Apache complaints to be aired. More than perhaps any other incident, the aftermath of the Camp Grant Massacre illustrates the prevailing attitudes that blocked justice for reservation Indians.

This tragedy had occurred in April 1871, when two leading citizens of Tucson led a group of 140 Papago Indians and Mexicans on an Indian hunting foray. The justification for the expedition was a set of attacks

falsely attributed to Apaches living in the vicinity of a US military station at Camp Grant. Disregarding the small matter of proof for their
allegations, the raiders struck without warning and caught the Apache
settlement while most of the men were absent. In fact, only eight of
the 144 Indians 'ravished, wounded . . . clubbed to death, hacked to
pieces or brained by rocks' were male.[37]

It was typical of the murderous mood in the American West that in
their coverage of what one historian has called 'the blackest page in the
Anglo-Saxon records of Arizona', the Denver *News* congratulated the
killers 'on the fact that permanent peace arrangements have been made
with so many, and we only regret that the number was not double'.[38]
Eastern opinion, however, was far from sympathetic to the action and
at President Grant's insistence, the ringleaders were eventually brought
to trial. After a five-day hearing it took just nineteen minutes' deliber-
ation for the jury to find the murderers not guilty.[39]

Recalling other instances of incurable bias, Britton Davis noted the
occasion he arrested a man for illegally selling whisky and ammunition
to San Carlos Apaches. He took him to be imprisoned in Tucson,
only to find the culprit back on the street within thirty minutes.[40] Yet
whisky dealers could have a devastating impact on reservation life.
The classic example was an incident in 1876, two years after Cochise's
death and only four years after his Chiricahua had been confirmed in
possession of their favourite territory. The affair began when the
deeply respected agent to this group of Apaches rebuked and threatened a station-keeper for peddling booze amongst his Indian charges.
However, having continued the trade in defiance of the agent's
authority, the station-keeper reaped the tragic rewards of his crime: his
Apache clients murdered him during their drunken stupor.

The same Tucson citizens who would later so blandly reprove the
whisky trader arrested by Britton Davis, now weighed in on behalf of
the dealer murdered by the Chiricahua. 'The kind of war needed' for
such Indians, railed the Tucson newspaper the *Arizona Citizen*, 'is
steady, unrelenting, hopeless, and undiscriminating war, slaying men,
women, and children . . . until every valley and crest and crag and
fastness shall send to high heaven the grateful incense of festering and
rotting Chiricahuas.'[41] Even worse than this genocidal blather was the
fact that the US authorities, with this incident as their pretext, now
shut down the Chiricahua reservation and sent John Clum in on his
round-up operation.

The dishonest behaviour that obliterated the best efforts of men like

General Crook, and which culminated in the policy of concentrating the Apaches at San Carlos, was not exclusive to this particular theatre. It was symptomatic of an entire pattern of relations between whites and Indians across the United States. Even in the 1770s, as settlers poured through the Appalachians, grabbing the territory around the Ohio River, the governor of Virginia, Lord Dunmore, wrote in support of the westering settlers:

> Do not conceive that government has any right to forbid their taking possession of a vast tract of country . . . which serves as a shelter to a few scattered tribes of Indians. Nor can they be easily brought to entertain any belief of the permanent obligation of treaties made with those people, whom they consider as but little removed from the brute creation.[42]

A century later, Francis Walker, the Commissioner of Indian Affairs, writing of the northern plains, expressed the same ideas with even greater candour when he suggested that 'There is no question of national dignity . . . involved in the treatment of savages by a civilized power.' Walker went on to explain the reservation system as the reduction of 'wild beasts to the condition of supplicants for charity'.[43]

As a continuation of these views and methods, the policy of Apache concentration is particularly revealing. For the unwanted geographical territory on which they planned to corral all the *Indeh* was the physical embodiment of that cramped mental space to which white Americans had assigned Indians in their imaginative world. This interior design pictured native peoples and their political claims upon the American continent as a minor distraction raised by beings unworthy of human status. Where they could not be eliminated by immediate destruction or physical removal, they might be held at bay by written agreement. But these contracts functioned only as expedients without binding significance. Like the documents establishing the Chiricahua and Warm Springs Apache reservations, they could be cancelled unilaterally or at short notice. They were usually empty words that echoed with four centuries of false white promises, right back to the smooth assurances of Hernan Cortés.

Inbuilt into such a set of prescriptions was its own justification. For when Indians responded with force to such injustice, they merely confirmed the savagery in which they had always been imprisoned in the white American conscience. Crook identified the syndrome with characteristic clarity: 'The American Indian commands respect for his rights only so long as he inspires terror from his rifle.'[44] The Chiricahua Apaches, dispossessed, discontent, herded on to the arid wasteland of San Carlos to squabble and be cheated by their white overseers, were soon to inspire respect for their rights in a manner that was as devastating as it was ultimately hopeless.

14

America's Greatest
Guerrilla Fighter

A lthough it was Geronimo who would later acquire renown amongst a white audience as the last great renegade against US domination, he was not the only Apache to challenge the reservation system at San Carlos. Nor were his exploits unrivalled in the annals of their resistance. In fact, it is another Chiricahua leader, Victorio, who has been unequivocally identified as 'America's greatest guerrilla fighter' by Dan Thrapp, his biographer and one of the principal white keepers of the Apache story.[1]

After Mangas Colorado's death in 1863, Victorio slowly earned the chieftaincy of the Warm Springs section of the Chiricahua. The murdered Apache statesman could not have had a more fitting successor. An approximate translation of Victorio's Apache name is 'The Conqueror', while one of his people later recalled that he was 'the most nearly perfect human being' he had ever seen.[2] Only a single photograph of him exists, but it is almost enough. Except for the piercing directness of the gaze, the face and shoulder-length hair appear like a bronze mask clamped within a frame of coarsely weathered timber. It registers the resolve and intelligence common to the faces of all Apache leaders. But in addition to these, one senses something of the qualities that marked Victorio's subsequent career: the military flair, the courage, determination in the face of hopeless odds, a capacity for ruthless violence.

Yet when reviewing the details of his individual case, one cannot help concluding that of all Apache leaders, Victorio was amongst those most unjustly victimised by the policy of concentration. Thrapp described him as being 'badgered, "removed", bullied, stolen from, shifted about, lied to and betrayed, separated from his family, starved, threatened, cajoled', until he was forced to respond in the campaign that will be for ever associated with his name.[3]

Ultimately, this was a conflict rooted in the land from which he and his people had sprung. For they had always shown a passionate affinity for the Mimbres and Black Range Mountains of south-western New Mexico, and especially for an area known as Ojo Caliente – a region of upland forest and wide lush valleys at the headwaters of the Alamosa River on the west bank of the Rio Grande. It was a geographical attachment that accounted for the designations by which the group was variously known, such as the Mimbres, or the Mimbrenos, the Warm Springs or Ojo Caliente Apaches, the last two names being inspired by the sacred fountain at the heart of their territory.[4]

Tragically, almost from the outset of hostilities in the Southwest, the idea that this Indian group must leave its cherished sanctuary seems to have been an unquestioned and irremovable fixture of American policy. As Thrapp has pointed out,

few ever considered acceding to their simple request to remain where they were, in their traditional homeland . . . whose mountains, valleys, deserts, and canyons they knew and loved. They must be moved. Why? Search the records from end to end, the thousands upon thousands of documents, and you will discover no valid reason. There was no reason. It was simply that, since they desired to remain, they must be moved.[5]

During Victorio's leadership the Warm Springs Apaches had no record of violence to compare with that of Cochise or Mangas Colorado. In fact, almost until the date of his final challenge to US authority there was no evidence to link his name to a single white death. The chief's one overriding wish seems to have been for his people to be left in peace in their homeland. Even after he had been roused to a state of antagonism, his whole war policy, except to express implacable opposition to removal, seems to have been a simple, physical reoccupation of Ojo Caliente's hallowed valleys.

Thus, when John Clum set out for south-west New Mexico in April 1877, to capture Geronimo and then shut down the Warm Springs agency on the pretext that they had harboured such a renegade, the fires of war were already starting to glow. Although Victorio agreed to leave with the agent for San Carlos, the realities of life on the sun-baked, malarial flats at the Arizonan reservation quickly proved too high a price for peace. Just three months later, and only weeks after Clum himself had resigned, Victorio roused over 320 of his people, they rustled together every mule and horse they could find and rode off into the darkness towards their old hunting-grounds.

By the end of September they had arrived back at Warm Springs, after losing more than thirty of their number, as captives or casualties in a string of indecisive skirmishes. Victorio then set about trying to re-establish his claim to the Warm Springs territory, negotiating with army officers stationed to the north of his old reservation. For almost a year an uncertain if peaceful stalemate obtained, but behind the scenes tragedy was struggling to be born.

In October 1878, the US government in Washington eventually arrived at its final decision. It reaffirmed a commitment to the policy of concentration and sent in the troops to do its bidding. As one historian has concluded, 'The myopic obstinacy of the government almost defies credibility.'[6] Later that month about 170 of the women, children and the elderly were loaded on to wagons for the 660-kilometre journey back to San Carlos. But just as Victorio had warned when rejecting the US demands, almost none of his warriors was amongst the transportees. Throughout the winter, the outlawed band now pursued a life of silent raids amongst the farmsteads and ranches of southern New Mexico. Then Victorio, his patience and faith in their word waning inexorably, made a final appeal to the white men to be allowed to remain at Ojo Caliente.

While Washington remained invincibly deaf to the wishes of a band of homesick savages, it did offer them a compromise: they might settle on a reservation occupied by another band of *Indeh*, the Mescalero Apaches, in the Sacramento Mountains 200 kilometres further to the east. It was not Warm Springs, but nor was it San Carlos, and Victorio presented himself at the agency in June 1879.

Then blind fate took a hand in shaping the next act of the drama. As Victorio waited nervously at his new home for confirmation of the US decision and the arrival of his women and children, a judge and prosecuting attorney happened to pass close to the reservation on a hunting and fishing excursion. By sheer chance, the Warm Springs Indians had got wind of news that they had been indicted on charges of horse-stealing and murder elsewhere in New Mexico. Victorio put these unrelated coincidences together and assumed that the judge's holiday party was actually out hunting for him. Rumour became panic and panic led, inexorably, to violence. As Thrapp put it in Yeats-like rhythms:

> In a passion, Victorio jerked the agent's beard, whistled in his horse herd, ordered the women into action, hurriedly packed his ponies, and with his fellows scampered toward the westward mountains once more. It was September 4, 1879. They were through with reservation life; from now on forever it would be war.[7]

Immediately Victorio returned to the Warm Springs area, slew the guard to an army horse herd and remounted his growing band of fighters. He had actually embarked on war with the United States of America supported by just forty warriors, but he quickly drew recruits from other Apache groups and at its largest his band numbered about 450 people.

Their first major confrontation with the troops pouring in from Arizona and across New Mexico to intercept them was a carefully planned ambush in the Black Range close to Ojo Caliente. Although fierce fighting continued all day, American casualties were relatively few – ten according to Thrapp – but the Apaches withdrew in good order and with a number of army horses and large amounts of booty.

Skirmishes recurred, but inconclusively, as Victorio made his circuitous route through the Black Range then south towards Mexico. While the army trailed them through the desert sands and lava beds towards the border, the Apaches worked in concert with the terrain and the climate to exact their toll. One water hole they repeatedly rode through until it assumed the consistency of thin mortar. Another they fouled with the entrails of a coyote. Eventually thirst began to undermine the pursuing force. 'The number of animals killed by the rearguard increased,' recalled one participant, 'the sun seemed to beat down hotter and hotter. There was no singing, no joking, no conversation, no smoking in the column, and the banjo of a colored man that used to enliven the men was silent.' In seventy-six hours, on just half a pint of water per man, they had ridden 200 kilometres. Yet, before these heroes could drink and give up the chase, they were ambushed by moonlight in old Mexico.[8]

Victorio stayed in the mountains for the first half of winter, then rode north in the new year. Troops were massed close to the border ready to block his passage, and one newspaper announced that the US army 'have the renegades about where they want them'.[9] Victorio then waltzed past, heading once more for the Black Range. It was claimed that the Apaches had killed as many as a hundred American civilians in the previous year's campaign. Now the casualties increased and Major Morrow, the officer who had chased Victorio throughout the previous fall, made a determined effort to get his man.

Four further engagements ensued as the Apaches were hounded between the Black Range and the San Andreas Mountains, and although none was conclusive, the balance of success lay heavily in Victorio's favour. And throughout the contest the Apaches had had no guaranteed supply of *matériel* whatsoever, except the little they could steal or capture. The same was also true for horses. They had always to mount themselves on stolen stock and, if necessary, they rode them to exhaustion, at which point they were always killed and often consumed. Between 600 and 1,000 was the estimated total by the spring of 1880. These tactics had ground Morrow's men to a temporary standstill. His commanding officer, General Hatch, reported that the horses were 'mere shadows' while the men's spirits, like their boots and outfits, were in shreds.[10]

It seemed incredible that, as the war with Victorio moved towards its climax and as the Americans, according to Thrapp, launched 'the greatest manhunt in the history of the Southwest', the Warm Springs Indians had remained ahead of them all.[11] But then the wonder lay in the nature of the Apache warrior. All the American participants who wrote an account of the wars attested to the Indians' legendary stamina. Britton Davis thought 'They were the most perfect specimens of the racing type of athlete that one could wish to see':

They were of medium height, few over five feet eight, but proportioned like deer. Small hands and feet; small bones; thin arms and legs, the latter sinewed as though with steel cords, so taut were the sinews and devoid of fat. Chests broad, deep, and full, the heritage from generations of mountain-dwelling ancestors, they moved along the trail with a smooth, effortless stride that seemed as tireless as a machine and as rhythmical. The thought of attempting to catch one of them in the mountains gave one a queer feeling of helplessness, but I enjoyed a sensation of the beautiful in watching them.[12]

Bourke wrote that campaigning Apaches could maintain 125 kilometres a day for three or four days, until any pursuer was completely thrown off the scent and in temperatures that would kill white men.[13]

John Clum, when he was heading towards the Warm Springs agency to arrest Geronimo, recounted how his Apache militia indulged in a two-hour war dance after completing a fifty-kilometre march through 'dust, cactus and a broiling sun'. As their chief 'smilingly explained, "they thought they were not getting sufficient exercise."' [14]

Although fighting warriors unencumbered by family and possessions were undoubtedly the most formidable opposition, Apache women were hardly less capable than their men. 'There is no tiger more dangerous than an infuriated squaw,' exclaimed John Bourke. 'She's a fiend incarnate.' [15] Davis described an occasion when a patrol was fired on after a skirmish, only to discover a young woman with a bullet wound just above the knee. She and her six-month-old infant were carried for almost two hours across a rugged, near-perpendicular canyon. As she waited to be operated upon by US surgeons a storm of freezing hail soaked her and the child to the skin. The next day they cut the leg off without anaesthetic or even a little whisky to numb the pain. The woman withstood the ordeal without a murmur, then was made to ride mule-back for another week to an army depot. Months later at San Carlos, Davis saw her again, running with the aid of crutches. [16]

A tale of even greater physical and spiritual resource was the odyssey performed by five Apache women who had been transported to Mexico City. After three years of slavery these Amazons escaped from their owners. Sleeping by day and walking by night, they covered more than 1,600 kilometres through country they had never seen before. They were able to cook food only once, but eventually arrived in Apacheria barefoot, armed with one knife and a single blanket. [17]

Without question the most celebrated of all Apache women in the late nineteenth century was Victorio's own sister, Lozen. Although it was not common in Indian society, Lozen was a fighter on equal terms with the male members of her band. She could withstand all the customary hardships of the Apache at war, and was skilled with both horse and rifle. Her most remarkable talent, known amongst her people as her 'power', was a capacity to locate the whereabouts of an enemy. Turning in a dervish-like trance she detected their presence through the palms of her hands, which were said to turn purple if attack were imminent. [18] Many members of the tribe believed implicitly in the existence and effectiveness of these mystical gifts. Indeed, they were the hallmark and currency of the Apache shaman. As we shall see, Geronimo himself claimed extraordinary powers, which were subsequently confirmed by the eye-witness testimony of other Apaches.

Beyond Lozen's mystical equivalent of an early warning system, Victorio had few other genuine advantages to offer his 160 warriors. Yet with these men he had maintained himself in the field for almost ten months against an enemy that outnumbered him by more than ten to one, including three cavalry regiments, two of infantry, a contingent of Texas rangers and a large number of Mexican troops. Moreover, Victorio's opponents enjoyed the benefits of a supply network entirely dedicated to their support. Even more incredible, perhaps, than this military achievement, itself an extraordinary feat of escapology engaging the entire complement of Apache war skills, was Victorio's ability to hold his people together, men, women and children, protecting and supplying them throughout the fighting. Despite all their hardships, none of his group seems ever to have doubted his decision to fight, nor his right to lead. Given these facts, it seems difficult to resist Thrapp's judgement of unparalleled Apache greatness.

While his record cannot be disputed, Victorio's life was destined to encompass all the elements of the tragic hero. He could keep moving and stay ahead of the lumbering American units, but time was not on his side. The simple process of attrition was beginning to count and he had also to contend with the rival talents of the US army's Apache guides. Eventually these forces caught up with him in his beloved Black Range, where he was surprised and savaged in a blind canyon by a party of Indian auxiliaries. In the midst of the fighting the scouts taunted that they had wounded the Warm Springs chief himself. Responding to the boast, one of the squaws shouted back that if their leader should die, they would eat him rather than let his body fall into enemy hands.[19]

One more time the Apaches struggled free of the trap, then headed again for the sanctuary of Mexico. This time, however, Mexico was waiting. Victorio had now lost some of his best men. Each was irreplaceable. For three more months he zigzagged across northern Mexico and western Texas, short of ammunition and desperate for a place to pause and rest his band. Eventually, in October 1880, he made the wrong choice.

While waiting for a small raiding party to acquire the ammunition they desperately needed, the Apache was taken by surprise at a place called Tres Castillos. Troops under a Mexican general, Joaquin Terrazas, completely surrounded the Warm Springs Indians. By coincidence, Lozen was absent, which for some Apaches explained the disaster. The defending force expended its limited ammunition then faced an onslaught from over 250 Mexican soldiers. Seventy-eight Apaches were slain, most of them warriors. A similar number of women and children were captured and enslaved. A Mexican soldier, a Tarahumara Indian, received the 2,000 pesos reward for killing Victorio, although this is rejected still by the Apaches themselves, who claim the great chief died by his own knife. Looking at the bronze and weathered oak in Victorio's only photographic portrait, one would not lightly disagree.

In Washington the Mexican victory was heralded as a 'noteworthy feat of arms which will exert so great an influence over the tranquility of both frontiers'.[20] As usual with regard to the Apaches, the bigwigs were off target. The tragic and unnecessarily violent tale of Victorio had run its course, but an equally violent epilogue was just then beginning. From the bloodbath at Tres Castillos had emerged seventeen survivors. Amongst these was a chief called Nana.

One US army officer once dismissed this elderly and lame Indian as 'palsied . . . and decrepit . . . barely able to accompany the squaws and children in their forays'.[21] It was indeed true that Nana was revered 'for his tenderness to the young, his consideration of the women, his courtesy to his fellow warriors and his complete devotion to his tribe'.[22] But his people also knew him as the fiercest and most implacable of all Apaches, shrewdest in military strategy and surpassing even Victorio himself.[23] Certainly, Victorio had always sought his advice and inspiration. In the ensuing few months, Nana was to show why.

Driven by a passion for vengeance that seems biblical in outline and intensity, Nana embarked on a raid across Mexico and the American Southwest that has few parallels. Thrapp called it 'legendary', while another Southwest historian, David Roberts, wrote that of all deeds of war performed by the Chiricahua it 'was arguably the most brilliant'.[24]

It began in June 1881, Nana gathering recruits and momentum as he rode. His average was 80 kilometres a day, although on some this rose to 120. So fast and so great were the distances covered that some newspapers reported the depredations as being committed by the entire Mescalero section of the Apache. About 1,400 Americans took the field, 1,000 of them regular troops, as Nana's force swept in and out of the Black Range. Few, however, had the misfortune to make any sort of contact. Those who managed to engage them, like the twenty-strong cavalry patrol that caught them in a last fierce gunfight before the Apaches regained their Mexican sanctuary, often reported such encounters in the official record as US victories. Typically, this last engagement resulted in the death of the cavalry officer, half his force being killed or wounded, while the Indians remained in command of the field.

In truth, the Apaches had fought and won seven serious fire fights, had ridden 5,000 kilometres, killed between thirty and fifty Americans, wounded many more and captured no fewer than 200 horses and mules. At the outset Nana's men had numbered fifteen. They had never been more than forty. Nana himself was about seventy-five years old. Palsied and decrepit he might have seemed; the old warrior had only just started.

15

Geronimo – The Last Renegade

After the tragedy of his family's massacre in Mexico during the 1850s, Geronimo claimed to have received a shaman's vision informing him of his invulnerability to the weapons of his enemies. Given the many gunshot wounds he survived during his long life, one is almost persuaded to believe in some protective 'power'. And never did it appear more effective than when he returned to San Carlos as Clum's prisoner in 1877.

Despite the Indian agent's avowed intention to see his captive speedily hanged, Geronimo was curiously reprieved soon after, then set free. Subsequent Chiricahua testimony suggested that Clum was pressured by other Apache leaders to release him, although this is not entirely certain.[1] Even Geronimo himself, in his autobiography, was unable to give a precise reason for his liberation.

Nor did he know in the autumn of 1880, as he bided his time on the San Carlos flats, that the torch of Apache opposition would pass to him in the wake of Victorio's death. Yet Geronimo was destined to carry that flame to the end of his people's military resistance, and then endure almost a quarter of a century of exile and imprisonment. That record alone was testimony to his stamina and resilience. However, it also brings into focus the deep character differences that separated him from the Chiricahua leader killed at Tres Castillos.

Although the actions and motives of Victorio were never so fully documented, one gains clear insight into his character from a variety of clues. We know, for instance, that he was an abstemious man and was never known to be drunk, exceptional amongst a people so famously vulnerable to the white man's stimulants.[2] Throughout his life he was also loyal to a single wife, when polygamy was the custom for Apache chiefs. However, it is the overall shape of his career as the Warms Springs leader that speaks most eloquently of Victorio's personality. That final fourteen months of war against insuperable odds, and his unwavering commitment to hold his beleaguered band together right until the tragic denouement, proclaim loudly an essential loyalty to the Apache life-way and an overriding unity of purpose.

In contrast to Victorio's spartan simplicity, Geronimo seems a bag of contradictions. There was, for sure, a similar passionate resistance to the white man, yet he oscillated between famous outbreaks and periodic attempts at settled reservation life, while in captivity he showed a willingness for at least partial assimilation, dabbling briefly in Christianity and developing a good grasp of hard Anglo-Saxon business. He was undoubtedly committed to his people, but he was never formally accepted as chief. He was blamed by some factions for the Chiricahua's later misfortunes. On one occasion, during a desperate Mexican ambush, he was accused of wanting to abandon the women and children to the enemy – an idea that seems unthinkable in Victorio.[3] Where the Warm Springs chief was monogamous, Geronimo had nine wives and outlived many of these and his children. Where Victorio was never known to have been intoxicated, Geronimo displayed a periodic reliance on alcohol which, as we shall see, played a large part in his life and in his death.

Geronimo was the most photographed Apache ever, yet this has hardly helped resolve the question of his true nature. In the case of Indians like Cochise and Crazy Horse it is the absence of any photograph that fires the imagination. With Geronimo it is the sheer abundance of images. Although there are several constants – the downward steel clamp of the scarred mouth and his brilliant eyes – the face always retains a sense of mystery. Perhaps for people of European culture the enigma lies in the sheer otherness of the Apache culture, which can only be understood by years of intimate contact.

Is it for this reason that the various contemporaneous accounts by his white opponents take us no closer to the inner man? Yet these sources do have a certain predictable consistency – they all condemn him as a demon. Naturally, Clum was the most inventive and vociferous, calling his *bête noire* surly, defiant, relentless, crafty, tricky, resourceful in wrongdoing, a renegade and trickster. For Britton Davis, one of the military officers succeeding Clum's regime, he was 'a thoroughly vicious, intractable and treacherous man . . . his word no matter how earnestly pledged was worthless.'[4]

The overriding, cumulative impression is a baffling paradox – a character both deeply inflexible yet unpredictable. For his subsequent interpreters, notably Angie Debo, his most meticulous biographer, and David Roberts, his most insightful, the qualities assume a more positive gloss, but the discrepancies remain. To the latter, for instance, he was:

Crafty, highly intelligent, a born manipulator, he gained a reputation even among warriors devoted to him for not always telling the truth. Geronimo was a worrier, a man torn by dark internal debates; there was a streak of the paranoid in him even before Janos . . . Rather than Cochise's iron purposiveness [and we could also add Victorio's] Geronimo's characteristic state was vacillation . . .[5]

While Debo similarly acknowledges the high intelligence, hardheadedness and practicality, she also argues that 'if one can follow his reasoning, he is seen as a man of essential integrity. He was deeply religious, and when a promise was made with oath and ceremony – mere poetic trimmings to the white man – he kept his pledge.'[6]

Perhaps the key word to help understand the apparent contradictions, and to supply an adhesive ingredient that binds together the differing assessments, is *survival*. Geronimo was above all a survivor. He was also a deeply curious and deeply alert man. These qualities went with the distrustfulness that characterised all Apache warriors. Yet his tragic personal history, especially the early loss of his mother, his wife Alope and their three children, had made distrust a condition of Geronimo's soul. When blended with his relentless will to survive (and no Apache face expressed the quality more completely), his hyper-suspicion made him approach every new situation with a Machiavellian rigour. And whatever suited the dictates of the moment governed his immediate responses. Such methods, of course, infuriated the Americans who came up against him (by and large, the officers fighting Geronimo were honourable men) and explain their universal verdict on him as a twister.

It also makes him appear a less noble figure than Victorio, who seemed to take the stoic's path to tragedy from the moment of his final breakout. Yet Geronimo's endurance beyond the vicissitudes of his tumultuous career supplies the overarching sense of unity, and represents no less an achievement. His indomitable commitment to survival

– the dodges, the famous outbreaks, the equally celebrated surrenders, even his shrewd financial dealings once the prison door had closed – is as important a legacy for the contemporary Apache as is Victorio's heroic legend.

These things require consideration before we go on to examine his final years of resistance, for along with the achievements we must take account of the extremes of violence that accompanied his record. Although in old age he was filled with sadness for some of his deeds, Geronimo, unlike Victorio, never paid with his own life for the death and suffering he inflicted on others. As Stephen Trimble has suggested, 'Today young Apaches must make sense out of Geronimo's violence, while honoring his skills.'[7] So, indeed, must all Americans, just as they must acknowledge the injustice which launched the final years of conflict.

With Clum's departure from San Carlos in 1877, the administration of the reservation had become a virtual paradise for embezzlers. Rations were manipulated to yield huge profits for both contractors and agents, the so-called Tucson Ring, while the supposed recipients themselves were almost starving. A single cup of flour was an individual's ration for a week. A small shoulder of beef was meant to last a family of twenty for the same period.[8] To see them through until the next inadequate hand-out, some Apaches were living off rats or rabbits. A subsequent inquiry into the San Carlos regime reported

> a course of procedure at the . . . Reservation . . . which is a disgrace to the civilization of the age and a foul blot upon the national escutcheon. Fraud, peculation, conspiracy, larceny, plots and counterplots seem to be the rule of action . . . The Grand Jury little thought when they began this investigation that they were about to open a Pandora's box of iniquities seldom surpassed in the annals of crime.[9]

Dire though the conditions had been, they were merely the tinder of rebellion. The spark was provided by a completely separate incident that has resonances well beyond the story of the Apache and closely parallels aspects of the conflict in the African Southwest (described in the following section).

The crisis centred on a frail, ascetic figure called Noch-ay-delklinne. This Apache shaman claimed to have communed with the spirits of their dead leaders, and prophesied a revival of Indian fortunes with the disappearance of the white men. His teachings, closely related to the ghost dance movement that was even then giving renewed hope to the demoralised Indians of the northern plains, also included a doctrine of non-violence. However, the settlers and military surrounding San Carlos viewed the prophet and his message in a very different light. Noch-ay-del-klinne's capacity to attract a following from amongst all sections of the Apache filled them with fears of a coordinated and unified uprising.

Yet it is surely indicative of the way the Euro-American image of the savage was filled with the shadows of the white subconscious, that they should now respond with such disproportionate force and aggression to this peaceful mystic, this messenger from the Apache's own dream world. Seeking to halt his growing influence, the San Carlos agent sent a contingent of over a hundred soldiers and scouts to his camp, with instructions for him to be arrested or killed. When this small army arrived to take its sole prisoner, the medicine man readily agreed to go quietly, but a number of Indians followed the posse, fearing for his safety. As the escort stopped for the night a tense situation slowly degenerated into a hostile standoff, and all that was needed was a single stray shot to ignite the fuse.

Within seconds of the first gunshot there was a general exchange of fire. The commanding officer screamed 'Kill the Medicine Man' and Noch-ay-del-klinne received a bullet through the leg. As he crawled away, another would-be assassin pushed his pistol barrel in the prophet's mouth and fired. When he survived this, a third guard smashed in his forehead with an axe and the terrible dreamer was dead. Eight soldiers and another eighteen Apaches were also killed in the battle.

Geronimo, his hair-trigger nerves jangling in the aftermath of the violent explosion, soon made ready to leave with seventy-three other men, women and children. It was 30 September 1881. Less than a year after Victorio's death, war had returned to the American Southwest.

In the breakout Geronimo, the Chiricahua shaman, was accompanied by another noted chief, Juh, and in the Sierra Madre Mountains of Mexico they linked up with Nana, after the old man's meteoric raid across the Southwest. Each of these two leaders was married to Geronimo's sisters, and the three brothers-in-law formed a formidable triumvirate. For a while their free band remained undetected in the Mexican range, but by April 1882 they were back on American soil.

The incursion was conceived and led by Geronimo himself, who was keen to bolster the Indians' fighting strength in the light of Mexican military manoeuvres against them.[10] Throughout the previous winter the free Apaches had sent word to relatives at San Carlos requesting that they join them in the Sierra Madre. When this failed to inspire a general exodus, Geronimo set out to recruit them. Ghosting past the soldiers set to guard the border, his party first assembled at a sheep farm south of the reservation, where Geronimo perpetrated the most infamous and best-documented of his many alleged murders. He and his warriors massacred a group of about sixteen Mexican men, women and children, stabbing and shooting them one by one, then apparently beating the infants to death with stones. A newspaper account recorded that one child had been roasted alive, while the head shepherd was mercilessly tortured until his skull was split open with an axe.[11]

After these brutal atrocities Geronimo moved north to a position just off the reservation, cut the telegraph wires to the San Carlos agency, then made his move on the morning of 19 April. Almost all of the surviving Warm Springs Apaches were amongst the 400 to 500 men, women and children who were stampeded into flight and who then straggled in a long and ill-concealed line towards the Mexican border. Many had been herded against their will. However, once the various raiding parties under Geronimo had slaughtered about fifty settlers, including a number of policemen, all of the Apaches realised that there was no going back. Unfortunately, going forward was barely any easier. Many Indians had lost their customary stamina during years of meagre San Carlos charity, and they had few supplies, weapons or horses. Although the Apache leader dispatched additional foraging parties, the resulting flow of supplies was insufficient to feed the hundreds of hungry Indians as they trudged southwards. A largely unmounted Indian group was also doomed to the pace of the weakest amongst them. At one point the whole band even had to stop to perform a puberty ritual for a girl who had just completed her first menses. That they could delay their tense and dangerous flight to honour the maidenhood of a single young female is a measure of the rite's critical importance in their religious and social calendar, and also provides a rare glimpse of the softer, more feminine aspect of Apache character.

Despite a number of forced night marches by the Chiricahua, the pursuing US cavalry and loyal Apache scouts closed relentlessly on their quarry, and, just before the border, engaged them in a brief exchange. The retreating Indians emerged largely unscathed from this but in old Mexico, disregarding international law, the Americans struck again in a fierce ambush during a rare lapse in Apache vigilance, as they danced to celebrate their successful escape. A later investigation revealed that they left behind fourteen dead warriors. A number of women and children had been killed or wounded, while another important loss was that of almost all their horses and possessions. Fearing a third American assault, the men concentrated at the rear of the column as it struggled on towards the Sierra Madre.

But in escaping one scene of misery, the vanguard of women and children ran headlong into a new and greater danger – a waiting force of Mexican soldiers. These troops had apparently been forewarned of the impending Apache exodus and had set out to catch them before they could reach their impenetrable mountain retreat. The Mexicans' timing could not have been better, their attack cutting broadside into a line of dispirited and weary refugees. Geronimo, described by one of those he had coerced into flight as 'the most intelligent and resourceful as well as the most vigorous and farsighted' of the leaders, tried to organise a desperate defence.[12] With about thirty other men he dug in and held off the Mexicans for the rest of the day, giving most of his people time to reach the sanctuary of higher ground. Then as darkness fell someone lit the surrounding bush and under the resulting smokescreen the Apaches were able to wriggle free of the trap.

Following Tres Castillos and now this second disaster – the Indian dead numbered at least seventy-five, the greater proportion being women and children, while a further twenty had been captured – the Warm Springs people of Victorio had virtually ceased to exist as a separate community. Those remaining now trudged on unhindered into the mountains and joined the other Apaches, a combination that represented the largest gathering of free Chiricahua since the 1870s. Despite the numbers their position was hardly secure. A few months after the enforced exodus from San Carlos, the Apache's most formidable American opponent, Nantan Lupan, the Tan Wolf, as the Chiricahua called General Crook, was back in the Southwest. Washington was intent on a final solution to the Apache 'problem'.

With characteristic thoroughness Crook set about reorganising the system that had disintegrated into chaos since his departure. Blaming the Apache outbreak on gross maladministration at San Carlos, Crook placed the reservation under military control, while the corruption of its previous administrators was investigated and exposed by a grand jury. Indian police were reinstated and the management of affairs was placed in the hands of officers of high integrity, like Britton Davis. The Apache were allowed to move back to the high country on the reservation, which was better for grazing and held more of their traditional harvests and game. Meanwhile Crook met and spoke to all the male occupants at San Carlos, listening to their grievances and re-establishing his old policy of self-administration and self-reliance for the peaceful Indians, and ruthless pursuit for any antagonists.

With the Indians re-adjusted to a settled life and loyal to their pact of cooperation with Crook, the Chiricahua in the Sierra Madre were cut off from a vital source of supplies and recruits. They could hunt and trade with surrounding Mexican communities, but any raiding was bound to stir the authorities into a military response. Equally, raids north of the border – especially for the ammunition essential for their American-made rifles – would lead them into inevitable conflict with the US military and eventually with Crook himself.

The Apaches in the Sierra Madre apparently recognised their fate. According to Nana's own grandson, 'Many were expressing the fear that reservation life was inevitable and that further resistance could result only in the extermination of our people.' On another occasion he suggested that 'Since Tres Castillos our people had known the outcome. Nana knew well how the struggle would end. His little band had fled so often, starved so often, slept so little, and suffered so long that death had no terrors.'[13] Both the old chief and Geronimo apparently preferred such a fate to captivity.

Yet the Apaches had not been without their successes. In March 1883 came one of those devastating Apache raids that plunged the white communities of the Southwest into terror. In less than a week the raiding party, questing for all-important ammunition, had left a trail of destruction, slaughtering twenty-six whites and seizing horses almost at will. And before the army could begin to find them, the Indians had vanished into Mexico. Just a single Apache had been killed. In terms of speed and intensity – its leader had apparently only ever slept on horseback during more than 1,000 kilometres – the raid rivalled the famous onslaught led by Nana. Bourke later judged that the Indians had passed through settled country occupied by 5,000 troops. None of these soldiers had even clapped eyes on their opponents.[14] Small wonder perhaps that the American settlers, in the great barrage of newsprint unleashed by the raid, frequently portrayed themselves as completely surrounded by savages as Custer himself.

Unknown to these white victims, however, the raiders had included amongst their number at least one who would prove an invaluable ally. He was an Indian called Tsoe. He was described by John Bourke as 'one of the handsomest men, physically, to be found in the world.'[15] Tsoe was an Apache, but he was related only by marriage to the Chiricahua, and midway through their ride he decided he had had enough of the renegade's free-ranging existence and had broken away, to slip back into San Carlos reservation a few weeks later. There he was promptly arrested by Britton Davis and taken to Crook.

For the Tan Wolf, this solitary Apache was the last piece in a complex jigsaw over which the general had mused for the last few months. New international agreements had finally been signed between Mexico and the USA, giving Crook an opportunity to penetrate deep into the southern mountains, and make direct contact with the Chiricahua. To find Apache, however, in the most desolate, inaccessible portion of their range would be almost impossible without a complete understanding of the terrain. Tsoe, or Peaches as he was known to the troops for his rosy complexion, had precisely that kind of detailed knowledge, and he readily agreed to lead Crook there.

On 1 May 1883, just weeks after the Apaches' last slashing raid, Crook's column was on the move towards the Sierra Madre. Both the plan and the force employed to execute it, which was heavily reliant on Apache scouts, typified Crook's methods and his gift for innovation. For the free Chiricahua never thought that the Americans would either dare or be able to track them to their final sanctuary. Nor was that belief ill-founded. During their struggle through the mountains to the Chiricahua camp, Bourke wrote that 'To look upon the country was a grand sensation, to travel in it, infernal.'[16]

The American soldiers toiled upwards through the Mexican range, each man trapped in an airless pocket of self-generated misery and heat, while the mules occasionally stumbled to their deaths along the precipitous ravines. For Tsoe, however, and the other Indian auxiliaries, who scaled the heights like deer, it was as if the excursion were all in a day's work. Bourke suggested that their guide 'never knew what it meant to be tired, cross or out of humor', and went on to adjudge the Apache 'the perfect, the ideal, scout of the whole world'.[17] They could keep up a pace of seven kilometres an hour for a distance of twenty-five, and when they stopped, Bourke eulogised, they could strike a fire with two sticks in just eight seconds.[18]

It was the kind of stamina and bushcraft which enabled Crook to reach his target in just a fortnight but, unfortunately, the general was absent when the vanguard first struck the enemy encampment. Aroused by the sudden contact the scouts instinctively attacked, Apache firing upon Apache as they rushed amongst the Chiricahua bivouacs, burning and looting, killing nine and rounding up their entire horse herd. Only after the skirmish had ceased did Crook himself eventually arrive, when the scouts rolled into the US camp loaded with spoils and a handful of captives.

The prisoners were quickly enlisted as go-betweens with the spokesmen for the renegade force. However, one of their most important leaders, Geronimo, was 200 kilometres away on a Mexican raid. Yet he was not completely out of touch with proceedings back in the mountains. Jason Betzinez, accompanying Geronimo on this particular expedition, later testified that the whole raiding party was seated around a fire, when the Apache shaman suddenly dropped the knife he was holding and announced: 'Men, our people whom we left at our base camp are now in the hands of US troops! What shall we do?' Betzinez published his account in 1959 after a lifetime absorbing the white man's ways and shedding the superstitions of his people. But he clung tenaciously to the story of Geronimo's clairvoyance, claiming that 'it came to pass as true as steel'.[19]

Geronimo and his party hurried back to the Sierra Madre, where they found affairs much as he had prophesied. He quickly conferred with his fellow leaders and together they opened negotiations with Crook himself. As the two sides assembled to discuss their grievances and possible terms for surrender, Bourke sized up the opposition. 'In muscular development, lung and heart power,' he wrote of the general corps of warriors, 'they were, without exception, the finest body of human beings I had ever looked upon.' Of the actual Chiricahua chiefs, he thought they were 'men of noticeable brain power, physically perfect and mentally acute – just the individuals to lead a forlorn hope in the face of every obstacle.'[20]

Just how forlorn their cause had become was brought home to the Chiricahua by the Americans' capacity to locate and storm their Mexican inner sanctum. Equally alarming were the constant reports of Mexican troop movements in the region. Many of the renegade band, especially the Warm Springs people, were weary of liberty and its end-less draining trials. After a week's patient negotiation they finally agreed to return to San Carlos. Crook himself gave safe conduct to a party of 325, including a number of prominent Chiricahua like the elderly Nana. Typically, Geronimo pledged to return to the reservation but requested more time to gather his people together, then vanished back into Mexico. Yet even the last renegade finally succumbed to the inevitable and, although it was nine months after Crook's expedition, he kept his word and headed back towards Arizona and civilisation.

According to the mindset in Washington, what civilisation entailed for the Apache was the abandonment of their hunter–gatherer past and their induction into the world of settled agriculture. This despite a dearth of fertile, well-irrigated land at San Carlos, and the fact that some of the best reservation country had already been parcelled out to white settlers.[21] Ever the realist, Geronimo had returned to Arizona with a large herd of stolen Mexican livestock to launch his people as cattle ranchers, which would better have suited their free-ranging traditions. But Washington, intent on beating the warrior's war lance into a ploughshare, confiscated the cattle and supplied the Apaches with pick, shovel, seed, harness and draught pony, then packed them off to become peasant farmers.

For almost two years, the Indians made genuine attempts to adjust to this alien way of life. Even Geronimo once proudly displayed a small blister on his palm as a badge of his new-won status as veteran sod-buster. In his 1884 report Crook wrote that 'for the first time in the history of that fierce people, every member of the Apache tribe is at peace.'[22] Yet beneath the surface of calm, discontents were brewing.

These were partly rooted in American intervention in two long-established Apache customs. The first was the making and drinking of *tiswin*, a crude, mildly alcoholic beer prepared from fermented corn. The ritual Saturnalia associated with this brew was invariably a riotous, and often violent, affair and the authorities wished to ban or, at least, curb its production. The second cause of friction was the established Apache methods of punishing their wives which, in cases of adultery, extended to cutting off the tip of the woman's nose. Sexual restraint was expected of both sexes in this conventionally chaste community and breaking its taboos was punished with corresponding severity.

By themselves the issues were not a *casus belli*. In fact, many Apaches recognised the harmful and repugnant aspects of both these old customs and wished to control them, but they equally resented white intrusion into their own social arrangements. And given the wider and traumatic assault upon the Apache's political, cultural and spiritual traditions – for the coercive attentions of Christian missionaries were another facet of life on the reservation – it is hardly surprising that such issues became matters of principle.

Another source of discontent was the habit amongst the American soldiers of trying to pick out the most infamous of the Chiricahua, when they came to the depot for their rations. Then, when their officers were not looking, the soldiers would point to the Indian and draw their hands slowly across their throats as a crude form of joke. For the Apaches this barrack-room needling had sinister implications. Were these soldiers possibly good men attempting to let the Indians know what lay in store? Apache suspicions were further aroused when the chief scouts on the reservation took to making the same morbid gesture. Exercised by its constant repetition, some of the Chiricahua became paranoid that they were soon to be arrested, perhaps imprisoned or even worse.

The most susceptible to the barrage of innuendo and rumour was the most suspicious and untameable bronco of them all, Geronimo. Eventually, goaded to distraction by their taunts, he lashed out and broke free once more. With 101 women, eight half-grown youths and thirty-five men, old Nana amongst them, he set off into the night of 17 May 1885. In one breathless ride they covered 200 kilometres. The only people to see them before they vanished into Mexico were those they killed en route.

Yet if one thing had been proved by the last big Chiricahua exodus – when their numbers had been far greater and more easily self-supporting – there was now no place left in old Apacheria, neither in Mexico nor in the American Southwest, for a band of free-roaming Indians. Geronimo's fourth and last outbreak was a wild and reckless coda to the history of Native American resistance. It had no future. Its conclusion was all but inevitable, and we need consider it only in brief outline. Yet even the bare statistics of his final fling make compelling reading.

It lasted for eighteen months and centred on an area of some 640 by 320 kilometres. The Indians had no base of supplies, no way of guaranteeing food or transportation. By the end they were being pursued by 5,000 regular and irregular American soldiers, 3,000 Mexican troops and about 1,000 other civilian vigilantes, scouts and Indian auxiliaries, many of them Apache – about 9,000 in total. During the period Geronimo's band killed about 100 Americans and Apache scouts and an unknown number of Mexicans, but a figure thought to exceed the casualty list north of the border. Losses amongst the Apaches amounted to eleven, including three minors and two women. None of these was inflicted by regular troops.

The whole adventure was punctuated by bizarre incidents and staggering escapades, one of the most extraordinary of which followed the American capture of a third of all the women and children, including Geronimo's own family. Setting out to retrieve his loved ones, the sixty-year-old Geronimo rode with four companions straight through Crook's dense screen of guards and patrols, slipped back into San Carlos and, under the noses of the troops in Fort Apache, collected his wife and daughter and returned to Mexico. Not a single soldier had seen them come or go, not 'even from a distance'.[23]

When, at last, American troops did make contact with the renegades, Geronimo finally promised to rendezvous with Nantan Lupan after a further two moons, at a place known as the Cañon de Embudos. The site's Spanish name passed into English-speaking legend as meaning the Canyon of Tricksters, possibly for what occurred there two months later. Crook set out on his mule one more time and found the Chiricahua group at the canyon just as Geronimo had pledged. They then sat facing each other and talked.

The historic moment was even recorded for posterity, a Tombstone photographer, C.S. Fly, somehow managing to wangle his way on to the American expedition. The resulting images, some of the most extraordinary in the Southwest's history, if not in all the American Indian wars, showed just how far the age-old European–tribal conflict had moved towards the kind of multi-media clash so familiar to the twentieth century. At last Geronimo and all the others agreed to surrender. With as much poetry as the arch-strategist could muster, he said:

> Once I moved about like the wind. Now I surrender to you and that is all . . . My heart is yours, and I hope yours will be mine . . . Whatever you tell me is true. We are all satisfied of that. I hope the day may come when my word shall be as strong with you as yours is with me.[24]

He tried desperately to convince the Americans of the deep, genuine fears that had precipitated his last ride. Given the oral traditions in Apache culture, honesty was an essential and cardinal virtue in their society. Once found out, no liar could ever be entrusted with important tribal business. These qualities were acknowledged and praised by men like Britton Davis and Bourke. Unfortunately, Geronimo himself was now seen as largely outside that tribal pattern. Given Crook's wearying sense of déjà vu, it is perhaps not surprising he did not believe a word the Apache shaman had spoken.

And the next day Geronimo had bolted. Alcohol, in the form of cheap whisky sold by an American lowlife called Tribollet, had inveigled its way into the Apaches' camp like an uncorked genie. Now the booze, in conjunction with the bootlegger's dire prophecies of imminent hanging, cast its evil spell and Geronimo was spooked into flight one last time. Enraged at his malign impact, Bourke wanted to hang Tribollet, a suspected agent for the Tucson Ring, as 'a foe to human society'.[25] But the damage was already done. Worse still, the military high command, vexed by this setback and by their own distant impotence, rejected the Tan Wolf's proposed surrender terms to the Apaches and goaded the already war-weary Crook to tender his resignation.

This made way for General Nelson Miles, a soldier with little genuine knowledge of Indians and a deep ignorance of the Apache. He rapidly got rid of Crook's scouts, thinking he could do the job quicker with white Americans. Very soon there were 5,000 troops in the field – about a third of the combat strength of the army – chasing twenty men and twenty women and children. However, General Miles was not one of those commanders who lost sight of the overall picture by venturing forth himself. He was, in fact, a career soldier with an eye to his place in history, and the achievement which seemed most likely to secure that glory was the capture of Geronimo.

Unfortunately, such a possibility looked as unlikely as ever. Geronimo and his reduced band now ran the army ragged. In some parts of Mexico the country was so stark it took the Americans thirty-six hours to get out of one ravine to its summit, and twelve pack animals were lost in the climb. And although the pursuing forces had managed to seize the renegades' entire equipment and horses on seven different occasions during the eighteen-month chase, each time the Indians had re-equipped themselves within days. When, after five more months, they were no nearer securing the ultimate prize, Miles eventually settled, like Crook before him, on a negotiated surrender brought about through the service of Apache scouts. The only difference was that Miles, unlike Crook, made promises to Geronimo that he never intended to keep.

Lured in by old Apache friends, the renegades promised to meet Miles at an agreed rendezvous. Like the location for Geronimo's meeting with Crook, the name of the spot seemed to hold a clue to the outcome: Skeleton Canyon heralded the death of Apache resistance. Soothed by Miles' false promises, the renegades were promptly packed on to a train and whistled away to the east, few of them ever to return. This was itself a betrayal of his surrender terms to Geronimo, but Miles' treachery extended far wider than this. While the general was being honoured for his great victory by the citizens of Tucson, his presentation sword studded with a fifty-seven-carat star of India sapphire and with a hilt made of solid gold (public subscriptions failed to cover the full price, so Miles met some of it himself), most of the Chiricahua population, including the Apache scouts without whom the surrender would never have been secured, were languishing in prison in Florida at the start of twenty-seven years captivity.[26]

An outraged John Bourke suggested that there was 'no more disgraceful page in the history of our relations with the American Indians than that which conceals the treachery visited upon the Chiricahuas who remained faithful in their allegiance to our people.'[27] This much, however, Miles' treachery had changed. The killing had stopped in the American Southwest, while in the east Apache dying had just begun. Within three and a half years, almost a quarter of the 498 Chiricahua transported into exile had succumbed to disease.

Before going on to consider aspects of this long incarceration, we should pause to make a number of comparisons with the tribal conflicts discussed earlier and also to attempt a final assessment of Apache resistance. The most obvious conclusion to be drawn was the extremely arduous nature of white conquest in Apacheria. Dan Thrapp believed it was 'the most costly, in human lives, of any in the history of America.'[28] One might even add that it involved more casualties on the European side than the combined Spanish conquests of the Mexica and the Inca. This says much about the martial qualities of the Apache who, it should also be emphasised, as a people numbered no more than the Tasmanians. Given these statistics one begins to see the Apache much as their eulogists have suggested – as one of the most skilful and courageous tribal opponents that any European power confronted anywhere on earth.

However, over the likes of the Tasmanian Aborigines they had one enormous advantage. They were never confined to a finite space like an island. Moreover, Apacheria – a mixture of desert and precipitous sierra – was even more inimical to European presence than were the damp forests and mountains of Van Diemen's Land. With his customary insight, Bourke noted the importance of human ecology in the white–tribal war of the Southwest: the 'two great points of superiority of the native or savage soldier over the representatives of civilized discipline are his absolute knowledge of the country and his perfect ability to take care of himself at all times and under all circumstances.'[29]

If anything, the Apaches' advantages over the Mexica of the sixteenth century were even greater. Most important of all was the fact that the *Indeh* had no tradition of open, pitched battles. Indeed, had they attempted to confront American forces in that manner they would have been as quickly annihilated as were the inhabitants of Tenochtitlan. It was Bourke, once again, who summed up precisely the Apache approach to warfare:

> In battle he is . . . the antithesis of the Caucasian. The Apache has no false ideas about courage; he would prefer to skulk like the coyote for hours, and then kill his enemy, or capture his herd, rather than, by injudicious exposure, receive a wound, fatal or otherwise. But he is no coward; on the contrary, he is entitled to rank among the bravest. The precautions taken for his safety prove that he is an exceptionally skillful soldier.[30]

Just as the Mexica must have despised the alien methods of the Spanish *conquistadores* as brutally dishonourable, so did many white Arizonans, incapable of Bourke's wide and sympathetic reflection, view the guerrilla tactics of the Apache as a kind of 'dirty' war. Snakes, serpents, coyotes, wolves and tigers form the basis for most white imagery on the tribe's combat style. That the military commanders of Tenochtitlan would have understood this bitter judgement expressed by the white Arizonan settlers on an unmanly and ungallant foe exposes one of the more interesting ironies of the Indians of the American Southwest. The fighting unit that bears closest comparison with the Apache is not to be found among the tribal people previously discussed, but in one of their European opponents: the *conquistadores* of the sixteenth century.

Like the Spanish knights, the Apache had long-standing traditions of enmity towards foreigners that programmed them for war from the very outset. Apaches distrusted not only whites, but anyone who lay outside the boundary of the tribe. The invasion of Apacheria by Europeans thus involved no disorienting culture shock for them as it had done for the Mexica. The *Indeh*'s Ishmael-like belief that every man's hand was against them was an important strategic benefit. It made them cautious, elusive, inaccessible, committed, ruthless.

During their contests in the Southwest, the Apache had another advantage, like the armies of Cortés or Pizarro, in not seeking primarily to defend territory. For the Mexica, by contrast, a major restricting consideration was their defence of the land, the granaries, the settled resources that underpinned their army's effectiveness. The conquering Spaniards had no such initial limitation. Like the Apache, they were plundering units. They could, and did, simply seize resources as required, without regard for any immediate consequence. The Apache likewise raided white and Mexican farmsteads almost at will and this ubiquitous, if enforced, commissariat was the key to their legendary mobility.

Another point of comparison was the Apache's superiority as individual fighters to the mass of their opponents. True, they did not have the concrete technological advantages enjoyed by each *conquistador* over his indigenous American foes, and they never enjoyed more firepower than their Mexican or American opponents. But what the Apache lacked in terms of hardware they made up for in fieldcraft and natural resilience. Crook once noted that you could engage Apaches in a fire fight without ever once actually seeing them. So often it was a case of a smaller but élite voluntary corps facing conscript Euro-American forces, many of whom were coerced into service. These differences in part neutralised the whites' advantages of number and arms technology and ensured the longevity of Apache resistance.

The final similarity between Apache and Spaniard was their joint use of extreme brutality and terror. Torture of captives, as we have seen, was a regular feature of Apache methods. The women were known to have beaten prisoners to death with stones, and to have impaled the bowels of living victims with wooden sticks.[31] During their flight into Mexico, some Apache raiders impaled a local girl and left her to die hanging from a meat hook through the back of her head.

It was this kind of episode that explained their monstrous reputation. It makes the likes of Sugarfoot Jack understandable and it also makes the Apache seem the least sympathetic of the three tribal peoples considered here. They had little of the vulnerability and general innocence of the Tasmanians, and unlike the metropolitan Mexica or the imperial Inca, the Apache had no readily visible cultural achievements to expose, by contrast, the scale of Spanish rapacity.

Yet it cannot be ignored that the Apache were a people fighting for survival against a foe who was not just anxious to create his own living space in the region. Nor were white settlers simply embarked upon a furious but righteous quest for justice after Indian atrocities. Their policy towards the Apache was often genocidal in scope, as the US Board of Indian Commissioners acknowledged with remarkable complacency in 1871: 'the attempt to exterminate them [the Apache] has been carried on at a cost of from three to four million dollars *per annum*, with no appreciable progress being made in accomplishing the extermination.'[32]

It was only after the failure of a policy of total military annihilation that the authorities gave consideration to any alternative. Yet even when this was officially adopted, white appetites remained largely undiminished, intent on a conquest of both the Apaches' geographical territory and of their internal landscape – their lifestyle, culture and beliefs. Such ethnocide was motivated throughout by the relentless, unforgiving logic of the savage stereotype. This European outpouring, which had been in full spate on the North American continent ever since the time of Cortés, washed on through Arizona and New Mexico in the nineteenth century: a deep and complex fear not just of Native Americans but even of the landscape itself. Such ingrained attitudes made bloodshed inevitable in a war of equally aggressive combatants. But it also led to violence in times of peace. The systematic abuse of the Apaches, even after they had acquiesced in reservation life, was typical of the institutionalised hatred and injustice to which Indians were subjected across the USA.

Given this background to the Christian conquest, one begins to see the efforts of the Apache diehards – Victorio, Nana, Geronimo – as a desperate and justifiable last stand for the survival and integrity of their own way of life. And in the last quarter of the twentieth century this is precisely the shift in focus that has occurred in Southwest historiography. A later generation of writers has initiated a process of revision that has resulted in a more positive interpretation of the Apache and their conflict with white settlers. On the one hand, anthropologists like Maurice Opler and a number of remarkable female authors, Eve Ball and Angie Debo most notably, have disinterred that part of Apache culture which was buried by the tumultuous violence – the rich, feminine, ritual life of an earth-bound, earth-hallowing people. At the same time, military specialists like Dan Thrapp and David Roberts have rehabilitated the marauding raids of Victorio and Nana and found in them a legitimate purpose denied by their white adversaries.

These new soundings of the Southwest's past have in turn taken hold amongst a wider audience. As indeed they should. If a modern pluralist America wishes to understand and commemorate its country's founders, then it must also recognise those other Americans who opposed that process and also understand why they did so. If society wishes to honour the exploits of a Custer and recall his tragic end, then it must honour in equal measure the heroic fall of a Victorio. If it seeks to celebrate General George Crook as the greatest Indian fighter in its history, then it should at least seek to know his principal foe, Geronimo, not as a tiger, nor even the greatest tiger, even less the greatest Indian, but simply as an Indian and as a man. This indeed suggests the complexity of truth.

16

The Caged Tiger

It is a measure of Geronimo's representative status that even in exile and defeat he continued to illustrate important facets not just of his own nation's wider experience, but of the whole relationship between Christian whites and tribal people. In this final chapter on the Apache we should consider in detail two aspects of his period in captivity: the evolving nature of his reputation and his use of alcohol. However, it is impossible to overlook a feature of the Chiricahua's collective fate that was equally typical of Native American experience – their dispossession.

Many of the Apaches exiled in Florida, then Alabama and, finally, in Oklahoma were those reservation Indians who had never participated in renegade outbreaks. A good number, indeed, were scouts and families of scouts, who had either knuckled down to the life of peasant farmers or served loyally in the US forces. Officers like Crook and Bourke knew that Geronimo and his last companions in resistance would never have been brought to surrender without the services of their fellow Apaches. Small wonder that they condemned the Florida exile as an act of gross betrayal. When General Miles oversaw the final round-up and herded the Chiricahua into railway box-cars – itself a traumatising experience, since most had never seen a train – these San Carlos Indians lost all their land, their stock and non-portable possessions without compensation.

By coincidence the year of this eviction also saw the proposal of a bill that would eventually inflict massive territorial losses upon almost all Native Americans. The Dawes Act, which passed into law in 1887, only months after the Chiricahua had been incarcerated at two old

252

Florida forts, was supposed to aid the Indians' absorption into the wider American community. Clearing the tribes off their land and on to reservations had made way for white settlement, but there were drawbacks to the system. For the Indians' isolation in these ghettos had actually fostered old group identities, allowed a continuation of their communal approach to resources and encouraged a resistance to the white man's higher civilisation.

It was the age-old problem faced by European conquistadors everywhere. Having defeated the savage, how could they then turn him into a primitive replica of themselves. For the Spaniards in sixteenth-century Mexico part of the answer was the *encomienda* system. 'As everyone knows,' wrote one *encomendero*, 'the Indians are weak by nature and are satisfied with having enough to get along on from day to day. And if there is any way to bring them out of their laziness and carelessness, it is to make them help the Spaniards in their commerce.' By labouring for their European bosses, the Americans would gain the benefit of wages, and would in time 'become fond of commerce and profits', thus being drawn into the white capitalist ethos.[1]

For the British in Tasmania the answer had been preparatory schooling at Robinson's Aboriginal camp on Flinders, with its educational mix of Victorian cleanliness and Evangelical Christianity. For nineteenth-century white Americans the solution lay in the principle of severalty: splitting reservations into separate parcels of land so that the new private owners would acquire the industry and self-interested individualism of the dominant culture. Unfortunately, the 'severalty law operated as most whites had hoped and most Indians had feared.'[2] There were supposed safeguards to prevent the Indians' rapid loss of their 'new' lands – the allotments could not be sold, leased or willed for twenty-five years – but many Native Americans were total innocents in the world of property management.

Some squandered their titles recklessly, while others were persuaded into unfavourable deals or lease agreements. In the first third of the twentieth century about half of all allotments passed from Indian hands, most of them sold or forfeit for non-payment of taxes.[3] Moreover, once portions of the reservation had been divided up for all those Indians eligible, the surplus became available for sale to whites. By the 1930s and the end of severalty, the Indians had lost about two-thirds of their total land holding, their territories dwindling from 139 to 48 million acres. The price they had paid to own property like a white man was an area of land greater in size than Belgium, the

Netherlands, Switzerland and the United Kingdom combined.

Geronimo and his people did not even have the opportunity to face the challenge of land ownership. As they boarded the train in September 1886 everything had been stripped from them. This much the guards let them keep the whole journey: the degrading stench of vomit and excrement in the insanitary wagons. Another item the Indians most probably acquired in transit was the tuberculosis bacillus that killed a quarter of them in less than four years. In return, what most whites wanted was a quick glimpse of the Chiricahua as they passed through on their way to Florida, and especially of Geronimo and his band of renegades.

When the tiger of the human species was finally brought to bay, the newspapers went into a frenzy. As Angie Debo noted, 'Never were so many headlines owed by so many to so few.'[4] Geronimo had become the most infamous Indian in the Western hemisphere, eclipsing even the great Sitting Bull. At San Antonio in Texas, where his train was delayed while the authorities decided on his final destination, the town 'held a Roman holiday, with hawkers selling photographs and souvenirs'.[5] After a Florida congressman had apparently made a strong pitch for his own neighbourhood, the coastal town of Pensacola won the right to serve as Geronimo's gaoler, at the nearby Fort Pickens. The town's promoters are said to have been exultant. He might have been the worst Indian in the world, but he was definitely good for business. Even the other, innocent San Carlos Apaches were a focus for travelling sightseers. When plans were mooted to move these Indians from their separate Florida prison the need for secrecy was underlined. The railroad bosses and their political lobbyists were bound to try and block the measure, because of the loss of business it would entail.

However, Geronimo himself was undoubtedly the star attraction. By February 1887 Fort Pickens was seldom receiving fewer than twenty visitors a day and, on some occasions, this rose to over 450.[6] Typically, the arch-realist made the best of a bad situation. He made and sold bows and arrows, quivers, or canes. In a slow, conscientious hand he learnt to print his name in capitals, and signed the items to further increase their value. He charged artists to pose for their paintings, while signed photographs were an old stand-by. Initially his autograph sold at ten to the dollar, but by the twentieth century and with inflation they were fifty cents a piece. Another of Geronimo's ingenious scams was to remove the buttons from his coat, or the hat from his head, and sell them to the punters gathered at railway stations to see him. When the train pulled away, the wily old shaman would sew more buttons back on and take out a fresh hat, which he had brought especially for the occasion.[7]

Geronimo reached his widest audiences towards the end of the century, and after the Chiricahua's removal from the east in 1894, to a new, semi-permanent establishment in Fort Sill, Oklahoma. From here he was allowed to travel under escort to a number of major public exhibitions and shows, the first being the Trans-Mississippi and International Exposition at Omaha in the fall of 1898. All went extremely smoothly except for one small alarm. Geronimo and some other Apaches had got thoroughly lost while out for a jaunt in the country and by the time they got back they found local headlines screaming:

GERONIMO AND NACHEE ESCAPE
APACHE MURDERERS THOUGHT TO BE ON
THEIR WAY BACK TO ARIZONA.[8]

At the time of this rumpus, Geronimo was in his mid-seventies. But his explosive reputation was by now as relentless as the warrior himself had been in his prime, and would endure to his death. In his 'home' state of Oklahoma it was a legend that was said to generate an audience of ten thousand at any single event and kept him in constant local demand.[9]

The climax to Geronimo's show business career was an event of global significance – the inauguration parade of President Theodore Roosevelt in Washington in 1904. The old Apache was part of a larger Indian display that was divided into two groups and meant to symbolise the *before* and *after* of white conquest. In the lead would ride a contingent of wild savages resplendent in traditional costume. Behind came a post-conquest group, educated at special Indian schools and sprucely decked out in Western suits. Seeing these civilised Indians, the spectators were meant to reflect on their achievements and the benefits to them of white culture. Unfortunately that was not quite how the audience reacted.

The Apache shaman was naturally one of the old contemptibles in the lead, but when he hove into view the crowds threw their hats into the air, shouting 'Hooray for Geronimo'. The man whose normal billing was 'the tiger of the human race' or 'the Apache terror' may have been a savage, but by the twentieth century the savage was acquiring cult chic, and Geronimo stole the show. Only Roosevelt, apparently, attracted more attention.[10] The sight of the great Chiricahua riding with quiet dignity through the concrete and steel canyons of the American capital may have allowed some spectators to gloat with satisfaction on their white victory, but there was also mingled with that triumphalist response a new, unfamiliar, more positive feeling towards the old warrior.

Hitherto, the fledgling US superpower had derived much of its ethos and national identity from the culture of its western frontier, a place where decent, ordinary white Americans created order and prosperity out of a wilderness peopled by savages. That sense of the nation's political and moral expansion, of its limitless potential for greatness, was bound up with its constant outward thrust into an unknown geography. Yet implicit, if half-hidden, in that crusade was a contradiction. In order for American civilisation to progress yet further, it needed somewhere to progress to. But where would the westering pioneer advance once the continent had been conquered all the way to the Pacific? As the settlers pushed on, the paradox became ever clearer. The American frontier had not just involved a simple triumph of light over darkness, settled over unexplored, civilisation over savagery. In the forging of the nation's soul each had required the other – light *and* darkness, settled *and* unexplored, civilisation *and* savagery – an essential, indivisible whole. With the taming of the last wild spaces, it was not only the native inhabitants who were vanquished. In all frontiersmen, white and red, something would die.

Geronimo lived on the cusp of this new development, and while he may have been the final symbol of how the West was won, he was also among the first icons for America's lost wilderness. No wonder so many photographers rushed to catch a glimmer of his indomitable flame. Moreover, it was a response rippling around the globe and which strengthened as the century unfolded. It was weakest of course where tribal peoples retained some autonomy or seemed to represent some form of political threat, as we shall see in German South West Africa. Partly its antecedents were in the 'noble savage' stereotype that had existed since the Renaissance, but it was also rooted in a wider change of attitudes towards nature and the importance of nature in human affairs. This in turn arose from a reaction against what was seen as the dull utilitarianism and banausic secularity of the industrialised West.

Non-human inhabitants of the natural world were equally affected by the change. The essential innocence of the large herbivore was naturally ripe for rehabilitation long before any savage predator like a wolf, or indeed an Apache, and in the late nineteenth century the survival of the American bison became a national priority for pioneer conservationists. And if the passenger pigeon had slipped too close to extinction for rescue, at least its final going – the death of an individual called Martha at Cincinnati Zoo in September 1914 – was recorded with due detail and solemnity. Thirty years before the inauguration parade of Theodore Roosevelt, the US government had created the country's first national parks and wildlife sanctuaries. Under the sympathetic direction of the new hunting-and-fishing president, the conservation of wildlife and natural landscapes became an important social and political movement.

Like Geronimo, tribal peoples generally were beneficiaries of the new passion for wilderness. They gained economically. A new if often mistaken value came to be attached to their indigenous customs. They acquired an unfamiliar respect in the world of whites, especially amongst academics. There were also new opportunities to be exploited, like the selling of one's buttons, or one's hat. Yet there was also a more complicated side to the relationship. For the ethic that had created the Indian reservation had also created the nature reserve. Tribal people were accorded a different worth but they remained essentially an adjunct to the world of the dominant whites. Just as national parks preserved a parcel of wilderness as a spiritual and recreational valve for the pressures of urban society, so were tribespeople often seen as adding that dash of savage pageantry, of atavistic colour, to the monotone of modern life.

The tribesman could even become, like Geronimo in his Wild West shows, a living entertainment, a peepshow, the stuff of glossy brochures. Even today that same pattern recurs. In modern-day Namibia, holiday safari advertisements aimed mainly at white European and American clients treat and celebrate the Himba village or the lion pride with the same voyeuristic enthusiasm. In its promotional gush for a tour entitled 'Papua New Guinea: Birds of Paradise and Bushmen', a contemporary wildlife-holiday outfit suggests that

New Guinea represents the ultimate birding dream . . . Until recently, the island's remoteness and lack of tourist infrastructure prevented this dream from becoming reality. Now, however, with the help of three beautifully appointed forest lodges, all connected by internal flights, we can explore the Papuan rainforest . . . in comfort and safety . . . We will also be able to observe many of Papua's colourful peoples, with their distinctive tribal dress and customs.[11]

The island's feather-decked aborigines, its extravagantly plumed birds, its damp enfolding forests, are all accorded a rough equality – three parts of an exotic fantasia – tantalisingly close and offering the authentic whiff of excitement, but all to be enjoyed 'in comfort and safety' like an al fresco opera. Such values and attitudes do not represent genocide, nor even ethnocide, but they reduce the tribesman to an artefact and a visual experience, to be substantiated by a photograph or through a tourist's souvenir.

The Western appetite for wilderness can and does have a deeply destructive impact on tribal societies – a fact illustrated by the fate of an African people whose reputation bears some resemblance to that of the Apache. The nomadic pastoralists of East Africa known as the Maasai were viewed by early European colonists as the black aristocrats of the open savannahs, feared or secretly admired for their warrior traditions and cultural integrity. The region's exceptionally rich megafauna, involving some of the largest concentrations left on the planet, had lived alongside these cattle-rearing people for hundreds of years.

In the twentieth century this happy co-existence of big game and Maasai was honoured by the creation of a series of wildlife parks in the heart of their territories. Initially established by the British colonial masters and largely with the consent of the local people, some of these sanctuaries, like Amboseli and Maasai Mara, eventually became world famous and formed the basis of a tourist industry that was critical to the economy of independent Kenya. Yet in 1974, the country's government, ever anxious for a larger inflow of Western tourist dollars, created new wildlife areas and evicted the Maasai from parts of their former grazing lands. Initial promises of compensation were never properly honoured and relations were further strained by the deep corruption amongst the local administration. The Maasai have lost, according to one commentator, several important dry-season grazing and watering areas in order to make way for eco-tourism.[12]

Confined to the inadequate grasslands around the edges of the wildlife reserves, the Maasai's ever expanding cattle herds have become too large for the available pasture and have overgrazed the land, converting the celebrated national parks into 'islands of bio-diversity in a sea of degradation'.[13] Moreover, the Maasai people, often deeply embittered by the priority given to wildlife and wildlife tourists, slaughtered some of the rarest and most sought-after animals, poisoning the lions and spearing rhinos.[14] They have been forced to trade their warrior culture for Kenyan shillings, putting on displays in fake villages and haggling with the Western visitor over the value of their dance routines once converted into video footage.

In Apacheria itself in the late 1990s a similar conflict of interests has arisen over the proposed reintroduction of the Mexican wolf. Western ecologists and conservationists, anxious over this creature's near-extinction, talk of 'the most biologically appropriate means of re-establishing wild populations and ensuring its long-term survival.'[15] The Mescalero Apache, meanwhile, who actually live close to the areas where *Canus lupus baileyi* will be set free, are worried about wolves devouring their cattle. The wild man and the wild beast are no longer, it seems, the soul-mates that the Christian West once assumed.

The internal and physical landscapes imposed by European dominance placed other social and psychological strains upon tribespeople that were as acute as they were often intangible. Frequently it was much easier to measure the symptoms than to identify their cause or assess their precise nature. Even Geronimo, whose crafty exploitation of most circumstances tends to disguise the massive adjustments demanded of him, was susceptible to these hidden pressures. One manifestation of his own troubled state was his regular refuge in strong alcohol.

Unlike most Native Americans north of Mexico, some of the tribes of the Southwest, including the Apache, had their own traditional drinks such as the nourishing tipple, *tiswin*. The recipe and custom were probably acquired from Mesoamerican Indians, who had enjoyed a greater range of alcoholic beverages even in the pre-Columbian period. *Tiswin* was not a very strong brew, but Apaches ritually fasted before indulging and relished the full effects of a long binge. Given this habit it is not surprising that they welcomed the more potent, dis-tilled alcohols that Europeans introduced to America.

The impact of these stimulants upon the Apache has been almost uniformly baleful right until the end of the twentieth century. At Fort

Apache and San Carlos, for instance, eighty-five per cent of all major crimes still involve drink.[16] Nor is alcohol just a problem in the Southwest. Statistics published in 1986 suggest that amongst all Native Americans the level of alcohol-related crime is very similar to that among the Apache.[17] Although these statistics can easily be distorted by a small number of repeat offenders, rates of suicide and homicide, both of which are strongly linked to drink, are about twice as high amongst Indians as amongst whites. The incidence of sclerosis of the liver is four times higher.[18]

These social problems may not have been so pervasive amongst the Apache in the first half of the nineteenth century, but when Geronimo was a young man the negative effects of alcohol were still dramatic. It had become almost standard practice, for example, amongst the communities of northern Mexico to try to deal with raiding Apaches by inducing bands to enter their town and to ply them with the products of civilisation, including liberal quantities of tequila or mescal. Then, when the Indians were sleeping off their hangovers, the Mexicans would slaughter the befuddled enemy. Despite their legendary wariness, Apaches regularly fell for the ploy, which suggests a deep and reckless craving for the bait. Even during his penultimate outbreak, Geronimo himself and Juh were caught in such an ambush. Both Apache leaders escaped on that occasion, but a couple of years later, after another drinking bout, Juh collapsed into a river and drowned, apparently drunk on mescal (although his son and other Apaches have denied that alcohol played any part in his death).[19]

While Apaches may have had their drinking traditions prior to the advent of Europeans in America, and although white Americans could not be held responsible for the bingeing pattern of Apache consumption, nevertheless the deep cultural shock inflicted by white conquest was undoubtedly, as the academic and author Elliott West has argued, a factor in the Indians' craving for alcohol's anaesthetic properties.

White immigrants drank to relieve the tensions growing from the initial isolation and the heavy labors of pioneering. As for the Indians, there may have been some biological basis for their habits, but their drinking seems mainly a response to – and a cause of – their deteriorating position. In alcohol they found brief escape from dispossession and cultural disruption. Rampant drunkenness worsened problems of disease and sped the unraveling of social structures, which in turn gave Indians more reason to drink. It was a brutal cycle helped along by traders, who understood that the demand for alcohol, unlike that for awls or blankets, increased with the product's use. So frontier drunkenness among whites and natives told of different tensions. One habit expressed the trials of conquest, the other the despair and dependence of the conquered.[20]

Recognising this shattering impact and the often violent consequences of drink, the US government outlawed the sale of strong liquor to Indians – an act that remained in force until 1953. Yet, as we have seen, unscrupulous dealers like Tribollet, whose drunken whisperings had inspired Geronimo's final flight, ignored these restrictions. Nor did local law officers much care to punish trangressions when they were discovered, as the testimony of Britton Davis has earlier shown. White conquistadors had long understood the offensive capability of this subtle weapon and at times exploited it ruthlessly.

In the late eighteenth century, Mexico's Spanish viceroy welcomed the Indians' taste for drink and openly advocated that it be spread to the still innocent Apache, both for the profits that would result and because it created 'a new need which forces them to recognize very clearly their obligatory dependence with regard to ourselves'.[21] It was a policy that echoed a long Spanish tradition with regard to native drug use and went back to the very beginnings of their conquest in the Americas.

In pre-Cortesian Mexico alcohol had been strictly controlled by the masters of Tenochtitlan. The Mexican emperor himself had once inveighed against his own people's favourite drink, *pulque*, as being 'like the whirlwind that destroys and tears down everything'.[22] Neither the young nor ordinary workers were meant to touch it, and only those over seventy years of age were given slightly more licence to indulge in a little festive drinking. Yet anyone found guilty of a second offence of drunkenness might be punished with death.[23]

Given these severe restrictions on alcohol, it is not surprising that the Mexican populace should take the opportunity to imbibe once the Spaniards assumed control. Yet the appetites unleashed by the conquest, and which the Spaniards actively promoted, suggest something far more joyless and desperate than the celebratory toast to a lost taboo. The Mexican practice was to drink to satiation, induce vomiting, then start again. Government laws were enacted banning *pulque*, but these had only a temporary impact.[24] In fact *pulque* became one of the major products of the Spanish haciendas, while state revenues from the drink were equal to half their income from the silver mines.[25] Following the Spanish conquest of the Incan empire a very similar pattern of alcohol abuse ensued there. And in both the Andes and Central America, Spanish authors, attempting to explain the massive population losses, cited drunkenness as a major cause of mortality.[26]

Another addiction that rose dramatically in the post-conquest Andes was the chewing of coca leaves, the raw product from which modern cocaine is derived. Coca had enjoyed magical and religious associations before the Spanish invasion and its use had been restricted, like alcohol, to the priestly and aristocratic classes. But once this prohibition was lifted coca production and consumption became important elements of the Andean economy. Once again, although the addiction was almost exclusively amongst the native Americans, the huge financial profits made from the drug were mainly controlled by Spanish entrepreneurs. It was a situation hardly calculated to engender cross-cultural sympathies.

The Europeans coerced the inhabitants of the Andean highlands to descend thousands of metres to work in the coca plantations, which flourished on the edges of tropical forests. The resulting change in altitude and climate, together with the labour itself, had a devastating impact on the workers. Many developed a condition known as 'mal de los Andes' that inflicted a gruesome death as it ate away the nose, lips and throat. Some authorities estimated that between a third and a half of those workers involved in coca production died during their five-month service. Even the Spanish king himself condemned this profligate consumption of human resources.[27] But, as one contemporary author noted, in the coca plantations there was 'one disease worse than all the rest: the unrestrained greed of the Spaniards.'[28]

Coca was simply too profitable for the coca magnates ever to trouble themselves unnecessarily about production methods. Moreover, coca worked neatly in rhythm with the other great source of Andean profits, the silver mines. The mildly narcotic leaf deadened feelings of pain or hunger and thirst in the over-worked miners and was thus in constant demand. One Spanish authority estimated that the total coca traffic to Potosi was worth 500,000 pesos annually. Besides this obvious economic incentive there were other ancillary pressures driving its production and sale. Without the continued use of this stimulant, the coca barons insisted, the miners could never sustain their high levels of silver production. They also argued that their harvest was the only item that the Inca people really craved, and represented the best means to draw them into the European monetary economy. As one Spanish authority wrote, 'without coca there would be no Peru.'[29]

In Europe's wider colonial empire, there were many other instances where stimulants were embraced by the native populations in almost exactly the same fatal fashion. The Caribs of the West Indies were slaves to British rum, while the French trappers and merchants of Canada, in order to guarantee a steady supply of furs from their Indian collaborators, plied tribes like the Huron and Ottawa with French brandy. In the Pacific the degenerate Aborigine dressed in European motley and slumped in a drunken stupor at the outskirts of town, as he whiled away his race's final days, was a standard image of colonial Australia. Nor was it a stereotype without justification. Aborigines showed and continue to show a similar propensity towards alcohol as the indigenous peoples of North America. They are the most arrested and imprisoned group in Australia, with arrest rates twenty times the non-Aboriginal population. In Western Australia this rate more than doubles again, and a third of all these arrests are alcohol-related.[30]

Given the almost universal character of alcohol abuse amongst tribal peoples, one is tempted to a number of speculative generalisations. The most obvious is that the tribal world's outer experience of social and cultural disintegration wrought by the European incursion found its inner corollary in the slow-motion chaos of alcoholic stupor. Drunkenness both expressed and momentarily released them from the loss of meaning in their lives. And it continues to do so. The incidence of alcohol abuse amongst Native Americans is closely correlated to those tribes who are experiencing, even now, the highest levels of cultural change.[31] In the American-dominated Marshall Islands, where the US superpower tested its nuclear arsenal, suicide rates amongst indigenous males aged between fifteen and nineteen years are twelve times higher than they are in America itself. Studies on other Micronesian islands with even higher rates of suicide have shown that half the victims had consumed alcohol prior to their deaths.[32]

The second obvious conclusion is that alcohol was a major contributory factor in the cycle of disintegration, a fact of which the Europeans often took full and cynical advantage. Few, however, had put it quite so crudely as the German General von Trotha when he justified his war of annihilation against the inhabitants of South West Africa: 'Conquered the colonies have to be, nothing of that can be withdrawn. The natives have to give way . . . Either by the bullet or via [the Christian] mission through brandy.'[33] Although few might say it, brandy was as effective a weapon in the clash with tribal society as the Mauser or the Maxim. In some ways it was better, since it had the added advantage of turning a handy profit.

Whatever the pressures imposed by white conquest, tribal peoples had some share in their own alcoholic downfall. It was they ultimately who chose to uncork the bottle. Many tribal leaders recognised and understood its deleterious impact and tried to set a different example. In fact temperance was often the mark of a great tribal champion. The Shawnee prophet Tecumseh, the Apache chief Victorio, and Hendrik Witbooi, the formidable Nama leader of South West Africa, are all exemplars of that tradition. It should equally be recognised that tribal society was not the only loser in this cross-cultural exchange of drugs. The conquered may have been susceptible to the bottle, but the conquerors were soon hooked on their own new vice.

Tobacco, one of the two great modern Western addictions, was a habit acquired from the New World in the sixteenth century. Amongst indigenous Americans, however, tobacco had been placed under similar restrictions to their own home-produced alcohols, and enjoyed much the same cultural status – an adjunct to religious ritual, taken sparingly and with discrimination. Geronimo, for instance, used cigarettes and tobacco as a ceremonial feature of his work as a shaman. But for Europeans it had none of this spiritual context and became a simple nicotine habit to be satisfied as the craving demanded. This reverse addiction displayed by Europeans suggests that it was not just the drug itself – tobacco or alcohol – that was so destructive, but its use in the complete absence of any long-standing tradition, the cultural and ritual associations that contained the stimulant and gave meaning to its effects.

One final speculation emerges from the pattern of widespread alcohol abuse amongst conquered tribespeople, but it has implications not so much for the latter as for the modern multi-racial Western societies of Europe, America and the South Pacific. If we can presume that the excessive use of a stimulant borrowed from another culture is an index of pervasive social alienation amongst the abusers, then what lessons can we possibly draw from the current figures concerning production and traffic to the West of cocaine, heroin and other hard drugs? What seismic cultural disorders do we infer from the estimated $200 billion worth of illegal narcotics annually imported into the USA?[34] What malaise in post-industrial British society can explain the country's 34,000 registered addicts – mainly using heroin and cocaine – or the eighty per cent increase in heroin seizures in 1995, to 1,118 kilos? When we know that this quantity breaks down to 658 million injections, whose pain and whose loss of life's meaning should we envisage?[35]

In the context of the individual tribal lives featured in this book alcohol constantly resurfaces, almost like an artist's visual motif, symbolising the moment of decay. When William Lanney, the King of the Tasmanians, slipped into his final illness in the Dog and Partridge, the bottle was naturally on hand to quicken his going. When the great hope of the last Aborigines, Walter George Arthur, overturned his boat and disappeared without trace, he had drowned as much in the booze as in the Tasman Sea. Samuel Maharero, the paramount chief of South West Africa's Herero tribe, was a hopeless alcoholic whose consumption rose at times to almost a bottle of strong spirits a day. Like other tribal chiefs in the region, Maharero's cardinal sin was not that he drank, but rather that he often drank and conducted his land negotiations at the same time. And if he did not always personally have a bottle available, it was a regular German courtesy to make sure that he did. Numerous land deals to the detriment of Africans were smoothed in this fashion.

Alcohol also had its place in Geronimo's last days. During his exile in Oklahoma the Chiricahua warrior would often recount to those coming to visit him how his Power had protected him from the bullets of his white enemies and he would strip down to show them the numerous old scars, slipping pebbles into the holes left by some.[36] Even as an old man he retained his sturdy good health, defying the ailments that carried off so many of his family and friends one by one. In 1896 Nana died, then Nana's wife, Geronimo's own sister, in 1907. Since his capture he had also buried two more wives and three children. Notwithstanding this resilience he remained susceptible to the white man's own more subtle power and found ways to obtain it despite the prohibition on liquor on the reservation. Perhaps during the final years alcohol served as a foil for the rage which rose periodically within him – to his death he regretted his surrender – but the white authorities took his binges as a sign of his continued intransigence.

Secrecy, therefore, surrounded his drinking habits. In February

1909 he had to inveigle a young Apache friend into obtaining him some whisky through a white soldier. Armed with the bottle, the shaman rode out to get drunk and then tried to find his way home in the dark. During the return journey Geronimo, now in his mid-eighties, fell off his horse and collapsed half-submerged in a small creek. A severe cold turned inexorably to pneumonia and the warrior's spirit finally began to ebb away. Sensing his end, he sent for his two remaining children, but the white authorities had one last small defeat to inflict. Instead of wiring the summons they posted it, and the Chiricahua died a day before their arrival.

But even at the last Geronimo had been thinking ahead, planning for contingencies, and he requested that on his death, his horse be tethered to a certain tree close to the site of burial. His final belongings should also be left hanging on the east side of the grave, where they could easily be found. And in three days, announced the indomitable old warrior, he would come back to collect them.[37]

The Germans in
South West Africa

'The bold enterprise shows up in the most brilliant light the ruthless energy of the German command.'

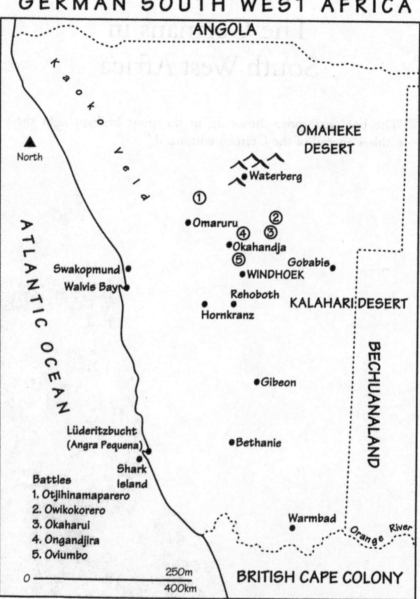

GERMAN SOUTH WEST AFRICA

ANGOLA

OMAHEKE
DESERT

▲
North

Kaoko Veld

Waterberg

①
Omaruru ●
②
④
③
Okahandja ●
⑤
Gobabis ●
WINDHOEK ●

Swakopmund ●
Walvis Bay ●

Rehoboth ●
KALAHARI DESERT

ATLANTIC OCEAN

Hornkranz ●

● Gibeon

BECHUANALAND

Lüderitzbucht
(Angra Pequena) ●

● Bethanie

Shark
Island

Battles
1. Otjihinamaparero
2. Owikokorero
3. Okaharui
4. Ongandjira
5. Oviumbo

Warmbad ●

Orange River

0 ——————— 250m
400km

BRITISH CAPE COLONY

17

A Freshly Slaughtered Goat

The affair that arose in the village of Warmbad in late October 1903 seemed, on the face of it, a trivial matter. Jan Abraham Christian was a minor tribal chief in the recently established colony of German South West Africa. His people, known as the Bondelswarts and numbering little more than a thousand souls, occupied the dry bush country in the southernmost portion of the colony, between the Karas Mountains and the Orange River.

According to one African eyewitness account, the fracas started when Jan Christian wanted a goat to minister to the needs of a young niece. The infant was apparently suffering from some form of inflammation, and tradition demanded that the warm stomach of a freshly slaughtered animal be used as medicine. Unfortunately, the Bondelswarts' own herds were grazing some way off in this harsh, hot, waterless semi-desert, while goats belonging to members of a neighbouring tribe, the Herero, happened to be passing through Warmbad. When Jan Christian asked the Herero to provide one of these they refused, at which point the chief ordered his men to seize the required animal.

The offended goatherds then took the matter to the local German official, a Lieutenant Jobst, and complained of the Bondelswarts' behaviour. Jobst immediately sent word to Jan Christian demanding that compensation be offered to the Herero. In return the chief dispatched a payment of eighteen shillings, which was accepted by the aggrieved party. With this financial settlement the sleepy village of Warmbad, as well as the office of the German magistrate, should have lapsed back into its habitual, heat-induced quietness.

Unfortunately, Jobst, incensed by the chief's behaviour, pressed on with the affair, ordering Christian to account for his actions in person. When he declined and sent six councillors to explain matters instead, they were arrested and when Christian ignored a second summons Jobst set off for Warmbad with at least eight men to arrest him. The young officer had not considered his actions in any depth. Not only was he in contravention of a treaty signed by his own colonial government, which granted Jan Christian jurisdiction over matters solely between African parties, he was bursting in upon the main settlement of a well armed and martially skilled people with the purpose of seizing their leader by force. It was an illegal, foolish and, ultimately tragic, course of action.

Its dénouement came after Jobst's men had entered Christian's house and dragged him struggling and humiliated into the full view of his people. The unanimous testimony of the Bondelswarts subsequently confirmed that when the chief tried to wrench himself free of his captors, the German sergeant present drew his revolver and summarily shot Christian through the head. The tribe's response was equally unhesitating, equally irrevocable. Within seconds Lieutenant Jobst, his sergeant and another German soldier slumped to the ground with fatal wounds.[1]

Like so much violence born of ignorance and crass bravado, it had been out of all relationship to its immediate cause. It might have been possible to locate a grotesque humour in the fact that four men had lost their lives over an eighteen-shilling goat, but it was an outcome void of rational purpose. Worse still, it could only result in further unreason. While the sound of those half-dozen gunshots might dissolve into the everyday hubbub of Warmbad life – the cries of children playing, the calls of birds, the barking of indifferent dogs – no exchange of this nature, especially when viewed across the racial and cultural gulf which separated Bondelswart from German colonists, could be forgiven or left to evaporate unnoticed.

In German South West Africa in 1903 such meaningless violence would lead to – would demand – further violence. And even as the blood of those four men mingled with the African dust, the encircling crowd must have recognised that their actions would bring down upon themselves a larger retribution from Europe's most powerful military nation. Equally, when the acknowledged leader of a proud and independent tribe had been unjustly murdered, the German settlers and their administration could have anticipated little but further armed resistance. However, no one foresaw the great wave of slaughter that rose up in that frenzied moment and which swept outwards to engulf the entire country.

Even a month later, after the Warmbad incident had steadily drifted into a wider, if somewhat desultory, inconclusive armed struggle between the colonial forces and the Bondelswarts, the German governor of South West Africa, Major Theodor Leutwein, was in no desperate hurry to leave the capital, Windhoek, and travel south to the theatre of conflict. During his ten-year period in office, the governor had overcome a succession of tribal revolts. There probably seemed little reason to assume that this uprising would demand greater attention or resources than the others he had successfully quelled in the past.

Yet this relaxed approach was not shared by some of his superiors in the Fatherland. When a report detailing the matter arrived on the desk of his Imperial Majesty, Kaiser Wilhelm II, the response was loud and violent. For the German Emperor the Bondelswarts affair was a 'war', an 'emergency' demanding 'large-scale reinforcements'. He railed at both the lack of data on 'developments, dispositions, terrain, etc.' and what he perceived as political interference in exclusively military matters. 'In such a situation,' he fumed, 'the Foreign Office and the Colonial Office have the temerity to *propose a reduction of our colonial force* to save money! Instead, they must be brought to battalion strength lest we lose all our colonial possessions!' Since the report documented a relatively minor disturbance involving a small tribe in only a minuscule fragment of one of Germany's four widely separated African colonies, the Kaiser's forebodings about the loss of his nation's entire overseas possessions must have seemed to his staff unnecessarily shrill, if not hysterical.[2]

Yet within weeks of the Kaiser's declamation, Germany would stand on the brink of losing its second largest and most widely settled overseas colony. An affair that had started with a commandeered goat would lead to a conflict with greater casualties than the Boer War. It would be the first serious military campaign of Wilhelminian Germany and the greatest armed struggle for this young nation since the Battle of Sedan in 1870. It would cost more than 500 million Marks, while casualty lists that ran into thousands would bring personal tragedy into villages and towns throughout the country. In the words of one commentator, it was 'Germany's bloodiest and most protracted colonial war'.[3]

For half the indigenous peoples of South West Africa, the three-and-a-half-year conflict was little short of a cataclysm. It would decimate several important tribal populations and destroy for ever the basis of their traditional lives. For almost all the territory's black inhabitants, once the military crisis had subsided, it would lead to an exploitative white colonial regime whose iron grip would not be released for almost ninety years.

18

A Darkness That May Be Felt

While for Kaiser Wilhelm II the Bondelswarts rebellion precipitated a vision of imperial collapse, for his principal officer in German South West Africa, it triggered a more parochial set of thoughts. Most pressing amongst Theodor Leutwein's narrow concerns, as he rode southwards to oversee operations, was a determination to ensure that public blame for the Warmbad shoot-out attached not to the German officer but to the Africans themselves.

Privately, however, Leutwein was in no doubt that Lieutenant Jobst had been at fault. 'This is not the way to treat a native [chief],' he complained to the Colonial Office. 'Rather we ought to do our utmost to strengthen his authority.'[1] It was a view shared by others among Leutwein's political officers, like the German magistrate at the politically important settlement of Gibeon, who wrote to his superior of the delicate balance of relations between the administration and the tribes in the colony's southern region, known as Namaqualand.

Incidents like that at Warmbad damage us in every respect, economically in Europe, in our prestige and with the natives . . . I sincerely hope that it can be definitely established that at Warmbad the first shot came from the side of the Bondels. That will create a possibility that he may be convinced that all the blame rests with the Bondels.[2]

The *he* in question whose reaction so exercised the German staff was one Hendrik Witbooi, a tribal leader, little more than five feet tall and in 1903 approaching his sixty-sixth year. Despite this advanced age and diminutive stature he is unquestionably the dominant African figure in the history of German South West Africa. From the numerous photographs of the man there seem to radiate the qualities which made him more powerful and influential than any chief in Namaqualand. Most striking are the iron-hard set of his mouth and jaw and the crystalline fixity of his stare. The universally acknowledged modesty, the quiet delivery and economy of speech, even the smallness of his physique, seemed to confirm, by contrast, the sense of inner control from which emanated his unquestioned public authority. In his own political memoirs Leutwein depicted Witbooi as 'never departing from what he felt to be right or his duty';

> full of understanding of the superior civilisation of the Europeans, yet not always loving its bearers; a born leader and ruler . . . [He] would have certainly become an immortal name in world history if fate had not caused him to be born on a minor African throne.[3]

Like most of the African tribes in the colony in the early part of the nineteenth century, the Witboois had enjoyed contact with European missionaries. For the young Hendrik, the Reverend Olpp of the Rhenish Missionary Society had been a particularly important influence in his life. Olpp himself wrote that 'If there is anyone . . . who is really earnest it is this young man. Up to now he has been one of my best scholars. He reads Dutch and Nama fairly readily and is taking enormous pains to learn to write a fair hand.'[4]

As important as his technical education was the deeply puritanical faith that the German teacher inculcated in his favourite pupil. It was a faith based less on the messages of the New Testament than on the language, tone and stories of the Old, from which Hendrik was accustomed to draw in illustration of his own actions and those of his political opponents. According to Dr Heinrich Vedder, himself a missionary, and author of the most important account of the territory's pre-colonial history, *South West Africa In Early Times*, Hendrik was subject to powerful visions and dreams, and spent long hours meditating at the grave of his grandfather, Kido Witbooi.[5]

Yet in harness with this mystical side of his character, Hendrik was also a deeply practical man. Unusually, in the eyes of his European contemporaries, he was both hard-working and abstemious, vehemently opposed to the strong alcohol that did so much to undermine the traditional life of his people. In his grasp of the region's politics, particularly the many implications of German military presence, he would later show a perspicacity unequalled by any other African leader.

From 1880 onwards Hendrik Witbooi had set about the consolidation of his position amongst his own Nama people and then waged a relentless campaign against the other tribes of South West Africa, with the intention of establishing himself as an unchallenged ruler. However, despite his exceptional qualities, his right to the status of paramount chief, even in his own region of Namaqualand, let alone in South West Africa in general, was based on nothing more substantial than superior military force. For, while Witbooi himself had been born in the territory, both his father, Moses, and his revered grandfather, Kido, had been newcomers to the area in the first decades of the nineteenth century. None of the three generations, therefore, had long-standing political claims on the territory.

Hendrik's personal ambition for power was part of a wider historical clash between rival African forces that had moved into the south-west region from opposing directions. Witbooi's own power base lay among the many related tribes that had pushed north across the Orange River from lands incorporated into the British Cape Colony. Known to Europeans as 'Hottentots' (a name now considered racist and offensive), these tribes were descended from the Cape's original inhabitants, the Khoikhoi, but had come to define themselves as a people called the Nama.

They were of the same basic ethnic stock as the San, the indigenous 'Bushmen', the first people of Africa whom the Khoikhoi had themselves displaced. Together these ancient Africans formed a single racial family known as the Khoisan. The two share a number of linguistic features, notably a variety of distinctive click sounds in their speech, as well as a range of physical attributes – the slight build and small size, a light yellow-brown skin colouration and distinctively Mongoloid facial characteristics. However, the Nama represented a significant social advance on their San neighbours, acquiring the use of iron tools and weapons, and exchanging a hunter–gatherer existence for one of nomadic pastoralism based on sheep.

The various Nama clans pushing across the Orange River had easily dislodged their San relatives, but their progress did not go unchallenged. Running in opposition to their northward thrust was the southward migration of peoples of Bantu origin. Believed to have originated in the great lakes region of East and Central Africa, these taller, darker-skinned, iron-using tribes had steadily pressed into the southern portion of the continent and reached modern-day Namibia possibly as early as the seventeenth century. Their southward migrations involved two distinct groups.

The more numerous of these were called the Ovambo. Although possessing herds of goats, sheep and cattle, they were essentially an agricultural people and occupied the hot fertile land straddling two of only three permanent watercourses in Namibia, the Kunene and Okavango Rivers, which today form large sections of the country's northern border with Angola. During the period of German rule it was a region that remained largely outside effective government, and was certainly ignored as a location for white settlement.

After the First World War, however, when the German colony was replaced by a South African administration, the Ovambo came increasingly under European control and were recruited as the main source of labour in the colony's mines and other industrial developments. Representing more than half the present population of Namibia, they also became a major force in the establishment of an independent African state. (Typically, the country's current president in 1998, Samuel Nujoma, is himself of Ovambo origin.) Yet in the pre-colonial period, the Ovambos' numerical superiority and undoubted military potential, coupled with their occupation of an unattractively hot and highly malarial region, ensured that they remained unchallenged and self-contained masters of their fertile territories.

In the period immediately before German occupation it was the far less populous Bantu tribe, inhabiting the high plateau to the south, which would occupy a central position, both geographically and politically, in South West African history. The Herero, unlike their Ovambo cousins, were primarily a cattle-herding people, whose staple diet was sour milk and cow's blood. They were considered to have a lighter skin and finer facial features than most other Bantu tribes, and were renowned for a well-developed sense of their own physical and cultural superiority. It was a belief for which they had at least some justification.

Charles Andersson, a Swedish explorer and trader during the pre-colonial period, described them as 'an exceedingly fine race of men . . . Their features are, besides, good and regular and many might serve as perfect models of the human figure. Their air and carriage, moreover, is very graceful and expressive.'[6] Andersson later wrote that one group of Herero accompanying an important chief was 'the finest body of men I have ever seen before or since'. Then as an immediate and damning rider he added that 'They were *all* arrant knaves.'[7]

At the centre of the Herero sense of self-worth, in fact at the heart of their society, were their herds of cattle. A key myth in the tribe's story of its own origins proclaimed that the first Herero had been given a bull and a cow by the Creator, while other peoples had to be content with inferior endowments. It was a legend that revealed the core of the Herero *Weltanschauung*. When this was challenged once by a German settler, one proud herdsman is reputed to have answered: 'Everyone is greedy. The European is devoted to dead metals. We are more intelligent, we get our joy out of living creatures.'[8] Typical of this joy was the extremely rich Herero vocabulary to describe the various markings and colours on their stock, totalling more than a thousand words. The German missionary, Heinrich Vedder, wrote that

> The Herero man devoted his entire time, strength, and personal attention – his very life in fact – to his cattle. In dry years he dug wells untiringly with a pointed stick hardened in the fire, and drew water from a depth of fifteen feet and more, pouring it into wooden troughs for his thirsty animals. All his efforts were directed to increasing the herd; his cattle were the sole object of his thoughts; his greatest pride was the condition of his oxen; his dignity and influence increased or declined in proportion to the number of stock which he owned; even his religion stood or fell in accordance with these possessions.[9]

By the mid-nineteenth century the Herero's immense cattle wealth was already legendary. In 1854 Charles Andersson described a single herd belonging to one chief that started to arrive in a broad flock early one day and was still arriving on the evening of the next.[10]

The paramount importance that the Herero attached to their cattle, and the ecological factors which shaped the limits of viable pasture in South West Africa, also determined the pattern of their encounters with the region's other tribes. Since the country's rainfall was unpredictable it meant that the Herero were obliged to follow its erratic course to satisfy their herds. One result was their repeated encroachment upon the lands of the Nama.

In the competition for good pasture the Herero's numerical superiority and physical powers gave them an initial advantage over the Nama. On the other hand, their unwillingness to slaughter live-stock even during periods of the most severe drought, coupled with an unparalleled capacity to rebuild their stock once better times returned, ensured that their herds were the constant envy of less frugal neighbours. It was a frequent occurrence for both the Nama and also the displaced San to make predatory attacks on Herero cattle. By the early nineteenth century a climate of deep enmity had developed between these Khoisan and Bantu peoples, while the pattern of raid and counter-raid had become both an integral part of the region's economy and a central dynamic in South West African affairs.

However, this pattern was decisively altered by the northward migration of five further tribes between 1815 and 1830 – the final such arrival of African peoples from beyond the Orange River. The new-comers were all detribalised Nama, invariably refugees from bonded labour and other oppressive treatment in the British colony to the south. All five, known collectively as Orlams ('the overland people') and including the Witbooi, tilted the balance of relations between Nama and Herero in favour of the former.

Although they were refugees from the Cape Colony, they brought with them from their former masters a knowledge of the Dutch lan-guage and the Dutch Reform Church, as well as a familiarity with Boer custom and dress. Most important of all, they had developed great skills in horsemanship and the use of firearms, often in military service for their European overlords. When a severe drought in 1833 led to Herero incursions into the territory of their southern neigh-bours, it was these formidable military assets that the Nama had in mind when they requested Orlam assistance.

The Nama–Orlam alliance, with its key military advantages, was the foundation for fifty years of Khoisan ascendancy in pre-colonial Namibia. Amongst Europeans that half-century has regularly been characterised as a dark age of unceasing murder and violence, from which the Africans themselves were only delivered by the arrival of German colonists. It is a judgement for which there was certainly some evidence. To take just one example, an Orlam raid on the important Herero settlement at Okahandja, in August 1850, escalated into a bloody massacre in which men, women and children were indiscriminately murdered. Charles Andersson claimed that women had their hands and feet cut off in order to remove their decorative coils of copper wire, while children's bowels were ripped open 'to gratify a savage thirst for blood'.[11]

The Herero unlucky enough to be taken captive could expect no better treatment. 'If one goes from Berseba further into the interior of the country,' wrote one missionary, 'one comes across masters who are really monsters. They do not hesitate to thrash a poor wretch with a sjambok until the skin breaks with every blow, exposing raw flesh, and sometimes, indeed, the place of chastisement is covered with blood, just as if a sheep were slaughtered there.' Another German missionary described some of the Herero slaves belonging to the Nama as 'nothing more than living skeletons . . . whose bodies bore innumerable marks of the sjambok.'[12]

As one might have expected, such attitudes and behaviour were not the exclusive preserve of the Nama. A Herero confession reproduced in a German colonial newspaper of 1900 is a gruesome measure of the tribe's habitual, almost casual brutality towards their southern neighbours. 'Returning from Hornkranz,' declared one unabashed murderer, 'we came across a few Hottentots [Nama] whom of course we killed.'

> I myself helped to kill one of them. First we cut off his ears saying to him, 'You will never again hear the [Herero] oxen lowing.' Then we cut off his nose saying, 'You shall never again smell [Herero] oxen.' Then we stabbed his eyes saying, 'Never again shall you see [Herero] oxen.' And we cut off his lips, saying 'You will never again eat [Herero] oxen.' And then finally we cut his throat.[13]

The Orlams' introduction of rifle and horse in the early nineteenth century unquestionably precipitated an intensification of the Nama–Herero conflict, but ultimately it was another of their cultural imports which would have far greater impact on the lives of South West Africa's inhabitants. Before the Orlam exodus from the Cape Province they had come into close contact with Christianity and had subsequently encouraged missionaries to join them once they had established themselves north of the Orange River.

Throughout the half-century of warfare following Orlam ascendancy, members of both the Wesleyan and Rhenish Missionary Societies had been active amongst many of the Nama and Herero communities and, apart from a handful of European traders and explorer-hunters, were the main source of information on this period. For many of them it was an arduous existence. Isolated and incapable of exerting strong influence on an unruly flock, one despondent Wesleyan residing with the Orlam spoke for many of his compatriots when he wrote:

> Alone with my small family, in want of the conveniences, and sometimes, of the necessities of life; a barren land, a stupid, ignorant and yet conceited people; missionaries far off, friends further still; no tidings from afar and those from neighbouring tribes, discouraging. Souls are perishing. Plunder, murder, and a darkness that may be felt.[14]

Europeans stationed with the Herero sensed that they too worked an infertile soil. 'Murder, immorality, lying, the three banners of Satan's empire waved freely here,' complained one missionary resident in the country for almost thirty years. 'The Hereros from Chief to servant, from rich to poor, are unashamed beggars and thieves. Polygamy, adultery and whoring are regarded as perfectly natural.'[15]

Although the missionaries had played a consistent and beneficial role in attempting to broker a truce in the Nama–Herero wars, their efforts, according to another eyewitness account, did little to improve matters. Not only did the two sides persistently renege on the cease-fire, but as soon as the external threat was eliminated they 'fought all the more fiercely amongst themselves'.

> Every small [Herero] chief who had a few cattle plundered and murdered the others who had rather more, and everyone who had been despoiled looked for a third at whose expense he could recoup his loss. Bloodshed and misery, murder and horror, were so prevalent throughout the land . . .[16]

While the pre-colonial years are consistently portrayed by the missionaries as a period of demonic anarchy, their position as unbiased chroniclers of South West Africa's affairs cannot be taken entirely on trust. For as representatives of an alien, militarily aggressive culture and with their own powerful contacts at the heart of European decision-making, the missionaries were in a strong position to influence the imperial appetite of their respective nations. And this is precisely the role they played. Repeated images of 'Bloodshed and misery, murder and horror' gave impetus to their lobbying, and then justified their political interference in South West Africa once it had borne fruit.

Theodor Leutwein acknowledged that 'Without the fact of a German mission . . . we would not have been able to take possession of the country with as little means at our disposal as was actually the case.'[17]

As early as 1864 the Rhenish Missionary Society had hoisted the Prussian flag over one of their establishments amongst the Herero, and in 1868 had asked for protection from the Prussian government. When this was not forthcoming and the British sent a representative in 1876 to explore the possibility of annexing South West Africa for themselves, the Society even lent support to this proposal as one offering them greater security and influence over their African charges. After this had come to nothing and Britain confined its acquisitions to the important port at Walvis Bay, the Society's own Inspector, Dr Friedrich Fabri, took up the cause of European occupation. His book *Bedarf Deutschland der Kolonien?* (*Does Germany Need Colonies?*) triggered a wave of agitation for an imperial policy, and from 1880 the Society openly called for German intervention in South West Africa.

Many Germans believed overseas colonies were a precondition of their status as a major European power. The budding German imperialists looked towards the huge territories of the British and concluded that it was this empire that brought Britain's great industrial strength, failing to appreciate that it was actually the other way round. Yet Fabri and his supporters were unwilling to be disabused and fortunately for the imperialists their dream of a place in the sun had caught the *Zeitgeist* of late-nineteenth-century Germany.

Prince Otto Edward Leopold von Bismarck, architect of the greater German nation and chancellor of the unified state since 1871, had long been opposed to overseas adventures as a distraction from Germany's overriding need to consolidate its position in Europe. However, by 1883, swayed partly by public clamour, Bismarck had swung round to the idea of colonies, particularly if they could be acquired and developed under the charter company system which Britain had used to create its great Indian empire. By this method the German state would theoretically be freed from financial and administrative responsibility for its overseas possessions, but could still enjoy all the prestige they would bring. The burdens of imperial management, meanwhile, would devolve on the companies which were commercially involved in the colonies.

Bismarck's increasing sympathy for a German empire ran in parallel with the efforts of a German tobacco and guano merchant, Adolf

Lüderitz, to acquire legal title to sections of the South West African coastline. On 25 August 1883 Lüderitz followed up an initial acquisition of the southern port of Angra Pequena with the purchase of a stretch of coast from the Orange River northwards for over 300 kilometres. For this massive tract Lüderitz paid one Orlam chief 260 Wesley Richards rifles and £600 sterling, the last to be paid in goods. However, since the supplier was allowed to define the value of the goods provided, the African owners were considerably short-changed. Moreover, both Lüderitz and Bam, the Rhenish Missionary who helped arrange the deal, deceived the Africans over the meaning of the term, '20 geographical miles', that was used to define the extent of the German purchase inland from the coast. Since a geographical mile was the equivalent of 7.4 kilometres – a fact of which the Africans were ignorant – the chief, Josef Frederiks, had signed away half his tribe's entire territory. Bam's part in the affair was doubly reprehensible since, by his own admission, he had helped conduct negotiations when Frederiks had been made drunk by the German agent.[18]

The role of the Rhenish Missionary Society in a deal that involved the transfer of so many arms to the territory was itself highly suspect. This behaviour – not to mention the fact that the Society's own trading company had been heavily involved for a number of years in supplying arms to the region – casts an oblique and ironic light on the missionaries' collective image of a pre-colonial dark age. If the country had been plunged into darkness then it was in part the shadow cast by Europe's encroachment.[19]

Lüderitz went on to cap his first successful deception with further treaties, this time for the coastline running northwards to the border with the Portuguese colony of Angola. In one agreement he secured title to a 700-kilometre stretch for only £20. Since he had again used the '20 geographical miles' figure to define the depth of his holding he had, in effect, swindled the tribe of its entire territories.[20]

Alarmed by the intense German interest in the African territories bordering its own colony in the Cape, the British government sought to assert its own claim to South West Africa. However, by the time officials in Cape Town and the Colonial Office at Westminster had coordinated their policy of acquisition, a German warship off South West Africa had already landed a party, planted the flag, and claimed the country in the name of the Kaiser.

As a kind of second tier to the process of legal appropriation initiated by Lüderitz, a colonial official, C.G. Büttner, himself a former missionary, set about acquiring treaties of protection with the various communities in South West Africa. By 1885 many tribes, including the Herero and a number of Orlam and Nama clans, had entered into an agreement with the Germans. Although these expedient documents were framed in conciliatory and innocuous terms, what their African signatories had acquired was not their own right to defence, but the intruder's right to assault and dispossess, once the opportunity should present itself.

If the indigenous Africans had had any hope of preventing their own gradual subjection to a European power, then political and military leadership of the highest order was essential. Of all South West Africans in the late nineteenth century, only one man was equipped to meet the threat of European aggression: Hendrik Witbooi. He was one of the first to recognise the ultimate implications of German protection and would be the last chief to accede to their suzerainty, and then only after a long period of armed conflict.

Yet in tandem with his rare perspicacity, Hendrik embodied the classic and fatal flaw of all tribal society. Rather than building a unified front amongst the various communities of the region, Hendrik showed an unwavering commitment to the age-old Khoisan–Bantu struggle. It was the key weakness in his political vision. Although his repeated assaults on the Herero would eventually yield the customary booty of stolen cattle, this hardly compensated for the strategic advantage available to both tribes had they formed an alliance in the face of the fledgling European colony. By the time the old Orlam warrior had set about mending fences with his Bantu enemy, and by the time he had realised fully the menace presented by the Germans, their troops were ashore and garrisoned. Before too much longer they had trained their sights on him.

19

A Place in the Sun

As an exercise in imperial rapacity nothing quite overshadows Spain's ruthless dissolution of American civilisations in the early sixteenth century. However, for sheer speed coupled with the scale of its territorial consumption, the 'Scramble for Africa', in which seven European nations swallowed up the world's second largest continent, was equally staggering. Almost the entire process was completed within a twenty-year period. In 1876, when Hendrik Witbooi was already in his late thirties, the largest European power in Africa was still ostensibly the Ottoman empire. By 1896, however, and before Witbooi's star had reached its zenith in the south-west, the continental carve-up was nearing completion.

In a single generation the British, the major beneficiaries of the scramble, had hacked out a swathe almost the entire length of Africa. Only Germany's colony in East Africa (later Tanganyika, then Tanzania) interrupted the broad red strip that stretched all the way from the Mediterranean shores to the South Atlantic coast. Running them a poor second were the French, who had acquired virtually the whole of Africa's north-western bulge including the ancient Islamic kingdom of Morocco. Even the small-time players, like the Portuguese and Belgians, had come away from the territorial feast completely sated. Just three of their land holdings – the Portuguese colonies of modern-day Angola and Mozambique, with the Belgian territories around the great river system of the Congo – were between them almost half the size of the entire United States of America. The new owners of the Congo had acquired lands seventy-six times greater than their own European nation.

Although late starters in the scramble, German imperialists could also be well pleased with their haul by the end of 1885. From being a country without any overseas possessions they had progressed to an African empire of more than 2.5 million square kilometres, not to mention a large chunk of the Pacific territories now know as Papua New Guinea. With their African dominions had come nominal suzerainty over 14,000,000 indigenous inhabitants. That many of these were still unaware of the fact was beside the point. Germany seized a total of four colonies – two smaller states in the more populous, culturally advanced west, called Togoland and Cameroon, and the larger territories of German East and South West Africa on each coast of the continent's southern half.

With these possessions, Europe's *nouveau* imperialists had staked their claim to a place in the sun, and the other scramblers accepted it largely without complaint. Even William Gladstone, the British prime minister whose government the Germans had so successfully outflanked in their seizure of the south-west, seemed to bear no grudge. Only days after Bismarck's coup, Gladstone announced to his Scottish constituents that he looked 'with satisfaction, sympathy and joy upon the extension of Germany in these desert places of the earth'.[1]

The remark might easily have been construed as ironic. For after the first flush of success had faded and the Germans surveyed their newly acquired territory in the harsh light of day, they could see far less cause for celebration. Their extension into the desert spaces of South West Africa had certainly given them a place in the sun. And that, in a nutshell, was the problem. The great star rising in the austral dawn was not the golden source that warmed the vineyards of Rhineland or shimmered on the lakes of Bavaria. Into the country's cloudless African skies rises a dazzling ball whose rays beat down with Saharan intensity. By mid-morning the glare radiating off the bleached desert landscapes obliges humans to shutter their gaze to a narrow and painful squint. By midday the thirstland can liquefy in its own savage heat haze, and to step out into this atmosphere can be as enervating as motion against a heavy tide.

Lying between latitudes 17 and 29 degrees south, the country is bordered to the east by the Kalahari Desert and to the west by the coastal Namib Desert. The latter, almost 2,000 kilometres long, is nourished by a southerly airstream which wells upwards in the deep Antarctic waters of the South Atlantic. Cold and dry, the Benguela

Current deposits under fifteen millimetres of rain on the Namib's shoreline. The desert's northern stretch, lying between Walvis Bay and the former Portuguese border on the Kunene River, is still known today as the Skeleton Coast. It is aptly named. Even now its long white beaches are dotted with the remains of half-decayed ships, wrecks which once gave this coastline a reputation as one of the most inhospitable in Africa. It was and, indeed, largely remains a world devoid of human presence, but partly for that reason it supports a rich marine ecosystem. In winter, penguins and long-winged albatross drift northwards with the Benguela Current, and in summer the white-sand beaches are crowded with fur-seals, which come ashore to mate and pup. Breeding cormorants form even greater congregations, and it was their stinking nesting-grounds that were the source of guano for traders like Lüderitz.

As one travels inland from the coast the land gradually climbs and, before descending again towards the Kalahari Basin in the east, it forms a central plateau. These highlands themselves rise again to an intermittent sequence of rugged mountains. Lying on a north–south axis and continuing for almost the country's entire length, they are the physical spine of modern-day Namibia, and it was the areas around these massifs that supported the main human populations. They also provided some of the country's best grazing pasture, particularly in the wetter, northern areas, which formed the Herero heartland. This region sustained not just the vast African cattle herds, but also large numbers of game, like kudu, springbok, zebra, elephant, rhino, giraffe. These, in turn, were the mainstay of the hunting San and, in times of hardship, also the Nama.

However, even this healthier, better-watered land was no Eden. The rains were certainly heavier than in the coastal region, but they were still unpredictable and could fail completely. A classic climatic indicator is *Eragrostis denudata*, the eight-day grass, which can complete its cycle of germination, flowering and seed production in just a week, to ensure its survival until the next uncertain rains. Everything that thrived in this land had to be drought-adapted, even the Nama and Herero, whose system of partial transhumance was itself a response to the joint vagaries of rainfall and pasture.

In their assessment of the colony's economic potential the Germans were obliged to take account of these adverse factors, as well as the severe transportation problems that prevailed in the region. The dense thorn bush that nourished the thick hides of the elephant and rhinoceros was far less kindly to human occupants. Pointing out the early hazards of bush travel, Charles Andersson wrote:

> The fish-hook principle on which most of these thorns are shaped, and the strength of each, make them most formidable enemies. At an average, each prickle will sustain a weight of seven pounds. Now, if the reader will be pleased to conceive a few scores of these to lay hold of a man at once, I think it will not be difficult to imagine the consequences.[2]

If travel on foot was difficult, journeying with a wagon and team was probably worse. 'To give a faint idea of the obstructions of this kind of travelling,' Andersson continued, 'we will suppose a person suddenly placed at the entrance of a primeval forest . . . the haunt of savage beasts, and with soil as yielding as that of an English sanddown; to this must be added a couple of ponderous vehicles . . . to each of which are yoked sixteen to twenty refractory, half-trained oxen.'[3] It was hardly surprising that the 300 kilometres from Walvis Bay to Windhoek involved a ten-day journey.

As an alternative to such ineffectual locomotion, one optimistic settler brought a steam engine ashore in 1896. Having taken three months to cover the thirty kilometres from Walvis Bay, the engine completed a few short journeys in the vicinity of Swakopmund, and was eventually abandoned on the outskirts of the town, where its useless hulk still stands today – a national monument to the early transport difficulties.

Nor were these the only challenges for a successful colony. Arid and almost waterless, South West Africa allowed few agricultural choices. The Germans could follow the example of the Herero and adapt themselves to the region's rainfall, pursuing the system of semi-nomadic pastoralism which many of the Dutch Boers had embraced south of the Orange River. However, even after taking a decision to rear cattle, they had then to confront other obstacles. Foremost was the fact that all the best land fell within the territories of either the Herero or the Nama. Equally problematic for European settlers was the acquisition of livestock, since the Herero were unwilling to trade anything but small numbers of their poorer-quality beasts. In his book *South-West Africa under German Rule 1894–1914*, Helmut Bley suggested that:

The Herero based their cattle-farming entirely on the size of their herds, and had no idea of building up the quality of their breeding-stock or husbanding their land. This meant not only that they occupied unnecessarily vast tracts of grazing-land but also that the Europeans were hampered in their efforts to establish a profitable cattle industry. The size of the Herero herds kept the price and quality of stock uneconomically low.[4]

Such a statement entirely overlooked the fact that the Africans had never conceived of themselves as participating in a 'profitable cattle industry'. Their animals were not commodities in an exchange economy, but a self-sufficient regime fulfilling all the tribe's spiritual, social and nutritional needs. That the Herero were so unwilling to sell their best cattle – behaviour that infuriated the early settlers – was a measure, not of their inadequacy as European-style cattle farmers, but of the integrity of their own system.

If both livestock and land were initially unavailable, the early colonists could at least speculate about the region's mining potential. They were certainly aware of the huge diamond fields located in the 1870s at Kimberley in the adjacent and geographically related Cape Province. Moreover, the copper mines at Otavi and Tsumeb in the north had long been known and exploited by the Ovambo to furnish themselves with the metal for tools and weapons. In time the country would indeed prove rich in diamonds and other valuable commodities like lead, zinc and uranium. As Lüderitz and his agents travelled the country making land purchases from the various tribes, they were literally walking over a fortune. Lüderitz at least had hoped as much and went to great lengths to acquire mining concessions to tribal land. 'I should be pleased,' he once wrote, 'if it turned out that the entire [colony] is a colossal mineral deposit, which, once it is mined, will leave the whole area one gaping hole.'[5] He would never come to realise the profits of these operations himself. Having run out of capital he was obliged to sell his entire South West African stakes very shortly after the initial purchase.

It was not just lack of capital that restricted the early development of mining. Another limiting factor was the absence of labour. Both the Nama and Herero were at relatively low densities and had all the resources necessary to maintain an independent lifestyle. They had little reason or incentive to become paid employees of the Germans. Besides, the earliest settlers in South West Africa took a dim view of their work capacity. Charles Andersson reflected the general European attitude towards the Nama when he wrote that '[they] are an excessively idle race. They may be seen basking in the sun for days together, in listless activity, frequently almost perishing from thirst or hunger.'[6] Writing several generations later, the missionary Vedder agreed that the Nama 'always deemed labour beneath his dignity', blaming it on 'his weak limbs and delicate physique', which disqualified 'him for hard work'.[7]

If the lazy Nama were not going to convert easily into the dust-caked, lung-infected proles who would dig out the fortunes of future German mine owners, Charles Andersson was equally doubtful about the labour potential of the Herero. 'They are idle creatures,' he noted. 'What is not done by the women is left to the slaves, who are either impoverished members of their own tribe or captured bushmen.'[8]

In their assessment of the colony's human materials the Germans had at least some assets they could weigh in the balance against the long list of negatives. The first was a small community known as the Basters or Bastards. They were the offspring of relationships between European, predominantly Boer, men and Khoisan women. Invariably disowned by their white fathers, the Basters moved northwards as a body and settled at the town of Rehoboth in 1870, after negotiating an agreement with the surrounding Nama. Despite European maltreatment, including enslavement even by their own fathers, the Basters clung to their European heritage, speaking Afrikaans and embracing Christianity.

When the new colonists arrived and claimed the country for the Reich, the Basters readily hitched their wagon to the rising German star. In all the colony's military clashes between African and European, the Germans could count on active Baster support or, at least, their sympathetic neutrality. Only with the arrival in 1915 of the conquering South African forces did the Basters abandon allegiance to their German overlords.

The other community which found grounds for mutual self-interest with the invading Europeans were a people called the Bergdamara or Damara. Of rather mysterious origins, but probably some of the earliest inhabitants of the region, these people divided into two communities: some were employed, often forcibly, by the Nama and Herero, for whom they served as cowherds, shepherds and menials. Those escaping this servitude lived among the mountains in small hunter–gatherer bands in the manner of the San. Pioneer Europeans

accused both the Herero and Nama of indiscriminately killing independent Damara communities, whom they apparently referred to as
'baboons', while the Nama name, *Chou-daman*, loosely translatable as
'shitty blacks', was supposed to reflect their indifference to personal
hygiene. Given this inter-tribal antagonism, Damara willingness to
cooperate with the Germans, although hardly born of deep affection,
was not difficult to understand.[9]

Hahn suggested that the Damara received their full freedom only
upon the military defeat of the Nama and Herero, when they were
given their own reserve and rights of self-regulation by the colonial
government. However, an indication of the new status accorded them
by their European allies is provided by Hahn's sweeping conviction
that the Damara was 'happiest when under a firm hand, which rules
his daily conduct and nips desires for insubordination and imperti-
nence in the bud.'[10] One statistic illustrating the firmness of that
German hand is the estimated 10,000 Damara − one-third of the
tribe's entire population − who, despite their neutrality or support for
the European cause, died in the war between 1904 and 1907. These
deaths came about because the German troops were unwilling to distinguish between hostile and friendly African communities.[11]

Once the Germans had completed their inventory of the country's
natural resources, it is difficult to see how they could have avoided the
obvious implications of any audit. A sun-drenched, drought-afflicted
land enveloped by desert, with a non-existent transport network,
highly restricted agricultural opportunities, unknown mineral resources and a sparse, well-armed indigenous population living at subsistence level, South West Africa was hardly El Dorado. Or, rather,
one might say that it was a classic El Dorado, and the fact that the
Germans persisted with their colonial adventure was a clear indication
of the ineradicable fantasies at work in most European empires.

It is worth examining the cherished notions which propelled
Germany's imperial policy, and measuring these aspirations against the
bare statistics eventually produced by their colonial effort. For their
economic experience in South West Africa was highly symptomatic of
most of the European colonies in Africa. Simultaneously, such a comparison reveals a fundamental shift in European attitudes towards overseas territory from those that had launched fifteenth-century Spain
into the New World.

The two main arguments that had initiated a German drive for empire–provision of *Lebensraum* for the Reich's expanding home population and the securing of a protected overseas trade – were to prove almost completely hollow in South West Africa, as, indeed, in all their overseas territories. By 1911 only 11,140 settlers had emigrated to the country, and this was the most popular destination of all the colonies. By the same year the total German population that had started a new life in the empire was under 17,000, a paltry figure when compared with the 981,000 who had departed for Russia by 1867, or the 128,000 leaving annually for the Americas during the 1870s.[12]

By the start of the First World War, thirty years after Germany's imperial adventure had begun, the colonies as a whole had hardly proved their supposed economic advantages. As a going concern they were hopeless. Not one of the main colonies was financially self-supporting, and by 1913 the entire colonial trade amounted to only £13 million, half of one per cent of the Fatherland's total commerce.[13] Belgium alone imported eighteen times more German goods than did South West Africa, and five times more than did all the African colonies together.[14] In 1912 colonial exports had come to exceed imports by £3,170,000; but this was hardly an impressive return, given the £100 million that the German taxpayer had eventually invested in the empire between 1884 and 1914.[15]

The best that could be made of these figures might be to present Germany's empire as an item of conspicuous consumption, an expensive luxury whose principal value was symbolic – a much-desired badge of imperial status for the world's most powerful military nation. Although this might have been typical of much of Europe's experience in Africa, it contrasted strongly with earlier periods of expansion. In fact, the German position in South West Africa was the inverse of that of the Spaniards in the Andes. There were no rooms filled with gold to defray the conquistadors' initial expenses, let alone bullion fleets to dazzle the home nation and bankroll its state policy. There were no get-rich-quick stories to lure in wave after wave of fresh adventurers. For the Germans in the nineteenth century, imperialism had become a cultural and ideological imperative, but it had very little foundation in hard-nosed, practical common sense.

What was equally noteworthy about the new German imperialism was the manner in which – in order to give the colony a vague semblance of economic viability – they seized lock, stock and barrel from its indigenous people whatever small subsistence resources there were in South West Africa. Although these German tactics involved no departure whatsoever from the methods of earlier conquistadors, what was striking was the manner in which they flouted totally the moral expectations of their age. For, far more than any of its predecessors, the new industrial Europe of the late nineteenth century saw itself in the business of colonies at least partly for the good of the colonised. Empire was now a field for philanthropists, and the slogan issued to his fellow whites by the great British explorer David Livingstone – 'Civilisation, Christianity and Commerce' – had become the clarion call for many colonists in Africa.

With the establishment in late-eighteenth-century Britain of a movement for the abolition of the African slave trade, Europeans had finally begun to awaken politically to their past exploitation of tribal societies. In 1791, William Pitt, the same prime minister who five years earlier had unleashed upon the Aborigines of Australia a policy of British penal settlements, spoke of 'the shame and guilt with which we are now covered' as a result of Britain's long tradition of African slave labour.[16] Once that specific battle had been won, firstly with the abolition of the trade in 1807 and then with the Slavery Abolition Act of 1833, humanitarian concerns widened to embrace the treatment of all Britain's imperial subjects. Humanitarian groups like the Aborigines Protection Society and Christian missionary organisations were increasingly seeking to influence colonial policy by awakening wider public concern on issues of political freedom and social justice.

Despite this background of humanitarian interest in colonial Africa, Germany, in an imperial career spanning just thirty years, embarked on two major colonial wars. As a result of these conflicts or the social dislocation they engendered, approximately 330,000 Africans lost their lives. It was an unenviable record. To be fair to the Germans much of it was barely more than representative of wider European practice in Africa. All seven powers used violent methods both to implement political control and in seizing Africa's resources. Compared with the ruthless system of extortion operating in King Leopold's private fiefdom of the Congo, the economic regime in South West Africa was positively amateurish. Belgian policies of torture and amputation for failure to meet economic targets, especially in wild-grown rubber, eventually led to the deaths of hundreds of thousands of Africans, while the royal profits accruing from these atrocities ran into millions of francs.

Yet there was one dimension to the policies in South West Africa that seemed both distinct and uniquely German. Once relations between the Teutonic colonists and their African subjects had descended into a state of open conflict, the crisis opened the way for German officers whose views on race and on Africans in particular gave rise to policies of outright genocide. Rather than suggesting some process of imperial atavism, the deliberate, almost clinical methods and detached attitudes towards the issue of racial extermination contained a deeply modern element. Rather than a return to the anarchic brutalities of the Spanish *conquistadores*, German atrocities in Africa seem to anticipate the radical, systematic inhumanity of a later holocaust – that against the Jews during Hitler's Third Reich.

20

The Empire Builders

Although the final, irrevocable breakdown in Euro–African relations did not occur until twenty years after the Germans' first occupation of South West Africa, the period before this war could hardly be characterised as a time of peaceful co-existence. From 1884 until that fateful confrontation in the Bondelswarts village of Warmbad, there were two decades of constant political acrimony and intermittent fighting.

The two German figures dominating this period of pre-war rancour were the colony's administrator, Captain Curt von François, and his eventual successor as governor, Major Theodor Leutwein. At first glance the two characters could not have seemed more contrasting. While François was rash and confrontational, his successor appeared hesitant and conciliatory. Where one seemed bellicose, the other was pacific, and while the captain sought instant military answers to colonial problems, the major aimed to achieve his objectives through long-term political manoeuvring.

Superficially, Leutwein, who held office in the colony twice as long as von François, from 1894 to 1904, seemed the more successful tactician. It was certainly during his decade in power that the German colony was transformed from an entity existing largely only on paper into a concrete political reality. While this was in part owing to Leutwein's greater personal qualities, a good deal of the achievement could be traced to the substantially increased resources committed by the home government.

The records of the two men had more in common than their personalities might initially suggest. Neither could ultimately be considered a success in South West Africa, since the careers of both ended in a form of dismissal. Even more striking was the fact that both ultimately found that their radically different policies in South West Africa produced an outcome that was the exact reverse of what they had intended. Von François, pursuing a line of military aggression towards the Nama, was to find himself politically and strategically outmanoeuvred by his chief opponent, Hendrik Witbooi. On the other hand, Leutwein's plan to overawe the indigenous inhabitants through largely peaceful political means eventually forced the Herero and Nama to launch an all-out war upon the Germans.

Although Curt von François never enjoyed the level of men or *matériel* that Leutwein eventually commanded, his own appointment in 1889 was an expression of Berlin's growing awareness of the need to commit physical resources to uphold its imperial authority. Only months after German marines had plunged the national flag into the hot Namibian sands – and despite Chancellor Bismarck's hopes of empire on the cheap through a policy of imperial chartered companies – it was obvious that no colonial offshoot of the Fatherland was going to blossom on these waterless shores completely unaided.

Adolf Lüderitz, the guano merchant who had helped sow the seeds of German empire, was himself forced by insolvency to sell his own dubiously acquired lands to the *Deutsche Kolonialgesellschaft für Sudwestafrika*. This newly formed corporate enterprise, although involving some of the wealthiest men in Germany and holding, on paper at least, 240,000 square kilometres of African territory, had committed only 468,000 Marks (about £24,000) to imperial development.[1] One German economist suggested that trying to achieve anything with 'such ridiculously small working capital, [was] about as absurd as the idea of a man who would try to cut a tunnel through the Alps with a pickaxe.'[2]

However, the company's derisory input into the colony was barely less than the German government's own initial investment. In 1888 there were still only three officials present in the country, including Dr Heinrich Goering, the colony's imperial commissioner (and father of the future Nazi leader Hermann Goering). With such a skeleton staff the Germans were in no position to press their authority upon their African subjects. In fact, only four years after the imperial adventure had been launched, Goering, faced with the threat of Herero violence, was forced to withdraw to British protection at Walvis Bay, and the German colony collapsed amidst general humiliation.

With this final exposure of the charter system by which Bismarck had hoped to build his colony, the German chancellor was obliged to adopt a more expensive policy to restore national honour. As a preliminary this involved the dispatch of twenty-one German troops under the command of von François – a force well short of the 400–500 that Goering had actually requested. However, the captain's arrival in South West Africa marked a change of emphasis in the colony's administration.

A traditional Prussian soldier to his finger-tips, von François was also a violent racist who saw little merit in his official orders to avoid any kind of confrontation with the Africans. 'The Europeans have failed to give the black man the right kind of treatment,' was his own opinion. 'Nothing but relentless severity will lead to success.'[3] In confirmation of these methods he moved the German military headquarters to Windhoek, brushing aside all Herero objections. Having fortified his new stronghold, he undertook the additional recruitment of Baster and Damara levies, while requesting reinforcements from Germany, which increased his European troop to fifty men by January 1890.

With Dr Goering's support von François set about implementing his policy of relentless severity, which involved two key objectives: firstly to strengthen the German position and prevent any combination of African forces against the revitalised but vulnerable colony; secondly, to oblige each of the different African communities to complete treaties of protection with the German authorities. In von François' narrow military mind both these goals eventually interlocked in a single violent purpose: the destruction of the Witbooi tribe.

The unwillingness of their leader, Hendrik Witbooi, to consider a protection treaty, and his persistent raids upon Herero livestock, had repeatedly exposed the ineffectuality of German rule in the colony. Captain von François had finally concluded that there could be no peace in South West Africa without inflicting a decisive defeat upon him. And in 1892 there were other pressing reasons to bring him to book. In that year German colonists had started to arrive in the country and would need peaceful conditions if they were to prosper. More important still was the fact that despite Witbooi's recent attack on the Herero, he had not entirely abandoned his offers of a ceasefire with his Bantu neighbours. Through the agency of the Baster leader, Hermanus van Wyk, Witbooi and Samuel reopened negotiations and these were finally concluded in a peace agreement in November 1892.

Von François recognised the inherent dangers for the European position in a united African front, and he immediately initiated plans for an attack on Witbooi's stronghold at Hornkranz. A visit to the settlement in July 1892, ostensibly a final attempt to persuade Hendrik into a treaty with the European government, had already given von François a chance to look over the country and plan his secret raid. The arrival of a further 215 German soldiers and two batteries of artillery in March of the following year was the signal for its immediate implementation.

The Hornkranz massacre that followed on 12 April 1893, and which forms the opening scene of this book's introductory chapter, constitutes a model of Europe's treachery towards tribal peoples, of its capacity for unprovoked violence and the ensuing self-justification. In the colony itself, however, it took far less time to expose the gulf between the Germans' official version and what had actually taken place at Hornkranz. Even the boasts of overwhelming military success were quickly deflated. Only hours after von François' achievements were fêted in Windhoek, it was reported that the Witbooi had captured forty German horses. The captain immediately negotiated purchase of 120 replacements from a German trader, only to learn subsequently that these too had been taken.

Having dismounted the German cavalry, the Witbooi were able to ride up to the walls of Windhoek jeering at the enemy's impotence. They then severely disrupted the capital's supplies by taking charge of a convoy of over twenty ox wagons. Two months later, having drawn to his banner Nama from all over the southern region, Hendrik struck again, this time wiping out a European experimental farm that had previously been established on Witbooi land without tribal consent. The Africans' haul included 2,350 Merino sheep, 125 oxen and 28 horses. By the end of 1893, only eight months after the Hornkranz raid, the tables had been completely turned.[4]

In the colony itself trade was paralysed. Von François was unable to guarantee European safety except in Windhoek itself. Stunned by the phoenix-like resurrection of a tribe he believed he had destroyed, the captain's only response was to call for artillery and more reinforcements. However, von François' final bolt had been fired. In Germany, Prince Arenberg announced in the Reichstag that 'Major François is not the right man in the right place and must be replaced by someone else . . . Witbooi is the real master of the country, and François is no match for him.'[5]

The Hornkranz massacre marked a natural caesura in South West African affairs. It brought to a close the militant policy of its author and terminated his career in the colony on an ignominious note. Witbooi, by contrast, had escaped death, remained at large and resumed mastery of the situation. However, the idea of his final submission had not been abandoned in Germany. A speech by Bismarck's replacement as imperial chancellor, Count Leo von Caprivi, delivered to the Reichstag in March 1893, signalled a fresh departure from the lackadaisical approach of his predecessor. 'South West Africa is ours . . .' Caprivi announced. 'This is not the moment for retrospection. How it all happened and whether it was a good thing or not is irrelevant now. It is ours, German territory, and it must remain so.'[6] The man sent out to ensure that it did would prove a far more shrewd, effective and enduring agent of German imperialism than anyone the Africans had previously encountered.

Theodor Leutwein, the son of a Lutheran pastor, was born on 9 May 1849 at Strampfelbronn, close to Germany's south-western border with France. Having studied law in Freiburg, he had then embarked on a military career, and by the time of his new appointment in South West Africa the recently promoted major was forty-four years old with little experience of active soldiering. He was, according to Helmut Bley, 'trained and sophisticated, self-assured but not overconfident, versed in Hegel and Moltke, "silent in seven languages", and yet with an amazing store of political naivety.'[7]

However, Leutwein was not going to repeat the errors of his predecessor. Instead of bludgeoning the Africans into submission as von François had intended, Leutwein aimed to compel them to an acceptance of German rule by a mixture of political manoeuvre and, if necessary, a cautious display of force. He claimed to be a student of British colonial history and sought to emulate the methods used by its administrators, especially the time-honoured policy of divide and rule. As long as he could ensure that the Africans failed to unite amongst themselves he would be able to pick off his opponents one at a time.

Shortly after his arrival in the country he gave a demonstration of his intended approach in his rapid suppression of the Khauas, the Nama tribe occupying the region to the west of Windhoek. They, like the Witbooi, had long refused to sign a protection treaty, while their chief, Andreas Lambert, had recently been accused of killing a German trader called Krebs. Having made a forced march from

Windhoek with a hundred troops and seized the tribe in a surprise attack, Leutwein then agreed to waive the murder charge against Lambert, if he signed a treaty with the German government. On his agreement to these forced demands the chief was released, when he immediately attempted to flee. He was promptly recaptured, court-martialled, found guilty of Krebs' murder and executed. This despite a general acknowledgement, even by the Germans themselves, that Krebs' actual killer had been a Witbooi – a survivor of the Hornkranz massacre and a man with considerable grounds for hostility towards white colonists.

Even though he had reported the death and returned the German's effects to Windhoek, Lambert was found guilty by association. Following the execution, Lambert's brother was unwillingly appointed acting chief in contravention of the Khauas custom on succession and, despite the fact that most of the tribe had fled, he and the remaining members were coerced into accepting German 'protection' and stripped of their arms and horses.[8]

Emboldened by such success, the governor soon felt able to take on the only tribe remaining outside his control, the Witbooi. It was clear from the outset that 'the Lord of the Water and King of Great Namaqualand', as Hendrik styled himself, was not going to be over-awed by the bullying tactics used against the Khauas Nama. Cautiously, Leutwein opened 'negotiations' with Hendrik in early May 1894, and when these had proved as fruitless as ever, the German leader offered a strategic two-month truce – the time required to ensure the arrival of 250 reinforcements from Europe. With these fresh troops at his back Leutwein was finally in a position to embark on a decisive engagement, which he opened on 27 August. Outgunned and starved of both food and ammunition, the Witbooi still maintained a fierce resistance. The Naukluft Mountains into which they had retreated were a forbidding wasteland of soaring red cliffs, jagged waterless peaks and treacherously narrow defiles. They proved perfect terrain for the Witbooi's guerrilla tactics and the Germans suffered severe casualties before their opponents were bombarded into final submission in September 1894.

From the moment of his arrival in South West Africa Leutwein had achieved a string of minor successes against indigenous opposition. However, with his triumph in the Naukluft Mountains he had scored a crucial victory. Hendrik had always been the major obstacle to dominion in South West Africa and with his defeat, the final plank of German military policy had been hammered into place. At the conclusion of a protection agreement with the Witbooi, Leutwein's stock should have soared. Instead, when the terms of the agreement were published in Windhoek and elsewhere, there was a storm of protest. The Witbooi, far from losing their illustrious leader and his foremost troops to a firing squad, were free to return to the lion's share of their former lands. Moreover, they had been allowed to keep their arms and ammunition, while the 'treaty of protection and friendship' stressed the voluntary nature of future cooperation.

In Germany the principal critic of the peace settlement was Captain von François, who complained that 'the war against Witbooi has cost the German Empire approximately four million Marks. The damage it has caused in the colony is at least as great. But . . . his tribe remains united . . . and he [Witbooi] receives a salary of 2,000 Marks.'[9] In defence of his measures Leutwein had pointed out to the Colonial Office in Germany that Hendrik had not been forced into unconditional surrender, but had simply accepted the peace terms offered. Total military defeat of the Witbooi tribe would have involved months and possibly years of further fighting, which Leutwein had no resources to undertake. The treaty he had got was the best that the German government could have hoped for in the circumstances. Leutwein's critics, however, distant from the realities of South West African conditions, or unwilling to acknowledge that he had succeeded where others had failed, were unconvinced. They accused Leutwein of leniency, a charge that was to become a constant refrain throughout his decade in office.

Much later, when his career in the colony had ended in the same kind of official censure that had doomed von François, Leutwein wrote an account of his governorship, *Elf Jahre Gouverneur in Deutsch-Südwestafrika*. Addressed to the intensely racist world of Germany's colonial establishment at the turn of the century, it was intended in part to rebut the accusation that he had been too soft on blacks.

Considered from the vantage point of the late twentieth century, Leutwein's concern to prove himself as indifferent to African welfare as the most extreme of his colonial colleagues can make parts of his book seem like a deliberate and perverse act of self-indictment. Typical was his boast to have made 'the native tribes serve our cause and to play them off one against the other. Even an adversary of this policy,' he added, 'must concede to me that it was more difficult, but also more serviceable, to influence the natives to kill each other for us than to expect streams of blood and streams of money from the Old Fatherland for their suppression.'[10]

While he was often as unfeeling as he frequently claimed, Leutwein was by no means the most extreme amongst German officials active in the country. Dr Paul Rohrbach, an adviser on the colony's economic development, was the proponent of an utterly ruthless brand of racism. 'The decision to colonise in South West Africa,' he wrote, in a passage notorious for its brutal justification of German policy, 'could mean nothing else but this, namely that the native tribes would have to give up their lands on which they have previously grazed their stock in order that the white man might have the land for the grazing of his stock.'

> When this attitude is questioned from the moral law standpoint, the answer is that for nations of the 'Kultur-position' of the South African natives, the loss of their free national barbarism and their development into a class of labourers in service of and dependent on the white people is primarily a 'law of existence' in the highest degree . . .

> By no argument whatsoever can it be shown that the preservation of any degree of national independence, national prosperity and political organisation by the races of South West Africa, would be of a greater or even of an equal advantage for the development of mankind in general or of the German people in particular, than the making of [such] races serviceable in the enjoyment of their former possessions by the white races.[11]

By this same chilling logic Rohrbach could later conclude that if the Africans had any inalienable rights as human beings, it was the right 'to the possession of the greatest possible working efficiency': the sole freedom, in short, to be the slaves of Europeans.[12]

Notions like these created the ideological matrix in which the colonial governor operated, and even had Leutwein wished his policies to reflect a greater concern for the country's indigenous occupants, men like Rohrbach were ever alert to deviations from their prescribed norms. In most expositions of their views, their touchstone was the inexorable logic of what European colonists were doing in Africa, the sheer scientific inevitability of Germany's triumph. By contrast, any expression of emotion was stigmatised as the colonist's cardinal sin – a view classically conveyed by the armchair imperialist, Dr Karl Dove, when he urged his views on Leutwein after one clash with Nama. 'It is to be hoped,' Dove wrote in a German newspaper, 'that the Imperial Governor will not be prevented by the sentimental humanitarianism of certain quarters from sending all the [Nama] falling into his hands to the gallows . . . There is no place for sickly sentimentalism!'[13]

While Leutwein could never have been charged with any excess of feeling for Africans, he did evince some sense of concern at his government's conduct. He showed a desire to stem the worst abuses of his fellow Germans, avoided unnecessary loss of life and, by a display of leniency after the Namas' military defeat, won the respect of no less a figure than Hendrik Witbooi. Moreover, Leutwein at least conceded that the German position in Africa did involve some degree of ethical conflict. 'Colonisation,' he once wrote, 'is always inhumane. It must ultimately amount to an encroachment on the rights of the original inhabitants in favour of the intruders. If this is unacceptable then one must oppose all colonisation, which at least would be a logical attitude.'[14]

In the final decade of the nineteenth century Leutwein was the nearest that the German South West African government came to a moral conscience. And when he stood amongst the ruins of his own failed policies that awareness would confer on him a near-tragic status. Tragic not because he had failed but because, unlike most of the other German officials in South West Africa, he glimpsed the injustice of the system over which he presided, he had an insight into its moral implications, but in the final analysis he lacked the qualities to mount any serious reform or propose an alternative course.

For most of Leutwein's governorship, of course, there seemed no reason to change tack. The Germans' superior physical force was usually sufficient to flatten immediate signs of opposition in the colony, without Leutwein having to question the justice of his actions, or to consider the subterranean discontents that lingered amongst the Africans once he and his soldiers had returned to Windhoek. What mattered to him, as he himself cynically acknowledged, was that 'However ruthless one's colonial policy, it is necessary to give one's actions a *semblance* of legality.'[15] Just how indifferent he could be to achieving the genuine article was shown by his treatment of the Bondelswarts in 1897–98.

This Nama tribe had expressed deep dissatisfaction at a German directive to identify all rifles – a measure seen as the first step towards complete disarmament of the Africans. Seeking to quell any rebellion, Leutwein immediately headed southwards with a hundred men and four guns, and placed the Bondelswarts and another tribe of Nama allies on trial. With Leutwein acting as both judge and prosecuting counsel they were found guilty and condemned to cover the cost of the German expedition. Since the Bondelswarts had no means to pay the fine they were forced to make compensation with their own land, which was what Leutwein had sought all along.

This fresh surrender of territory intensified a process of impoverishment that the Bondelswarts had suffered since 1890, when their alcohol-soaked chief had signed away the better portion of their domain to a British land and mining syndicate. By 1894 a number of white farms had already been carved out of their territories, and the Bondelswarts took steps to depose their incompetent leader. Leutwein immediately responded, rushing to the defence of the 'best friend we [have] in the south of the Protectorate' and intimidating the would-be rebels with an artillery display.[16] To the British land company, Leutwein counselled dispossession by stealth, and upheld their request not to have the land–cession contract made public. His notion of colonial justice was clearly illustrated by his remarks on approving the non-publication of the contract:

> I consider this a *legitimate* request because by the time the syndicate has selected the 512 farms of 10,000 Cape acres apiece to which it is entitled in 15 years from now, there will not be much left for the natives. If they learn about this now, revolution is inevitable, but if they are familiarised with it *by and by* it will be possible to satisfy them. [author's italics][17]

For Leutwein the word 'legitimate' had come to connote, not what was equitable and right in a given situation, but what best suited European self-interest irrespective of its impact on African lives.

The governor's step-by-step approach to dismantling African power in the German colony was facilitated, in the case of the Nama, by the fragmentary nature of their tribal society. Because of their wide dispersal in the country, Nama discontent was geographically isolated and invariably confined to a single small population. Except in the case of the Witbooi, a moderate-sized detachment of European troops and a few guns had always been sufficient to suppress any act of defiance. However, the much larger and much more powerful Herero nation could not be overawed in the same way. Yet it was obvious to the German governor that if any viable European colony was going to develop, then the Herero's economic dominance and large grazing territories would have to be wrested from them. Nothing better demonstrates the suppleness of Leutwein's methods, nor the deep cynicism that lay at the root of his policies, than his manipulation of this people.

It had been a godsend to him that at the outset of his governorship the Hereros had been distracted by a succession dispute. Their new chief would become, alongside Hendrik Witbooi, one of the two key African figures in the tragic drama which overtook the country only a few years later. However, Samuel Maharero would provide his people with a leadership as vacillating and short-sighted as Witbooi's was strong and decisive. Educated by missionaries and a convert to Christianity, Samuel represented the new generation of European-influenced Africans. By the time of his election to the chieftaincy he had already travelled by ship to Cape Town, had mixed in British society, met the governor of the colony, and had adopted many of the outward customs of the colonising powers. His dwelling was a comfortable Western-style house, white tropical suits were a mark of his chiefly rank, while brandy, wine and schnapps were all part of his expensive taste in European luxuries. Von François thought him vain and sensual, while Leutwein considered him a drunkard and a womaniser.[18]

The Westernised and manipulable Samuel might have been the natural choice for the Germans – indeed, their open support for him was to prove a decisive factor in his election – but with his own people he was far from popular. Under the traditional Herero system of inheritance the candidacy of his cousin, Nikodemus, who was both a traditionalist and a proven leader, took precedence over that of Samuel. Although Samuel eventually prevailed in the election, the fact that he did so in the teeth of substantial opposition meant that he looked increasingly to the new European power in the land in order to bolster his position with his tribe. This collusion with the colonists, which was to become a constant feature of his leadership, would in time have catastrophic consequences for the Herero people. It would leave them preoccupied with internal politics and badly divided at a critically threatening moment in their history.

Geronimo the Chiricahua shaman at San Carlos in 1884, aged about sixty.

Despite US army officers'
dismissiveness, Nana at
seventy-five performed
one of the most brilliant
deeds of the Apache wars.

A classic portrait of General George Crook
on campaign – mounted on his mule,
Apache, and in civilian dress.

Only a single photograph of Victorio exists, but it is almost enough.

The peace conference at the Cañon de los Embudos, March 1886.
Geronimo faces the camera with Nana to his left; Crook and Bourke are
second and third on the right hand side.

Geronimo with some of the last Chiricahua holdouts,
including Naiche, the son of Cochise, to his left.

Captain John Gregory Bourke,
one of the most talented US army
officers in the nineteenth century.

Hendrik Witbooi, the formidable Nama leader.

Vain, complacent and an
alcoholic, the Herero leader
Samuel Maharero was an
unlikely rebel against the
might of the German Empire.

Colonel Theodor Leutwein,
Governor of German South
West Africa, 1894–1904.

The conqueror of the Herero,
General Lothar von Trotha:
'I shall annihilate the revolting
tribes with rivers of blood and
rivers of gold.'

The Herero leader, Nikodemus, before his execution for armed
rebellion against the Germans.

Leutwein immediately set about exploiting these divisions, first by acknowledging Samuel Maharero as the paramount chief and then supporting his rival Nikodemus in his own bid for recognition as a leader largely independent of Maharero's authority. Congratulating himself on the shrewdness of this tactic, Leutwein laboured the point to the German chancellor Caprivi: 'It is self-evident that a politically divided Herero nation is more easy to deal with than a united and coherent one.'[19]

With the new European power in the land apparently at his back, Samuel's paramountcy among the Herero looked unassailable. And, indeed, during his decade of close cooperation with Leutwein the chief was able to exploit his position both to defeat his Herero opponents and to build his own internal empire, often with land and possessions taken from his rivals.

However, the office of paramount chief was a deeply ambiguous symbol of African authority, serving, in the final analysis, not to uphold Herero self-government, but to enable a gradual German erosion of the tribe's autonomy. Even the title's pedigree was highly questionable. Hugo von François, brother to the former military commander in South West Africa, and well versed in the country's affairs, believed that it was simply an invention of the whites designed for their own ends, but without any 'factually existing legal status amongst the natives'.[20]

Moreover, it was widely recognised amongst experienced settlers that tribal authority, even that of a so-called supreme chief like Samuel, was by its very nature both consensual and democratic. There was no single leader invested with outright authority to dictate Herero policy. The fact that older colonists knew this indicates a deep and persistent hypocrisy in German dealings with the tribe. They understood the divided nature of Herero command structures, and yet simultaneously insisted on the paramount chief's capacity to control all his people whenever they called upon him to do so. As the point at which the colonists exerted pressure on tribal affairs, Maharero became a major focus for his people's gathering discontent. If during his decade of empire building Leutwein seemed the Cortés of German South West Africa, then Samuel was undoubtedly his kidnapped emperor.

From the outset his rôle as paramount chief placed him in a virtually impossible position, and it would be unfair to suggest that his self-serving machinations were completely responsible for the decline in African fortunes between 1894 and 1904. However, his persistent willingness to consider his own interests and his personal position within the tribe above the larger strategic concerns of his people was a critical factor in the relentless haemorrhage of Herero strength. Leutwein himself acknowledged that Samuel's friendship 'enabled us to remain masters of Hereroland despite our modest protective force. In order to please us, he did more harm to his people than we could ever have done by relying on our strength alone.'[21] Although his leadership during the Africans' tragic rebellion would go some way to compensate, it did not atone completely for his earlier role in the nation's downfall.

A typical example was his willingness to enter into an agreement with Leutwein in December 1894 that delimited the southern boundary of Hereroland. On the face of it, a demarcation of respective territories seemed a sensible means of avoiding possible conflict. Unfortunately, neat lines drawn on a map took no account of the region's actual ecological conditions or the traditional but fluctuating Herero needs for good grazing and surface water, wherever they might be. While the very ink was drying on the paper, Herero cowherds were violating the provisions of a treaty of which they knew little and comprehended less. The Herero language did not even possess a word for a 'boundary'. Maharero knew this, but had other motives for offering consent, like his government salary of 2,000 Marks for policing the agreement. Moreover, the Herero land that Samuel blithely signed away for German settlement was largely at the expense of the eastern Herero, whose chief was Samuel's arch opponent, Nikodemus. As it stood in its original form the treaty was both short-sighted and unworkable, and it took very little time to expose its flaws.

The eastern Herero, deeply resentful of Samuel's presumption in taking decisions on their behalf, continued to graze their stock well south of the agreed line. Even the Herero supposedly under Samuel's direct authority refused to be bound by the treaty's terms. After more than twelve months of repeated transgressions Leutwein sought a final resolution of the boundary question. At a meeting in January 1896 the German governor granted a southward extension of Herero territory to a line just west of Windhoek. This fulfilled Samuel's wishes and regularised his people's *de facto* occupation of all the intervening territory.

While this seemed a pure concession to African demands, it was also a clever ploy by Leutwein to divide the Herero leadership once again. For while the governor had been seen to accede to Samuel's wishes, he deliberately rejected Nikodemus' request to have the south-eastern town of Gobabis and its hinterland of prime pasture formally ascribed to his ownership. By favouring one and spurning the other Leutwein had breathed fresh life into the old Samuel–Nikodemus dispute, which was exacerbated by the paramount chief's voluble insistence on punishment for any who violated the new terms of the agreement.[22]

Within three months of sowing the seed of discord, Leutwein reaped its violent harvest. Galled by the obvious bias in the boundary treaty and impelled by the demands of a severe drought, the eastern Herero simply ignored the agreed border in the interests of their cattle. The fact that they were denied access to the Gobabis area at this critical time, and were increasingly squeezed by an influx of white settlers, only served to worsen relations. Eventually it was a mixed force of eastern Herero with a group of aggrieved Nama that wiped out a German patrol and advanced on the government military post at Gobabis.

Despite this coalition of Bantu and Khoisan forces, the rebellion was doomed almost from the outset. Even within the eastern Herero, the rebels were isolated from the community's Christian members, who refused to fight, and were actively opposed by Hendrik Witbooi and Samuel Maharero, who joined forces with the Germans. While the attack on Gobabis was only narrowly defeated, at a subsequent battle the eastern Herero under their chief, Kahimemua, were completely crushed. With a price on their heads, Nikodemus and Kahimemua finally gave themselves up and were taken for trial.

While most of the Eurocentric historiography has never questioned the two leaders' complicity in the uprising, Gerhard Pool, author of a recent biography of Samuel Maharero, has pointed to the contradictory nature of the evidence concerning Nikodemus, and demonstrated that even some prominent whites well placed to form an accurate judgement, like the German missionary at Samuel's headquarters, Okahandja, were deeply unhappy about a guilty verdict. Unfortunately for the accused, their individual testimonies during the trial tended to work against the possibility of a joint acquittal. For while Nikodemus pleaded his innocence throughout, Kahimemua based his defence on the assertion that, as a subordinate, he was simply carrying out the other chief's orders.[23]

Whatever the truth, their conviction was certainly the most convenient verdict. For Leutwein it presented an opportunity to demonstrate the smack of firm government, while simultaneously eliminating the main rival to Germany's principal Herero ally. For his own part, Samuel wasted no time in calling for Nikodemus' execution, nor did Leutwein's deputy, Friedrich von Lindequist, who, as prosecuting counsel, seemed animated by a deep hostility to the accused man. Finally, on the morning of 13 June 1896, amidst an atmosphere of Herero bitterness that persisted for generations, both Nikodemus and Kahimemua were shot by firing squad at a place that came to be known subsequently as Nikodemus Mountain.

Other rebels were sent to Windhoek as forced labour, while some of their womenfolk were pressed into service as prostitutes for the German troops. On top of a fine of 12,000 cattle, the eastern Herero also incurred losses of large areas of good pasture, which were handed over for white settlement. At the close of the 'War of the Boundary', as the conflict came to be known, the Herero were in no doubt that they had suffered a major defeat.

Nor did it mark the end of their misfortunes. Once again, Samuel was at the centre of an issue that probably did more to inflame Afro-German relations than any other – the controversy over credit-trade and land sales. The Herero had long been accustomed to a few pioneer Europeans with wagonfuls of consumer goods trading in their midst. In fact, the supplies of arms brought by men like the Swedish explorer Charles Andersson had been critical to their overthrow of Orlam dominance. However, this former situation bore little relationship to the large pack of settlers who took to trading with Africans during the 1890s as a prelude to the development of their new land-holdings.

German anxiety to acquire African livestock ran up against the Herero's deep religious attachment to their herds and their widespread unwillingness to sell any but the poorest-quality beasts. It was a potential cultural impasse that drove some Europeans to unscrupulous methods, while a general African unfamiliarity with money laid them open to easy exploitation. To illustrate 'the ignorance of the veld-living Herero', one German observer recalled a typical scenario:

A trader camps near a Herero village. To him are driven oxen which the Herero wishes to sell. 'How much do you want for the oxen?' says the trader. 'Fifty pounds sterling,' replies the Herero. 'Good,' says the trader, 'here you have a coat valued at £20, trousers worth £10, and coffee and tobacco worth £20, that is in all £50.' . . . this sort of trading is exceptional and quite original; it requires to be learned and the newcomer will have to pay for his experience, before he is able to emulate the dodges and tricks of the old traders.[24]

One of the most invidious of European dodges was the offering of goods on credit. Such a measure inevitably involved the cooperation and at times the downright cupidity of the Africans themselves to take effect, but there is no doubt that some traders abused the system. A profit margin of a hundred per cent or more was customary amongst the veld traders, not to mention the seventy per cent imposed on goods by the merchant suppliers.[25] And these charges took account neither of the interest levied on outstanding debt, nor the whites' habitual undervaluing of the Herero's main currency – their livestock. One trader openly boasted that for every 3,000 Marks owed to him by Africans, he obtained 4,000 to 4,500 Marks' worth of cattle.[26] A graphic description of this type of malpractice was offered by one Herero chief in a statement to British officials:

> Often, when we refused to buy goods, even on credit, the trader would simply off-load goods and leave them, saying that we could pay when we liked, but in a few weeks he would come back and demand his money or cattle in lieu thereof. He would then go and pick out our very best cows he could find. Very often one man's cattle were taken to pay other people's debts. If we objected and tried to resist the police would be sent for and, what with the floggings and the threats of shooting, it was useless for our poor people to resist . . . They fixed their own prices for the goods, but would never let us place our own valuation on the cattle. They said a cow was worth 20 Marks only. For a bag of meal they took eight cows . . . For a pair of boots a cow was taken . . . Often when credit had been given, they came back and claimed what they called interest on the debt. Once I got a bag of meal on credit, and later on the trader came and took eight cows for the debt and two more cows for what he called credit; thus it cost me ten cows altogether.[27]

Not all the traders were dishonest: it was estimated by one contemporary observer that of the fifty men trading in 1904, about a third were guilty of serious misconduct.[28] Nor were all these misunderstandings over trade the fault of the Europeans. A myopic improvidence was widespread amongst the Herero, while the profligate squandering of resources by their paramount chief set the worst possible example to his people.

One indication of the expensive tastes Samuel maintained on credit was his alcohol bill with a single trading company in the month of December 1896, which included 11 bottles of beer, 57 bottles of wine and 27 bottles of assorted spirits. The total for the whole of that year amounted to 74 bottles of beer, 73 bottles of wine and 104 of hard liquor, including 37 bottles of brandy. Not only did Samuel borrow heavily to support his own habits, but his people often took purchases from traders in his name and then neglected to pay. The European merchants, unable to locate the individual responsible for an outstanding bill, simply debited Samuel's general account.[29] Given these factors and his own spendthrift lifestyle it is hardly surprising that the supreme chief owed 70,000 Marks by 1901.[30]

In order to cover these debts Samuel soon embarked on a reckless sale of tribal lands – behaviour that was not only misguided, but in contravention of tribal tradition, which decreed Hereroland the inalienable property of the people. The Germans knew the Herero custom on this issue but, as on the question of the powers attaching to the paramountcy, ignored it as long as land titles continued to wind up in European hands. After 1897 the pace of territorial transfer quickened in the wake of a severe rinderpest epidemic that decimated the Herero's uninoculated herds. While estimates of German cattle loss vary between five and fifty per cent, Herero losses were put at eighty to ninety per cent.[31] In the quest for money to pay for vaccinations, the Africans were compelled to part with their only remaining asset – land.

As if these torments had been insufficient, the Herero were then struck again like biblical victims of some Mosaic curse. This time it was an outbreak of typhus, which swept through a community that had been deprived of its traditional milk diet. And as the century came to its dreadful close the Herero suffered two further visitations, a swarm of locusts and then one of the region's recurrent periods of drought. The impact of these successive plagues was appalling. An estimated 10,000 Herero died, while those precious herds which had once been the envy of South West Africa were largely gone.[32] A census taken in 1902 revealed that 1,051 European ranchers now held as many cattle as the entire Herero nation of over 80,000 people.[33]

Throughout these terrible years of hardship the downward spiral of credit-trade, debt and land sale whirled inexorably on. At the heart of this maelstrom was the pathetic figure of the paramount chief who, like some bewildered sorcerer's apprentice, gazed on impotently as the forces of destruction he had helped to summon steadily devoured his people. Yet his only reaction was to take refuge in alcohol and to continue to sell land with casual abandon.

Herero headmen would literally wake one morning to find European settlers newly arrived and erecting homesteads in their midst. When challenged, the colonists would show the African occupants a sale agreement acquired in Windhoek, but sanctioned originally by the hand of their drunken chief in Okahandja. Then the tables would be turned completely, and the Herero, now confused and betrayed, would themselves be ordered to vacate properties which had been tribal land for generations.

A focal point for this type of sale was the extensive Herero territory crossed by the recently constructed railway between Swakopmund and Windhoek. These areas of prime grazing were much sought after by whites for their new transport facilities, and Samuel was only too happy to comply. By 1902 it was estimated that in the previous two or three years about 100,000 hectares had been lost in this fashion.[34] By 1903 the total area that had been transferred to white ownership amounted to 3,500,000 hectares – more than a quarter of all Hereroland.[35]

The growing crisis over land sales precipitated two main responses from the government. Pressed by concerned missionaries and other observers, Leutwein considered restrictions on credit-trading. An initial effort to control it was abandoned in 1899 only weeks after its introduction, because of the howl of protest from the traders themselves. The next attempt to bring order into the realm of African debt took over four years to implement. Only after a commission of inquiry from Berlin had investigated the problem in 1902 was a definite procedure agreed upon. This ordinance decreed that traders had twelve months (after a deadline of November 1903) in which to settle all debts, after which period the debt would be cancelled. Backed by police and even soldiers, and sometimes resorting to violence, the traders pursued these outstanding debts with ever greater urgency – 'like a pack of ravenous wolves', in the words of one British commentator. The Credit Ordinance's announcement led to 106,000 claims, a good number of them false or usuriously inflated, and in the long run it served merely to increase the abuses it was supposed to check.[36]

The other colonial measure to safeguard the Herero from the complete loss of their territories was the creation of a 'reserve'. In the eyes of the government this would be a core area of inalienable land. However, it was never intended that this should represent the whole of the African holdings, nor were the Herero compelled to live there. They would have free movement outside its boundaries, while the non-reserve lands could be grazed or leased or even sold as they wished. Unfortunately, many did not fully grasp the government's intention, but saw the reserve scheme as yet another device to prise them off their traditional homeland.

This misunderstanding persisted until the latter part of 1903, when the strains in Afro-German relations were moving rapidly towards complete breakdown. Already assailed by rapacious debt-collectors, the Herero chiefs were confronted in September by a further bombshell – an announcement of the proposed borders of the reserve. Excluding important tribal areas, poor in grazing and lacking sufficient water, the reserve was immediately condemned by the more traditional Herero leaders as far too small.

Then came a final shock – news of government plans to build an additional railway, this time cutting north right through the heart of Hereroland to the copper mines at Otavi. Reflecting on the huge and critical losses they had already incurred in the vicinity of the Windhoek line, the Herero could only contemplate the worst.

As early as March 1903 the Herero leaders may have started to discuss the calamitous impact of white encroachment and to consider a decisive response. However, it was probably not until early December 1903 that Samuel Maharero himself had been convinced of the need to abandon his pleasure-seeking existence at Okahandja and take up arms against the 'friend', whose empire-building in South West Africa had been so closely interwoven with Samuel's own. As the year came to its close, circumstances had conspired to ensure that the individual concerned, Theodor Leutwein, would be too distant to influence decisions being taken against him at Okahandja. A minor fracas concerning the seizure of a goat at the small southern town of Warmbad had escalated into a gun battle between a hot-headed German officer and members of the Bondelswarts tribe. Now came reports that a rebellion had ensued. As Christmas approached it was not the news the governor had hoped for.

Instead of a happy period in Windhoek amongst friends and colleagues on his tenth Christmas in the colony, he could look forward to long dusty rides in the hottest season. Instead of a round of cele-brations, he would have to put on his military uniform and ride out with his troops, as he had done so many times in the previous decade.

What Leutwein did not consider on his tenth Christmas in German South West Africa, and what he had never seen – blinded by his white supremacist values and his perception of Africans as subhuman creatures important only as units of colonial labour – was that his personal empire had been riveted down on top of the aspirations of its tribal inhabitants and over their welling sense of injustice. As Leutwein plodded endlessly southwards, covering half the length of a colony he had done so much to construct, he still did not detect the great sub-terranean forces that were about to break through its false foundation. By the time he saw Windhoek again, German South West Africa would be consumed by a terrible war, in which his own career, his policies and hundreds of German soldiers and settlers would all be destroyed.

21

Cruelty and Brutality

A s on so many occasions in Samuel Maharero's life, it was largely external circumstances that had forced him to act in the first days of 1904. With the position of his people deteriorating almost weekly and with so many young warriors baying for German blood, the paramount chief had either to respond immediately or be swept aside by the strength of Herero feeling.

Once he had finally decided to lead his people, events then also had a hand in choosing the precise moment of his call to arms. The Bondelswarts uprising, which itself had hinged on the ludicrous disagreement over a goat, was the pivot on which the Herero revolt swung into action. In late December Leutwein, unable to effect a speedy resolution of the southern unrest, had ordered a third of the colony's four field companies to join him at Warmbad. This left only 232 men in Windhoek capable of bearing arms. There would never be a more favourable moment, and the paramount chief seized it with both hands.[1]

However, propelled on to centre stage in the unlikely role of rebel leader, Samuel opened with a remarkable gesture of clemency. 'To all the headmen in my country,' he wrote on 11 January 1904, 'I have ordered all my people to refrain from touching any of the following: Missionaries, English, Basters, Bergdamaras, Namas, Boers. We do not touch them. Do not do this. I have sworn an oath that this decision will not become known, not even to the missionaries. Enough.'[2] Like the Herero decision to spare women and children, the chief's edict was humane, but it also showed a grasp of strategy, since it sought to limit the Germans' allies in the coming conflict. Unfortunately, what

Samuel had not bargained for was the instinctive loyalty of the Baster community for their European overlords. On receipt of Maharero's letters requesting military assistance both from himself and Hendrik Witbooi, the Baster leader Hermanus van Wyk passed the documents straight on to Leutwein.

At first the German governor, like many in the colony, could hardly believe that a man who had been as supine as Samuel could now have taken up arms against them. Indeed, in the initial stages of the uprising, Samuel's track record of compliance was one of the Africans' main assets. Despite a number of signs – increasingly belli-cose Herero behaviour and their feverish purchase of horses, saddles, arms and other equipment – the war took the Europeans completely unawares.

Just as they were stunned by its outbreak, so the Germans were mystified by its causes. But rather than confront the overwhelming evidence of their systematic assault upon Herero life, the whites in South West Africa lashed out in all directions in their search for a scapegoat. Their choices are worth analysing, not only for their be-wildering inaccuracy, but also for their revelations about the colonial psyche.

The first target was the Germans' imperial rivals to the south – the British. Both the captain of a German gunboat, whose crew would play a role in combating the Herero, and initially Leutwein himself gave support to the notion that British *agents provocateurs* had helped incite the hostilities. When, in the absence of any genuine evidence, the anti-British campaign collapsed, the colony found a ready substi-tute in their own missionaries.

That the missionaries had been exempted from hostilities on Samuel's orders, and had then refused – unlike all other whites in the colony – to take up arms against the Africans, were now offered as proof that they had made common cause with the Herero. The furore of slander fed on the weakest evidence. When, for example, the mis-sionaries had failed to bury dead German soldiers during a siege of Okahandja this was taken as evidence of their traitorous behaviour. That they had actually been prevented from reaching the corpses by a hail of German bullets seemed to count for very little. In fact, nothing could have been further from the truth than the charge of missionary involvement in the Herero uprising. As Horst Drechsler has pointed out, 'Even their much reviled "neutrality" was a myth. The plain fact was that the missionaries never missed an opportunity to intervene in favour of their fellow-countrymen.'[3]

Like many aggressors the Germans projected the greatest blame onto the actual victims of their violence: the Africans themselves. It was a given in the colony that to explain Herero unrest one need look no further than the ignorant conceit and savagery of the primitive. It was hardly surprising, therefore, that an official German inquiry ascribed the causes of war 'to the arrogance of the natives and to their confidence in their superiority over the Germans'.[4] It was a morally convenient line to take, since Africa could be blamed on two counts, first for the outbreak of 'motiveless' bloodshed and later for the hysterical retribution which was brought down upon it by the Germans. Leutwein himself, towards the close of the fighting and after he had been removed from military command, concluded that the 'freedom-loving Herero' had been increasingly pressurised by the 'progressive extension of German rule . . . But, and this is decisive, they had the impression that in regard to this rule of the German they were in the last resort the stronger side.'[5]

Leutwein had good reason to blame the Herero, if only to deflect attention from his own part in the war, and as he cast around for further excuses he alighted on one that is especially illuminating of European attitudes. Prior to Hendrik Witbooi's decision to lead the Nama in revolt in late 1904, it came to light that a follower of the Ethiopian Movement had been active in the region. This black 'prophet', called Sheppert Stürmann, was part of an African Christian community that opposed foreign missionaries for their role in the advance of imperialism and which preached African redemption from colonial oppression. Incapable of following the well-marked trail of solid, rational evidence which guided the way to Witbooi's decision, Leutwein seized upon Stürmann as a providential *deus ex machina* to explain away the Nama's mysterious sense of grievance. What better key for unlocking the ways of Africa – that black, benighted land of unreason – than the fanatical hand of the religious mystic? 'The rising,' Leutwein let it be known, '[was] "unquestionably" to be attributed to the machinations of this man.'[6] It was symptomatic of this classic European distortion of 'the dark continent', itself a fragment of the same mythology, that the German press should describe Witbooi as South West Africa's 'Mahdi' – a figure who have been for a generation of Europeans the archetypal image of savage black madness.[7]

No matter how much Leutwein might have wished to deflect

blame, it was inevitable that in their scramble to absolve themselves of responsibility others would pass the burden on and upwards. However, it was the old charge of excessive leniency towards Africans which formed the main thrust of their accusations against him. 'Throughout the country,' railed one colonial organisation, 'the natives who . . . have for years been pampered and made immoderate in their demands through the Governor's blandishments are now in a state of ferment . . .' From the twisted logic of these statements it was only a small step into complete madness: it was not the years of colonial abuse that had provoked the Herero into a desperate revolt – in fact, the reverse – the uprising had been caused by 'unreasonable treatment of the colonists' themselves.[8] Africa had risen as a result of abuses inflicted not upon itself, but on its white oppressors by their own colonial administration.

In addition to these accusations from fellow whites, the outpouring of Herero hatred and violence towards Germans forced Leutwein to confront his most cherished illusions about the fairness of his administration. According to Helmut Bley, the governor had genuinely endeavoured to have himself accepted as the representative of a legitimate government, taking 'care to emphasise to the Africans that a normal state-system, bound by its constitution and statutes, was in control', and was attending equally to the interests of both black and white.[9] When a trader once referred to the administration as 'his government', Leutwein admonished him for his presumption.[10] Yet, while he had often claimed, in disputes with African parties, that his actions were in strict accordance with the legal processes of the legitimate state, Leutwein had only ever insisted on the letter of the law when white self-interest was served by so doing.

As Bley also pointed out, 'Leutwein had never contemplated equipping the Africans to defend their rights in the court of law', and invariably they had to endure a profound bias in the colony's judicial processes.[11] Part of the reason for the Bondelswart uprising, for instance, was the settlers' published demand that all Africans regard whites as superior beings and that in court only the testimony of seven African witnesses could outweigh evidence presented by a single white person.

One of the most important sources of evidence on the denial of African rights is provided by the judicial records during Leutwein's office. These reveal that the murder of six Europeans by Africans resulted in the imposition of fifteen death sentences and a single prison sentence. The courts in which whites were tried for murdering three Africans handed down terms of imprisonment for two years, one year and three months respectively.

These cases give no indication of the many instances when settlers simply took matters into their own hands and administered beatings (euphemised as 'paternal chastisement') at their own whim. 'Our people were compelled to work on farms,' testified one Herero chief after the revolt, 'and the farmers had them chained up by the police and flogged without mercy for the slightest little thing.'[12] In his assessment of the causes of hostilities, one missionary suggested that 'the average German looks down upon the natives as being about on the same level as the higher primates (baboon being their favourite term for the natives) and treats them like animals.'[13] When the German Reichstag sought to criticise the settlers' arbitrary and violent behaviour, they responded with a petition in which they argued:

> From time immemorial our natives have grown used to laziness, brutality and stupidity. The dirtier they are, the more they feel at ease. Any white man who has lived among natives finds it impossible to regard them as human beings at all in any European sense. They need centuries of training as human beings, with endless patience, strictness and justice . . .[14]

Part of the 'training' offered by the settlers to African women, at least, was sexual violation, which was seldom reported, let alone punished. Exactly why such offences carried so little risk of retribution is indicated by the fate of an African whose wife was raped by three Germans. When he tried to intervene he himself was maltreated and dragged off to the police, who gave him fifty lashes for assaulting a white man.[15] It is a measure of the enduring colonial attitudes towards African womanhood that the missionary writer Reverend Vedder claimed a quarter of a century later that for Damara women 'to have a child by a white man is . . . considered an honour and distinction'.[16]

One case involving sexual misconduct that did eventually reach the law courts occurred only months before the Herero uprising, and involved a German trader named Dietrich and a young African couple celebrating the birth of a new baby. Both the offspring of Herero chiefs, Barmenias and Louisa Zerua were approached by Dietrich for a lift while travelling home in their wagon. After they had stopped for the night, Barmenias was disturbed by screams then gunshots and rose to find Louisa dead, their baby injured and the German running off into the darkness. It was later revealed that Dietrich, after plying her husband with alcohol, had made advances to Louisa and shot her when she refused to submit. At his trial the judges accepted Dietrich's defence that he started shooting under the drunken impression that he was being attacked, although even Leutwein admitted that this was a total fabrication.[17] On his acquittal, a furore of protest led to a retrial and the German was eventually sentenced to three years' imprisonment. Conveniently for the convicted murderer, the war intervened and he was released and recruited as a non-commissioned officer.[18]

These abuses of the judicial process had a far-reaching impact upon the Herero. Later they would cite the murder of Louisa Zerua and Dietrich's exoneration as a factor in their decision to take up arms. In his own letter to Leutwein giving the reasons for war, Samuel referred to the absence of legal redress: 'How many Hereros have been killed by white people, particularly traders, with rifles and in the prisons. And always when I brought these cases to Windhuk [*sic*] the blood of the people was valued at no more than a few head of small stock.'[19]

In conjunction with their losses of cattle and land, their exclusion from the processes of justice left the Herero with the conviction that they were fighting for the preservation of their national life. The German charge that the Herero were motivated by an arrogant presumption of their own martial superiority is not borne out by their leaders' own assessments. In his letters to other African chiefs requesting support for the uprising, Samuel suggested an awareness of their desperate plight. To Hendrik Witbooi he wrote: 'Let us die fighting rather than die as a result of maltreatment, imprisonment or some other calamity.'[20] To the Baster leader, Hermanus van Wyk, he announced his wish 'that out weak nation[s] all over Africa should stand up against the Germans, let them rather finish us off and let them live alone in our country.'[21] Chief Zacharias Zerua, father-in-law to the woman murdered by Dietrich, was even more pessimistic. According to his son, 'He knew that if we rose we would be crushed in battle . . . We were driven to desperation by the cruelty and injustice of the Germans.'[22]

However they might have rated their prospects, the Herero's opening advances were swift and decisive, momentarily paralysing the colony. Between 12 and 18 January 1904 parties of Africans entered isolated and undefended white farmsteads, sometimes seizing the occupants while they slept. Occasionally settlers would be confronted by their own farmhands. Possibly, in those moments of stunned confusion, some of the old German masters had time to reflect that the brutal beatings they had administered and dismissed as 'paternal chastisement' had converted their assailants into killers, who now bludgeoned them to death and crudely mutilated their corpses. Traders were also killed. Schröder, the man who had boasted he could get 4,000–4,500 Marks for every 3,000 owed by a Herero, was amongst those who paid the ultimate price for greed.

Yet Samuel's instruction to leave unharmed all women, children and non-German whites was largely obeyed. Only the Okahandja contingent violated the order, murdering six Boers, including wives and a single minor. Of all those slaughtered in the first phase of the war, estimated at between 123 and 150, seven were Afrikaans-speaking and three were female.[23]

The total secrecy that had accompanied these opening attacks precluded any defensive measures by the Germans and gave the Herero the bulk of European cattle and small livestock. Yet Samuel and his other chiefs had lost some important strategic opportunities. The need for complete surprise, for instance, robbed them of the assistance of 600 Herero men working on the Otavi railway, who were immediately interned at the outbreak of war. The Africans had also failed to strengthen their position with regard to arms and ammunition, which they desperately lacked. Although some estimates put their arsenal at 4,000 guns, Leutwein thought it included only 2,500, with little ammunition. Moreover, by failing immediately to seize the capital, Windhoek, the Herero missed the chance to solve their shortage at one fell swoop. This left them at a grievous disadvantage from the outset. One historian has suggested that the Germans' five Maxims alone almost equalled the Herero's total firepower.[24]

While the main fortified settlements were all surrounded, the Herero failed to overrun them. Typically, the town of Okahandja was seized on the first day of fighting and its stores looted and burnt. However, apart from a few settlers caught off guard, most whites took refuge in the fort, which was isolated from the outside world when Samuel had both the railway and telegraph lines cut. The Herero, unlike their formidable Bantu cousins to the east, the Zulu, were unwilling to attack at night, and disdained the notion of fighting amongst buildings as unmanly. Lacking the necessary equipment to breach the walls, they were probably also reluctant to face the combined fire of the besieged garrison. Seventy-one men thus held off the Africans during the ensuing days, and while German troops from Windhoek were driven back on 12 and 13 January, a relief force of a hundred men with 50,000 rounds of ammunition broke through two days later.

Okahandja had been reinforced, but it remained to Captain Viktor Franke of the Second Field Company, which had been on its way south to assist the suppression of the Bondelswarts, to wrest the initiative firmly away from the Africans. By 15 January Franke had reached Gibeon, the headquarters of the Witbooi, when he heard the news from Windhoek. Realising the seriousness of the fighting to the north, he immediately turned his men around. They covered 380 kilometres in the next four and a half days, and after finding Windhoek shaken but not challenged, they pressed on to Okahandja. Franke's troops relieved the town on 27 January, the Kaiser's forty-fifth birthday. And again they moved north, this time for the important Herero settlement of Omaruru.

Thus far, the German ride from Gibeon had been without violent incident. Now they faced serious opposition. First was Samuel's rearguard, covering his retreat into the Onjati Mountains to the west of Okahandja. Only after a six-hour battle were Franke's men able to continue the march for Omaruru. By the time they relieved the town on 4 February the Germans had had a full taste of Herero resolve. The men they had jeered at as baboons had held them in another fierce eight-hour fire-fight. Herero losses were heavy, estimated at a hundred, but almost a fifth of the German troops were also dead or wounded.

The Herero, in failing to capture and destroy Windhoek and Okahandja, had lost their one serious opportunity to deal the Germans a major blow. Moreover, the railways were quickly restored, a large force of marines had reinforced Leutwein's troops, and the governor himself, after negotiating a hasty ceasefire with the Bondelswarts, had returned by ship to take command in the north. He and the other colonists could thank Franke's ride for restoring the European position. The official German historians went further, claiming it had 'taught anew how far men can surpass the boundaries of human endurance when a strong and unbendable will rules.'[25]

With an additional 1,340 troops ashore by 1 March, Leutwein put into effect his plans to bring the conflict to an end. His three principal objectives were to clear the Africans from around his main lines of communication with the outside world (the railway to the port of Swakopmund); to prevent the Herero and their large numbers of captured livestock from escaping across the border into Bechuanaland; and to keep the different Herero forces from uniting and to engage and defeat them one by one. In order to achieve his objectives he divided his force into four sections.

By 4 March two of these units had successfully cleared the areas south and west of Okahandja, having engaged the Herero in three heated but indecisive exchanges. The first true victory celebrations were reserved for the tongue-twisting battle of Otjihinamaparero, after troops under Major von Estorff had ridden north to engage the western section of the Herero. Since the force of about a thousand Africans had suffered, at their enemy's reckoning, only fifty casualties, and had then retreated eastwards toward the main Herero concentration, Estorff had not inflicted a resounding defeat, nor had he maintained the western Herero's isolation as Leutwein had wanted. But the German press and their Kaiser were not to be balked. The newspapers enlarged the significance of Otjihinamaparero, while Estorff's own report made it 'sound vaguely like a second Sedan' and Wilhelm's message of congratulation spoke of 'the brave and steady behaviour of my soldiers and marines'.[26]

Then came a more euphonious-sounding battle – Owikokorero. Only this one was not such a cause for jubilation. This one was an African victory.

Leutwein's eastern section was under the command of Major von Glasenapp, newly arrived from Germany with a force completely unfamiliar with African conditions. The colony's veterans looked with dismay at its inexperienced and complacent officers, with their cases of champagne, boxes of cigars and their hunting rifles. Von Glasenapp's allotted task was to coordinate with the garrison at Gobabis and block the Herero's route to Bechuanaland. However, since the Africans had risen in order to preserve their national life, fleeing across the desert was not likely to be a part of their immediate strategy.

Nevertheless, the major, not content with his unglamorous role, straightaway exceeded the orders and set out in search of the leader of the eastern Herero, Tjetjo. Undeterred by the increasing exhaustion of his troops and their lack of horses – there were only 80 among 412 men – he divided them into two units and gave chase across arid waterless country, averaging thirty-three kilometres a day for a month. For his newly arrived soldiers, supported only by interminably slow wagon transports, 'the scarce waterholes and the great distances between them were a nightmare.'[27] By 12 March disease resulting from the polluted water had begun to take its toll.

Yet von Glasenapp, impatient of victory, left his main contingent to make camp and pushed on with a patrol of forty-six men and eleven officers. On the following day they caught up with a handful of Africans in charge of a large number of cattle. When these cowherds fled, the Germans took control of the stock and rode on through the dense bush until mid-afternoon.

Then, as they emerged from the thorn scrub to cross a large clearing, they came under unexpected attack. The Germans, scrambling for the little natural cover available, were under the mistaken impression that they had caught up with only a small group of stragglers. In fact, they had just run into a trap carefully laid by Tjetjo's rearguard. When von Glasenapp attempted to retrieve their position and ordered their one Maxim to be mounted, the Africans intensified their fire, ripping through the broken line. The machine-gun was never brought into operation and it was only when the surviving Europeans reached their supply wagon that they were able to organise an effective retreat. In half an hour, nineteen men and seven of the officers, including Hugo von François, had been killed.[28] For the Germans, Owikokorero had been a reverse as significant as their victory at Otjihinamaparero. A shaken von Glasenapp now ordered an immediate halt.

Not that this was the end of his tribulations. For the next three weeks his men were carefully watched by Tjetjo's scouts, and when the Germans pulled back towards Leutwein's main force, the un-detected Herero shadowed their movements. On the morning of 3 April, with the 237 German troops strung out over two and a half kilometres, a small Herero party suddenly appeared to draw the European fire. While the rearguard was thus distracted, the Africans surrounded it on three sides, cutting off half the force. On realising that he was under attack, von Glasenapp raced back and threw his entire unit into the battle, bombarding the Africans with two field pieces. Only after four hours of heavy fighting did the Herero break off their frontal assaults and melt back into the bush. It had been a ferocious contest. The Africans left forty-two of their men at Okaharui, while forty-nine, a quarter of the German force, were either dead or wounded.

Many of these troops had only been in South West Africa for a matter of weeks, and as the wagons full of wounded rattled away over the desert sands they carried off the original German boast that the war against the Herero would be little more than a glorified game shoot. Nor was morale the only casualty. According to one commentator Okaharui 'heralded the collapse of the eastern detachment'.[29] For what the Herero had started, typhus completed. From the original contingent of 534, only 151 were still on their feet, and on 5 May 1904 it was decided to disband it.[30]

The communication difficulties which had been in part responsible for von Glasenapp's problems now spared Leutwein news of these reverses until he himself had faced the Herero in battle. He had initially been reluctant to confront them until he could mobilise all the reinforcements pouring into the colony during February and March. With the arrival of 1,567 troops, 1,000 horses, 10 artillery pieces and 6 machine guns he was eventually able to field a force of 2,500 men.[31] By the time he gave his orders to attack Samuel's main force, the Germans had more armed combatants than the Africans.

On paper the odds were overwhelmingly in favour of the Europeans. Yet Leutwein had great difficulties making his technical superiority count, and of his three initial objectives he had achieved only one: the Herero had not escaped to Bechuanaland with most of the colony's livestock. But since this had never been their intention, it could hardly be considered a major German triumph. Moreover, if they ever had tried to leave, the Germans had scarcely shown themselves capable of preventing it.

When Leutwein set out from Okahandja on 7 April with 800 Germans and 160 African auxiliaries he was almost as keen to quell the growing white opposition to his command as he was to defeat his African opponents. Two days later at the battle of Ongandjira he was offered an opportunity to do both. About 3,000 Herero, bolstered by news of Tjetjo's victory at Owikokorero, had grouped in a loose semi-circle at the foot of a series of steep ridges. While Samuel directed the African right, the left was commanded by Assa Riarua, the formidable son of Samuel's great rival Riarua, and the man considered central to the Herero decision to fight. His forces waited with great discipline, protected behind a thick thorn hedge three metres high and stretching almost two kilometres.

Only when the Germans had approached to within 200 metres did Assa Riarua order a barrage on the exposed German left flank.

Repeatedly Leutwein had to reinforce his left to check this attack, bringing up both machine-guns and artillery, which were used to great effect. Even so, the Africans made two desperate charges at the European positions, urged on by Herero women hurling abuse at the enemy and chanting to their warriors: 'Who owns Hereroland? We own Hereroland!'[32]

Gradually superior German firepower began to tell and the Africans pulled back, scaling the slopes behind them. When a third Herero mounted force, watching the battle's progress from the African right, rode down to try to intervene, the Germans charged furiously to prevent any reinforcement. However, by the time they had climbed to the ridge tops formerly held by Samuel's men they were surprised to find them already evacuated.

Given the large number of combatants, Ongandjira involved relatively few casualties – African losses were about a hundred and the Germans' under twenty – while both sides had grounds for disappointment. Samuel apparently executed some of his men, accusing them of cowardice. Leutwein captured Herero letters informing him for the first time of the defeat at Owikokorero. It was an added vexation for the governor just when he had failed to achieve the sweeping victory which the armchair generals in Berlin believed was easily within his grasp. Opposition to his conduct of the war was growing. Leutwein badly needed a quick, decisive conquest to silence his critics.

Unfortunately, at the Battle of Oviumbo four days later, the result was about as inconclusive as at Ongandjira. Worse, that elusive, much-needed victory had come within a hair's breadth of being achieved. But not by Leutwein; by Samuel. The German governor's skilful extrication of his men from what might have been a complete catastrophe was not the kind of triumph the Berlin top brass had in mind. After the outcome on that exhausting, unlucky 13 April, Leutwein's fate in South West Africa was largely sealed.

Oviumbo had taken place on terrain that favoured the Herero, and, as at Ongandjira, they arrayed themselves in an arc around important waterholes. On this occasion, Samuel neutralised the impact of German artillery by fighting on level, densely vegetated ground, where the enemy were unable to see their target or establish range on the highly mobile African force. By the afternoon, the Germans were completely surrounded and compressed into a rectangular defensive formation. Towards evening, unknown to Samuel, they were also seriously short of ammunition. However, instead of pressing home a major advantage, the Herero leader slipped away under cover of darkness while snipers kept the Germans pinned down. Not surprisingly, Leutwein was equally relieved at the onset of nightfall and the opportunity to retreat. Now badly shaken, he returned to Okahandja to await yet further reinforcements and the intense criticism that his failure was bound to draw.

He had already been reprimanded in February for his attempts to open negotiations with Samuel, and had been told then by the director of the Colonial Department that only unconditional surrender would be acceptable to Berlin. In defence of his measures, Leutwein had argued that consideration for the future of the colony should have a bearing on military conduct. 'I do not concur,' he wrote, 'with those fanatics who want to see the Herero destroyed altogether. Apart from the fact that a people of some 60,000 to 70,000 is not so easy to annihilate, I would consider such a move a grave mistake from an economic point of view. We need the Herero as cattle breeders . . . and especially as labourers.'[33]

Harsh and cynical as it may have been, Leutwein's attitude came increasingly to seem like the voice of sweet and kindly reason when compared with the military policy subsequently endorsed by his superiors. Backed by the German emperor himself, the Chief of General Staff, Count von Schlieffen, took over direction of the war. Now both he and the Kaiser had become convinced of the need for a replacement commander-in-chief in South West Africa. The officer they eventually chose to succeed Leutwein reflected the dominant mood both of the German people and the settlers within the colony.

Ever since those fateful days in January when many of their neighbours had been clubbed and horribly mutilated on their own ranches, the settlers had been consumed by an overwhelming desire for revenge. 'All you hear these days,' wrote one missionary, 'is words like "make a clean sweep, hang them, shoot them to the last man, give no quarter". I shudder to think what may happen in the months ahead. The Germans will doubtless exact a grim vengeance.'[34]

The fact that in the following five months they did nothing of the kind was, in a sense, the worst possible outcome. For the Herero's successes in the field were deeply humiliating to a nation reputed to possess the world's most powerful and efficient military machine. German anger and frustration increased almost daily, and in the absence of concrete results, the war was fought all the more furiously on paper. What amounted to a national propaganda campaign included frequent allegations of Herero atrocities on German women and children. Typical was a passage in Gustav Frenssen's *Peter Moor's Journey to South West Africa*, written to generate national feeling for a conflict which had been overshadowed by reports of the Russo-Japanese War then raging in Mongolia. 'In South West Africa,' announced one of the novel's characters, 'the blacks, like cowards, have treacherously murdered all the farmers and their wives and children.'[35] That these words, like so much of contemporary writing on the war, were an exaggeration was beside the point. Fact or fiction, they fuelled an anxiety to retrieve the nation's honour and inflict a savage retribution.

Representative of this was an extraordinary letter, found amongst Wilhelm II's correspondence, from an enraged member of the public offering advice on how to vanquish the unexpectedly difficult African foe. Its author suggested 'that our soldiers, whenever they withdraw, thoroughly poison their water supplies.'

> After all, we are not fighting against an enemy respecting the rules of fairness, but against savages. Never must we allow the Negroes to prevail. The consequences of such a victory would be dire indeed since even now the Negroes believe that Africa belongs to them, rather than to the Lord above.[36]

Given the dramatic urgency surrounding the German need for victory, the stage was set for the appointment of a commander capable of implementing the most ruthless measures. In Adrian Dietrich Lothar von Trotha, the German high command had found a man willing to do their bidding — and more.

Born in 1848, von Trotha was the scion of an old aristocratic family who, in the classic Junker tradition, had followed his father into the Prussian army. He had experienced armed combat as early as 1866, in the Seven Weeks War against Austria. However, his first encounter with non-European opposition had not come until 1894 when, as military commander in German East Africa, he had successfully suppressed the Wahehe revolt. After further years in Germany and promotion to the rank of major-general by 1900, von Trotha commanded the First East-Asiatic Infantry Brigade in the combined European suppression of the Chinese Boxer Uprising.

In May 1904, the date of his appointment as commander in South

West Africa, von Trotha was a powerfully built 55-year-old with heavy Kitchener-like whiskers. In photographs from the period his face expressed firmness to the point of severity, and was matched by a reputation, earned during his colonial years, for iron-fisted brutality and a deep disdain of 'rebellious natives'. 'I know enough tribes in Africa,' he wrote some months after his arrival in German South West Africa. 'They are all alike. They only respond to force. It was and is my policy to use force with terrorism and even brutality. I shall anni-hilate the revolting tribes with rivers of blood and rivers of gold. Only after a complete uprooting will something emerge.'[37]

It was a chilling indication of what Theodor Leutwein, who had retained his position as the colony's civil governor, could expect from the new commander. Cold, inflexible, narrow-minded, von Trotha had jettisoned all considerations but outright victory. He had no time to question what had sparked the uprising, nor whether the Herero should have a role in the colony once war had ended. His only con-cern was their imminent destruction.

Even Leutwein himself was hardly given more consideration. On reading the reports of the war up to the time of his arrival, von Trotha sneered: 'To me it seems like the aimless running around of a lot of rats with their tails entangled in the vicinity east of Okahandja.'[38] While sailing to Africa, von Trotha had forbidden Leutwein to pro-ceed with a proclamation offering amnesty to all innocent Herero. He had then ordered a general disengagement until preparations for a final showdown could be implemented. For two months following his arrival on 13 June 1904, he oversaw the establishment of an elaborate communications system and supply dumps for the units which he now ringed around the Herero positions in the Waterberg Mountains.

The dinosaur footprints that are stamped into the ancient sandstone of these relict mountains are testimony to their great age and to the mil-lions of years of vertebrate occupancy. In places brick-red cliffs rise sheer out of the earth to form plateaux topped by rich vegetation. Dense stands of trees – silver terminalia, weeping wattle, wild syringa, flame acacia and mimosa – hold the rainfall like a sponge, converting it at times into a green haven high above the region's parched bushveld. It had been, and indeed remains, a natural focus for wild game, and for centuries it was a Herero stronghold, a welcome retreat in times of hardship, both environmental and military.

Now Samuel and his people, possibly numbering as many as 50,000, had gathered there to await the German onslaught. Over 200 kilometres north of Windhoek, the Herero's Waterberg encampment stretched the enemy's supply lines to the limit and took them into an area with which few were acquainted. To the Herero, however, the Waterberg area was deeply familiar and provided the best possible grazing at a moment of gathering crisis.

Exactly how extreme this crisis was becoming was apparent to Samuel as his patrols brought in report after report of the massive build-up of German forces. Von Trotha now had an army approaching 5,000 men, with 10,000 horses, thirty artillery pieces and twelve machine-gun units. His plan was to surround the Herero position at the southern edge of the mountains with six detachments, co-ordinating movements through a signal post stationed on the top of the Waterberg. The encircling units were to prevent any Herero escape while the massively superior firepower of the Germans was 'to annihilate these masses with a simultaneous blow'.[39] Stations would then be set up to complete a search-and-destroy operation against those who had slipped the net.

However, von Trotha's plan had one strategic anomaly that others had not failed to notice. To the south-east he had deployed only a comparatively small unit under Major van der Heyde. Later Leutwein's son claimed that his father and Major von Estorff had both warned von Trotha of the dangers inherent in this battle formation. In the event of a Herero breakthrough in this quarter, both men argued, the Africans would be forced to retreat into the jaws of a vast waterless expanse known as the Omaheke. Unless they could somehow cross this wasteland and continue into Bechuanaland it would be certain death for the whole tribe. But von Trotha was adamant. So too were the general staff in Berlin, who felt that 'such an outcome of the battle could only be even more desirable in the eyes of the German Command because the enemy would then seal his own fate, being doomed to die of thirst in the arid sandveld.'[40] This was a possible outcome which von Trotha, bent on annihilation, seemed happy to contemplate.

On 11 August 1904, the day chosen for attack, the general's plans started to go awry almost immediately. By early morning Samuel's forces were engaged in fierce fighting against the main German section, which had attacked from the south. Yet neither of the two flanking units, including that under Major van der Heyde, was able to support von Trotha as had been intended. After hours of combat the

German artillery and machine-guns eventually began to impose themselves on the battle, and with von Trotha's eventual seizure of the main waterholes – which Samuel had stubbornly defended and without which his people would be unable to maintain resistance – the Herero position was critical. Assailed from three different directions and with von Trotha's unit controlling the south, the 50,000 Africans and their cattle were squeezed into a rectangle, sixteen kilometres by eight, that was now being hammered by German cannon.

Major van der Heyde, meanwhile, had had no impact on the course of the day's fighting. On the night before the battle he had got completely lost in the dense bush and only stumbled on the right route when he heard the sound of German artillery pounding the Herero positions. By the afternoon it was less a case of him engaging the Herero, than them confronting him – the only link in the German chain without the strength to contain their headlong flight. As the retreating Herero swept south-eastwards it was only nightfall that saved van der Heyde's section from complete annihilation.

Totally exhausted by a complex manoeuvre that had hardly achieved greater success than those commanded by Leutwein – Herero casualties were apparently relatively light – the German forces could now relax for the next twenty-four hours.[41] For, although they had not inflicted a major defeat and although the enemy had escaped, they had merely leapt straight through the trapdoor into the trap. To Horst Drechsler, von Trotha's deliberate disposition of his forces to permit such an outcome was a calculated act of genocide.[42] However, for sympathetic historians it was at worst an oversight, and at best an expression of the professional soldier's self-justifying precept that all war was brutal. Whichever interpretation comes closest to von Trotha's initial intentions, it cannot be doubted that when the Germans went in pursuit on 13 August they inflicted dreadful slaughter upon their opponents.

Gustav Frenssen, compiling his fictional account from the first-hand experience of German soldiers, gave a graphic picture of the Herero exodus.

In the path of their flight lay . . . cattle and men, dead and dying and staring blankly . . . A number of babies lay helplessly languishing by mothers whose breasts hung down long and flabby. Others were lying alone, still living, with eyes and nose full of flies . . . All this life lay scattered there, both man and beast, broken in the knees, helpless, still in agony or already motionless . . .

> At noon we halted by the waterholes which were filled to the brim with corpses. We pulled them out by means of the ox teams from the field pieces, but there was only a little stinking bloody water in the depths . . .[43]

The official history of the campaign, while acknowledging that von Trotha ordered the execution of all male combatants, claimed that he gave instructions for women and children to be spared.[44] Gerhard Pool also, stressing the impact of Herero suffering on even the most hardened troopers, described how the general found an abandoned infant at a waterhole and put the child in the care of a Herero woman; how another two-year-old girl was discovered by German soldiers and fed on goat's milk before they took her along in a wagon.[45]

Yet these humane gestures must be set against other, less endearing incidents. A Baster interpreter, for example, recalled on oath an occasion when von Trotha was present at the discovery of two old Herero women who had fallen behind through exhaustion. Both were shot at the waterhole where they rested. Another young woman was first questioned by the general himself, then bayoneted on his instruction. Then there was the testimony from another Baster guide, which told how German soldiers found a baby boy in the bushes, and proceeded to throw the terrified infant from one to the other like a ball. After they had tired of this form of torture, one of them fixed his bayonet and asked for the child to be tossed in his direction, when he transfixed its body with the blade. As the youngster writhed in his death agony the other troopers greeted the feat with guffaws of laughter.[46]

Other eyewitnesses, some of them European, gave evidence confirming this new phase of unopposed slaughter: of young girls and women raped before being bayoneted; of an elderly lady gathering wild vegetables, shot through the forehead at point-blank range; of old women, some of them blind, burnt alive in the hut where they lay; of a large body of warriors, disarmed and herded into a kraal, then slaughtered to a man; of another large group, lured in under truce for negotiations, and mown down with rifle and cannon; of Herero men slowly strangled with fencing wire, and left hanging in rows like crows; of men, women and children packed into a high thorn and log enclosure, doused with lamp oil and burnt to a cinder.[47]

Von Trotha's policy of no prisoners and no quarter, a violation of international law, gradually became known in Germany through letters home from his troops. But the general excused himself on the grounds that he had neither the supplies to feed prisoners, nor could he allow captive Africans to infect his men with disease. And in the Reichstag the colonial director faced down allegations of German misconduct with righteous indignation, claiming that 'cruelty and brutality are alien to the German character . . .'.[48]

In fact, cruelty and brutality went on and on until the Germans could follow the retreating Herero no further. For the choking dust, bitterly cold winter nights, the sheer desiccating emptiness of the Omaheke spared no living creature, neither African nor European. Eventually the Germans' horses and mules, exhausted by the chase, collapsed beneath them. Then the men, forced to drink at stinking waterholes littered with human and animal carcasses, started to die from typhoid. On 30 September, von Trotha order the pursuit to be called off, but not before he had put into effect the recommendations of Wilhelm II's anonymous correspondent, and poisoned the waterholes.

Regular German units stationed along 250 kilometres of the desert's western fringe formed a chain to prevent any return. The Herero, meanwhile, imprisoned in the Omaheke, dug desperately in its lifeless sands for water. In some places the Germans found a hundred separate holes, each two to three metres deep. In their craving for moisture some had drunk at the women's breasts, or slit the throats of their cattle and drunk the blood. Others had disembowelled oxen and squeezed the stomach contents in the hope of a few final drops of fluid. These measures had given about a thousand, including Samuel Maharero, the strength to reach British territory in Bechuanaland, but most simply succumbed to their exhaustion and lay down to die.

A lucky few turned north and escaped to Ovamboland. Those who tried to break through back towards the east were confronted by the German troops. In his diary, von Trotha recorded an occasion when women and children had come to him begging for water. He had ordered them to be forced back into the bush at gunpoint. Alarmed by the ceaseless carnage, some of the old African officers like Major von Estorff asked von Trotha to negotiate, but the general demanded that the slaughter go on. Gerhard Pool recorded that 'von Estorff was so dissatisfied with this answer, that, rightly or wrongly, he labelled von Trotha a poor statesman and a cold-blooded person.'[49]

Had any doubt on the issue remained, the general laid it to rest a week later. On 1 October 1904, he put out the proclamation with which his name will be for ever associated. It was his *Vernichtungs Befehl*, his 'Extermination Order', and in its dozen or so lines von Trotha offered the world a summation of his genocidal hatred of Africa and Africans, a life-negating testament to Namibia's darkest hour:

> I, the great general of the German troops, send this letter to the Herero People. Hereros are no longer German subjects. They have murdered, stolen, they have cut off the noses, ears, and other bodily parts of wounded soldiers and now, because of cowardice, they will fight no more. I say to the people: anyone who delivers one of the Herero captains to my station as a prisoner will receive 1,000 Marks. He who brings in Samuel Maharero will receive 5,000 Marks. All the Hereros must leave the land. If the people do not do this, then I will force them to do it with the great guns. Any Herero found within the German borders with or without a gun, with or without cattle, will be shot. I shall no longer receive any women or children; I will drive them back to their people or I will shoot them. This is my decision for the Herero people.
>
> The Great General of the Mighty Kaiser [50]

Not surprisingly, a number in the old colonial government were deeply disturbed by the general's methods, but for Leutwein, von Trotha's hateful vision of a *tabula rasa* was a total negation of everything he had sought to achieve in South West Africa. Initially sidelined by the general, he was then stripped of most of his political responsibility. This was more than Leutwein would endure, and he now asked to be relieved of his duties.

But von Trotha was undeterred. In a report to the general staff he placed the Herero's destruction in the context of his wider vision for Africa. 'This uprising,' he wrote, 'is and remains the beginning of a racial struggle, which I foresaw for East Africa as early as 1897 in my reports to the Imperial Chancellor.'[51] The Herero war had represented many things, but it had never been explicitly a racial war. Occasionally, at great risk to themselves, the Africans had ensured the safety of German women and children, while Samuel had even forbidden his men to harm German traders with whom he had long and friendly relations. Violence was specifically targeted at those identified as the authors of colonial oppression. Von Trotha's assessment was, therefore, a gross over-simplification.

Yet, by virtue of this crude analysis and his brutal methods, the general had steadily changed the nature of the conflict. Typically, the Germans now slaughtered Africans within the war zone – Herero, Damara, even San – without attempting to distinguish friendly from hostile parties. Those not immediately assaulted, like the Nama, were nevertheless threatened with violence in the very near future.

Sensing the indiscriminate nature of German vengeance, the Nama chose to pre-empt the inevitable. Forty-eight hours after the publication of the *Versnichtungs Befehl*, the news came through that Hendrik Witbooi had declared war on the Germans. There was a double irony in this heroic and pathetic gesture by the ageing Nama leader. While it had fulfilled General von Trotha's false prophecy of racial struggle, it had exposed the fallacy on which he had based his policy of genocide. For rather than submit meekly to the German terror, as the general believed they must, the Africans had risen up bravely and recklessly to confront it.

The reasons for the Nama's belated decision to fight, although obscure to a European community intent on scapegoats, were not difficult to fathom. For twenty years they had suffered the encroachment of European power, and by January 1904 many communities had been tricked or squeezed off large portions of their land, while all were in the same state of virtual rightlessness endured by the Herero. Yet since the outbreak of war, a number of Germans had made no secret of the fact that they welcomed the crisis as an opportunity to advance this process even further. Settlers called for the Nama to be disarmed, their tribal organisation dissolved and the people confined to reserves. Such proposals were widely repeated in the colony's newspapers and were hardly likely to be overlooked by German-speaking Nama.

While Leutwein condemned this public speculation as both danger-ous and premature, in private he was in agreement with the erosion of Nama independence. 'Once the Herero are defeated and disarmed,' he wrote to Berlin, 'we will disarm the south. Destruction of the tribal organisations, the institution of locations and pass laws, will take place after the Hereros have been defeated.'[52] As always with Leutwein, his ultimate objectives were barely distinguishable from those of the most extreme colonists. The only significant difference was his concern to attain his goals a little at a time.

Yet to the Africans Leutwein's methods had at least represented some kind of brake on the more aggressive imperialists. It was he, furthermore, who had established cordial relations over the years with a number of the Nama captains, especially Hendrik Witbooi. His replacement by General von Trotha in late 1904 had broken that personal link. Simultaneously, and in apparent confirmation of the rumoured crackdown in Namaqualand, the Germans had increased the size of their southern garrison. It seemed to Witbooi that the writing was on the wall.

Then came more disconcerting news. Hendrik had earlier sent a hundred soldiers to act as scouts for the Germans against the Herero – part of a contingent he had traditionally provided during the previous decade, to assist Leutwein at times of Afro-German conflict. On this occasion, however, a number of the men had deserted and returned home with news of the atrocities committed by von Trotha's forces, of the systematic elimination of the Herero, and of the abuses inflicted on the Witbooi auxiliaries themselves. The last of these allegations, acknowledged and lamented by the German governor himself, was a violation of the tribe's status as an ally. Hendrik was horrified. Already susceptible to the dicta of his inner voice, he was now further swayed (as Leutwein was later to over-emphasise) by the fighting talk of the Ethiopian Movement 'prophet', Sheppert Stürmann. In his letter to the governor justifying the decision to fight, Witbooi expressed deep remorse that he had for so long cooperated with the Germans. Now was his moment to redeem himself from past follies. To the other Nama captains, Hendrik urged that now was the moment to redeem Africa for Africans.

Most responded. The Bondelswarts, who had triggered the entire war, were one of the few tribes that were split. A number of them were seized immediately by the Germans before they could answer the call to arms. Yet one of their leaders, Jacob Morenga, had been involved in hostilities ever since the original conflict had ignited back in November 1903. When Leutwein had patched up relations with the tribe to enable his departure for the war in the north, this 'renegade' Bondelswart was outlawed and a price placed on his head.

Morenga, in fact, was of mixed blood, the offspring of a Herero–Nama union, and considered by Leutwein to combine the martial virtues of both peoples. Before the war he had been working at a copper mine in the British Cape, but had returned on hearing of the hostilities. He had enjoyed an excellent mission-school education, was fluent in English, German and Afrikaans and proved a brilliant guerrilla tactician. If Witbooi has become in more recent times a heroic model for the country (indeed, Hendrik's unforgiving eyes gaze out on contemporary Namibian life from all denominations of its currency) then Morenga should at least be honoured as an embodiment of African unity for the newly independent state. For he was, as the German historian Horst Drechsler pointed out, the first indigenous leader in South West Africa to be untouched by the old inter-tribal rivalries.[53] His vision of military resistance to the Germans did not fade at the borders of Bondelswart territory, but embraced the whole nation, while his partisan army combined elements from many tribes, including the Herero. That his defeat and death could only be engineered through German and British co-operation in some ways reflected the threat that this 'new man' posed to the imperial policies of both nations.

By the time of Witbooi's decisive call to arms, Morenga had already established himself as a focus for resistance, vilified in the European newspapers as 'an elusive brigand', but acknowledged by indigenes and colonists alike as a type of African Robin Hood.[54] Like Samuel, he forbade his men to harm non-combatants and also took and paroled prisoners. After successfully storming one military post he informed the authorities so they could give medical attention to the wounded. Whenever he raided European farms and disarmed the occupants, he provided them with detailed requisition orders for the items taken. His style of combat also included a sense of humour. After an ambush that deprived a German company of all its horses, he wrote a note to the immobilised commander requesting that he look after his nags better, to ensure they were worthy of theft. Such exploits earned the respect not only of his European adversaries, but of a flock of African recruits. His guerrilla force grew from only eleven at the time of Waterberg, to about 400 by early 1905.

Morenga's men represented about a fifth of an entire Nama force of just 2,000 soldiers, and theoretically it should have been a deeply uneven contest, a brief epilogue to the tale of slaughter in Hereroland. Shortly after Hendrik's declaration, the Germans had more than 15,000 men, 500 officers, 60 artillery and machine-gun units, 20,000 horses, not to mention almost limitless reserves of reinforcements, ammunition and equipment. The final outcome was always, in a sense, a foregone conclusion. Yet the war in the south lasted three times as long as that in Hereroland, and involved more than 200 engagements. It would account for as many German lives and cost the taxpayer considerably more. It would defeat von Trotha's military imagination, while his career in German South West Africa would end in the same ambiguous manner as Leutwein's.

While the Nama lacked the numerical superiority enjoyed by the Herero, they benefited from a range of logistical and tactical advantages. The Germans had no railway in the south to supply themselves. Provisions to the only port at Lüderitzbucht had then to be lugged by wagon across the Namib's shifting sands, a tortuous journey of 250 kilometres that could take three and a half weeks. Namaqualand was also hotter, drier and more broken by mountains and steep-sided gorges, of which the Nama made full use in their hit-and-run tactics. Their deep knowledge of the country paid another crucial dividend. 'In the interior,' wrote one frustrated officer, 'there were . . . numerous waterholes, but they were known to the natives and not to us. Hendrik Witbooi can live with his people for months on end out in the Kalahari Desert and yet our maps showed the area to be completely waterless.'[55]

Not only was the terrain better suited to the Africans, the type of combat was also in their favour. Nama methods were fundamentally different from those of the Herero. In any conflict, the latter had always to take their cattle herds into strategic consideration, fighting only in areas where they could water and graze their animals. At the end of an engagement they needed to hold their ground to make their slow and cattle-hindered exit. For these reasons, and also to utilise their numerical strength against the Germans, they favoured pitched battles, in which European firepower and discipline had eventually carried the day. The Nama, however, operating in small groups unencumbered by livestock or family units, were elusive, mobile and flexible.

Mobility and flexibility were not the Germans' major assets, nor was imagination von Trotha's strongest suit. He had been favoured earlier by a style of warfare that suited his own forces, and the fact that he could call freely on the resources of an embarrassed, if not infuriated, German state. But in Namaqualand, where the Africans simply melted away before his men could lumber out to find them, the general was at a loss to know what to do. His instinctive reaction was to call for further massive support, requesting the construction of a railway line to the southern interior. When this was turned down he called for a suspension of operations, which was read as a signal in Berlin that the ideas had run out. The Director of the Colonial

Department wrote: 'It is difficult to interpret this as anything else but a statement of bankruptcy on the part of General von Trotha . . . Count von Schlieffen and his associates largely share my opinion.'[56]

By 1905 widespread disillusionment with the war had set in amongst the German troops. When their grievances started to appear in the German press, the military authorities responded with a number of executions amongst the ranks and dismissed the criticism as the work of a few troublemakers. But the protests continued. The Reichstag heard complaints that parents and relatives were notified of combatants' deaths by open postcard.[57] The local press also began to carp at von Trotha's inability to bring hostilities to a close. In October one German correspondent reported that the general's effort to repeat his encircling tactics of the Waterberg had resulted in 1,200 German troops closing in on nothing but the dry, clear, sparkling ether of Namaqualand, while Witbooi and his men were 200 kilometres further to the south. The correspondent went on:

This war is being conducted against a people who possess neither money nor resources of their own. The greater portion of the material with which they wage war against us they have captured from ourselves. The cattle with which they replenish their stock they have taken from us, and many of their weapons are our own army rifles. Up to date we have not succeeded in capturing even one of their chief leaders. The losses which we have inflicted upon them are more than outweighed by our own casualties, which have upon almost every occasion been greater than the enemy's. That is the result of one year's campaigning which has already cost 200 million Marks.[58]

It was not difficult to draw the unspoken conclusion. Nor would von Trotha have disagreed. He did, however, want to depart with honour, and only days after the correspondent had filed his copy, fortune smiled on the general.

On 29 October, while leading an attack on a German supply convoy, Hendrik Witbooi was wounded. The old warrior, then in his sixty-eighth year, had inspired his men to fight for over twelve months, constantly eluding the Germans and raiding at will. There were no signs that he had intended to give up the struggle. That chance bullet, however, in the absence of medical attention, was a decisive blow against the Nama's determination to continue. One British source gave Witbooi a hero's burial on the field of battle: 'His only requiem was the screeching of shells and the whistling of German bullets.'[59] According to this account, Hendrik's son and a few followers laid him in a shallow grave disguised to avoid German detection, while the rest of the Witbooi force held off the European advance.

Less than a month later, the German commander, who had described the news of Hendrik's death as a 'beautiful message', felt he now had grounds to retire in the manner he intended.[60] To cap it all he had received further great tidings. In the same year that one of his countrymen had published the special theory of relativity and a fellow German speaker issued his *Jokes and their Relations to the Unconscious*, the general himself had earned the renown of his nation. Just days before his embarkation on 19 November 1905, he learnt that his legacy to South West Africa – a thousand African dead for each of his sixty steps up the gang plank – had won him the order Pour le Mérite from the Kaiser. The honour, however, carried the slightest of taints. On the occasion of his award, a lowly captain and a major were decorated with the same medal. The first of these, Captain Franke, the man who had led the relief of Windhoek, was acknowledged as the true 'popular hero of the South West Africa War'.[61]

The four principal players in the war – Theodor Leutwein, Samuel Maharero, Lothar von Trotha and Hendrik Witbooi – had all now vanished from the scene. With Samuel's exile in Bechuanaland his nation had been reduced to a shattered remnant, while Hendrik's death had robbed the Nama of their outstanding leader, and his own Witbooi people of the will to continue. A large body of them capitulated with one of their sub-chiefs only a week after the German general's departure. Although the colony would remain on a war footing for a further eighteen months, it was the beginning of the end of the Nama rising. By February 1906 the Witbooi diehards had also had enough.

Only a few small bands remained at large and the war was closing much as it had opened. The men of Warmbad, who had watched in growing anger as their chief had been seized by the impulsive Lieutenant Jobst almost three years before, and whose retaliatory action had sparked the African revolt, were now among the last in the field. Foremost amongst them was Morenga. In 1905 the Germans had lost two major battles to his forces and even the general staff conceded that 'His conduct of the war has something grand about it and is in its form far superior to that of all the other native leaders. All in all, an outstanding soldier, to whom we as the enemy do not wish to deny our respect.'[62] They did, however, neglect to respect international borders, and when Morenga's men retreated into the territory of British South Africa in March 1906, the Germans followed, launching a surprise attack in which the African leader was wounded. When Morenga gave himself up to British police two months later, the German authorities were euphoric.

The war had ground on for far too long. Even von Trotha's stomach for the fight had weakened before his exit. From the blood and thunder of his Extermination Order, he had shifted to a position where the Nama were offered food and employment if they gave themselves up. After his departure the German military authorities abandoned the hard line altogether, and when one Bondelswarts group finally laid down their arms in December 1906, a negotiated truce allowed them 1,500 head of cattle, the retention of their lands as free people and 300 sheep together with a team of oxen for their captain.

From a position where, over the heads of a civil administration, the commanding officer had demanded the Africans' total submission or annihilation, matters had come full circle. Now it was the colony's governor, Friedrich von Lindequist (the man who had prosecuted Nikodemus a decade earlier), who called for the Nama's unconditional surrender, while the military offered to negotiate. Three years of costly fighting had forced the learning curve to rise steeply and they intended to end the war by political manoeuvre.

One Nama force under their leader Simon Kooper was pursued deep inside British territory by a German detachment three times the size of their own and ambushed, in violation of international law. After Kooper had fought this attack off with huge losses amongst his men, the Germans finally bought him off in 1908. Kooper settled in Bechuanaland until his death in 1913, drawing £60 of German gold a year, disguised as a British pension in return for good behaviour.

Although Kooper had been the last Nama leader to abandon the struggle, for the Germans his removal had been a subordinate goal. After Hendrik Witbooi, Morenga had always represented the greatest threat. While his seizure by the Cape police had been balm for German nerves, his release more than a year later, in June 1907, brought the colony once again to fever pitch. The governor described it as 'like an electric shock, causing great excitement among the natives, all the way to the north'.[63] Although the state of war had been lifted three months earlier, news of his return led to the cancellation of troop ships to Germany, and a large force, including twelve companies, three field batteries, four platoons of mountain artillery and four machine-guns, was assembled in the south. One man who seemed to have learnt nothing from the years of fighting was the Kaiser. He now ordered his men to 'put a price of 20,000 Marks on Morenga's head and to wipe out the whole bunch without mercy'.[64] German soldiers had been attempting to achieve this without any success since 1903, and at least then Morenga had been in the colony.

Now they needed subtler methods. The new German governor, therefore, wrote to his opposite number in the Cape, playing on the mutual benefits of Morenga's elimination, while a German staff officer was duly attached to the British border police. When the African leader made a break for the border, the Europeans were given their opportunity. Morenga was trailed to the southern edge of the Kalahari, and after a four-hour gun battle on Friday 20 September 1907, he, his brother and two of his cousins were shot dead. It remained only to square Kooper in his Bechuanaland lair, and the fire of rebellion was finally out.

The South West African war could never have been in any sense a close-run thing. Like the Apache, the people of South West Africa could field only a small, irreplaceable force, while their subsistence resources could only dwindle, unless enlarged by further capture. The Germans, on the other hand, had only to wait for the massive build-up of troops and *matériel* to enjoy an overwhelming superiority in all areas. Time, therefore, had always been on their side.

However, if victory had never been in doubt, it had certainly been dearly bought. Germany's 'bloodiest and most protracted colonial war' had lasted four years, involved 17,000 European troops, wasted the lives of 2,000 and cost 600 million Marks, the equivalent of £20 million sterling. And, had they but known, within seven years of Morenga's death the Germans would surrender their bitterly contested colony to the invading forces of British South Africa.

For the losing side, the war was nothing short of a catastrophe. It was, according to one historian, 'one of the five great revolts against early colonial rule in Africa'.[65] It was also the last major war in the scramble for Africa and it had cost the colonised peoples everything.

The Nama and the Herero lost between a half and three-quarters of their total numbers. They were reduced to a landless proletariat, ground under by one of the most oppressive colonial regimes on the continent. Even 'liberation' by the British forces of 1914 would bring little change in their fortunes, and it would take a further seventy-five years of struggle, latterly on the field of combat, before their rights were genuinely restored.

22

Never Must We Allow the Negroes to Prevail

After it had become apparent to General von Trotha that the Herero's complete extirpation was a goal impossible of attainment, he had been forced to seek assistance from a community he had consistently reviled. The Rhenish Missionary Society, retaining some of the credibility enjoyed in peacetime, was charged with trawling Hereroland to locate remaining African bands and to encourage their assembly at special reception stations. By May 1906 these camps held 14,769 people – a rump population, largely reduced to skin and bone, that was then subjected to a second phase of persecution.

A work-force of 2,200 Herero men, women and children had already been deployed by the colony's administrators on the Otavi railway. The rest of the camps' inmates now joined them in a system of virtual slave labour, while the camps themselves were closed in August 1906 on the pretext that such a concentration of Herero represented a threat to the colony.[1]

By the end of 1905 the German authorities had prepared the legislation to underpin the process of enslavement. Central to this was an Expropriation Order which Wilhelm II, taking time out amidst the royal family's Christmas celebrations, brought into effect on 26 December. It was an ill-timed expression of Christian heartlessness, legitimising the seizure of the 'entire moveable and fixed property of the tribe' – their land and cattle.[2] A resolution passed by the Reichstag, which called for the Herero's retention of pasture sufficient to maintain their traditional economic life, was circumvented by the Colonial Department and the colony's administration. Since the Herero had no cattle, ran the callous and dishonest solecism, they had

343

no need of any land. In May 1907 the whole of Nama territory, except that of the Berseba tribe, joined Hereroland as government property.

In the early days the colonists' treatment of their captive labour force was little short of a continuation of von Trotha's policy of annihilation by other means. Typical were the cruelties inflicted on those sent to work in Swakopmund. 'They suffered greatly from the cold,' wrote the missionary Heinrich Vedder:

> Their clothing had long since been torn to tatters. Men and women without went about in sacking, their only protection from the cold. Many got inflammation of the lungs and died. During the worst period an average of 30 died daily. It was the way the system worked.[3]

When Vedder and others questioned the system, they received evasive replies. The Okahandja commandant in charge of prisoner distribution, while acknowledging that Africans 'should be strong and healthy in the interests of labour and also of humanity', refused to limit service to those capable of performing it. The old, the lame, the sick had to go to make up numbers. It was also difficult, he argued, 'to send back the weak Hereros interned in Swakopmund as suggested . . . because there are no replacements for them.'[4] Absent from this moral *non sequitur* was any concern to safeguard the work-force, even simply as a non-renewable resource. In its place was the logic of El Dorado – an all-consuming mania for the satisfaction of immediate European needs, irrespective of its human cost.

For the Nama, if anything, matters were worse. Paul Rohrbach, the colony's economic adviser, accurately reflected settler attitudes when he wrote that 'the Hottentots are generally regarded . . . as useless . . . providing no justification for the preservation of the race . . . [This] led to their losses being regarded with indifference, if not with satisfaction.'[5] By March 1907 the Germans must have been well pleased with their administration's progress in this field.

In holiday guidebooks to contemporary Namibia, Shark Island receives notice usually as the site of a plaque commemorating the German merchant who gave his name to the port opposite, Lüderitz. Perhaps the guidebooks' white authors considered it too insignificant, too macabre or too shameful to record that Shark Island was also the Germans' chosen location for Nama internment. Within weeks of their transfer in September 1906, itself a violation of the agreed surrender terms, Shark had become a mass grave for the imprisoned Nama. Starved, overworked, and susceptible to its cold climate, their numbers dwindled daily. In just one four-week period, 276 perished. Von Estorff, the German officer opposed to von Trotha's merciless policies, now wrote a report recommending the return of at least women and children to a more wholesome climate.

With all the frozen inhumanity of an SS officer or, indeed, of a British official in charge of concentration camps in the Boer War (the example cited by the German bureaucrat to justify his own actions) the request was turned down, on the grounds that it endangered security in the colony. By April 1908, seven months after the Nama's deportation, 1,032 of 1,795 had died. Of the 245 men still alive by that date, only twenty-five were in a condition to work. These methods were replicated wherever prisoners were held. According to the Germans' own report, more than forty-five per cent, 7,682 of approximately 17,000 Herero and Nama, had died between 1904 and 1907.[6]

The exact scale of the tragedy inflicted on the people of South West Africa between these years has been an issue of vigorous and recurrent debate. Clearly, the greater the number of casualties, the more firmly could Germany's accusers press the charge of genocide. However, any accurate assessment depends on the reliability of two other statistics: the before and after censuses of Herero and Nama populations. Only one of these – an official estimate from 1911, giving figures of 15,130 Herero and 9,781 Nama – has been accepted as the number of survivors.[7] Debate centres, therefore, on the tribes' pre-war totals.

Various counts had been done before the conflict and were acknowledged in their time as reliable. In 1874 the Reverend Irle, a missionary amongst the Herero, suggested between 70,000 and 80,000 for that tribe, and 20,000 Nama. In his own book, Leutwein accepted these figures as an accurate reflection of tribal populations on his arrival in 1894. A further German estimate, published by Captain Schwabe a decade later, also supported these totals.[8] In 1905 the British newspaper *The Times*, using German military information, suggested a Herero population of between 60,000 and 80,000, and possibly as high as 100,000.[9] Even in 1908, when international questions over German methods had already started to arise, the novelist Frenssen wrote of a 'savage furious people numbering sixty thousand'.[10]

Why should a range of estimates all in general agreement and acceptable at the time of publication suddenly cease to be valid for subsequent authors on South West African history? What deep and unspoken anxieties compelled the Reverend Vedder to such extraordinary circumlocution when discussing Herero numbers in the 1920s? 'One would not be wrong,' he wrote after his estimate of 33,000, 'in assuming that *in ancient times* they were double this number.' [author's italics][11] Why should Israel Goldblatt write: 'It is impossible to arrive at any reliable figure of the number of Hereros who were killed or who died during the campaign and it is therefore impossible to be able to state . . . that only one tenth of the population survived'?[12] Why should Gerhard Pool suggest 'the historian is unable to give accurate figures concerning the number of Hereros at the outbreak of the war, the number who were present at Waterberg in August, those who died during the war and the number that survived'?[13]

Why? Because it was a way of deflecting attention from and of blurring the whole issue of German atrocities. For Vedder it was almost as if to have stated a number outright would have been to utter the hated charge of genocide itself. And, in a sense, it was. For, to offer any ante-bellum figures for Herero and Nama populations is to indicate the scale of their decline as a result of German policies What many historians wanted to avoid acknowledging was that approximately three-quarters of the Herero and more than half the Nama died in the three-year period. Perhaps even more damning was the sixty per cent reduction of the Damara: they had not even been party to the conflict. A total of about 75,000 African inhabitants perished in the war.[14]

Even if one accepts that the precise number of African casualties was uncertain, there is little doubt that a policy of extermination enjoyed wide German support. Leutwein had written in the early stages of the war 'of those fanatics who want to see the Herero destroyed altogether' – a statement closely echoing the missionary who had noted the settlers' constant boast to 'Make a clean sweep, hang them, shoot them to the last man'.[15] Significantly, Leutwein had countered such views, partly on the grounds 'that a people of some 60,000 to 70,000 is not so easy to annihilate'.[16] It is apparent from both of these sources that von Trotha's announcement of his *Vernichtungs Befehl* reflected a general mood amongst settlers and was the articulation of their own pre-existing objectives.

The general's extreme methods also enjoyed support in Berlin, even at the highest levels. As we have seen, the possibility of the Herero's desert exodus had been anticipated well before the Battle of Waterberg and approved by the general staff. Moreover, the official report concerning events after the battle positively crowed over the subsequent German thoroughness:

> This bold enterprise shows up in the most brilliant light the ruthless energy of the German command in pursuing their beaten enemy. No pains, no sacrifices were spared in eliminating the last remnants of enemy resistance. Like a wounded beast the enemy was tracked down from one water-hole to the next, until finally he became the victim of his own environment. The arid Omaheke was to complete what the German army had begun: the extermination of the Herero nation . . .[17]

When it came to assessing the morality of such an outcome the authors were completely resolute. How could the Germans be in any way culpable, when they and the Sandveld had served merely as agents in some divine judicial process? 'The court had now concluded its work of punishment,' the report continued. 'The Hereros had ceased to exist as an independent tribe.'

Although von Trotha's *Vernichtungs Befehl* was eventually countermanded by his superiors, von Schlieffen, the Chief of General Staff, had initially upheld it. It was only the furore of opposition in the Reichstag, from Leutwein, the missionaries and sections of the German public, that forced him to reconsider. But in a subsequent assessment of the general's measures, it was not any moral implication that troubled Schlieffen. 'General von Trotha's intention is admirable,' he wrote. 'Unfortunately he does not have the power necessary to implement his plans. He must remain at the edge of the Omaheke and cannot drive the Herero out.'[18] Schlieffen's worries centred on its practical feasibility.

Since he recognised that von Trotha's plan 'could not be carried through successfully in the face of the present opinion', he yielded to the views of the German chancellor, Prince von Bülow, who wrote to the Kaiser asking for the order to be rescinded.[19] Wilhelm II was apparently 'extremely reluctant' to abandon his general. Only after thirteen days' delay was von Trotha finally ordered to reverse his policy.[20]

It is clear that there had been an important lobby throughout all layers of German society predisposed to a policy of extermination, but why should this have been the case? The question is all the more intriguing in view of the fact that at the outset of the German imperial career in 1884, Bismarck had himself convened a conference in Berlin, attended by the colonising powers of Europe, which had agreed new standards of humanitarian conduct. Hollow as these public statements may always have been, the Germans had not simply overlooked the moral and physical welfare of Africans, but pursued policies that were an absolute negation of their proclaimed intention.

The reason for this lies only partly in their axiomatic perception of Africans as inferiors. Paradoxically, the critical factor driving them towards a genocidal policy was a concern that these tribal peoples had shown potential well beyond their allotted station. True, until the outbreak of war, the Germans had acted, like all European colonists, on the assumption that they were not dealing with equals. Just as the embryonic science of anthropology envisioned a gradual pattern of historical improvement amongst the human species, culminating in white European, industrial man, so living African society must obey that same rigid teleological process. At each step, the rough slouch of its primitives would be modified, until it had metamorphosed totally into the buoyant march of twentieth-century civilisation. And if it was necessary to use violence in order to cram this perceived scheme of millennial change into just twenty years of colonial activity, then so be it.

The settlers' petition defending their use of whips was a classic expression of that coercive ideology. The Africans, they argued, had grown used to laziness, brutality and stupidity from 'time immemorial'. So much so that 'any white man . . . finds it almost impossible to regard them as human beings.' The answer was 'centuries of training as human beings'. Since no individual German had the luxury of such a time span, they must force the tempo like jockeys in a race, with constant use of the sjambok, the hippo- or rhino-hide whip. German settlers excused their brutal behaviour by placing it within the context of an intrinsic 'law' ('the natural right of the strongest' was how one Windhoek editorial put it), so that when they applied the accelerator to social change, when they thrashed Africans into accepting European models of land-ownership and land-use, they were simply acting as automatic cogs in determinist machinery.[21] By spurring on only what was inevitable, they were absolved from any moral debate.

Fused with these social Darwinian notions was the quasi-religious, and deeply contradictory, conviction that evolution did, in fact, fulfil a moral purpose: the development of the most powerful, the most advanced, most intelligent civilisation on earth. Europeans were at once the apex of a determinist process, but also the free agents of their own superiority. It was their duty to impose themselves on the rest of the world. As one of the characters in Frenssen's war novel announces: 'To the nobler and more vigorous belongs the world. That is the justice of God.'[22] Violence to Africans and to African society, in the cause of their assimilation into European society, had a moral imperative – it was being cruel to be kind. A Windhoek official, the inappropriately named Karl Dove, expressed it in inverse form when he wrote 'Leniency towards the natives is cruelty to the whites'[23] – an eerie pre-echo of another German writing in justification of a more radical programme of social change: 'Kindness here . . . would be just about the greatest cruelty to our own people' – the words of Adolf Hitler on the eve of the final solution.[24]

However, in South West Africa there was an additional element that helps explain the Germans' recourse to a genocidal policy. For twenty years European expropriation had gone on unabated and largely unchallenged. Although there had been armed responses, notably by Hendrik Witbooi, there had been nothing to halt, let alone reverse, colonial encroachment. There had been, therefore, no serious challenge to the ideas on which Germany's nascent imperialism had been founded. With the war of 1904 all this was suddenly thrown into confusion.

The Herero's uprising occasioned a deep sense of outrage, which operated on two distinct levels. By murdering scores of farmers and cutting off their testicles, the Africans had violated in the most direct, brutal fashion the physical and political body of the Germans. However, this they could perhaps understand. It was at least behaviour that fitted the Europeans' *a priori* vision of Africans. What were they if not savages, devoid of moral standards, barbarous devourers of human flesh? What was more difficult to come to terms with was the way in which the Herero had violated the roles the Germans had allotted them in their imaginative schema.

Every system of communication had reaffirmed an image of blacks as inferiors, half humans, cowardly, ignorant baboons, born to succumb to a higher civilisation, to labour and toil in the interests of a superior German race. Yet the Herero had had the temerity to renounce these fictive stereotypes, to assert their own reality and independence, inflicting grievous losses on German populations and then holding their own on the field of combat. The Herero uprising, minor in terms of its military challenge to the German state, was the most profound threat to the conceptual framework on which they had based their imperialism. And the longer German soldiers failed to subdue these half-naked savages, the deeper was the trauma for a people who had been constantly reassured that they were the greatest military nation on earth.

The resulting confusion, though never acknowledged, was implicit in much that the Germans said or did. It was, for instance, classically illustrated in the letter sent to the Kaiser and quoted in the previous chapter, which recommended the poisoning of their water supply. This should be done, argued its author, 'in order to give that race an idea of the power we wield over them.' If such a stratagem were an expression of the Germans' overwhelming superiority it was also, surely, an indication of military insecurity, resorted to out of deep fears for an opponent who had suddenly revealed new, unexpected powers. And that precise anxiety was acknowledged, when he added: 'Never must we allow the Negroes to prevail.'[25]

The provision of von Trotha with such overwhelmingly superior forces was itself an expression of their unstable oscillation between presumed dominance and vulnerability. On the one hand, it demonstrated the Germans' invincible military strength, yet it also implied the perceived magnitude of threat posed by the Herero. Von Trotha made even more explicit that polarity in the German response when he wrote: 'there could be no question of negotiations . . . unless we wanted to betray our impotence and confusion.'[26] According to this logic, killing had developed its own imperative, out of the Germans' neurotic fears of insecurity. Schlieffen echoed the refusal to negotiate, because, as he put it, 'After what has happened the co-existence of whites and blacks will be very difficult . . . Race war, once it has broken out, can only be ended by the destruction of one of the parties.'[27]

Negotiation was out of the question because it would have demanded that the Germans permit the truth about Africans to percolate through the lifeless crust of prejudice and misconception on which they had based their treatment. They would have had, literally, to re-imagine who they were fighting and their entire relationship to these other people. Emotionally and intellectually that would have been too costly and too painful. Better to soldier on, pouring in resources – to a total equivalent in modern values of US $1.5 billion – until the bitter end, until the object that had occasioned such inner turmoil was removed altogether. South West Africa 'should be just that colony,' wrote von Trotha, the man who personified the German identity crisis, 'where the European himself can work . . . with a fair amount of security.'[28] That inner state could only be predicated on the complete elimination of the Herero.

The refusal to renegotiate their image of the African helps explain much about the nature of the German campaign. It sheds light on the obsessive search for excuses and scapegoats: anything that enabled the *a priori* version of Africa to remain intact; anything that released them from any painful self-examination. It helps account for the persistence in a military policy that was completely disproportionate either to the military threat or to the economic value of the colony itself. For to have allowed the Negro to prevail would have undermined Germany's entire imperial adventure. Finally, it helps clarify why the Germans refused to discriminate hostile from 'friendly' African, Herero from Damara. Better to get rid of them all than to engage in any complicated sifting of their own black stereotypes.

The subsequent instability in the German image of their African opponent resulted also in a number of extraordinary ironies, of which the Germans remained determinedly unaware. One of the most striking arose from their portrayal of the fighting Herero as bestial cowards: 'I saw a black, half-naked figure like an ape, holding his gun in his mouth and climbing with hands and feet into a tree'; 'the blacks, like cowards, have treacherously murdered all the farmers, and their wives and children' (Frenssen); 'they have murdered and robbed and cut off the ears and noses and other parts of the body of wounded soldiers, and now out of cowardice they refuse to fight' (von Trotha).[29]

Yet a European nation at war required its formal infrastructure of praise to support and validate the deeds of its soldiers. And so there were the customary distribution of medals, the necessary words of commendation. After Otjihinamaparero, for instance, there was Wilhelm II's message of congratulation extolling the bravery of his soldiers and marines. In January 1905 *The Times*, in its audit of military honours, reported that 'So far 39 officers and 286 men have met a hero's death.'[30] Yet until that point nobody seemed to question how one became a hero by fighting ignorant, cowardly baboons. When the

General Staff eventually addressed the contradiction and conceded the corollary of German valour – that the Africans had been a brave and intelligent opposition – they hit on a novel formula for expressing their regard. The Herero had not been as brave as Germans, but more formidable enemies than the Boers.[31] It was a highly revealing comparison, suggesting an adversary that by no means diminished the reputation of the German troops. Yet by choosing the Boers, a white people widely regarded as having gone native (but also, incidentally, a nation that had almost fought off the might of the British empire), the General Staff had fallen short of offering the Herero martial parity with a European nation.

The more central and tragic irony of the war is that nothing had more completely blurred the presumed moral and intellectual distinctions between the two races. Yet never had the two been more completely and ruthlessly separated than in the war's aftermath. The events between 1904 and 1907 imposed a psychological chasm between the black and white peoples of South West Africa which has only been allowed to heal towards the close of the twentieth century.

On an ethical plane, the Herero and Nama had clearly sought to prove a general moral worth and the justice of their case through the military standards they adopted. Almost without exception they spared women, children, non-German whites and non-combatant Africans. The charges of indiscriminate murder that formed a part of the Germans' anti-African propaganda seem all the more vicious in view of the considerable efforts taken by Herero and Nama fighters to separate out the innocent from among their opponents. In fact, leaders like Jacob Morenga adopted standards more reminiscent of medieval chivalry than of modern warfare.

In justification of their own methods, von Trotha had made great play of the Germans' deep abhorrence of the Herero's castration of the dead. It was singled out for specific emphasis in the *Vernichtungs Befehl* as a practice that made forfeit any subsequent right to humane treatment. Yet as the missionary Irle pointed out, the castrations had often been done 'in the case of whites who have raped their [African] womenfolk in the most brutal manner.'[32]

If the moral case was generally in the Africans' favour, the distinctions between their respective mental capacities, as expressed through military competence, was at least blurred. The Germans had certainly won the war against the Herero convincingly, but victory had not relied on outstanding generalship. Neither Leutwein nor von Trotha had shown exceptional tactical supremacy over the Herero. At Oviumbo, implementing the lessons learnt at Ongandjira, Samuel had carefully neutralised German firepower by exploiting the terrain and dense bush, and had come within a whisker of a major victory. At Owikokorero and Okaharui other commanders had successfully exploited the tactics of ambush. Before von Trotha's arrival both casualty figures and military successes were almost equally divided between the two parties.

The Nama, if anything, had shown themselves to be tactically in advance of their opponents. Far fewer in number, they had inflicted as many losses, sustained the war for longer and exhausted more German resources than the Herero. They had proved themselves masters of guerrilla warfare, skilfully exploiting their knowledge of the environment and surprise tactics. Because of the Herero's reliance upon their cattle herds and Samuel's apparent concern to surround himself with his people, von Trotha had been allowed to bring his enormously superior firepower to bear on the campaign. The Nama, by contrast, never gave the opportunity for a pitched battle and in those circumstances the general was at a loss to know how to confront them.

For the people of South West Africa the war had involved the most dramatic assertion of their rights and qualities as human beings. By their actions – their civilised treatment of the innocent, their tactical competence, not to mention their courage – they had blurred the racial distinctions which the colonists had so cherished and which had formed the basis of their imperial ideology. Almost as if shattered by such an assault on their *Weltanschauung*, the Germans reacted with a policy of rigid racial segregation once victory was secured.

Although all land had been legally transferred to white ownership by the Expropriation Order of 1905, provision had been made for the governor to grant permission for land rights at his discretion. In the event, the governor never exercised this prerogative during the period of German rule. The right of Africans to rear cattle or horses was only allowed exceptionally after 1912.[33]

These measures were supported by a ban on more than ten families or individual labourers living on a single plot. 'Every tribal organisation,' wrote the deputy governor, 'will cease. Werfs [settlements] deep in the bush which try to avoid political supervision will not be tolerated. They would provide focal points for memories of tribal life and days when the Africans owned the land.'[34] This systematic coercion fulfilled a double objective: it sought to eliminate completely indigenous culture and gave the Africans only one option for survival. However, as the Reverend Vedder put it, with staggering complacency: 'The compulsion to work was not regarded as an injustice, for having lost their former possessions of cattle they realised the necessity to earn their living by manual labour.'[35]

Just in case they failed to appreciate the necessity, pass laws were instituted making it an offence to be without a recognised means of livelihood – in effect a job on a German farm. Those without such a work contract were without legal rights and could be arrested for vagrancy. Eventually every indigenous male over the age of eight had to carry an identity card. Without it he could receive neither food nor lodging. Although these prescriptions appear to anticipate later German treatment of Nazi-reviled minorities, in fact, they drew upon legal precedents initiated in British South Africa as early as 1807, an ideological debt that shows that there was nothing peculiarly Germanic about this brand of racism.[36]

Another reminder of 'the necessity and dignity of labour' – as one leading British imperialist, Joseph Chamberlain, liked to talk of African servitude – was the ubiquitous sjambok.[37] The use of this heavy whip mushroomed enormously after the war. The administration's records showed a nine-fold increase in cases between 1907 and 1912. These documented incidents represented only a fraction of the total, since only the most notorious cases of unofficial punishment ever came to public attention. One such case, against a psychotic farmer called Ludwig Cramer, involved whippings so severe that two women died and two other pregnant victims, their backs a mass of pustulant scars, miscarried. For these crimes Cramer received twenty-seven months' imprisonment.[38]

In a colony that suffered in 1903 from a male to female ratio of over five to one, it was inevitable that the Germans would use African women to satisfy less abnormal urges. However, in 1907 this *Schmutzwirtschaft* – dirty work – as it was called, was eventually forbidden by colonial legislation. The government outlawed mixed marriages, while the governor condemned any sexual relations between black and white as 'not only a crime against the purity of the German race . . . but [they] could also be a severe threat to the whole position of the white man in SWA.'[39]

There was, however, an even greater threat to the German position, which would reveal itself just eight years after the Herero and Nama uprisings. In 1914 South West Africa was unwillingly embroiled in a second, larger conflict. When Britain and Germany went to war in Europe, white troops from South Africa invaded the neighbouring colony and quickly swept aside all resistance, holding the territory for the next four years. Then in 1919, at the Paris Peace Conference, Germany was legally stripped of its colonies which, under the terms of the new Covenant of the League of Nations, were designated as mandated territories.

Old German East Africa became Tanganyika under an Anglo administration, while Togoland and Cameroon were each divided between the French and British. Given German South West Africa's contiguity with the Union of South Africa, it was to be placed under the supervision of its white neighbours. However, the German territories were not intended as spoils of war for the victors. Rather than symbols of European prestige, they were to be expressions of Christian conscience and humane Western values. Since the mandated territories were, in the words of the League of Nations, 'inhabited by peoples not yet able to stand by themselves under the strenuous conditions of the modern world, there should be applied the principle that the well-being and development of such people form a sacred trust of civilization.'[40]

From the very beginning, the allied forces had viewed themselves as liberators in the land of the Herero and Nama, and proclaimed to its inhabitants a new era of freedom. In a spirit of justice they had also exposed the worst aspects of the German regime, cataloguing them in a document entitled *Report on the Natives of South-West Africa and their Treatment by Germany*, which gained notoriety as the 'Blue Book'. It was a devastating account of their colonial methods and of the real causes of the Herero and Nama uprisings. It remains to this day one of the most important English-language accounts of the period and easily convinced its readers of the underlying subtext: that Germany was unfit to be an imperial power. Based partly on its findings, the repatriation of 6,000 German settlers was quickly implemented. To suggest the fresh start that was to be given to South West Africa, the South African prime minister General Jan Smuts announced that the 'mandatory state should look upon its position as a great trust and honour, not as an office of profit or a position of private advantage for it or its nationals.'[41]

Then the new white rulers, secure in their new possessions, started to reveal an older set of attitudes behind the rhetoric. By 1926 the white population had doubled, despite the German expulsions.

Africans were eventually given inalienable reserves, but these represented the driest, least productive sandveld, often short of water and poor in grazing. The vast majority of this African territory comprised the areas – the Kaokoveld, Ovamboland and Okavango – climatically least hospitable to white settlement. The remainder, essentially the old areas once occupied by the Herero and Nama, was declared a police zone in which Africans were only permitted by virtue of a work permit – the Germans' old pass laws by a new name. Eventually 260,000 black Africans enjoyed sixteen million hectares, compared with the forty million hectares held by just 73,000 whites.[42]

In other areas of administration the mandatory nation gradually revealed the deep continuities between its own objectives and those of its European predecessors. By the 1940s only ten per cent of the country's total expenditure went on the native areas, and the majority of this was on administration. One other representative sample of its racially divided priorities was that while fifty-three government schools catered for the educational needs of 38,000 whites, a third of a million black Africans had to make do with just five establishments.[43] Per capita expenditure on education for white and black children was allocated at a ratio of 112 to one.[44] And even as late as the 1970s the average white income was 3,000 rands, while that for blacks was just 125, and half of all the economically active Africans were in subsistence agriculture with a cash income of just thirty rand a year.

The new European power in South West Africa had quickly recognised that in order to control the country's future development, they needed also to dictate its past. Thus, the old image of German misgovernment underwent deep revisions. In many ways the fate of the Blue Book, that record of vile colonial aggression drawn up by British army officers, symbolised the wider struggle for South West Africa itself. Reversing the opinions so forcefully expressed in the Blue Book's pages, General Smuts soon announced that the 'Germans of South West Africa, whose successful and conscientious work I highly appreciate, will materially help in building an enduring European civilization on the African continent, which is the main task of the Union.'[45] The Germans themselves, of course, had immediately dismissed the Blue Book as noxious propaganda, countering its allegations in 1919 with their own parallel exposé of British colonial atrocities. It was also systematically ignored by later German historians.

In 1926 the white legislative assembly in Windhoek added their voice to the chorus of Blue Book condemnations. The methods and atrocities it recorded had become a severe embarrassment not just to the Germans but to all the European colonists, and it was decreed that the heretical text should be treated accordingly. Thereafter all copies of the report in the territory's official files and libraries were to be burnt, while recommendations were made to the British and South African governments that all copies in their public libraries should also be removed and destroyed.[46]

Not content with an ideological rehabilitation of the old colonial power, South African administrators paid the Germans the ultimate compliment by repeating their methods. In 1922 the Bondelswarts, exasperated by the false promises and their continued dispossession at the hands of the new regime, had rebelled once more. This time, however, it was South African men and technology that went to crush them. When 150 Bondelswart men rode off to the hills to renew their fifty-year struggle, they were subjected to aerial bombardment. One hundred were killed before being bombed into submission. White fatalities numbered just two.[47]

The disproportion of black to white losses suggested once more that note of heroic futility which had characterised African resistance ever since the time of Hendrik Witbooi. And for a further six decades both heroism and futility would resurface in equal measure on the battle-fields of South West Africa. It was not until 1990 that Namibia, the last African colony but one to achieve independence from its European rulers, was finally created.

23
They Built No Houses
and Dug No Wells

In a book that documents some of the bleakest episodes in Europe's relationship with tribal societies there is a risk of engendering in readers what Frederick Turner III has called 'a counter-productive orgy of racial self-hatred'.[1] Before attempting any final conclusions in this chapter we need first to recall the reasons why such a response would be misguided. Most significant and, certainly, most depressing is that genocide, attempted genocide and ruthless dispossession are policies with a long pedigree, recorded in the histories of the Greeks and Romans and even further back in the Old Testament.

Mass brutality and mechanised slaughter have been amongst the defining characteristics of this present century. In the First World War the Turkish government of the Ottoman Empire, pursuing a policy that inspired Adolf Hitler to his own nightmare excesses, forcibly deported its minority population of Armenians. At least 600,000 of them died during the violent purges, while as many more were permanently exiled from their ancient homeland. Even in the final quarter of the century, Pol Pot's fanatical Khmer Rouge demonstrated in Cambodia that the prospect of a human *tabula rasa* has never lost its hideous appeal. As many as 2,000,000 of the country's inhabitants perished in just five years as a result of disease, starvation and outright massacre. Similarly in Central Asia, more than 1,000,000 Tibetans are believed to have died and continue to die under Chinese occupation (and this is only a fraction of the 32–64,000,000 dead credited to the communist regime between 1949 and 1971).[2]

In Africa since Europe's decolonisation, military conflict, often inter-tribal in character, has brought almost perennial catastrophe to some part of the continent. During the Nigerian civil war of the late 1960s, the developed world was stunned by its first television pictures of African children starving helplessly to death in the self-styled republic of Biafra. The total number of victims from the conflict and its resulting famine may have been as many as a million.[3] Yet thirty years later, Western countries have become almost habituated to the imagery of African disaster. Typically, in the massive, multi-ethnic state of Sudan, the forty-year-old civil war, despite involving more casualties than Biafra – an estimated 1.3 million dead – and the displacement of many more millions, has continued almost unnoticed by the outside world.[4]

Not so the Rwandan massacres of 1994, which emphasises how far popular perception of these horrors can be almost a question of chance or fashion. Yet even the inter-ethnic strife between the Tutsis and Hutus, in both Rwanda and the neighbouring state of Burundi, has a history of mass slaughter stretching back over three decades that has been more or less unreported.

These episodes of violence – and there are others, like the Indonesian atrocities in East Timor and Irian Jaya – put into perspective any European crimes against tribal society. They crowd the dock with a welter of other offenders. They demonstrate that former tribal peoples, once incorporated into the modern nation state and equipped with the latest weapons technology, can just as easily inflict mass slaughter on each other and even on their own. Although in Rwanda and Zaire the only technology required for genocide, once unleashed by modern methods of political propaganda, was a two-dollar machete.

There is also an additional complication with over-emphasising Europe's exclusive guilt: it perpetuates a one-dimensional image of tribal peoples as helpless victims – innocent and sympathetic, but also weak, passive and incompetent. What David Stannard has written of pre-Columbian America could be extended to all tribal societies: 'the very plain fact is that the many tens of millions of people who lived in the Americas prior to 1492 were human – neither subhuman, nor superhuman – just human.'[5] When pre-industrial tribes responded to the threat of European encroachment they invariably demonstrated that they were also creative, determined and courageous human beings.

If the last two in the quartet of portraits presented here show anything, they reveal the severe difficulties in Europe's march towards victory.

The Apaches resisted white intrusion for 300 years and were only finally defeated after a quarter-century of concerted warfare with US forces and the expenditure of many millions of dollars. In the conflict for South West Africa, the Herero and Nama campaigns endured for longer than the struggle of Dutch colonists against the British in the neighbouring Boer War.

Yet, equally, if the Apaches are to be liberated from the one-dimensional image of the innocent victim, then we must accept all that this entails. If we are to recognise the military brilliance of Victorio or the granitic resolve of Nana, we need also to acknowledge Apache excesses, which were both abominable and militarily pointless. We must take account of incidents like the death of George Taylor, a 21-year-old Scotsman, out walking to see a friend one spring evening in 1873. An Apache band captured him unarmed and took him to a sheltered spot where they stripped him, tied his limbs, and started firing with their bows. Taking care not to hit a vital spot they eventually shot over 150 arrows into his body. When the army found him, the grass was flattened where he had rolled over and over in agony. As he did so the arrow shafts broke off, leaving the heads buried deep within his flesh. Loss of blood eventually caused him to lapse into unconsciousness when the Apaches finished him off, probably by castration. The US officer recording his death thought the method too 'beastly' to disclose.[6]

The fact is that tribal peoples were often capable of methods just as brutal as those inflicted upon them by their European conquerors. The classic examples were the Mexica. Their own use of ruthless force in campaigns against their tribal subjects was well recorded and left Tenochtitlan in hated isolation when Cortés broke in amongst them. In North America the 'Civilised Tribes' like the Cherokee, Chickasaw and Choctaw were perfectly happy during the early part of the nineteenth century to borrow the institution of black slavery from their European neighbours, along with other elements of white civilisation. Similarly, the Iroquois, while their democratic political arrangements would serve as an inspiration for those of the fledgling American state, were another tribe equally content to adopt the white man's gifts and use them against their Indian rivals. During the eighteenth century they maintained their dominance in the American fur trade with European firearms and participated in the military devastation of the Huron and Illinois, who lacked the new weapons.

As we have already noted, these rivalries, wherever they occurred –

Mexica versus Tlaxcalans, Tonto Apaches versus Chiricahua Apaches, Nama versus Herero – were critical to the European triumph. On the lower horizon visible to many tribal people their ancient enmities loomed larger than the relatively new threat from whites. If they were heroic and creative agents in their own defence, they were often equally resourceful participants in their neighbour's downfall. Their repeated failure to reconcile inter-tribal political differences and to harmonise access to economic resources are almost as constant factors in their defeat as European numerical and armed supremacy.

There is further evidence of which we need to take account in presenting Europe's defence. One inescapable fact in Mexico was the regular offering of human life to the American gods. No matter what degree of detachment we might bring to the practice, it is hard to conceive of it as an adornment to any human society. It is equally and indubitably true that the Tupinamba and Tupinikin tribes of coastal Brazil regularly ate each other following capture in battle. The Caribs of the Antilles were also anthropophagous, and gave their name to the habit's more usual label – 'cannibalism'. Inhabitants of the Belgian Congo in the late nineteenth century could live out to the letter Europe's savage stereotype for them. In one famous incident a British explorer unwittingly paid for a demonstration of cannibalism. At a price of six cotton handkerchiefs some members of the Wacusu tribe happily brought forward a victim, a ten-year-old girl, dispatched, dismembered and washed the flesh ready for the table, all in a matter of seconds.[7]

This type of behaviour shattered critical European taboos. It justified Western conquest and emphasised the higher code of their own Christian culture. The religion of the colonists propounded a set of core values which placed at the heart of human relations a number of unassailable ideals. Following the violence of their conquests, and however much coercion may have been used in the process of dissemination, these values and beliefs were spread and took root amongst many of the subjected tribal peoples. And it is difficult not to see the transplanted ideals of Christianity as an advance on a religion that relied on gouging out the hearts of sacrificial victims with obsidian blades. These ideals were part of the Europeans' understanding of themselves and of their great gift to the tribal world.

The problem was that across four continents, European colonists used their civilisation as a powerful shield for their actions. The conquistadors behaved as if *they* were representatives of the essential values preserved at Europe's heart, in its places of scholarship, in its centres of spiritual, cultural and artistic achievement. Yet at the imperial periphery – in Peru or in Mexico, or on the Amazon, or the Congo, or the Australian outback, or on the fringes of the Omaheke, or in the deserts and sierras of the American Southwest – this sense of superiority could amount to little more than a capacity to exert the European will through more advanced weaponry. It was often technology without moral guidance, power without responsibility. Sometimes the sum of Europe's greater achievement was the opportunity to treat tribal societies as animals without masters, or as a worthless species to be eliminated like vermin.

The Europeans' higher technology was much more than simply the physical means of their conquest. It shaped their intellectual and moral world, informing their comparative understanding of society and reassuring them how far they had advanced over their tribal subjects. In fact technological achievement coloured Europe's entire perception of what it meant to be human.

Technological and cultural progress was seen as a measure of the distance between man and his simian origins. It separated him from the apes of the forest. It was his triumph over the limitations of nature and time, and carried implications of moral and spiritual improvement. And in almost every source of imagery in the Western canon these abstract notions of cultural progress were expressed in the language of physical, linear movement. (The very word itself, *progress*, exemplifies that conflation of moral and physical advance.) European society was perceived as being on a journey away from its primitive past, towards a more enlightened future.

Imperialism, that great outward thrust upon the geographical world, was naturally incorporated into this cluster of ideas. For the participants, their physical expansion over the globe assumed moral and cultural qualities. It was itself an indicator of Europe's forward momentum. Conquest was progress. And it was a positive self-image that embraced even its darkest manifestations, like the search for El Dorado. This myth resulted in some of the worst excesses in Europe's colonial record, yet it was seen in its day – and continues to be treated – as a noble quest, whose main moral lesson was the heroic effort and example of the doomed European explorers, rather than the iniquities they committed in its name.

Europe's ingrained perception of human culture as a linear development had deeply sinister implications for those who seemed not to be making the same progressive journey. For tribal societies were invariably orientated towards a different set of goals. In their religious myths and beliefs, the principal journey undertaken by humans was circular in nature. The tribe and its ancestors were often held in a permanent, ongoing cyclical relationship with the earth and the totality of other life forms.

A classic indicator of this cyclical orientation was the calendar system of the pre-Columbian Maya. These Central American people were mesmerised both by time's operation and by its measurement, and in their long history had evolved three forms of calendar. By the time of Pedro de Alvarado's bloody campaign of subjugation in the 1520s the Maya employed a system involving a cycle of *katuns*, a span of 260 years that broke down into thirteen twenty-year periods. These complex arrangements offered a compelling insight into Mayan scientific attainment. At the moment of Spanish conquest, for instance, they could calculate the solar year more accurately than the invaders and could 'measure time precisely over millions, even billions of years'.[8] Yet it also expressed their view of time as a recurrent phenomenon. As the great stretches of time unfolded, the Maya believed that the events of the past would eventually return in the future. In fact, their preoccupation with time's mysteries was an index of their entire cultural and spiritual development. Small wonder that when they attempted to express the meaning of Europe's ruthless destruction of their world, they characterised it as time gone mad.[9]

The Spaniards, if they were ever aware of Mayan attitudes at all, were indifferent to the circular dynamic in their beliefs, viewing their society instead as physically and spiritually static. A major element in the European onslaught upon Mayan society was a violent desecration of their art, literature and scientific records. This myopic bigotry was replicated worldwide. As we have seen in Australia, white colonial officials even in this century believed the Aborigines had failed to achieve full humanity.[10] The black savages were locked within a developmental sump, incapable of progress. In the case of the Mexica, matters were, if anything, even worse, since they had moved into the channels of human development, but were not destined for the forward spiritual journey made by Europeans. They were headed backwards – a declension into the bloody pools of corruption left by their ghastly sacrifices.

The challenge perceived by Europeans once conquest was achieved was to erase these false notions and inculcate that forward-looking, linear and progressive mentality enjoyed by themselves. Hard labour was seen as the paramount remedy, and had the added advantage of wringing profit from the defective subjects. In fact economic exploitation was usually the real goal of putting tribal people to work, but its vaunted ideological purpose was to implant that rational, goal-oriented, acquisitive mindset by which European humanity functioned. This rationalisation was perfectly expressed by William Prescott in his description of the Spanish holocaust on Hispaniola:

> The Indians would not labour without compulsion, and . . . unless they laboured, they could not be brought into communication with the whites, nor be converted to Christianity . . . The simple people, accustomed all their days to a life of indolence and ease, sunk under the oppressions of their masters, and the population wasted away with even more frightful rapidity than did the aborigines of our own country, under the operation of other causes.[11]

Gone from this description is the Auschwitz-like inhumanity of Spanish methods. Instead, the Arawaks' inability to work is characterised almost as a failure to assume full human characteristics. They simply could not be lured from their idle stasis. Here, in nineteenth-century form, is a justification of the Nazi slogan, *Arbeit macht frei*.

Yet, if tribal people could not be given access to the colonists' superior mindset through work, if, in short, they showed resistance, politically, militarily or ideologically, to European subjugation, then the gap between their respective material cultures served as a justification for colonial methods. Gustav Frenssen, in his war novel *Peter Moor's Journey to South West Africa*, articulated this attitude with a compelling accuracy and insight that seems almost outside the author's own intention. Speaking of the Herero, one of his German characters announces: 'These blacks have deserved death before God and man, not because they have murdered two hundred farmers and have revolted against us, but because they have built no houses and dug no wells.'[12] In many parts of the European empire this was close to a universal truth. Technological inferiority equalled moral inferiority and, at times, moral worthlessness.

European peoples should acknowledge that the number of tribal peoples who died because they built no houses and dug no wells amounts to one of the great acts of human destruction, comparable to the Nazi Holocaust, or the Stalinist purges of the Soviet Union, or the mass slaughters of communist China. The exact numbers can never genuinely be known and most attempts at calculation, since they carry such weighty political implications, are quickly buried beneath the counter-claims of rival assessors.

Nevertheless, the most widely acknowledged estimates for America north of Mexico, for large parts of Central and South America, especially the Mexican and Incan empires, for Australia and New Zealand indicate population losses of between eighty and ninety per cent. Although even these calculations, it should also be stressed, are regularly and spectacularly ignored. While David Stannard argues that 'few informed scholars any longer contend that' there were not roughly 8,000,000 to 12,000,000 people living in pre-Columbian America north of Mexico, Sir Martin Gilbert, one of Britain's most celebrated historians, feels free to do so. In *The Routledge Atlas of American History* he uses a figure of 'approximately one million Indians'. To put this figure in context, it represents a human population density for North America at the end of the fifteenth century that is less than twice that for modern-day Greenland, a country which is mainly covered by polar icecap, in parts over 4,000 metres thick, and which is ninety-five per cent uninhabitable.[13] Here, in microcosm and in its most apparently innocent but pernicious form, is Europe's denial of tribal history and tribal achievement.

Another of the facts that few would dispute is that while most of the deaths may have been inflicted by the original inhabitants of Europe, these particular genocidal Europeans were microbial. Tribal losses throughout the world were significantly or mainly caused by European disease, to which the colonised tribes had almost no immunity. Even the common cold could have a devastating impact. In the Americas, however, indigenous populations were swept by successive epidemics of real killers, such as smallpox, measles, tuberculosis, influenza, malaria, typhoid, sometimes even before the physical arrival of the colonists themselves, as in Inca Peru.

Yet while it is beyond dispute that disease was the primary agent in the demographic collapse, and while the role of European colonists in this process was usually inadvertent (but not always: the disease-impregnated blanket sometimes became one more potent weapon in the West's armoury), it is equally indisputable that these consequences marched in tune with European wishes. Colonists wanted the land and resources previously owned by its indigenous inhabitants. Disease wrought havoc on indigenous America's capacity to resist the *conquistadores*. In the Inca empire it undermined political stability. In Mexico it cut swathes through the nation's military classes. In Australia the advancing colonists found that their invisible pathogens had cleared out the Aborigines as effectively as a bush fire might rid the land of vermin. Even where disease decimated those people of some use to the ruling Europeans – like the Andean labourers slaving in Potosi, who should at least have held the status of economic assets – the colonists showed a flagrant disregard for the human dimension to the tragedy. Typically, the Spaniards in Peru overcame the inconvenience of disease and its consequent labour losses by placing the same demands on an ever-shrinking pool of Inca survivors.[14]

Sometimes Europeans welcomed disease as a God-given blessing. It proved the savage's worthlessness. It demonstrated that his ultimate fate was extinction, as it reaffirmed the white man in his right to rule. Yet while disease might have served then as a symbol of European supremacy, it cannot serve now as an alibi proving European innocence.

Another recurrent theme often used to diminish any European sense of responsibility is that violent abuse of tribal subjects was behaviour confined to an age of cruder moral standards and now long since abandoned. One of the problems for the Tasmanian Aborigines, argued Clive Turnbull, was the fact that Van Diemen's Land 'was settled in the early part of the nineteenth century, before the humanitarian movement had gathered momentum.'[15] Yet, as this book's four portraits demonstrate, Europeans from the sixteenth to the twentieth century could behave towards tribal society – and then justify that treatment – in an almost identical fashion.

Nor should anyone cherish the notion that the present age is any exception to the pattern of the last half-millennium. Today tribal societies continue to experience the kinds of persecution they endured hundreds of years ago. Sometimes the communities suffering are descendants of the very same people whose lives were devastated by the original European conquerors. In Guatemala, for example, 470 years after Pedro de Alvarado first raised his sword to begin his assault on its people and culture, the Maya continue to endure his legacy of Spanish persecution. These indigenous people, who represent fifty to eighty per cent of the country's current population, still use their ancestral languages, wear their traditional costumes, celebrate ancient deities and abide by the original Mayan calendar. And for many of them life is still a weary struggle against European prejudice. The life expectancy of the Maya is currently seventeen years less than their Ladino neighbours (those of mixed and Spanish descent). In the early 1980s two-thirds of all Maya lived in poverty. By 1987 the same proportion lived in extreme poverty, while the overall figure for those in poverty had risen to eighty-three per cent. A report compiled in 1979 showed that of all the countries in Latin America, Guatemala had the worst land distribution record, with ninety-eight per cent of the Mayan population either landless or with insufficient land to support themselves.[16]

An insurgent movement, largely drawn from and supported by rural Maya communities, gathered momentum in the late 1970s in response to the inequalities in Guatemalan society. To counter this indigenous unrest, a Ladino military dictatorship seized power in 1978 and instituted policies that eventually resulted in a state of virtual civil war. Most notorious was a system of death squads, secret paramilitary units which roamed the countryside seizing and murdering Mayan people presumed to be sympathetic to the guerrillas. The number of those assassinated since 1980 was put at 50,000, while those displaced from the largely Mayan highland region of Guatemala at the height of the violence were estimated at over 1,000,000.[17]

In other parts of Latin America the same pattern of discrimination and abuse is widely replicated. In Venezuela, of the country's 315,000 Indians, only one per cent have legally binding title to their forest lands. And even these deeds are flagrantly ignored. Typically, a tribe of 850 members called the Kari'na of Monagas state was declared 'extinct' by a municipal council which wished to sell their land to oil and cattle-ranching interests. Another tribe, the Yukpa, who wished to establish legal title to their own lands, were ruled by the presiding judge to have no rights even to a lawyer's services in the case. In the state of Estado Bolivar, the Indians have been forbidden to engage in small-scale mining operations on the grounds that they would pollute water supplies, yet over sixty foreign companies have been granted concessions and operate with impunity in the same area.[18]

In Brazil the persecution of Amazonia's indigenous communities has become virtually a metaphor for all tribal suffering. And with good reason: in the early part of this century eighty-seven different Indian groups were wiped out during contact with the colonial frontier.[19] Although today some tribes have become the focus of high-profile campaigns, such as the establishment of a 160,000-square-kilometre park for the Yanomami in both Brazil and Venezuela, there are still major threats to indigenous Indians and their ancestral forests. Thus, in January 1996 the Brazilian government passed decree 1775, which permits a legal challenge to the status of any Indian reserve, even those based on agreements that are hundreds of years old. So far it is thought that logging, cattle-ranching and mining companies have registered nearly 2,000 claims on over eighty indigenous areas.[20]

In North America the same dual process continues. On the one hand, there has been a heart-searching re-evaluation by some white Americans of their historic impact upon the continent's first inhabitants, coupled with a material improvement in the lives of some Native American communities. The legal entitlement, for example, of many tribes to have casinos on their reservation lands has led to Indian-run gambling operations worth $5.4 billion in 1992, which represents one in every fifty dollars wagered in the US.[21] Yet this new source of revenue, largely launched after the Indian Gaming and Regulatory Act of 1988, has to be laid alongside less favourable statistics. In 1990 Native Americans as a whole had the highest levels of poverty and unemployment of any ethnic or social group in the US.[22]

Even the most positive developments in white–tribal relations carry within them elements of an older, more confrontational and exploitative ethos. The Hollywood film *Dances With Wolves* classically illustrates this complex of issues. In 1990 Kevin Costner's epic Western, about a nineteenth-century US officer and his unfolding relationship with a group of Lakota Sioux, was an enormous critical success that won seven Oscars. Part of its popularity, in addition to its leading star's Hollywood appeal, lay in the highly sensitive and sympathetic portrayal of Indian culture, especially the philosophical and spiritual dimensions to the Lakota's hunter-gatherer lifestyle. The film was also a major box-office hit, making over $500,000,000, while Costner himself was believed to have netted $50,000,000. Yet the heroes of the piece, the Lakota Sioux, remain grindingly poor. Their reservations include seven of the country's most impoverished thirty-two counties, and Shannon county on the Pine Ridge reservation is the very poorest in all the United States.

An even more acute irony was the fact that Costner sought to cap his movie profits by developing a multi-million-dollar luxury resort on lands bought from the Lakota, and named after his character from the film, John Dunbar. An element in this development was an attempted purchase of part of the Black Hills, which are lands sacred to the Lakota and the subject of the tribe's ongoing legal battle for compensation and territorial restitution after the US government seized them in 1877. (The Black Hills, one of the richest mineral areas in the world, with enormous deposits of gold, silver, copper, iron, tungsten, coal, graphite, lithia, mica, tantalite, beryl, caesium, andalucite, sulphur, quartz, topaz, zircon and uranium, have already yielded $250 billion in gold alone, of which the Indians have received not a single penny.) Costner's efforts to acquire and build a golf course on ground hallowed by the Lakota and still considered their own is viewed by some in the tribe as an act of gross betrayal.[23]

Yet *Dances With Wolves* and the story surrounding it also contains a number of more positive elements. Not least is the fact that the Lakota Sioux have maintained a legal battle for the return of the Black Hills for over a century, demonstrating an unshakable belief in the justice of their case and typifying the wider endurance of tribal resistance and culture almost worldwide. The Lakota use of American legal procedures, despite decades of official obstruction, also illustrates a capacity to master aspects of the dominant culture and to turn them to their benefit. The Lakota, for example, have been offered a compensation settlement of $400,000,000 for the loss of their 7.3 million acres.[24]

Notwithstanding Costner's later business project, his film *Dances With Wolves* was itself an attempt from the other side to make a positive adjustment in white–tribal relations. It exposed the moral ambiguities of American colonial politics and reversed a number of classic military stereotypes that had been previously ingrained in the Hollywood Western. Here, the part of the mindless savage was taken not by the painted Redskin, but by marauding US soldiers who scalped and butchered their Lakota victims. If only in cinematic terms, history was rewritten, and that alone contained a seed of genuine hope in the white–tribal conflict.

For the events of this history, even those most distant in time, are not an inert tale without consequence. They should not be ignored or – as has more usually happened – buried under a welter of self-serving distortion. Over five centuries Europeans, armed with a set of invincible stereotypes, devoured tribal society across four continents. The image of the bestial and pitiless savage which licensed this onslaught was never more a portrait of the Mexica, or the Inca, or the Nama, the Herero, the Tasmanians, or even the tigers of humankind, the Apache, than it was an image of Europe's own destructive capacity. It is a prevailing irony of this story that as the tide of European conquest engulfed tribal peoples, so the colonists' civilisation succumbed to a savage whom they had so violently condemned. But the savage was within themselves. To continue to deny this truth will only ensure that the past remains a dark and fatal shadow in the present and for the future.

Select Bibliography

General

Blackburn, J., *The White Men: The first response of aboriginal peoples to the white man*, London, 1979.

Braudel, F., *Civilisation and Capitalism: 15th–18th Century*, Volumes I–III, London, 1984.

Braudel, F., *The Mediterranean*, London, 1992.

Braudel, F., *A History of Civilizations*, London, 1994.

Bridges, L., *The Uttermost Part of the Earth*, London, 1987.

Calder, A., *Revolutionary Empire: The Rise of the English-Speaking Empires from the Fifteenth Century to the 1780s*, London, 1981.

Erasmus, D., *Praise of Folly*, London, 1993.

Fogel, R.W., *Without Consent or Contract: The Rise and Fall of American Slavery*, London, 1989.

Fromm, E., *The Anatomy of Human Destructiveness*, London, 1977.

Greenblatt, S., *Marvelous Possessions: The Wonder of the New World*, Oxford, 1992.

Hobbes, T., *Leviathan*, London, 1985.

Hulme, P. and Whitehead, N., *Wild Majesty: Encounters with Caribs from Columbus to the Present Day*, Oxford, 1992.

Leakey, R., *The Making of Mankind*, London, 1981.

Locke, J., *Political Writings*, London, 1993.

More, T., *Utopia*, London, 1992.

Nisbet, R., *The History of the Idea of Progress*, London, 1980.

Rousseau, J.J., *A Discourse on Inequality*, London, 1984.

Walvin, J., *Black Ivory: A History of British Slavery*, London, 1992.

371

The Conquest of Mexico

Arzans de Orsúa y Vela, B., *Tales of Potosi*, Ed. R. Padden, Providence, 1975.

Bakewell, P.J., *Silver Mining and Society in Colonial Mexico, Zacatecas 1546–1700*, Cambridge, 1971.

Bazant, J., *A Concise History of Mexico*, Cambridge, 1977.

Bethel, L., *Central America since Independence*, Cambridge, 1991.

Blanco, H., *Land or Death: The Peasant Struggle in Peru*, London, 1972.

Cieza de Léon, P. de *The Incas of Pedro de Cieza de Léon*, Norman, 1959.

Clendinnen, I., *Aztecs*, Cambridge, 1993.

Collis, M., *Cortés and Montezuma*, London, 1994.

Cook, N.D., *Demographic Collapse, Indian Peru, 1520–1620*, Cambridge, 1981.

Cortés, H., *Letters of Hernando Cortés, 1519–1526*, Tr. J. Bayard Morris, London, 1928.

Diaz, B., *The Conquest of New Spain*, Tr. J. M. Cohen, London, 1963.

Elliott, J.H., *Imperial Spain 1469–1716*, London, 1970.

Fernández-Armesto, F., *Columbus*, Oxford, 1991.

Friede, J. and Keen, B. (eds.), *Bartolomé de Las Casas in History*, DeKalb, 1971.

Gibson, C., *The Aztecs under Spanish Rule*, Stanford, 1964.

Hamilton, E.J., *American Treasure and the Price Rise Revolution in Spain*, Cambridge, Mass., 1934.

Hanke, L., *The Imperial City of Potosí*, The Hague, 1956.

Hassig, R., *Mexico and the Spanish Conquest*, London, 1994.

Hemming, J., *The Conquest of the Incas*, London, 1970.

Hemming, J., *The Search for El Dorado*, London, 1978.

Hemming, J., *Red Gold: The Conquest of the Brazilian Indians*, London, 1978.

Hyams, E. and Ordish, G., *The Last Of The Incas*, London, 1963.

Innes, H., *The Conquistadors*, London, 1969.

Las Casas, B. de, *A Short Account of the Destruction of the Indies*, London, 1992.

Litvinoff, B., *Fourteen Ninety-Two: The Year and the Era*, London, 1991.

Manchester, W., *A World Lit Only By Fire: The Medieval Mind and the Renaissance*, London, 1993.

Means, P. A., *Fall of the Inca Empire and the Spanish Rule in Peru*

1530–1780, New York, 1971.

Naipaul, V.S., *The Loss of El Dorado*, London, 1969.

Sahagún, B. de, *Florentine Codex (General History of the Things of New Spain), Book 12*, Tr. A.J.O. Anderson and C.E. Dibble, Utah, 1975.

Prescott, W.H., *The Conquest of Mexico*, London, 1965.

Salmoral, M.L., *America 1492: Portrait of a Continent 500 Years Ago*, Oxford, 1990.

Simpson, L.B., *The Encomienda in New Spain*, Berkeley, 1966.

Soustelle, J., *The Daily Life of the Aztecs: On the Eve of the Spanish Conquest*, London, 1961.

Stannard, D.E., *American Holocaust: The Conquest of the New World*, Oxford, 1992.

Stern, S.J., *Peru's Indian Peoples and the Challenge of Spanish Conquest: Huamanga to 1640*, Madison, 1993.

Thomas, H., *The Conquest of Mexico*, London, 1993.

Todorov, T., *The Conquest of America*, New York, 1984.

Townsend, R.F., *The Aztecs*, London, 1992.

Vaillant, G.C., *The Aztecs of Mexico*, London, 1950.

von Hagen, V.W., *The Ancient Sun Kingdoms of the Americas*, London, 1962.

von Hagen, V.W., *The Golden Man: The Quest for El Dorado*, Farnborough, 1974.

Wachtel, N., *The Vision of the Vanquished: The Spanish Conquest of Peru through Indian Eyes 1530–1570*, Hassocks, 1977.

Whitaker, A.P., *The Huancavelica Mercury Mine*, Cambridge, Mass., 1941.

White, J.M., *Cortés and the Downfall of the Aztec Empire: A Study in a Conflict of Cultures*, London, 1971.

Wright, R., *Stolen Continents: The Indian Story*, London, 1992.

The British In Tasmania

Bates, D., *The Passing of the Aborigines*, London, 1938.

Bonwick, J., *Daily Life and the Origin of the Tasmanians*, London, 1870.

British Parliamentary Papers: Correspondence and Papers Relating to the Government and the Affairs of the Australian Colonies, 1830–1836, Dublin, 1970.

Calder, J.E., *The Native Tribes of Tasmania*, Hobart, 1972.

Carter, P., *The Road to Botany Bay*, London, 1987.

Clark, M., *A History of Australia*, Ed. Michael Cathcart, London, 1993.

Davies, D., *The Last of the Tasmanians*, London, 1973.

Giblin, R.W., *The Early History of Tasmania, 1642–1804*, London, 1928.

Harris, S., *It's Coming Yet . . . An Aboriginal Treaty Within Australia Between Australians*, Canberra, 1979.

Hughes, R., *The Fatal Shore*, London, 1987.

Livingston, W.S. and Louis, W.R. (eds.), *Australia, New Zealand and the Pacific Islands since the First World War*, Austin, 1979.

Moorehead, A., *The Fatal Impact*, London, 1966.

Morris, J., *Heaven's Command: An Imperial Progress*, London, 1973.

Plomley, N.J.B., *Friendly Mission: The Tasmanian Journal and Papers of George Augustus Robinson, 1829–1834*, Hobart, 1966.

Reece, R.H.W., *Aborigines and Colonists: Aborigines and Colonial Society in New South Wales in the 1830s and 1840s*, Sydney, 1974.

Reynolds, H., *The Other Side of the Frontier: Aboriginal Resistance to the European Invasion of Australia*, London, 1982.

Robson, L., *A History of Tasmania. Vol. I*, Oxford, 1983.

Ryan, L., *The Aboriginal Tasmanians*, St Lucia, 1981.

Sutton, P. (ed.), *Dreamings: The Art of Aboriginal Australia*, Victoria, 1988.

Travers, R., *The Tasmanians: The Story of a Doomed Race*, Melbourne, 1968.

Turnbull, C., *Black War*, London, 1948.

Walker, J.B., *Early Tasmania*, Hobart, 1914.

The Dispossession of the Apache

Adams, A.B., *Geronimo: An Illustrated Biography*, New York, 1971.

Ball, E., *In the Days of Victorio*, London, 1973.

Ball, E., *Indeh: An Apache Odyssey*, Utah, 1980.

Barrett, S.M. (ed.), *Geronimo: His Own Story*, London, 1970.

Betzinez, J. (with W.S. Nye), *I Fought With Geronimo*, Lincoln, 1987.

Bolt, C., *American Indian Policy and American Reform*, London, 1987.

Bourke, J.G., *On the Border with Crook*, Chicago, 1962.

Bourke, J.G., *An Apache Campaign in the Sierra Madre*, New York, 1958.

Brill, C., *Conquest of the Southern Plains*, Oklahoma City, 1938.

Brogan, H., *Longman History of the United States of America*, London, 1985.

Brown, D., *Bury My Heart at Wounded Knee*, London, 1975.

Cremony, J.C., *Life Among the Apaches*, New York, 1991.

Clum, W., *Apache Agent: The Story of John P. Clum*, Boston, 1936.

Conner, D.E., *Joseph Reddeford Walker and the Arizona Adventure*, Norman, 1956.

Crook, G., *General George Crook: His Autobiography*, Ed. M.F. Schmitt, Norman, 1946.

Davis, B., *The Truth About Geronimo*, New Haven, 1929.

Debo, A., *Geronimo: The Man, His Time, His Place*, London, 1993.

Drinnon, R., *Facing West: The Metaphysics of Indian-Hating and Empire Building*, Minneapolis, 1980.

Falk, O., *The Geronimo Campaign*, New York, 1969.

Horsman, R., *Race and Manifest Destiny: The Origins of American Racial Anglo-Saxonism*, Cambridge, Mass., 1981.

Jacobs, W., *Dispossessing the American Indian*, New York, 1972.

Jahoda, G., *The Trail of Tears: The American Indian Removals 1831–1855*, London, 1976.

Josephy, A.M. Jr, *Now That the Buffalo's Gone: A Study of Today's American Indians*, Norman, 1984.

Josephy, A.M. Jr, *500 Nations: An Illustrated History of North American Indians*, London, 1995.

Kelly, L.C., *The Assault on Assimilation: John Collier and the Origins of Indian Policy Reform*, Albuquerque, 1983.

Lockwood, F., *The Apache Indians*, Lincoln, 1987.

Matthiessen, P., *In the Spirit of Crazy Horse*, London, 1992.

Milner II, C.A., O'Connor, C.A., and Sandweiss, M.A. (eds.), *The Oxford History of the American West*, Oxford, 1994.

Opler, M.E., *An Apache Life-Way: the economic, social, and religious institutions of the Chiricahua Indians*, New York, 1965.

Opler, M.E., *Apache Odyssey: A Journey between Two Worlds*, New York, 1969.

Porter, J.C., *Paper Medicine Man: John Gregory Bourke and His American West*, Norman, 1986.

Roberts, D., *Once They Moved Like the Wind: Cochise, Geronimo and the Apache Wars*, New York, 1993.

Slotkin, R., *Regeneration Through Violence: The Mythology of the American Frontier, 1600–1860*, Middletown, 1973.

Thrapp, D.L., *Conquest of Apacheria*, Norman, 1967.

Thrapp, D.L., *Victorio and the Mimbres Apache*, Norman, 1974.

Trimble, S., *The People: Indians of the American Southwest*, Santa Fe, 1993.

Unruh, J.D., *The Plains Across: Emigrants, Wagon Trains and the*

American West, London, 1992.

Watts, T.D. and Wright R. Jr, (eds.), *Alcoholism in Minority Populations*, Springfield, 1989.

The Germans in South West Africa

Adu Boahen, A. (ed.), *General History of Africa VII: African under Colonial Domination 1880–1935*, London, 1985.

Andersson, C.J., *Lake Ngami*, Cape Town, 1967.

Bley, H., *South-West Africa under German Rule 1894–1914*, Evanston, 1971.

Bridgman, J.M., *The Revolt of the Herero*, Berkeley, 1981.

Calvert, A.F., *South West Africa during the German Occupation 1884–1914*, London, 1915.

Calvert, A.F., *German African Empire*, London, 1916.

Cline, C.E.D., *E.D. Morel 1873–1924: The Strategies of Protest*, Belfast, 1980.

Davidson, B., *Africa in History*, London, 1992.

Drechsler, H., *Let Us Die Fighting: The Struggle of the Herero and Nama against German Imperialism (1884–1915)*, London, 1980.

First, R., *South West Africa*, London, 1963.

Frieslich, R., *The Last Tribal War: A History of the Bondelswart Uprising Which Took Place in South West Africa in 1922*, Cape Town, 1964.

Frenssen, G., *Peter Moor's Journey to South West Africa*, Boston, 1908.

Gann, L.H. and Duignan, P., *The Rulers of German Africa, 1887–1914*, Stanford, 1977.

Gifford, P. and Louis, W.R., *Britain and Germany in Africa: Imperial Rivalry and Colonial Rule*, London, 1967.

Emerson, B., *Leopold II of the Belgians: King of Colonialism*, London, 1979.

Goldblatt, I., *History of South West Africa*, Cape Town, 1971.

Gorges, E.H.M., *Report on the Natives of South-West Africa and Their Treatment by Germany*, London, 1918.

Hahn, C.H.L., Vedder, H. and Fourie, L., *The Native Tribes of South West Africa*, London, 1966.

Henderson, W.O., *Studies in German Colonial History*, London, 1962.

Kibodya, G. (ed.), *Aspects of South African History*, Dar es Salaam, 1968.

Mostert, N., *Frontiers: The Epic of South Africa's Creation and the Tragedy of the Xhosa People*, London, 1992.

Select Bibliography

Ogot, B., *Zamani: A Survey of East African History*, Nairobi, 1974.

Pakenham, T., *The Scramble for Africa*, London, 1991.

Pool, G., *Samuel Maharero*, Windhoek, 1991.

Steer, G.L., *Judgement on German Africa*, London, 1939.

Taylor, A.J.P., *Germany's First Bid for Colonies*, London, 1938.

Townsend, M., *The Rise and Fall of Germany's Colonial Empire*, New York, 1966.

Troup, F., *In Face of Fear: Michael Scott's Challenge to South Africa*, London, 1950.

Vedder, H., *South West Africa in Early Times*, London, 1966.

Wellington, J., *South West Africa and Its Human Issues*, Oxford, 1967.

Notes

Introduction: All Christendom will here have refreshment and gain

1. Drechsler, *Let Us Die Fighting*, p. 70.
2. Gorges, *Report on the Natives of South-West Africa*, pp. 26–7.
3. Drechsler, *Let Us Die Fighting*, pp. 70–71.
4. Gorges, *Report on the Natives of South-West Africa*, p. 27.
5. Drechsler, *Let Us Die Fighting*, p. 71.
6. Stannard, *American Holocaust*, pp. 266–8.
7. Walvin, *Black Ivory*, pp. 36–7, 317–18.
8. Pakenham, *The Scramble for Africa*, p. 622; Gorges, *Report on the Natives of South-West Africa*, p. 35; Adu Boahen, *General History of Africa VII*, pp. 475–6.
9. Suter and Stearman, *Aboriginal Australians*, Minority Rights Group Report, No. 35, p. 4; Macdonald, *The Maori of Aotearoa-New Zealand*, Minority Rights Group Report, No. 70, p. 5; Moorehead, *The Fatal Impact*, p. 88.
10. See Stannard, *American Holocaust*, p. 72, for the higher estimate, and Thomas, *The Conquest of Mexico*, p. 67, for the lower.
11. Hulme and Whitehead, *Wild Majesty*, p. 12.
12. Hulme and Whitehead, *Wild Majesty*, p. 13.
13. Reynolds, *The Other Side of the Frontier*, p. 34.
14. Blackburn, *The White Men*, p. 101.
15. Diaz del Castillo, *The Conquest of New Spain*, p. 185.
16. Hulme and Whitehead, *Wild Majesty*, p. 10.
17. Hemming, *Red Gold*, p. 15.
18. Hemming, *Red Gold*, p. 15.

19. More, *Utopia*, p. 136.
20. More, *Utopia*, p. 79.
21. Hulme and Whitehead, *Wild Majesty*, p. 12.
22. More, *Utopia*, p. 85.
23. Harris, *It's Coming Yet*, p. 36.
24. Bley, *South-West Africa*, p. 97.
25. Hulme and Whitehead, *Wild Majesty*, p. 15.
26. de Las Casas, *A Short Account*, p. 28.
27. Mostert, *Frontiers*, pp. 107–8.
28. Mostert, *Frontiers*, p. 117.
29. Mostert, *Frontiers*, p. 108.
30. Locke, *Political Writings*, pp. 282–3.
31. Wiedemann, *Greek and Roman Slavery*, pp. 18–19.
32. Calder, *Revolutionary Empire*, p. 7.
33. Prescott, *The Conquest of Mexico*, p. 39.
34. Walvin, *Black Ivory*, p. 16.
35. Walvin, *Black Ivory*, p. 64.
36. Fogel, *Without Consent*, p. 37.
37. Wiedner, 'Forced Labor in Colonial Peru', *The Americas*, Washington DC, 16, no. 4, pp. 357–83; Hemming, *The Conquest of the Incas*, p. 372.
38. Todorov, *The Conquest of America*, p. 138.
39. Braudel, *Civilization and Capitalism*, Volume III, p. 429.
40. Bley, *South-West Africa*, p. 31.
41. Prescott, *The Conquest of Mexico*, pp. 139–40.
42. The compendia examined are the *Cambridge Encyclopedia*, the *Cambridge Fact Finder*, the *Collins Paperback Encyclopedia*, the *Encyclopaedia Britannica*, the *Guinness Encyclopedia* 1995, the *Hutchinson Encyclopedia* 1996, the *Hutchinson Unabridged Encyclopedia*, the *Macmillan Encyclopedia* 1997, the *Readers Digest Book of Facts* and the *Readers Digest Illustrated Dictionary of Essential Knowledge*. The *Enclyclopaedia Britannica* is the only one to give any data on the war in German South West Africa, suggesting the Herero population fell from 70,000 to 16,000 and that the Nama were reduced by two-fifths (volume 27, p. 871). The *Readers Digest Book of Facts* is exceptional in not having an entry for the Black Hole of Calcutta, but then nor does it have one for Calcutta itself. The two quotations on the Mexica are from the *Cambridge Encyclopedia* (p. 96) and the *Macmillan Encyclopedia* 1997 (p. 103) respectively.

Rivers of Blood, Rivers of Gold

1   The March

1. Manchester, *A World Lit Only by Fire*, p. 240.
2. Vaillant, *The Aztecs of Mexico*, p. 24.
3. Turner, *Geronimo*, p. 16.
4. White, *Cortés*, p. 64.
5. Innes, *The Conquistadors*, p. 75.
6. de Sahagún, *Florentine Codex*, p. 25.
7. de Sahagún, *Florentine Codex*, p. 19.
8. de Sahagún, *Florentine Codex*, quoted in Wright, *Stolen Continents*, p. 29.

2   The Kidnap

1. Thomas, *The Conquest of Mexico*, p. 307.
2. Soustelle, *Daily Life*, p. 244.
3. Soustelle, *Daily Life*, pp. 52–3.
4. Diaz del Castillo, *The Conquest of New Spain*, p. 199.
5. Cortés, *Letters*, p. 95.
6. Vaillant, *The Aztecs of Mexico*, p. 149.
7. Soustelle, *Daily Life*, p. 68.
8. Soustelle, *Daily Life*, p. 84.
9. Thomas, *The Conquest of Mexico*, pp. 615–17.
10. Thomas, *The Conquest of Mexico*, p. 647, note 14.
11. Thomas, *The Conquest of Mexico*, p. 188.
12. Vaillant, *The Aztecs of Mexico*, pp. 196–7.
13. There are now widely diverging opinions on the levels of sacrifice and on the specific practice of cannibalism in pre-Cortesian Mexico. Hugh Thomas, for example, suggests that sacrificed victims were regularly eaten by the Mexican nobility. See *The Conquest of Mexico*, p. 25. However, Ronald Wright and David Stannard represent the more sceptical wing of opinion, and suggest that the image of a country swimming in blood was largely an exaggeration that served the propaganda interests of the original *conquistadores*. See *Stolen Continents*, p. 25 and *American Holocaust*, pp. 79–80.
14. Soustelle, *Daily Life*, p. 99.
15. von Hagen, *The Ancient Sun Kingdoms*, p. 56.
16. Thomas, *The Conquest of Mexico*, pp. 25–6.

17. Thomas, *The Conquest of Mexico*, p. xii.
18. Stannard, *American Holocaust*, p. 80.
19. Soustelle, *Daily Life*, p. 99.
20. Wright, *Stolen Continents*, pp. 25–35.
21. Innes, *The Conquistadors*, p. 195.
22. Prescott, *The Conquest of Mexico*, Volume II, p. 283.
23. Cortés, *Letters*, p. 24.
24. Diaz del Castillo, *The Conquest of New Spain*, p. 35.
25. de Las Casas, *A Short Account*, p. 15.
26. Simpson, *Encomienda*, p. 28.
27. Cortés, *Letters*, pp. 23–33.
28. Cortés, *Letters*, p. 129.
29. Diaz del Castillo, *The Conquest of New Spain*, p. 75.
30. Diaz del Castillo, *The Conquest of New Spain*, pp. 68, 126.
31. Cortés, *Letters*, pp. 212–24.
32. Innes, *The Conquistadors*, p. 124.
33. Wright, *Stolen Continents*, p. 31.

3   *The Night of Sorrow*

1. Diaz del Castillo, *The Conquest of New Spain*, pp. 235–6.
2. Prescott, *The Conquest of Mexico*, Volume II, p. 40.
3. de Sahagún, *Florentine Codex*, p. 55.
4. Prescott, *The Conquest of Mexico*, Volume II, p. 50; also Thomas, *The Conquest of Mexico*, p. 386.
5. Thomas, *The Conquest of Mexico*, p. 391.
6. Thomas, *The Conquest of Mexico*, p. 411.
7. Prescott, *The Conquest of Mexico*, Volume II, p. 104.
8. de Sahagún, *Florentine Codex*, p. 72.
9. Thomas, *The Conquest of Mexico*, p. 411.

4   *The Siege*

1. Prescott, *The Conquest of Mexico*, Volume II, p. 286.
2. Prescott, *The Conquest of Mexico*, Volume II, p. 282.
3. For a detailed consideration of the complex subject of the Mexican population at the moment of its encounter with Europe, see Thomas, *The Conquest of Mexico*, pp. 609–14. Stannard accepts

an estimate of 25,000,000 for Mexico at the time of Columbus' first journey; see *American Holocaust*, p. 33.

4. Soustelle, *Daily Life*, p. 207.
5. Diaz del Castillo, *The Conquest of New Spain*, p. 125.
6. Vaillant, *The Aztecs of Mexico*, p. 49.
7. Braudel, *Civilization and Capitalism*, Volume I, pp. 383–8.
8. Cortés, *Letters*, p. 123.
9. Braudel, *The Mediterranean*, p. 321.
10. Diaz del Castillo, *The Conquest of New Spain*, p. 130.
11. Diaz del Castillo, *The Conquest of New Spain*, p. 187.
12. Cortés, *Letters*, p. 48.
13. Cortés, *Letters*, p. 124.
14. Cortés, *Letters*, p. 43.
15. For a detailed analysis of the military advantages enjoyed by the Europeans see Hassig, *Mexico and the Spanish Conquest*.
16. Wright, *Stolen Continents*, p. 44.
17. Cortés, *Letters*, p. 196.
18. Diaz del Castillo, *The Conquest of New Spain*, p. 346.
19. Diaz del Castillo, *The Conquest of New Spain*, p. 345.
20. Prescott, *The Conquest of Mexico*, Volume II, pp. 277–8; also Thomas, *The Conquest of Mexico*, p. 528.
21. White, *Cortés*, p. 267.

5   The Besieging

1. Branigan and Jarrett, *The Mediterranean Lands*, London, 1975, p. 201.
2. Litvinoff, *Fourteen Ninety-Two*, p. 50.
3. Elliott, *Imperial Spain*, p. 108.
4. Elliott, *Imperial Spain*, p. 13.
5. Braudel, *The Mediterranean*, pp. 321–5.
6. Braudel, *The Mediterranean*, p. 241.
7. de Las Casas, *A Short Account*, p. xxii.
8. Braudel, *The Mediterranean*, p. 280.
9. Braudel, *The Mediterranean*, p. 532.
10. Diaz del Castillo, *The Conquest of New Spain*, p. 68.
11. Cortés, *Letters*, pp. 23, 68, 80.
12. Thomas, *The Conquest of Mexico*, p. 161.
13. Diaz del Castillo, *The Conquest of New Spain*, p. 108.

14. Thomas, *The Conquest of Mexico*, p. 213.
15. Diaz del Castillo, *The Conquest of New Spain*, p. 56.
16. Todorov, *The Conquest of America*, p. 42.
17. Thomas, *The Conquest of Mexico*, p. 172.
18. Diaz del Castillo, *The Conquest of New Spain*, p. 77.
19. Wright, *Stolen Continents*, p. 19.
20. Diaz del Castillo, *The Conquest of New Spain*, pp. 31, 73, 83, 95, 182.
21. Thomas, *The Conquest of Mexico*, p. 156.
22. Todorov, *The Conquest of America*, p. 59.
23. Cortés, *Letters*, p. 53.
24. Hassig, *Mexico and the Spanish Conquest*, p. 146.
25. Cortés, *Letters*, pp. 167, 209.
26. Prescott, *The Conquest of Mexico*, Volume II, p. 365.
27. Prescott, *The Conquest of Mexico*, Volume II, p. 317.

6 Gold – The Castration of the Sun

1. Braudel, *The Mediterranean*, p. 318.
2. Braudel, *The Mediterranean*, p. 334.
3. Cortés, *Letters*, p. 95.
4. Prescott, *The Conquest of Mexico*, Volume I, p. 213.
5. Cortés, *Letters*, p. 21.
6. de Sahagún, *Florentine Codex*, p. 31.
7. Stannard, *American Holocaust*, p. 80.
8. Diaz del Castillo, *The Conquest of New Spain*, p. 349.
9. Cortés, *Letters*, p. 279.
10. Hemming, *The Conquest of the Incas*, p. 29.
11. von Hagen, *The Ancient Sun Kingdoms*, p. 248.
12. de Léon, *The Incas*, p. 138.
13. Braudel, *Civilization and Capitalism*, Volume I, p. 424.
14. von Hagen, *The Ancient Sun Kingdoms*, p. 292.
15. de Léon, *The Incas*, p. 144.
16. de Gamboa, *History of the Incas*, p. 10.
17. de Léon, *The Incas*, p. 158.
18. Means, *Fall of the Inca Empire*, p. 11.
19. Means, *Fall of the Inca Empire*, pp. 10–11.
20. Wright, *Stolen Continents*, p. 73.
21. Means, *Fall of the Inca Empire*, pp. 17, 29.

22. Hemming, *The Conquest of the Incas*, p. 43.
23. Friede and Keen (eds.), *Bartolomé de Las Casas*, p. 36.
24. von Hagen, *The Ancient Sun Kingdoms*, p. 320.
25. Hemming, *The Conquest of the Incas*, p. 81.
26. Hemming, *The Search for El Dorado*, p. 46.
27. Hemming, *The Conquest of the Incas*, p. 81.
28. de Léon, *The Incas*, p. 157.
29. Hemming, *The Search for El Dorado*, p. 56.
30. Hemming, *The Search for El Dorado*, p. 70.
31. Hemming, *The Search for El Dorado*, p. 39.
32. de Aguado, *Historia de Venezuela*, quoted in Hemming, *The Search for El Dorado*, pp. 20–21.
33. Federmann, *Historia indiana*, quoted in Hemming, *The Search for El Dorado*, p. 29.
34. Hemming, *The Search for El Dorado*, p. 107.
35. Hemming, *The Search for El Dorado*, p. 47.
36. von Hagen, *The Golden Man*, p. 283.
37. Hemming, *The Search for El Dorado*, p. 50.
38. Todorov, *The Conquest of America*, pp. 142–3.
39. von Hagen, *The Golden Man*, p. 104.
40. Hemming, *The Search for El Dorado*, p. 127.
41. Brian Inglis, *Roger Casement*, London, 1974, p. 49.
42. Inglis, *Roger Casement*, p. 74.
43. McLynn, *Stanley: The Sorcerer's Apprentice*, p. 104.
44. Hemming, *The Search for El Dorado*, p. 70.
45. Fernández-Armesto, *Columbus*, p. 139.
46. Gibson, *The Aztecs*, p. 78.
47. Gibson, *The Aztecs*, p. 78.
48. Todorov, *The Conquest of America*, p. 134.
49. Todorov, *The Conquest of America*, p. 135.
50. Hanke, *The Imperial City*, p. 1.
51. Hamilton, *American Treasure*, p. 33.
52. Hemming, *The Conquest of the Incas*, p. 370.
53. Means, *Fall of the Inca Empire*, p. 180.
54. Hemming, *The Conquest of the Incas*, pp. 369–73.
55. Stern, *Peru's Indian Peoples*, p. 85.
56. Hemming, *The Conquest of the Incas*, p. 409.
57. Hanke, *The Imperial City*, p. 19.
58. Padden, *Tales of Potosi*, p. xx.
59. Hanke, *The Imperial City*, p. 25.

60. Stannard, *American Holocaust*, p. 215.
61. Hamilton, *American Treasure*, p. 189.
62. Todorov, *The Conquest of America*, p. 133; see also Hassig, *Mexico and the Spanish Conquest*, p. 152, and Cook, *Demographic Collapse*, p. 114.
63. Friede and Keen (eds.), *Bartolomé de Las Casas*, p. 32.
64. Friede and Keen (eds.), *Bartolomé de Las Casas*, p. 13.
65. Friede and Keen (eds.), *Bartolomé de Las Casas*, p. 13.
66. Wachtel, *The Vision of the Vanquished*, p. 202.

7   The Bones of King Billy

1. Travers, *The Tasmanians*, p. 220.
2. Hughes, *The Fatal Shore*, p. 424.
3. Ryan, *The Aboriginal Tasmanians*, pp. 216–7.
4. Walvin, *Black Ivory*, p. 9.
5. Walvin, *Black Ivory*, p. 8.
6. Walvin, *Black Ivory*, p. 8; Hughes, *The Fatal Shore*, p. 40.
7. Hughes, *The Fatal Shore*, p. 77.
8. Hughes, *The Fatal Shore*, p. 72.
9. Hughes, *The Fatal Shore*, p. 83.
10. Clark, *History*, p. 15.
11. Hughes, *The Fatal Shore*, p. 100.
12. Hughes, *The Fatal Shore*, p. 102.
13. Hughes, *The Fatal Shore*, p. 414.
14. Robson, *A History of Tasmania*, Volume I, p. 46.
15. Calder, *The Native Tribes*, p. 6.
16. Travers, *The Tasmanians*, p. 89.

8   The Black Crows

1. Bonwick, *Daily Life*, p. 100.
2. Ryan, *The Aboriginal Tasmanians*, p. 214.
3. Ryan, *The Aboriginal Tasmanians*, p. 14.
4. Plomley, *Friendly Mission*, p. 62.
5. Harris, *It's Coming Yet*, p. 31.
6. Bonwick, *Daily Life*, p. 17; Travers, *The Tasmanians*, p. 22.
7. Walker, *Early Tasmania*, p. 238.

8. Ryan, *The Aboriginal Tasmanians*, p. 10.
9. Walker, *Early Tasmania*, p. 243.
10. Davies, *The Last of the Tasmanians*, pp. 233–4.
11. Calder, *The Native Tribes*, p. 54; Travers, *The Tasmanians*, p. 135.
12. Davies, *The Last of the Tasmanians*, p. 16.
13. Carter, *The Road to Botany Bay*, p. 64.
14. Travers, *The Tasmanians*, p. 117.
15. Reynolds, *The Other Side of the Frontier*, p. 71.
16. Plomley, *Friendly Mission*, p. 23.
17. Plomley, *Friendly Mission*, p. 357.
18. Robson, *A History of Tasmania*, Volume I, p. 230.
19. Robson, *A History of Tasmania*, Volume I, p. 230.
20. Robson, *A History of Tasmania*, Volume I, p. 234.
21. Ryan, *The Aboriginal Tasmanians*, p. 77.
22. Travers, *The Tasmanians*, p. 109.
23. Davies, *The Last of the Tasmanians*, pp. 62–8.
24. Davies, *The Last of the Tasmanians*, p. 62; Hughes, *The Fatal Shore*, p. 414.
25. Travers, *The Tasmanians*, p. 109.
26. Hughes, *The Fatal Shore*, p. 230.
27. Plomley, *Friendly Mission*, pp. 26–8.
28. Turnbull, *Black War*, p. 67.
29. Turnbull, *Black War*, p. 60.

9   The Black War

1. Ryan, *The Aboriginal Tasmanians*, p. 139.
2. Travers, *The Tasmanians*, p. 147.
3. Plomley, *Friendly Mission*, p. 346.
4. Plomley, *Friendly Mission*, p. 346.
5. Davies, *The Last of the Tasmanians*, p. 65.
6. Davies, *The Last of the Tasmanians*, p. 61.
7. Ryan, *The Aboriginal Tasmanians*, pp. 135–7; Plomley, *Friendly Mission*, pp. 181–2.
8. Ryan, *The Aboriginal Tasmanians*, p. 99; Calder, *The Native Tribes*, p. 23.
9. *British Parliamentary Papers*, p. 210.
10. Travers, *The Tasmanians*, p. 145.
11. Calder, *The Native Tribes*, pp. 8–13.

12. Calder, *The Native Tribes*, pp. 8–9
13. Calder, *The Native Tribes*, p. 75.
14. Reynolds, *The Other Side of the Frontier*, p. 136.
15. de Gamboa, *History of the Incas*, p. 27.
16. Travers, *The Tasmanians*, p. 149.
17. Plomley, *Friendly Mission*, p. 89
18. Ryan, *The Aboriginal Tasmanians*, p. 107.
19. Turnbull, *Black War*, p. 118.
20. Travers, *The Tasmanians*, p. 148.
21. Hughes, *The Fatal Shore*, p. 371.
22. Hughes, *The Fatal Shore*, p. 377
23. Travers, *The Tasmanians*, pp. 112–16; Turnbull, *Black War*, p. 27.
24. Ryan, *The Aboriginal Tasmanians*, pp. 107–10.
25. Davies, *The Last of the Tasmanians*, p. 70.
26. *British Parliamentary Papers*, p. 228.
27. Davies, *The Last of the Tasmanians*, pp. 64–6.
28. de Las Casas, *A Short History*, p. 15.
29. Davies, *The Last of the Tasmanians*, pp. 66–7.
30. Harris, *It's Coming Yet*, p. 36.
31. Davies, *The Last of the Tasmanians*, p. 47.
32. Davies, *The Last of the Tasmanians*, p. 67.
33. Ryan, *The Aboriginal Tasmanians*, pp. 99–102.
34. Davies, *The Last of the Tasmanians*, p. 119.
35. Davies, *The Last of the Tasmanians*, p. 117.
36. Turnbull, *Black War*, p. 119.
37. See Travers, *The Tasmanians*, pp. 167–78; Davies, *The Last of the Tasmanians*, pp. 111–32; Ryan, *The Aboriginal Tasmanians*, pp. 110–12.
38. Plomley, *Friendly Mission*, p. 293.

10   The Conciliator

1. Plomley, *Friendly Mission*, p. 276.
2. Plomley, *Friendly Mission*, p. 66.
3. Plomley, *Friendly Mission*, p. 89.
4. Plomley, *Friendly Mission*, p. 332.
5. Plomley, *Friendly Mission*, p. 287.
6. Davies, *The Last of the Tasmanians*, p. 174.
7. de Las Casas, *A Short Account*, p. xiii.

8. Bourke, *On the Border*, p. 112.
9. Bates, *The Passing of the Aborigines*, p. xi.
10. *British Parliamentary Papers*, p. 253.
11. *British Parliamentary Papers*, p. 248.
12. Davies, *The Last of the Tasmanians*, pp. 195–6.
13. Ryan, *The Aboriginal Tasmanians*, pp. 187–9.
14. Davies, *The Last of the Tasmanians*, pp. 233–4.
15. Travers, *The Tasmanians*, p. 200.
16. Ryan, *The Aboriginal Tasmanians*, p. 186.
17. Davies, *The Last of the Tasmanians*, p. 194.
18. Ryan, *The Aboriginal Tasmanians*, p. 193.
19. Ryan, *The Aboriginal Tasmanians*, p. 190.

11   The Last Tasmanian

1. Davies, *The Last of the Tasmanians*, p. 202.
2. Ryan, *The Aboriginal Tasmanians*, p. 203.
3. Calder, *The Native Tribes*, p. 43
4. Ryan, *The Aboriginal Tasmanians*, p. 212.
5. Travers, *The Tasmanians*, pp. 21–8; Ryan, *The Aboriginal Tasmanians*, p. 212.
6. Travers, *The Tasmanians*, pp. 213–14; Davies, *The Last of the Tasmanians*, pp. 200–202.
7. Travers, *The Tasmanians*, p. 36.
8. Calder, *The Native Tribes*, p. 11.
9. Calder, *The Native Tribes*, p. 8.
10. Bonwick, *Daily Life*, p. 18.
11. Walker, *Early Tasmania*, p. 231.
12. Travers, *The Tasmanians*, p. 36.
13. Prescott, *The Conquest of Mexico*, Volume I, p. 36.
14. Bates, *The Passing of the Aborigines*, p. 67.
15. Gorges, *Report on the Natives*, pp. 95–6.
16. Ryan, *The Aboriginal Tasmanians*, p. 3.
17. Hughes, *The Fatal Shore*, p. 275.
18. Reynolds, *The Other Side of the Frontier*, p. 121.
19. Reece, *Aborigines and Colonists*, pp. 23–4.
20. Suter and Stearman, *Aboriginal Australians*, Minority Rights Group Report, p. 5.
21. Reece, *Aborigines and Colonists*, p. 54.

22. Livingston and Louis, *Australia, New Zealand and the Pacific Islands*, p. 150.
23. Macdonald, *The Maori of Aotearoa-New Zealand*, Minority Rights Group Report, p. 6.
24. Livingston and Louis, *Australia, New Zealand and the Pacific Islands*, p. 170.
25. Macdonald, *The Maori of Aotearoa-New Zealand*, Minority Rights Group Report, p. 13.
26. Kircher, *The Kanaks of New Caledonia*, Minority Rights Group Report, p. 6.
27. Kircher, *The Kanaks*, Minority Rights Group Report, p. 6.
28. Kircher, *The Kanaks*, Minority Rights Group Report, p. 14.
29. Kircher, *The Kanaks*, Minority Rights Group Report, p. 16.
30. Weingartner, *The Pacific: Nuclear Testing and Minorities*, Minority Rights Group Report, p. 16.
31. Weingartner, *The Pacific*, Minority Rights Group Report, p. 20.
32. Weingartner, *The Pacific*, Minority Rights Group Report, p. 20.
33. Turnbull, *Black War*, introduction.
34. Ryan, *The Aboriginal Tasmanians*, p. 224.

12   The Tiger of the Human Species

1. Conner, *Joseph Reddeford Walker*, p. 151.
2. Conner, *Joseph Reddeford Walker*, p. 268.
3. Conner, *Joseph Reddeford Walker*, pp. 266–7.
4. Cremony, *Life Among the Apaches*, p. 313.
5. Cremony, *Life Among the Apaches*, p. 266.
6. Cremony, *Life Among the Apaches*, pp. 33–4.
7. Bourke, *On the Border*, p. 113.
8. Clum, *Apache Agent*, pp. 41, 12.
9. Thrapp, *Conquest of Apacheria*, p. 256.
10. Clum, *Apache Agent*, p. 292.
11. Bourke, *An Apache Campaign*, p. 108.
12. Ball, *Indeh*, p. 29.
13. Barrett (ed.), *Geronimo*, p. 64.
14. Barrett (ed.), *Geronimo*, p. 64.
15. Josephy, *500 Nations*, p. 319; Wright, *Stolen Continents*, p. 212.
16. D.R. Wrone and Nelson, *Who's the Savage?*, Greenwich, Conn., 1973 pp. 232–3; R.S. Wright, *Stolen Continents*, p. 47.

17. Wright, *Stolen Continents*, p. 213.
18. Jahoda, *The Trail of Tears*, p. 78.
19. Barrett (ed.), *Geronimo*, p. 73.
20. Barrett (ed.), *Geronimo*, p. 75.
21. Thrapp, *Conquest of Apacheria*, p. 40.
22. Trimble, *The People*, p. 266.
23. Roberts, *Once They Moved*, p. 108.
24. Davis, *The Truth About Geronimo*, p. 88.
25. White, *Cortés*, p. 318.
26. Bryant, 'Entering the Global Economy' in Milner II, O'Connor and Sandweiss (eds.), *The Oxford History of the American West*, p. 213.
27. Horsman, *Race and Manifest Destiny*, p. 167.
28. Richard Fitter, *Wildlife for Man*, London, 1986, p. 187.

13 The Enemy and the People

1. Matthiessen, *In the Spirit of Crazy Horse*, p. 12.
2. Dippie, 'The Visual West' in Milner II, O'Connor and Sandweiss (eds.), *The Oxford History of the American West*, pp. 676–80.
3. Josephy, *500 Nations*, p. 391.
4. Matthiessen, *In the Spirit of Crazy Horse*, p. 12.
5. Thrapp, *Conquest of Apacheria*, p. 270.
6. Debo, *Geronimo*, p. 99.
7. Clum, *Apache Agent*, pp. 221–4.
8. Ball, *Indeh*, p. 15.
9. Cremony, *Life Among the Apaches*, p. 28.
10. Opler, *An Apache Life-Way*, p. 354.
11. Davis, *The Truth About Geronimo*, p. 4; Roberts, *Once They Moved*, p. 54.
12. Davis, *The Truth About Geronimo*, pp. 30–31.
13. Quoted in Ball, *In The Days of Victorio*, p. 65.
14. Betzinez, *I Fought With Geronimo*, pp. 67–8.
15. Thrapp, *Conquest of Apacheria*, p. vii; see also Bourke, *On the Border*, p. 113.
16. Cremony, *Life Among the Apaches*, p. 267.
17. Roberts, *Once They Moved*, p. 89; see also Thrapp, *Victorio*, p. 72.
18. Cremony, *Life Among the Apaches*, p. 177.
19. Conner, *Joseph Reddeford Walker*, p. 39.

20. Conner, *Joseph Reddeford Walker*, pp. 34–42.
21. Barrett (ed.), *Geronimo*, p. 102; Trimble, *The People*, p. 259.
22. Ball, *In the Days of Victorio*, p. 29.
23. Thrapp, *Conquest of Apacheria*, p. 18.
24. Clum, *Apache Agent*, p. 122.
25. Porter, *Paper Medicine Man*, p. 12.
26. Porter, *Paper Medicine Man*, p. 12.
27. Matthiessen, *In the Spirit of Crazy Horse*, p. 11.
28. Bourke, *On the Border*, p. 145.
29. Thrapp, *Conquest of Apacheria*, p. 126.
30. Porter, *Paper Medicine Man*, p. 19.
31. Bourke, *On the Border*, p. 445.
32. Betzinez, *I Fought With Geronimo*, pp. 120–21.
33. Bourke, *On the Border*, p. 437.
34. Thrapp, *Conquest of Apacheria*, p. 146.
35. Bourke, *On the Border*, p. 442.
36. Davis, *The Truth About Geronimo*, p. 42.
37. Thrapp, *Conquest of Apacheria*, p. 90.
38. Lockwood, *The Apache Indians*, p. 178; Roberts, *Once They Moved*, p. 74.
39. Thrapp, *Conquest of Apacheria*, p. 92.
40. Davis, *The Truth About Geronimo*, p. 60.
41. Debo, *Geronimo*, p. 97.
42. Josephy, *500 Nations*, p. 260.
43. Quoted in Matthiessen, *In the Spirit of Crazy Horse*, p. 9.
44. Bourke, *On the Border*, p. 234.

14 *America's Greatest Guerrilla Fighter*

1. Thrapp, *Victorio*, p. ix.
2. Roberts, *Once They Moved*, p. 55.
3. Thrapp, *Victorio*, p. ix.
4. See Debo, *Geronimo*, pp. 9–12; Debo argues that the Mimbres and Ojo Caliente or Warm Springs Chiricahua were distinct sections of the tribe.
5. Thrapp, *Victorio*, p. 99.
6. Roberts, *Once They Moved*, p. 174.
7. Thrapp, *Conquest of Apacheria*, p. 181.
8. Thrapp, *Conquest of Apacheria*, p. 187.

9. Thrapp, *Conquest of Apacheria*, p. 190.
10. Thrapp, *Conquest of Apacheria*, p. 193.
11. Thrapp, *Conquest of Apacheria*, p. 203.
12. Davis, *The Truth About Geronimo*, p. 80.
13. Bourke, *On the Border*, p. 134.
14. Clum, *Apache Agent*, p. 207.
15. Bourke, *An Apache Campaign*, p. 107.
16. Davis, *The Truth About Geronimo*, p. 25.
17. Ball, *In The Days of Victorio*, p. 188; Debo, *Geronimo*, pp. 230–31.
18. Thrapp, *Victorio*, p. 374.
19. Thrapp, *Conquest of Apacheria*, p. 201.
20. Thrapp, *Victorio*, p. 308.
21. Roberts, *Once They Moved*, p. 193.
22. Debo, *Geronimo*, p. 73.
23. Ball, *In The Days of Victorio*, p. 87.
24. Thrapp, *Conquest of Apacheria*, p. 215; Roberts, *Once They Moved*, p. 194.

15   Geronimo – The Last Renegade

1. Ball, *Indeh*, pp. 39–40.
2. Thrapp, *Victorio*, p. 58.
3. Debo, *Geronimo*, pp. 151–2.
4. Davis, *The Truth About Geronimo*, p. 142.
5. Roberts, *Once They Moved*, p. 121.
6. Debo, *Geronimo*, p. xi.
7. Trimble, *The People*, p. 267.
8. Thrapp, *Conquest of Apacheria*, p. 258.
9. Bourke, *On the Border*, p. 439.
10. Debo, *Geronimo*, pp. 138–9.
11. Thrapp, *Conquest of Apacheria*, pp. 237–8; Debo, *Geronimo*, pp. 139–41.
12. Betzinez, *I Fought With Geronimo*, p. 58.
13. Ball, *In the Days of Victorio*, pp. 163, 195.
14. Porter, *Paper Medicine Man*, p. 151.
15. Bourke, *An Apache Campaign*, p. 52.
16. Bourke, *An Apache Campaign*, p. 83.
17. Bourke, *An Apache Campaign*, pp. 52, 38.
18. Bourke, *An Apache Campaign*, p. 42.

19. Betzinez, *I Fought With Geronimo*, p. 115.
20. Bourke, *An Apache Campaign*, pp. 102, 118–19.
21. Davis, *The Truth About Geronimo*, p. 102.
22. Debo, *Geronimo*, p. 233.
23. Roberts, *Once They Moved*, pp. 262–3.
24. Debo, *Geronimo*, p. 262.
25. Bourke, *On the Border*, pp. 480–81.
26. Falk, *The Geronimo Campaign*, p. 160.
27. Bourke, *On the Border*, p. 485.
28. Thrapp, *Conquest of Apacheria*, p. 366.
29. Bourke, *An Apache Campaign*, p. 46.
30. Bourke, *An Apache Campaign*, p. 50.
31. Roberts, *Once They Moved*, pp. 44–6.
32. Clum, *Apache Agent*, p. 187.

16   The Caged Tiger

1. Gibson, *The Aztecs*, p. 132.
2. Bolt, *American Indian Policy*, p. 100.
3. Bolt, *American Indian Policy*, p. 100.
4. Debo, *Geronimo*, p. 3.
5. Debo, *Geronimo*, p. 325.
6. Debo, *Geronimo*, p. 326.
7. Debo, *Geronimo*, pp. 400–5.
8. Debo, *Geronimo*, p. 407.
9. Debo, *Geronimo*, p. 423.
10. Debo, *Geronimo*, pp. 416–19.
11. Ornitholidays brochure 1997, p. 71.
12. Monbiot, *No Man's Land*, London, 1994, p. 81.
13. Monbiot, *No Man's Land*, p. 83.
14. Affairs in Maasailand have improved recently, especially near Amboseli where the local Maasai have themselves converted their pastures into private game sanctuaries. Cattle are grazed in these areas only in extreme and life-threatening conditions. Otherwise the principal source of revenue is from tourists on photographic safaris. The current Maasai practice of culling some game species for their meat and skins may eventually be replaced with licensed tourist hunting – an innovation that could open up new and important economic opportunities for the Maasai. See David

Lovatt Smith, 'The Maasai and their role in the past and future of Amboseli National Park', in *Swara*, March–April 1996, pp. 18–21.

15. Jonathan Owen, *BBC Wildlife*, Dec. 1996, p. 61.
16. Trimble, *The People*, p. 285.
17. May, 'Alcohol Abuse and Alcoholism Among American Indians: An Overview' in Watts and Wright (eds.), *Alcoholism in Minority Populations*, p. 108.
18. May, 'Alcohol Abuse and Alcoholism Among American Indians: An Overview' in Watts and Wright (eds.), *Alcoholism in Minority Populations*, p. 105.
19. Debo, *Geronimo*, pp. 194–5.
20. West, 'American Frontier' in Milner II, O'Connor and Sandweiss (eds.), *The Oxford History of the American West*, p. 141.
21. Braudel, *Civilization and Capitalism*, Volume I, pp. 248–9.
22. Soustelle, *Daily Life*, p. 156.
23. Thomas, *The Conquest of Mexico*, p. 18.
24. Gibson, *The Aztecs*, p. 150.
25. Braudel, *Civilization and Capitalism*, Volume I, p. 248.
26. Friede and Keen (eds.), *Bartolomé de Las Casas*, p. 13; Wachtel, *The Vision of the Vanquished*, p. 98.
27. Hemming, *The Conquest of the Incas*, p. 368.
28. Hemming, *The Conquest of the Incas*, p. 369.
29. Wachtel, *The Vision of the Vanquished*, p. 146.
30. Hunter, *Aboriginal Health and History*, p. 90.
31. May, 'Alcohol Abuse and Alcoholism Among American Indians: An Overview' in Watts and Wright (eds.), *Alcoholism in Minority Populations*, p. 108.
32. Hunter, *Aboriginal Health and History*, pp. 136–7.
33. Pool, *Samuel Maharero*, p. 248.
34. Robinson, *The Laundrymen*, pp. 173–4.
35. *Independent*, 25 July 1995, 19 March 1996.
36. Debo, *Geronimo*, p. 384.
37. Debo, *Geronimo*, pp. 440–42.

17 A Freshly Slaughtered Goat

1. Gorges, *Report on the Natives*, pp. 92–3.
2. Drechsler, *Let Us Die Fighting*, p. 108.
3. Drechsler, *Let Us Die Fighting*, p. 144.

18 A Darkness That May Be Felt

1. Drechsler, *Let Us Die Fighting*, p. 107.
2. Gorges, *Report on the Natives*, p. 93.
3. Bley, *South-West Africa*, p. 39.
4. Vedder, *South West Africa*, p. 473.
5. Vedder, *South West Africa*, p. 477.
6. Andersson, *Lake Ngami*, p. 49.
7. Andersson, *Lake Ngami*, p. 143.
8. Bridgman, *The Revolt of the Herero*, p. 17.
9. Vedder, *South West Africa*, p. 47.
10. Andersson, *Lake Ngami*, p. 115.
11. Andersson, *Lake Ngami*, pp. 121–3.
12. Wellington, *South West Africa*, pp. 153–4.
13. Wellington, *South West Africa*, p. 148.
14. Goldblatt, *History of South West Africa*, p. 23.
15. Goldblatt, *History of South West Africa*, p. 21.
16. Vedder, *South West Africa*, p. 251.
17. Pool, *Samuel Maharero*, p. 64.
18. Drechsler, *Let Us Die Fighting*, pp. 23–4; Goldblatt, *History of South West Africa*, p. 102.
19. Drechsler, *Let Us Die Fighting*, p. 18.
20. Drechsler, *Let Us Die Fighting*, pp. 24–5.

19 A Place in the Sun

1. Quoted in Pakenham, *The Scramble for Africa*, p. 216.
2. Andersson, *Lake Ngami*, p. 152.
3. Andersson, *Lake Ngami*, p. 157.
4. Bley, *South-West Africa*, p. 58.
5. Drechsler, *Let Us Die Fighting*, p. 22.
6. Andersson, *Lake Ngami*, p. 335.
7. Hahn, Vedder and Fourie, *The Native Tribes of South West Africa*, pp. 127–8.
8. Andersson, *Lake Ngami*, p. 231.
9. Hahn, Vedder and Fourie, *The Native Tribes of South West Africa*, pp. 39–44.
10. Hahn, Vedder and Fourie, *The Native Tribes of South West Africa*, p. 77.

11. Drechsler, *Let Us Die Fighting*, p. 214.
12. Henderson, *Studies*, p.132 and Townsend, *The Rise and Fall of Germany's Colonial Empire*, pp. 36–7.
13. Henderson, *Studies*, p. 38.
14. Gann and Duignan, *The Rulers of German Africa*, p. 26.
15. Henderson, *Studies*, p. 53.
16. Quoted in Mostert, *Frontiers*, p. 286.

20   The Empire Builders

1. Drechsler, *Let Us Die Fighting*, p. 30.
2. Gorges, *Report on the Natives*, p. 15.
3. Drechsler, *Let Us Die Fighting*, p. 43.
4. Drechsler, *Let Us Die Fighting*, pp. 71–3.
5. Drechsler, *Let Us Die Fighting*, p. 73.
6. Drechsler, *Let Us Die Fighting*, p. 69.
7. Bley, *South-West Africa*, p. xiv.
8. Gorges, *Report on the Natives*, pp. 79–82.
9. Drechsler, *Let Us Die Fighting*, p. 78.
10. Gorges, *Report on the Natives*, p. 10.
11. Gorges, *Report on the Natives*, pp. 18–19.
12. Wellington, *South West Africa*, p. 196.
13. Drechsler, *Let Us Die Fighting*, p. 93.
14. Bley, *South-West Africa*, p. 68.
15. Drechsler, *Let Us Die Fighting*, p. 81.
16. Drechsler, *Let Us Die Fighting*, p. 82.
17. Drechsler, *Let Us Die Fighting*, p. 83.
18. Gorges, *Report on the Natives*, p. 42.
19. Drechsler, *Let Us Die Fighting*, p. 84.
20. Pool, *Samuel Maharero*, p. 97.
21. Drechsler, *Let Us Die Fighting*, p. 87.
22. Gorges, *Report on the Natives*, p. 45.
23. Pool, *Samuel Maharero*, pp. 138–51.
24. Gorges, *Report on the Natives*, p. 47.
25. Pool, *Samuel Maharero*, p. 166.
26. Pool, *Samuel Maharero*, p. 166.
27. Gorges, *Report on the Natives*, p. 47.
28. Pool, *Samuel Maharero*, p. 167.
29. Pool, *Samuel Maharero*, p. 168.

30. Pool, *Samuel Maharero*, p. 176.
31. Drechsler, *Let Us Die Fighting*, p. 98; Bridgman, *The Revolt of the Herero*, p. 50.
32. Drechsler, *Let Us Die Fighting*, p. 98.
33. Bridgman, *The Revolt of the Herero*, p. 50.
34. Pool, *Samuel Maharero*, p. 181.
35. Bridgman, *The Revolt of the Herero*, p. 51
36. Gorges, *Report on the Natives*, pp. 50–51.

21   Cruelty and Brutality

1. Pool, *Samuel Maharero*, p. 197.
2. Pool, *Samuel Maharero*, p. 202.
3. Drechsler, *Let Us Die Fighting*, p. 140.
4. *The Times*, 6 December 1904.
5. Goldblatt, *History of South West Africa*, p. 138.
6. *The Times*, 12 November 1904.
7. *The Times*, 18 October 1904.
8. Drechsler, *Let Us Die Fighting*, p. 142.
9. Bley, *South-West Africa*, p. 7.
10. Bley, *South-West Africa*, p. 43.
11. Bley, *South-West Africa*, p. 102.
12. Gorges, *Report on the Natives*, p. 54.
13. Bridgman, *The Revolt of the Herero*, p. 62.
14. Bley, *South-West Africa*, p. 97.
15. Drechsler, *Let Us Die Fighting*, p. 134.
16. Hahn, Vedder and Fourie, *The Native Tribes of South West Africa*, p. 53.
17. Bridgman, *The Revolt of the Herero*, p. 62.
18. Gorges, *Report on the Natives*, pp. 54–5; Drechsler, *Let Us Die Fighting*, p. 135
19. Gorges, *Report on the Natives*, p. 56.
20. Drechsler, *Let Us Die Fighting*, p. 143.
21. Pool, *Samuel Maharero*, p. 204.
22. Gorges, *Report on the Natives*, p. 58.
23. Bridgman, *The Revolt of the Herero*, p. 74.
24. Bridgman, *The Revolt of the Herero*, p. 67.
25. Bridgman, *The Revolt of the Herero*, p. 81.
26. Bridgman, *The Revolt of the Herero*, pp. 96–7.

27. Pool, *Samuel Maharero*, p. 221.
28. Pool, *Samuel Maharero*, p. 224.
29. Drechsler, *Let Us Die Fighting*, p. 149.
30. Drechsler, *Let Us Die Fighting*, p. 148.
31. Bridgman, *The Revolt of the Herero*, p. 87.
32. Bridgman, *The Revolt of the Herero*, p. 102.
33. Drechsler, *Let Us Die Fighting*, p. 148.
34. Drechsler, *Let Us Die Fighting*, p. 145.
35. Frenssen, *Peter Moor's Journey*, p. 6.
36. Drechsler, *Let Us Die Fighting*, p. 147.
37. Imperial Colonial Office, File No. 2089, pp. 100–102, von Trotha to Leutwein, 5 November 1904, author's own translation.
38. Pool, *Samuel Maharero*, p. 245.
39. Pool, *Samuel Maharero*, p. 251.
40. Drechsler, *Let Us Die Fighting*, p. 155.
41. Drechsler, *Let Us Die Fighting*, p. 156.
42. Drechsler, *Let Us Die Fighting*, pp. 155–6.
43. Frenssen, *Peter Moor's Journey*, p. 189.
44. Bridgman, *The Revolt of the Herero*, p. 125.
45. Pool, *Samuel Maharero*, p. 264.
46. Gorges, *Report on the Natives*, pp. 63–5.
47. Gorges, *Report on the Natives*, pp. 64–7.
48. Drechsler, *Let Us Die Fighting*, p. 151.
49. Pool, *Samuel Maharero*, p. 270.
50. Bridgman, *The Revolt of the Herero*, p. 128.
51. Drechsler, *Let Us Die Fighting*, p. 161.
52. Goldblatt, *History of South West Africa*, p. 130.
53. Drechsler, 'Jacob Morenga: A New Kind of South-West African Leader', in W. Marhov (ed.), *African Studies*, 1967, pp. 95–105.
54. *The Times*, 25 May 1905.
55. Bridgman, *The Revolt of the Herero*, p. 12.
56. Drechsler, *Let Us Die Fighting*, p. 187.
57. *The Times*, 14 January 1905.
58. *The Times*, 20 October 1905.
59. Gorges, *Report on the Natives*, p. 96.
60. Bridgman, *The Revolt of the Herero*, p. 153.
61. *The Times*, 7 November 1905.
62. Drechsler, 'Jacob Morenga: A New Kind of South-West African Leader', in W. Marhov (ed.), *African Studies*, 1967, p. 100.
63. Drechsler, *Let Us Die Fighting*, p. 201.

64. Drechsler, *Let Us Die Fighting*, p. 201.
65. John Iliffe, 'The Herero and Nama Risings: South-West Africa, 1904–7', in G. Kibodya (ed.), *Aspects of South African History*, 1968, p. 95.

22 *Never Must We Allow the Negroes to Prevail*

  1. Drechsler, *Let Us Die Fighting*, p. 208.
  2. Bley, *South-West Africa*, p. 166.
  3. Goldblatt, *History of South West Africa*, p. 146.
  4. Goldblatt, *History of South West Africa*, p. 146.
  5. Goldblatt, *History of South West Africa*, p. 147.
  6. Drechsler, *Let Us Die Fighting*, p. 212.
  7. Drechsler, *Let Us Die Fighting*, p. 214.
  8. Gorges, *Report on the Natives*, pp. 33–4.
  9. *The Times*, 4 December 1905.
  10. Frenssen, *Peter Moor's Journey*, p. 189.
  11. Hahn, Vedder and Fourie, *The Native Tribes of South West Africa*, p. 156.
  12. Goldblatt, *History of South West Africa*, p. 133.
  13. Pool, *Samuel Maharero*, p. 280.
  14. Gorges, *Report on the Natives*, p. 35. Note, however, that Drechsler accepts a smaller figure than Gorges for the number of Bergdamara casualties, resulting in a lower overall total of about 75,000 African victims. See Drechsler, *Let Us Die Fighting*, pp. 214, 219, note 189.
  15. Drechsler, *Let Us Die Fighting*, p. 145.
  16. Drechsler, *Let Us Die Fighting*, p. 148.
  17. Bley, *South-West Africa*, p. 161–3.
  18. Bley, *South-West Africa*, p. 166.
  19. Bley, *South-West Africa*, p. 165.
  20. Drechsler, *Let Us Die Fighting*, p. 164.
  21. Bley, *South-West Africa*, p. 221.
  22. Frenssen, *Peter Moor's Journey*, p. 233.
  23. Gorges, *Report on the Natives*, p. 49.
  24. Alan Bullock, *Hitler and Stalin: Parallel Lives*, London, 1991, p. 895.
  25. Drechsler, *Let Us Die Fighting*, p. 147.
  26. Drechsler, *Let Us Die Fighting*, p. 161.
  27. Bley, *South-West Africa*, p. 165.
  28. Pool, *Samuel Maharero*, p. 248.

29. Frenssen, *Peter Moor's Journey*, pp. 98 and 6; Bridgman, *The Revolt of the Herero*, p. 128.

30. *The Times*, 18 January 1905.

31. *The Times*, 21 March 1906.

32. Drechsler, *Let Us Die Fighting*, p. 146.

33. Bley, *South-West Africa*, p. 172.

34. Bley, *South-West Africa*, p. 223.

35. Hahn, Vedder and Fourie, *The Native Tribes of South West Africa*, p. 162.

36. Mostert, *Frontiers*, pp. 348–9.

37. Townsend, *The Rise and Fall of Germany's Colonial Empire*, p. 286.

38. Gorges, *Report on the Natives*, p. 162.

39. Bley, *South-West Africa*, p. 212.

40. Troup, *In Face of Fear*, p. 58.

41. Troup, *In Face of Fear*, p. 60.

42. First, *South West Africa*, p. 142.

43. Troup, *In Face of Fear*, p. 72.

44. Fraenkel and Murray, *The Namibians*, Minority Rights Group Report, p. 8.

45. First, *South West Africa*, p. 49.

46. Drechsler, *Let Us Die Fighting*, pp. 9–10.

47. First, *South West Africa*, p. 101.

23 They Built No Houses and Dug No Wells

1. Barrett (ed.), *Geronimo*, introduction, p. 26.

2. R. Hicks, *Hidden Tibet: The Land and Its People*, Shaftesbury, 1988, p. 63.

3. Kuper, *International Action Against Genocide*, Minority Rights Group Report, p. 6.

4. Verney et al, *Sudan: Conflict and minorities*, Minority Rights Group Report, p. 9.

5. Stannard, *American Holocaust*, p. 51.

6. Thrapp, *The Conquest of Apacheria*, p. 134.

7. F. McLynn, *Stanley: The Sorcerer's Apprentice*, London, 1991, p. 237.

8. Wright, *Stolen Continents*, p. 50.

9. Wachtel, *The Vision of the Vanquished*, p. 31.

10. Harris, *It's Coming Yet*, p. 36.

11. Prescott, *The Conquest of Mexico*, Volume I, pp. 139–40.
12. Frenssen, *Peter Moor's Journey*, p. 233.
13. Stannard, *American Holocaust*, p. 268; Gilbert, *The Routledge Atlas of American History*, London, 1993, p. 2.
14. Hemming, *The Conquest of the Incas*, p. 409.
15. Turnbull, *Black War*, introduction.
16. Wearne, *The Maya of Guatemala*, Minority Rights Group Report, pp. 12–13.
17. Wearne, *The Maya of Guatemala*, Minority Rights Group Report, p. 23.
18. Oliver Tickell, 'Land Fever Could Wipe Out Indians', *BBC Wildlife*, January 1996, p. 59.
19. Gray, *The Amerindians of South America*, Minority Rights Group Report, p. 8.
20. Damien Lewis, 'Indians Set To Lose Forest Lands', *BBC Wildlife*, June 1996, p. 71.
21. Rogers Worthington, '. . . and where it stops, nobody knows', *Chicago Tribune Magazine*, 22 August 1993.
22. Sharkey, 'Indian giver', *Guardian Weekend*, 8 April 1995, p. 32.
23. Sharkey, 'Indian giver', *Guardian Weekend*, 8 April 1995, pp. 27–32.
24. Sharkey, 'Indian giver', *Guardian Weekend*, 8 April 1995, p. 30.

Notes

11. Peacock, The Colour of Mercy, Volume 1, pp. 150–51.
12. Ingham, Peter More, January 28, p.73
13. ...quoted ... in ... Colbert, The Reconstruction of ...History, London, 2002, p. ...
14. Blomqvist, Final Account of the Boer, b. 304.
15. Turnbull, Black War, introduction.
16. Weaire, The Maya of Guatemala Without Rights, Group Report, pp. 12–13
17. Weaire, The Maya in Guatemala Without Rights, Group Location, p. 21
18. Oliver, Tickell, Land Never Could Wipe Out Infamy, BBC ... January 1996, p. 50.
19. Gray, ... declaration of South America, Minority Rights Group Report, p. 8.
20. Vidal, ..., Indians See To Lose Forest Land ..., BBC Wildlife June 1996, p. ...
21. Rogers, Washington, ...Land where reasons nobody knows, Chicago Tribune Magazine, 24 August 1995
22. Starkey, Indian river, Guardian Weekend, 8 April 1995, p. ...
23. Starkey, Indian river, Guardian Weekend, 8 April 1995, pp. 27–32.
24. Starkey, Indian river, Guardian Weekend, 8 April 1995, p. 30.

Index

Index